JESUS

FAITH AND REASON
Studies in Catholic Theology and Philosophy

The series aims at publishing scholarly studies that serve the project of "faith seeking understanding." We hope to assist in making available in English valuable work being done by theologians and philosophers abroad; in this regard we recognize a special place for the ongoing renaissance in French-language Thomistic theology and philosophy. In addition to translations, we intend to publish collections of essays and monographs from a range of perspectives, united by their common commitment to the ecclesial and sapiential work of "faith seeking understanding" so as to build up the Church and proclaim the Gospel afresh.

PUBLISHED VOLUMES

Serge-Thomas Bonino, OP, ed., *Surnaturel: Reflections on Nature and Grace*
Gilles Emery, OP, *Trinity, Church, and the Human Person: Thomistic Essays*
Lawrence Feingold, *The Natural Desire to See God*
Matthew L. Lamb, *Eternity, Time, and the Life of Wisdom*
Guy Mansini, OSB, *The Word Has Dwelt among Us*
Thomas Joseph White, OP, *Wisdom in the Face of Modernity*

JESUS

ESSAYS IN CHRISTOLOGY

Thomas G. Weinandy, OFM, Cap.

SAPIENTIA PRESS

OF AVE MARIA UNIVERSITY

Sapientia Press
of Ave Maria University
5050 Ave Maria Blvd.
Ave Maria, FL 34142
800-537-5487

Distributed by:
The Catholic University of America Press
c/o HFS
P.O. Box 50370
Baltimore, MD 21211
800-537-5487

Cover Image: Mosaic dome of the Florence Baptistery. Photograph courtesy of Mary Ann Sullivan, Bluffton University.

Printed in the United States of America.

Library of Congress Control Number: 2013950269

ISBN: 978-1-932589-65-8

For the Holy Family
Joseph, Mary, and Jesus

Contents

Preface

Our contemporary world is embroiled in numerous conflicts—wars, terrorism, violent crime, and ethnic cleansing—as well as challenged by myriad social ills—human trafficking, poverty, hunger, single-parent families, and economic injustice. There is equally a host of moral issues that fragment our global culture—abortion, same-sex marriage, euthanasia, religious freedom, recreational drug use, and the environment. All of the above and more have immense practical and shared repercussions upon our common national life and universal community values.

In light of the above, to publish a substantial volume of essays on Christology hardly seems warranted and much less helpful given the needs and concerns of the time. How could a collection of academic essays on the biblical understanding of Jesus or erudite musings on the doctrinal history of Christology or debates as to the person and work of Jesus be relevant to what plagues our world and splinters our societies? Even essays on Jesus and the Christian life may appear to be mere spiritual ruminations that provide a psychic reassurance and an emotional antidepressant but do not fearlessly confront hard reality and authentically address imperative issues.

As the author of these essays, I am convinced that the topics they address are of supreme importance for advancing a knowledge and love of Jesus as the definitive Lord and universal Savior. Precisely because he is our Lord and Savior, he is, in his very person and life-giving salvific presence, indispensable for furthering humankind's determined struggle to promote, defend, and secure peace, justice, and personal and civic virtue. Only in the light of Christ can we clearly perceive and adequately address the evils and concerns of our contemporary world. Although these essays are often philosophical and theological in nature, the truth they attempt to express bears the life of the Holy Spirit, a life that can convert hearts and enlighten minds and so transform all peoples and nations. Only in Christ and his Spirit do men and women live in the truth and love of the Father and so become brothers and sisters. The Christological essays in this volume are divided into four parts that represent the above rationale.

Christology and the Bible

The three essays in Part I examine the biblical understanding of Jesus. Chapters 1 and 2 are extended commentaries on the first two volumes of Pope Benedict's *Jesus of Nazareth*. The importance of these essays resides not only in providing a commentary of what Benedict perceives within the biblical account of Jesus, but also in examining the manner in which he interprets these biblical accounts. For Benedict, the New Testament provides historical data concerning the life of Jesus and also professes a theological interpretation that elicits from the reader an act of faith. The Scriptures, for Benedict, are the revelational spring from which Christian doctrine flows—the marvelous mysteries of the faith. Thus Benedict not only facilitates our understanding of the biblical account of the person and work of Jesus, but he also simultaneously teaches us to read the sacred word as it was intended to be pondered: through eyes of faith illumined by the light of the Holy Spirit. These two essays provide key elements of Benedict's understanding of the biblical Jesus and in so doing highlight his exegetical methodology, a methodology that is inherent within the biblical text itself. These essays contribute to our contemporary appreciation of Jesus as the Christ as well as develop a richer and more rewarding manner of contemporary biblical exegesis.

Chapter 3 treats Thomas Aquinas's *Commentary on the Letter to the Hebrews*. Within the present revival of Thomistic studies there is, appropriately, a renewed interest in Aquinas's biblical commentaries. This is an important development, for Aquinas was primarily an interpreter of the sacred text, and it is this anointed word that is the foundational impetus for his more philosophical and systematic works. Only in the context of Aquinas's understanding of Scripture can one fully grasp and appreciate the mature theology contained in his two *Summae*.

What makes his *Commentary* especially interesting and significant is that he is examining an inspired text that systematically treats Jesus and his work of salvation, and it does so by demonstrating how Jesus and his salvific acts—the Cross and Resurrection—fulfill the Old Testament. This essay not only provides the logic and content of Aquinas's commentary but also focuses on his understanding of Jesus, in keeping with Hebrews itself, as being the singular Lord and universal Savior.

Christology: Historical and Systematic

Part II addresses Christological issues of an historical nature, centering primarily on the Fathers, the early Councils, and Aquinas. They are systematic in that they deal with doctrinal issues that arise from within the Church's Christological received tradition.

The essays in Part II examine the Christology of Ignatius of Antioch as founded with the New Testament and as a prelude to the Council of Chalcedon. They explicate the Christologies of Athanasius and Cyril of Alexandria, arguing that their understanding of the Incarnation provides a Christological conception and expression that would be sanctioned by the Councils of Nicea, Ephesus, and Chalcedon. Chapter 8 discusses Aquinas's Christology, an understanding that brings to maturity the patristic and conciliar tradition.

Chapters 9, 10, 11, and 12 explore various related historical and systematic Christological themes: the Christology of Walter Kasper; the relationship between Christology and the Trinity; the role and place of Mary, as the new Eve, within the Incarnation; and the human acts of Jesus as they form and instantiate the acts that are the sacraments.

The fact that these essays are mainly doctrinally historical in nature does not deprive them of their contemporary relevance. As is evident in Part III, the Church's tradition provides the living stones upon which a vibrant and timely Christology can be built. To reject these living incarnational stones is offer a Christology that becomes merely a pile of worthless dead rocks.

Christology and Contemporary Issues

The nine essays that make up Part III deal with concerns that are of present interest. Chapters 13–16 examine proffered Christologies that are not in accord with the Church's living tradition and so tender views of the Incarnation that are neither scripturally, doctrinally, or soteriologically acceptable, thus making Jesus irrelevant to the lives of people and their genuine concerns. Simply put, these counterfeit and spurious Christologies destroy the life-giving faith of the Church and so jeopardize the salvation of unsuspecting innocent men and women.

The remaining essays are positive in nature and so much more enjoyable (and even fun) to read. Chapters 17, 18, and 19 address the issue of Jesus's human consciousness and knowledge, along with the question of whether or not Jesus possessed, while on earth, the beatific vision. Chapter 20 examines a range of contemporary Christological issues that arise from the Creed of the Council of Chalcedon; for example, Christology from above and below, Jesus's miracles, and Jesus and religious pluralism. Chapter 21 is a treatment of Jesus in relation to Islam.

Essential to the theological task is defending and promoting the truth of Jesus as the incarnate Son of God and Savior of the world. The essays in Part III attempt ardently to achieve both.

Christology and the Christian Life

Part IV provides essays that are of a more spiritual nature, examining how Christology pertains to our growth in holiness and fosters our love for Jesus as our Lord and Savior. These chapters are more diverse than the previous ones, treating the humility of God and Jesus, the name of Jesus, his being lifted up, his Eucharistic commentary on his passion and death, and his praying and enacting the Our Father while offering his life to the Father on the Cross.

Chapter 27 is a short essay that attempts to recover the good name of Thomas the Apostle. He is universally known as "the Doubting Thomas" and yet no other apostle, not even Mary, makes a more clear profession of faith in who Jesus is: "My Lord and my God." He is not the apostle of doubt. He is the apostle of faith!

Chapter 28, on Jesus as "the Cosmic Christ," argues that his primacy resides not only in that all was created by and for him, but also in that he achieved his primacy through his obedient incarnation and loving death on the Cross. In his glorious resurrection and ascension, the Father bestowed upon him his primacy over heaven and earth, the reward and recompense of his mighty deeds, thus becoming the Supreme Lord and Universal Savior of the whole cosmos. There is no one greater than Jesus.

Two essays aim to deepen the prayer of the faithful. Chapter 29 offers a form of Eucharistic adoration through contemplating the mysteries of Jesus. Chapter 30 is a commentary on Athanasius's Christological and soteriological praying of the Psalms, in which we find an Athanasius that is scripturally penetrating and spiritually perceptive. Both wish to nurture a love for Jesus and an appreciation of who his is and what he has done on our behalf.

Chapter 31 discusses a most unlikely source for a theology of the Incarnation and salvation—Mark Twain's *The Adventures of Huckleberry Finn*. Although some readers may find this interpretation far-fetched, I am confident that all will enjoy it as a fitting conclusion to this volume.

As acknowledged above, the world we live in is overwhelmingly beleaguered with evil, exhausted with relentless tears, and confronted by issues and problems, the resolution of which will have long-term effects for good or evil. Nonetheless, there is genuine hope and joy, as these essays bear witness. This hope resides in our faith in Jesus—our Lord and Savior. His love overcomes all evil and bestows upon all who believe the assured confidence that his truth, goodness, and justice will triumph in this life and for all eternity. At the end of time, all of the faithful and all of the angels, in the love and joy of the Holy Spirit, will bend their knees and profess in one voice that Jesus Christ is Lord to the glory of God the Father. May all praise and honor and glory be to the Lamb once slain and who now lives forever and ever.

The essays contained in this volume were written over a rather lengthy period of time. Many people were instrumental in helping me write them—especially academic friends and colleagues who have prompted me to think more deeply about the Incarnation and in so doing have helped foster my love for that great mystery. I thank them for their learned advice and spiritual wisdom.

I especially wish to thank Matthew Levering, who suggested that these essays be collected in one volume, and Roger Nutt, of Sapientia Press of Ave Maria University, for so enthusiastically taking up this initiative. They have bestowed upon me a great honor. This volume would not have been possible without the assistance of Ashleigh McKown. With great skill and patience, she performed all of the editorial work, ensuring that the style, grammar, and footnotes for all the various and diverse essays are in proper order. To her I own a great deal of gratitude.

Thanks are also owed to the journals, periodicals, and publishers that first published these essays and generously allowed them to be reprinted in this volume.

Lastly, I want to express my gratefulness to God the Father for sending his Son into the world; my praise to God the Son, our Lord Jesus Christ, for his obedient love in becoming man; and my joy to God the Holy Spirit, by whose power the Word was made flesh in the womb of Mary and so dwelt among us.

The Solemnity of All Saints, 2013

PART I

CHRISTOLOGY AND THE BIBLE

CHAPTER 1

Pope Benedict XVI
A Biblical Portrayal of Jesus

Pope Benedict's *Jesus of Nazareth: From the Baptism in the Jordan to the Transfiguration* (New York: Doubleday, 2007) is a marvelous book. Its attractiveness lies not simply in the depth of its theology or in its clarity of expression, but also in the serene and prayerful manner in which it is written—a serenity and prayerfulness that are conveyed to the heart and mind of the reader. I do not mean to imply that it is fundamentally a book of meditations, no matter how spiritually beneficial this book may be. It is a robust theological work that addresses authentic contemporary biblical, historical, philosophical, and doctrinal issues, though some scholars may rightly feel that Benedict at times too quickly draws conclusions from somewhat inadequate or insufficient argumentation. Some scholars might also quibble that Benedict quotes most frequently, both positively and negatively, authors of an older generation. Yet a close examination of his sources shows that Benedict is conversant with contemporary scholarship even if one would have appreciated his commenting on a particular scholar's work.

What makes his book refreshingly unique is that all of the various academic and scholarly concerns are pondered from within the living household of faith—the confident and vibrant faith of the Catholic Church to which Pope Benedict ardently adheres with a loving heart and inquiring mind. It exemplifies the true meaning of the Augustinian dictum of faith

Originally published as "Pope Benedict XVI: A Biblical Portrayal of Jesus," *Nova et Vetera* 7, no. 1 (2009): 19–34. Reprinted by permission.

seeking to understand. It is precisely because Benedict believes in Jesus that he is seeking to understand him more deeply. The beauty of this book is its prayerful, intellectual quest for a more profound biblical and theological understanding of Jesus, and, having discovered it, interior serenity and intellectual joy ensues.

Jesus and Biblical Hermeneutics

If the purpose of *Jesus of Nazareth* is to provide a more profound understanding of Jesus, the manner in which this end is achieved is equally important. For Benedict, the Bible is the fount of our knowledge of Jesus and the well to which the Church continually returns so as to quench her thirst for Jesus that is never fully satisfied. At the very onset of his study, Benedict takes up the fundamental issue of how the Bible is to be read and studied. If one's philosophical presuppositions and historical methodology for reading the Bible are such that an authentic knowledge of Jesus is unattainable and further study will lead only to unproven hypotheses about who Jesus is, then the Bible is no longer the wellspring of faith's life; rather, it becomes a poisoned spring that first enfeebles and ultimately kills faith.

While admitting that the historical-critical method has advanced our scholarly understanding of the Bible and its formation, Benedict notes that many contemporary studies of the biblical Jesus have not actually advanced our understanding of him. Instead they are "like photographs of their authors and the ideals they hold." The impression is given that "we have very little certain knowledge of Jesus and that only at a later stage did faith in his divinity shape the image we have of him." For Benedict, this situation is critical. Faith's "point of reference is being placed in doubt: Intimate friendship with Jesus, on which everything depends, is in danger of clutching at thin air" (xii). Later, in an even more critical assessment of contemporary biblical scholarship, Benedict states: "The alleged findings of scholarly exegesis have been used to put together the most dreadful books that destroy the figure of Jesus and dismantle the faith." The foundational error resides within "the so-called modern worldview, whose fundamental dogma is that God cannot act in history" (35). What Benedict bluntly terms "the Antichrist,"

with an air of scholarly excellence, tells us that any exegesis that reads the Bible from the perspective of faith in the living God, in order to listen to what God has to say, is fundamentalism; he wants to convince us that only *his* kind of exegesis, the supposedly purely scientific kind, in which God says nothing and has nothing to say, is able to keep abreast of the times. (36)

These are strong words, and such criticisms punctuate Benedict's book throughout. By way of contrast, Benedict's own biblical methodology and scholarly arguments, which are principally founded upon Vatican II's *Dei Verbum* and the Pontifical Biblical Commission's *The Interpretation of the Bible in the Church* (1993) and *The Jewish People and Their Scriptures in the Christian Bible* (2001), foster a much more confident approach for obtaining the truth contained within the biblical proclamation and thus offer a more reliable and objective understanding of Jesus.

For Benedict, the historical-critical method cannot be abandoned, for the Christian faith is founded upon historical events. "*Et incarnatus est*—when we say these words, we acknowledge God's actual entry into real history" (xv). But the historical-critical method does not exhaust the interpretive task. While it is able to consider the various books of the Bible in their historical contexts and discern their various sources, "the unity of all of these writings as one 'Bible,' however, is not something it can recognize as an immediate historical datum" (xvii). For Benedict, the content of the Bible must not merely be interpreted historically but also, above all, theologically. "If you want to understand the Scripture in the spirit in which it is written, you have to attend to the content and to the unity of Scripture as a whole" (xviii). While the Bible is composed of many different "books" written in various historical eras in various literary genres, its unity is a theological datum. This theological datum is not imposed upon it, but is found within it. That theological datum is Jesus Christ himself, who unites both the Old and the New Testaments.

This Christological hermeneutic, which sees Jesus Christ as the key to the whole and learns from him how to understand the Bible as a unity, presupposes a prior act of faith. It cannot be the conclusion of a purely historical method. But this act of faith is based upon reason—historical reason—and so makes it possible to see the internal unity of Scripture. (xix)

Benedict provides here some significant and fruitful insights. Yes, we need to know what historical events took place, but it is only through faith that we recognize these historical events as divine revelatory actions and so are able to grasp, in faith, their theological significance as a whole. For Benedict, Jesus provides not only a historical unity to the Bible, in that all historical revelation leads to him and finds its completion in him, but he also simultaneously provides the theological hermeneutic for interpreting this historical unity, in that the historical revelation prior to him Jesus can only be fully understood theologically in light of its being completed in him. What is most novel and insightful is that Benedict argues that Jesus himself teaches us how we are to understand the unity of biblical revelation. He understood himself and his mission and so revealed his own identity and mission only from within the totality of this prior biblical revelation. Jesus embodies the whole of the Old Testament revelation. In his person, Jesus completes and in his mission fulfills the Old Testament's veiled, though originally intended, meaning and in so doing elevates it to a new level of clarity.

Benedict's above understanding allows him to do two things throughout the course of his book. First, because he sees the Bible as a unity, Benedict is eager to demonstrate the theological interrelationship between the Old and the New Testaments, especially the manner in which New Testament revelation cannot be fully understood without a thorough understanding of the Old Testament, and simultaneously how the New Testament completes the Old and so provides a deeper understanding of it. Because he judges, in faith, that the Old and New Testaments contain the entire history of God's revelatory action, Benedict is rejecting the oblique Marcionism contained in some contemporary biblical scholarship, which limits the meaning of a particular Old Testament book solely to its historical context. Second, again because of this biblical unity, Benedict is not afraid to interweave passages from a variety of biblical books after the manner of the Fathers of the Church so as to develop a theological point, particularly concerning the person and work of Christ. Some scholars may consider this the unjustified mixing of apples and oranges, but Benedict is convinced that while there are many different authors from both covenants, together they are, each in their own distinct manner, professing and proclaiming one and the same Gospel. It is therefore completely fitting to knit their various revelatory truths into a configuration that does justice to the whole. For Benedict, "'Canonical exegesis'—reading the individual texts of the Bible in the context of the whole—is an essential dimension of exegesis" (xix; see also 191). Benedict defends his own method of exegesis by stating, "I have merely tried to go beyond purely historical-critical exegesis so as to apply new methodological insights that allow us to offer a properly theological interpretation of the Bible" (xxiii). I have allotted a significant amount of space for presenting Benedict's biblical and theological methodology because I believe he has articulated a methodology that not only pertains to his own book, but also provides a Christian/Catholic alternative for doing theology. On the one hand, there is no doubt that this book's primary concern is to enunciate an authentic biblical understanding of Jesus that supports the Church's later doctrine development. On the other hand, one cannot help but sense that Benedict is also attempting in this process to rescue Scripture from a pseudoacademic environment where it has languished for decades and to return it to its proper environment; that is, the living household of faith, the Church. His method not only allows biblical scholars to be true to their exegetical principles, but also provides new opportunities to engage in authentic theological inquiry, something scholars' own historical-critical method hindered them from fully undertaking. For Benedict, biblical scholars ought not to be shackled by a method that does not allow them full and free access to the entire biblical text as a unity. Benedict's methodology once more allows systematic theologians (of which he is one) access to the biblical text. The Bible is no longer under the strict governance of an elite biblical academy, but now that the Bible may be interpreted from within a theological and ecclesial perspective, actual theologians can once more rightly claim it as their own. It is from within this methodological context that Benedict proceeds to examine in the body of his book key historical events and teachings within the life of Jesus as presented in the Gospels.

Jesus: The New Moses

Benedict begins his study with Deuteronomy, where Moses promises the people that God will "raise up for you a prophet like me from among you" (Dt. 18:15). Such a promise was necessary because the Israelites' entrance into the Promised Land did not fully constitute their salvation. Israel must await a new Moses in whom their full liberation would be fulfilled. For Benedict, this new Moses "will be granted what was refused to the first one—a real, immediate vision of the face of God, and thus the ability to speak entirely from seeing, not just from looking at God's back" (5–6; see also 265). This new Moses would then establish a greater covenant. It is from within this context that Benedict believes that the prologue of John's Gospel must be read. "No one has ever seen God; it is the only Son, who is nearest to the Father's heart, who has made him known" (Jn. 1:18). Jesus, as the new Moses, "lives before the face of God, not just as a friend, but as a Son; he lives in the most intimate unity with the Father" (6). Much later in his book Benedict emphatically reiterates this same point. "Only the one who is God sees God—Jesus. He truly speaks from his vision of the Father, from unceasing dialogue with the Father, a dialogue that is his life" (265–66). What Jesus reveals is not a product of human reasoning, but a result from his human prayer, which is "a participation in this filial communion with the Father" (7).

Here Benedicts expresses for the first time what I consider to be the major theme of his book. Jesus is the incarnate Son of God who bestows upon all believers what he himself shares—a filial intimacy and knowledge of the Father. Benedict will orchestrate this signature theme under various modalities throughout the entirety of his book until it reaches its crescendo with the great "I am" of John's Gospel.

The Baptism of Jesus: Entering into the Depths of Sin

Following the Gospel narratives, Benedict emphasizes Jesus's historicity and so his communion with the whole history of humankind. In Luke, Jesus's primogenitor is not father Abraham, as in Matthew's Gospel, but father Adam. Thus Jesus is literally "the son of man" (10). The baptism of Jesus also highlights his solidarity not merely with some generic and sanitized form of humanity but rather his solidarity with the sinful race of Adam. Benedict perceives already in Jesus's baptism "a confession of guilt and a plea for forgiveness in order to make a new beginning" (17), and thus a foreshadowing of his death and resurrection.

Looking at the events in light of the Cross and Resurrection, Christians realized what happened: Jesus loaded the burden of all mankind's guilt upon his shoulders; he bore it down into the depths of the Jordan. He inaugurated his public activity by stepping into the place of sinners. His inaugural gesture is an anticipation of the Cross (18).

Benedict perceptively appreciates in Jesus's baptism, to which the above alludes, the foreshadowing of what it truly means for Jesus to have assumed a humanity from fallen Adam in that he must bear the burden of sin to its ultimate end. Echoing Irenaeus, Benedict sees Jesus recapitulating, assuming within his own historical humanity, the whole of humankind's sinful history. Furthermore, without any apology or even a slight questioning pause of the pen, Benedict appropriates a familiar, though controversial, von Balthasarian theme. He clearly acknowledges that Jesus, the son of Adam, enters into the domain of the devil. Benedict does alter the emphasis of this theme, however.

His entering into the sin of others is a descent into the "inferno." But he does not descend merely in the role of a spectator, as in Dante's *Inferno*. Rather, he goes down in the role of one whose suffering-with-others is a transforming suffering that turns the underworld around, knocking down and flinging open the gates of the abyss. His Baptism is a descent into the house of the evil one, combat with the "strong man" (cf. Lk 11:22) who holds men captive." (20)

Notice that Jesus's descent into hell is not some passive event for Benedict. It is not simply or only the submissive experience of abandonment accompanied by its consuming anguish. Rather, for Benedict, Jesus descends into the domain of Satan in order to do combat so as to free humankind from hell's captivity; that is, from the sufferings of sin, death, and damnation. Moreover, this descent into hell does not simply occur after Jesus's death; rather, it "accompanies him along his entire journey. He must recapitulate the whole of history from its beginnings—from Adam on; he must go through, suffer through, the whole of it, in order to transform it" (26). Later Benedict once again emphasizes that it is not only after his death "but already by his death and during his whole life, that Jesus 'descends into hell,' as it were, into the domain of our temptations and defeats, in order to take us by the hand and carry us upward" (161; see also 99). Benedict is keenly aware that only if the Son of God, having become man of the sinful race of Adam, actually experiences the full effects of sin—temptation, suffering, and death—and so breaches sin's very domicile—hell—can he overthrow it and lift us up into the new abode of heavenly life. This journey of descent not only expressed Jesus's love for us, but also the love of the Father in rescuing his Son from the demonic realm of sin and death. Jesus descended "into the abyss of death, into the night of abandonment, and into the desolation of the defenseless. He ventured *this* leap as an act of God's love for men.

And so he knew that, ultimately, when he leaped he could only fall into the kindly hands of the Father" (38).

At Jesus's baptism, where he first publicly begins his descent into the abyss, the love and protection of the Father were already present. It is here, when Jesus first aligns himself with sinful humanity and assumes to himself its ultimate fatal consequences, that the Father sent forth his Spirit upon him and declared his identity as the beloved Son, and, as the Anointed One, his "kingly and priestly dignity were formally bestowed upon him for all time in the presence of Israel" (26).

While Benedict does not shy away from the language of descent and even that of "descent into hell," he gives to such notions a much more active and broader perspective than is normally understood. While Jesus may experience the depths of sin and the suffering that ensues from it, he turns such experiences into the means whereby he conquers sin and vanquishes death and so triumphs over Satan. But it is here that one would wish for some soteriological mechanism to come into play. How does taking on the sin and guilt of humankind and so suffering its effects even to the depths of hell bring about hell's demise? Benedict does not clearly say.

I argue that it is precisely in his love that this transformation occurs. In love, the Son of God assumed our sinful humanity and on the Cross assumed its curse to the end—even entering into the abyss. Moreover, on the Cross he simultaneously offered, in love, his life as a sacrifice to the Father in reparation for all of humankind's sin. He entered hell as the one who so much loved his brothers and sisters in Adam as to assume their punishment, as well as the one who lovingly offered his sinless and holy life to the Father on behalf of his sinful brothers and sisters. It is this twofold love that freed sinful humankind from hell's condemnation and made it possible for humankind to be transformed into righteous sons and daughters of the Father after the likeness of Jesus, the Son. Interestingly and perhaps tellingly, Benedict never did bring up this theme in his second volume.

Jesus and the Kingdom of God

Whereas Jesus preached the coming of God's kingdom, Benedict notes, the apostolic Church proclaimed Jesus as the Christ. This was not a mutation of the original Gospel, but rather the Church's awareness that the kingdom of God is embodied in the person of Jesus himself. It is "not simply in Jesus's physical presence that the 'Kingdom' is located; rather, it is in his action, accomplished in the Holy Spirit" (60). For Benedict, then, the kingdom of God is not some human-engineered utopia in which God ultimately disappears (54). Rather, in Jesus, "God has here and now entered actively into history in a wholly new way" (60). "What did Jesus actually bring, if not world peace, universal prosperity, and a better world? What has he brought?" Benedict's biblical answer to these and similar questions echoes throughout his book. "The answer is very simple: God" (44; see also 354). This understanding of the kingdom of God is similarly perceived within the Sermon on the Mount, which Benedict perceptively interprets in a Christological manner.

It is unanimously understood that Matthew portrays Jesus in the Sermon on the Mount as the new Moses. In interpreting the Sermon, however, Benedict advances his theme that Jesus, as the Son of God incarnate, establishes an intimacy with God. Unlike the Israelites' harrowing experience of God's presence on Mount Sinai, God now "speaks intimately, as one man to another" (67). Moreover, the Beatitudes present "a veiled interior biography of Jesus," for they "display the mystery of Christ himself, and they call us into communion with him" (74). Jesus himself is the one who is poor in spirit, who is meek, who seeks for righteousness, and the like, and as such he reveals his intimate union with God. Such intimacy is to be the life of the Church who practices the Beatitudes and of those who are her members. This is specifically seen in the Beatitude that the pure of heart will see God.

For it belongs to his [Jesus's] nature that he sees God, that he stands face-to-face with him, in permanent interior discourse—in a relationship of Sonship. In other words, this Beatitude is profoundly Christological. We will see God when we enter into the "mind of Christ" (Phil. 2:5). Purification of heart occurs as a consequence of following Christ, of becoming one with him. (95)

As the above exemplifies, the closer one draws to Jesus and thus to God, the more one becomes truly human. The Sermon on the Mount teaches us "how to be a human being." But to be such we must live "in relation to God" (128).

If Jesus himself embodies the Beatitudes that fulfill the Ten Commandments, for Benedict, Jesus also personifies and fulfills the Torah. Benedict notes the recognized reading that Jesus, when he states "You have heard it said … but I say to you," has appropriated to himself "the same exalted level as the Lawgiver—as God" (102). But then Benedict once more draws upon his constant theme. The Torah is holy because it comes forth from the all-holy God, but if Jesus, with a display of divine authority, is altering the Torah, then he, too, must be the all-holy God.

Jesus understands himself as the Torah—as the word of God in person. The tremendous prologue of John's Gospel—"in the beginning was the Word and the Word was with God, and the Word was God" (Jn. 1:1)—says nothing different from what the Jesus of the Sermon on the Mount and the Jesus of the Synoptic Gospels says. The Jesus of the Fourth Gospel and the Jesus of the Synoptics is one and the same: the true "historical" Jesus. (110–11)

Here we observe how subtly, and yet unmistakably, the Synoptics profess the divinity of Jesus. It is not, as is often assumed within scholarly circles, that the Synoptics portray the earthly, human, historical Jesus while the Gospel of John divinizes him to the detriment of human historicity. Rather, Benedict clearly shows that, in a profound appraisal of the Gospels, both are proclaiming the same truth in different manners, and in so doing enhancing our understanding of who Jesus is.

This bears itself out when Benedict comments on John, chapter 6, where Jesus proclaims that he is the true bread of life. While God gave the Israelites the manna in the desert, the real food that he gave them, of which manna is a symbol, was his words of life—the Torah. "So the Torah is 'bread' from God, then. And yet it shows us only the back, so to speak. It is a 'shadow.' 'For the bread of God is that which comes down from heaven, and gives life to the world' (Jn. 6:33)" (267). Jesus is the real bread of life and so Jesus is the fulfillment of the Torah. "The Law has become a *person*. When we encounter Jesus we feed on the living God himself, so to speak; we truly eat 'bread from heaven'" (268). This finds its ultimate fulfillment in the Eucharist, where the eternal Word/Torah nourishes us on his resurrected body and blood.

Jesus and the Our Father

If the Sermon on the Mount reveals that Jesus is truly the Son of God and therefore demonstrates just how close God is to us, and also teaches us how to be human by being related to God through Jesus, the Our Father is at the heart of this revelation. Benedict observes astutely that thoughts normally precede our words. But this is not always the case when it comes to prayer. Especially in the Psalms and the liturgy, our words of prayer precede our thoughts; actually, the words of the Psalms and the liturgy conform our minds to the truths expressed in such prayers, and so we actually pray in conformity with the inspiration of the Holy Spirit (130–31). This is also the case when we pray the Our Father.

The Our Father arose from Jesus's own life of prayer, from his filial "dialogue with the Father" (133). Benedict observes the relationship between the Our Father and the Ten Commandments, and in so doing the intimate connection between the Old and New Testaments emphasizes once again that we can be human only in relationship to the Father. "The Our Father, then, like the Ten Commandments, begins by establishing the primacy of God, which then leads naturally to a consideration of the right way of being human" (134). While we pray to the Father, that address can only be made in Jesus because he "is 'the Son' in the strict sense—he is one substance with the Father. He wants to draw all of us into his humanity and so into his Sonship, into his total belonging to God" (138). The Our Father exemplifies a central Christian mystery. Through his humanity, Jesus unites us to his own sonship and so provides the means to become children of the Father. "We are not ready-made children of God from the start, but we are meant to become so increasingly by growing more and more deeply in communion with Jesus. Our sonship turns out to be identical with following Christ" (138). Benedict understands our relationship to the Father in and through his Son to be the essence of what it means to be human and warns of the consequences of its absence. Commenting on the petition—"deliver us from evil"—he states: "The Our Father in general and this petition in particular are trying to tell us that it is only when you have lost God that you have lost yourself; then you are nothing more than a random product of evolution" (166).

The Parables as the Mystery of Jesus

In introducing his chapter on the parables, Benedict once more highlights the paucity of much contemporary liberal biblical scholarship, though "in its day it was viewed as the *ne plus ultra* of scientific rigor and reliable historiography and was regarded even by Catholic exegetes with envy and admiration." The reason is that it reduces the parables to entertaining morality tales and Jesus to that of a wise guru. Similar to the interpretation of the Sermon on the Mount, "this type of interpretation that makes Jesus a moralist, for all of its significant historical insight, remains theologically impoverished, and does not even come close to the real figure of Jesus" (186).

Not surprisingly, as he did when interpreting the Sermon on the Mount and the Our Father, Benedict once again recognizes that the parables concern the mystery of who Jesus is (188). With admirable insight, Benedict also informs us that "it is on the Cross that the parables are unlocked" (190).

The parables speak in a hidden way, then, of the mystery of the Cross; they do not only speak of it—they are part of it themselves. For precisely because they allow the mystery of Jesus's divinity to be seen, they lead to contradiction. It is just when they emerge into a final clarity, as in the parable of the unjust vintners (cf. Mk. 12:1–12), that they become stations of the way of the Cross. In the parables Jesus is not only the sower who scatters the seed of God's word, but also the seed that falls into the earth in order to die and so to bear fruit. (191)

Jesus is the only beloved divine Son of the Father whom the vintners will kill, and yet his death will be the seed that bears much fruit. This same theme is woven into Benedict's interpretation of the parable of Lazarus and the rich man, which he also reads in light of raising Lazarus of Bethany from the dead. "Do we not recognize in the figure of Lazarus—lying at the rich man's door covered in sores—the mystery of Jesus, who 'suffered outside the city walls' (Heb. 13:12) and, stretched naked on the Cross, was delivered over to the mockery and contempt of the mob, his body 'full of blood and wounds'? ... Moreover, as the rich man asked Abraham to send Lazarus to his brothers because they would believe someone who rose from they dead, so Jesus, is "the true Lazarus" [both of the parable and of the actually raising], who "*has* risen from the dead—and he has come to tell us so" (216–17).

In a manner reminiscent of the Fathers of the Church, Benedict has beautifully woven together various passages of Scripture so as to offer a deeper understanding of the parables and miracles, an understanding that enables us to discern the mystery of who Jesus is as the Son of God incarnate and of his passion, death, and resurrection.

The Johannine Portrayal of Jesus

Benedict's study of the Synoptic Gospels covers approximately two-thirds of his book. One of his primary aims is to demonstrate that these Gospels, in many and various ways, truly do proclaim the divinity of Jesus. "Listening to the Synoptics, we have realized that the mystery of Jesus's oneness with the Father is ever present and determines everything, even thought it remains hidden beneath his humanity" (218). While this truth only gradually penetrated the hearts and minds of Jesus's disciples, his opponents clearly perceived the significance of what Jesus was saying and doing, and they ardently rejected it as blasphemous. However, "in John, Jesus's divinity appears unveiled" (219).

Because Jesus's divinity is so evident in John's Gospel, many scholars have rejected its historicity. Benedict launches into a passionate, lengthy, and ultimately effective defense of its historicity (218–38). For Benedict, the disciple whom Jesus loved has not abandoned history, but, through prayerful reflection under the guidance of the Holy Spirit, he has faithfully presented the words and actions of Jesus and in so doing has penetrated their inner meaning and significance. "Just as Jesus, the Son, knows about the mystery of the Father from resting in his heart, so too the Evangelist has gained his intimate knowledge from his inward repose in Jesus' heart" (222–23). In response to those who argue that John's Gospel does not bear witness to history but is intended simply to strength the faith of the early Church, Benedict perceptively queries:

What faith does it "testify" to if, so to speak, it has left history behind? How does it strengthen faith if it presents itself as a historical testimony—and does so quite emphatically—but then does not report history? ... A faith that discards history in this manner really turns into "Gnosticism." It leaves flesh, incarnation—just what true history is—behind. (228)

Having defended the historicity of John's Gospel, Benedict discusses four Johannine images: water, vine and wine, bread, and the shepherd. It is not possible to comment in detail on all or any one of these images. Nonetheless, it is not surprising, given the established pattern of his book, that Benedict perceives that all of these images have to do with Jesus, as the Son of God incarnate, granting access to his Father in the Holy Spirit. Moreover, the images of water, vine and wine, and bread find their fulfillment in the sacraments of Baptism and the Eucharist. Through Baptism the Christian is united to Christ, the vine, and so comes to share in the new life of the Holy Spirit as children of the Father. Likewise, Jesus, the vine, continually nourishes this life through the Eucharist. Benedict perceives that those who follow Jesus as the shepherd have access to the Father through him. This is why the Church is commissioned to preach the Gospel to all nations and peoples: "There is only one Shepherd" (284).

Peter's Profession and the Transfiguration

Having examined a variety of Jesus's teachings and actions by and through which he revealed the mystery of himself as the Son incarnate, Benedict focuses on two events that lie at the heart of this mystery: Peter's profession of faith and the Transfiguration. While Benedict has linked throughout his book the Incarnation with the Cross, he now deepens this connection in a most thoughtful manner.

Benedict first notes that Jesus questions his disciples about his identity as he sets out to Jerusalem—the journey of the Cross—a journey that his disciples must also undertake if they are to be his faithful followers. This provides the context of Jesus's query, "Who do the people say that I am?" While the responses of John the Baptist, Elijah, and Jeremiah are those of prophets, they all prefigure some form of suffering and death as well as the eschatological events through which Israel would be restored. Nonetheless, while they may approximate who Jesus is, they fall far short. Jesus is more than just a prophet. For Benedict, this distinction is crucial within the context of global religions. "Today it is fashionable to regard Jesus as one of the great religious founders who were granted a profound experience of God" (293). But such an understanding is always a human experience that at best obtains fragments of divine truth. "The individual decides what he is going to accept from the various 'experiences,' what he finds helpful and what he finds alien. There is no definitive commitment here" (293). Peter's confession elevates Jesus to a unique and singular status that differs in kind from the founders of other religions.

While Benedict notes that the wording of Peter's confession differs in the three Synoptics, the real issue is not in attempting to sort out which one is authentically the historical, the *ipsima verba Petri*. Rather, it is to grasp, in faith, the truth that the Gospels are proclaiming. Scholars discern two ways of interpreting Peter's confession that they often see as opposed to one another—as expressing Jesus's ontological nature or as expressing his role or function within salvation history. For Benedict, Peter's profession is both. In all three forms, his profession states something that is "'substantive'— you *are* the Christ, the Christ of God, the Christ, the Son of the living God" (298). Yet this proclamation of who Jesus is must equally be understood within its salvific context—the mystery of the Cross and Resurrection. Benedict concludes:

At certain key moments, the disciples came to the astonishing realization: This is God himself. They were unable to put all this together into a perfect response. Instead they rightly drew upon the Old Testament's words of promise: Christ, the Anointed One, Son of God, Lord. These are the key words on which their confession focused, while still tentatively searching for a way forward. It could arrive at its complete form only when Thomas, touching the wounds of the Risen Lord, cried out, in amazement: "My Lord and my God" (Jn. 20:28) ... Only by touching Jesus' wounds and encounter his Resurrection are we able to grasp them [Thomas's words], and then they become our mission. (304–5).

While Peter rightly professed that Jesus was the Christ, the Son of living God, he did not place such a profession in relationship to the Cross and so his faith was defective. "Jesus' divinity belongs with the Cross—only when we put the two together do we recognize Jesus correctly" (305).

There is an intimate connection between Peter's profession of faith and the Transfiguration. Benedict notes that Peter's profession would have occurred on the great Day of Atonement, the one day of the year where the high priest would have solemnly pronounced the name of Yahweh. This reinforces the interpretation that Jesus is truly God, and also that his mission is inherently tied to the Cross. The following week would be the Feast of Tabernacles, the Transfiguration occurring on the final day of the feast. Luke sets the Transfiguration within the context of Jesus praying. For Benedict, the Transfiguration "displays visibly what happens when Jesus talks with his Father: the profound interpenetration of his being with God, which then becomes pure light. In his oneness with the Father, Jesus is himself 'light from light'" (310). Unlike the light that shone upon Moses, the light of the Transfiguration comes forth from within Jesus himself.

While it would appear that Peter's remark about setting up three tents, one for Jesus and one each for Moses and Elijah, is but confused nonsense, Benedict sees it as a direct reference to the Feast of Tabernacles itself. God dwelt within the Tabernacle, but now through the Incarnation, God literally "has pitched the tent of his body among us and has thus inaugurated the messianic age" (315). Moreover, as the holy cloud, the *shekinah*, hovered over the Tent of Meeting displaying the presence of God, so now "Jesus is the holy tent above whom the cloud of God's presence now stands and spreads to 'overshadow' the others as well" (316). As noted above, the Father's exhortation to listen to his Son, who is flanked by Moses and Elijah, both indicates his continuity with the Torah and the Prophets and his being the new Torah and the fulfillment of God's promises.

The Identity of Jesus

Benedict brings his book to a close by examining the titles of Jesus that clearly identify him as God: Christ, Lord, Son of Man, the Son, and the "I Am."

Benedict rightly notes that one must distinguish the title "Son of God" from that of "the Son," which Jesus himself employs. In the Prologue, John sets the context for Jesus's use of the title. "No one has ever seen God; it is the only Son, who is nearest to the Father's heart, who has made him known" (Jn. 1:18). The truth of this statement, Benedict again states, arises out of the Jesus's prayerful filial dialogue with the Father. "At the same time, it also becomes clear what 'the Son' is and what this term means: perfect communion in knowledge, which is at the same time communion in being. Unity in knowing is possible only because it is a unity of being" (340). This biblical understanding of the term "Son" along with other biblical evidence provided by Benedict throughout his book rightly give rise to the Council of Nicea's *homoousios*. "This philosophical term serves ... to safeguard the reliability of the *biblical* term" (320).

Jesus's self-revelation is most strikingly seen in his use of "I am." This phrase was first used in Exodus 3:14 where God reveals his name as "I am who I am." God designates himself as "I am." Deutero-Isaiah emphasizes that the Israelites will know that "I am he" (Is. 43:10). For Benedict, when Jesus says, "I am," he is not simply placing himself along side of the Father, but "because he is the Son, he has every right to utter with his own lips the Father's self-designation" (348). But Jesus's self-designation as God by appropriating to himself the very name of God, "I am," also reveals that as God incarnate he is to die on the Cross. "When you have lifted up the Son of man, then you will know that I am he" (Jn. 8:28). As Benedict states, "On the Cross, his Sonship, his oneness with the Father, becomes visible ... The burning bush is the Cross. The highest claim of revelation, the 'I am he,' and the Cross of Jesus are inseparably one" (349).

It must not be thought that Jesus's use of the "I am" is exclusive to John's Gospel and so historically suspect. It is also found in the Synoptics, though in a less conspicuous manner. In Mark, for example, Jesus walks on the water as he approaches the disciples on the stormy lake. They are frightened at his sight, but he assures them: "Take heart, it is I [I am he]; have no fear" (Mk. 6:50). Benedict observes that within the Bible men are overwhelmed with fear when confronted by the presence of God. "It is this 'divine terror' that comes over the disciples here. For walking on the waters is a divine preroga-tive: God 'alone stretched out the heavens, and trampled the waves of the sea,' we read in the book of Job (Jb. 9:8; cf. Ps. 76:20 in the Septuagint version; Is. 43:16). The Jesus who walks upon the waters is not simply the familiar Jesus; in this new Jesus they suddenly recognize the presence of God himself" (352).

A Personal Relationship with Jesus

As the above discussion demonstrates, Benedict is keen to show that, be-cause of his unique relationship with the Father, Jesus is the eternal Son of God incarnate. What also becomes evident in so many ways throughout his book is that this relationship is available to those who believe in Jesus. In an almost Protestant Evangelical fashion, Benedict stresses that it is through our personal relationship with Jesus, our friendship with Jesus, by means of faith and the sacraments, that we come to share in his own personal rela-tionship with the Father (see, e.g., xii, xxiv, 24, 138). This, I believe, is signif-icant. It reveals Benedict's pastoral awareness that contemporary men and women are seeking personal relationships that are authentic and loving. For Benedict, this human "personalism" can be obtained only if one first has a personal relationship with Jesus, who allows one to share in the divine life of the Father through the love of the Holy Spirit. It is through our sharing in the life and love of the Trinity that we can truly share our lives with one another in love. As Benedict states:

In the end, man needs just one thing, in which everything else is included; but he must first delve beyond his superficial wishes and longings in order to learn to recognize what it is that he truly needs and truly wants. He needs God. And so we now realize what ultimately lies behind all the Johannine images: Jesus gives us "life" because he gives us God. He can give God because he himself is one with God, because he is the Son. He himself is the gift—he is "life." (353–54)

In providing the reader with an authentic biblical portrayal of Jesus, Benedict has offered the reader an opportunity to meet Jesus himself, and in so doing allowed the reader to come to a deeper personal relationship with him. Benedict has learned from Jesus himself that this is the true purpose of theology and the hoped for goal of faith—to encounter the living God in Christ Jesus.

CHAPTER 2

The Son's Filial Relationship to the Father

Jesus as the New Moses

UNDER POPE BENEDICT'S rubric of Jesus being the new Moses, the Christological hermeneutical key to his two-volume work *Jesus of Nazareth* is his understanding of the biblical proclamation of Jesus's filial relationship to the Father.

The Centrality of Jesus's Relationship to the Father

At the onset of his first volume, Benedict states that only if the historical Jesus is actually anchored in God does he become real. He continues:

This is also the point around which I will construct my own book. It sees Jesus in light of his communion with the Father, which is the true center of his personality; without it, we cannot understand him at all, and it is from this center that he makes himself present to us still today. (1:xiv)

Throughout both volumes, Benedict never forgets that if we are to grasp who Jesus is, we must ever more deeply understand his relationship to the Father, for it is his relationship to the Father that reveals Jesus to be his only begotten Son. In anticipating his interpretation of the Sermon on the Mount, Benedict states, "Above all, what we will see in the next chapter is

Originally published as "The Son's Filial Relationship to the Father: Jesus as the New Moses," *Nova et Vetera* 11, no. 1 (2013): 253–64. Reprinted by permission.

that Jesus always speaks as the Son, that the relation between Father and Son is always present as the background of his message" (1:63).

Benedict could subsequently write:

From our study of the Sermon on the Mount, but also from our interpretation of the Our Father, we have seen that the deepest theme of Jesus' preaching was his own mystery, the mystery of the Son in whom God is among us and keeps his word; he announces the Kingdom of God as coming and as having come in his person. (1:188)

As he begins his study of images of Jesus in John's Gospel, which will manifest even more clearly Jesus's unique relationship to the Father, Benedict concludes:

Listening to the Synoptics, we have realized that the mystery of Jesus' oneness with the Father is ever present and determines everything, even though it remains hidden beneath his humanity. (1:218)

In volume two, this same Christology hermeneutic is present. In examining Jesus's high priestly prayer, where he speaks of the Father consecrating him in the truth, Benedict states: "Thus one may say that this consecration of Jesus by the Father is identical with the Incarnation: it expresses both total unity with the Father and total existence for the world" (2:87).

To examine the mystery of Jesus, as the incarnate Son, through his relationship with the Father, is not in itself novel. Many other Scripture scholars and theologians have commented previously on this mystery. What makes Benedict's treatment unique and noteworthy is the centrality he gives to it and the manner in which he develops it. Jesus's words and deeds reveal him to be the only Son of the Father, and for Benedict, Jesus did this primarily by fulfilling an Old Testament prophecy or elevating an Old Testament event in a new and never previously considered manner. If the Christological hermeneutical key lies in Jesus's relationship to the Father, then in order to grasp fully and perceive clearly the manner of Jesus's relationship to the Father, one must turn to the Old Testament, for it is from within the Old Testament that the mystery of Jesus was hidden and now made manifest.

Theological Exegesis

Benedict's exegetical methodology not only authorizes him to read the Bible with the eyes of faith, but also, in faith, enables him to establish Jesus as the exegetical key for interpreting the Old Testament. While Benedict acknowledges the legitimacy of the historical critical method, he argues that left to itself it can render the Bible sterile, not permitting the full content of revelation to become manifest. In his second volume, he states starkly:

If scholarly exegesis is not to exhaust itself in constantly new hypotheses, becoming theologically irrelevant, it must take a methodological step forward and see itself once again as a theological discipline, without abandoning its historical character. (2:xiv)

One is only able to discern the fullness of who Jesus is and the comprehensive significance of his words and deeds if one advances beyond the historical critical method. This Benedict proposes to do in *Jesus of Nazareth*.

Following Vatican II's Constitution on Divine Revelation, Benedict states that "if you want to understand the Scripture in the spirit in which it is written, you have to attend to the content and to the unity of Scripture as a whole" (1:xviii). The person of Jesus Christ is the one who unifies the whole Bible—the Old and the New Testament. "This Christological hermeneutic, which sees Jesus Christ as the key to the whole and learns from him how to understand the Bible as a unity, presupposes a prior act of faith" (1:xix). What is of immense significance here is that Benedict does not simply see Jesus as the key to understanding the whole of the Bible; we must learn from him as to how to interpret the Bible. Jesus consciously places his words and actions within the context of Old Testament revelation. His own words and actions, in the context of the Old Testament revelation, provide the exegetical tool for understanding who he is and what he is salvifically doing. In so doing, Jesus reveals how he fulfills and brings to completion the whole previous history of salvation. He fulfills it and brings it to completion in a manner that no one could have ever imagined, yet having done so, all the previous revelational content of salvation history is illuminated anew and constitutes in Jesus the realization of the Father's eternal plan of salvation.

The scholarly community therefore "must recognize that a properly developed faith-hermeneutic is appropriate to the text and can be combined with a historical hermeneutic, aware of its limits, so as to form a method-ological whole" (2:xv). This "faith-hermeneutic" authorizes one to engage in what Benedict calls "canonical exegesis" or "theological exegesis." Bene-dict concludes: "It is obvious that the way I look at the figure of Jesus goes beyond what much contemporary exegesis ... has to say" (1:xxiii). In his books, Benedict has "tried to go beyond purely historical-critical exegesis so as to apply new methodological insights that allow us to offer a properly theological interpretation of the Bible" (1:xxiii). Again, Benedict ultimately believes that he has attempted in both volumes to do properly what Vatican II encouraged.

Fundamentally this is a matter [his exegetical method] of finally putting into prac-tice the methodological principles formulated for exegesis by the Second Vatican Council (in *Dei Verbum*, 12), a task that unfortunately has scarcely been attempted. (2:xv)

There is only one example of Benedict's theological or canonical exe-gesis in which he is able to perceive and articulate many facets of what it means for Jesus to be the Son of the Father. Throughout both volumes, one theme that Benedict consistently brings to the fore is the various ways Jesus portrays himself as the new Moses. In so doing, both Jesus and Moses take on new significance. Jesus, in word and deed, aligns himself with a word said and deed done by Moses, thus designating himself as the new Moses. Jesus's "Moses-like" words and deeds advance and elevate something that Moses said and did to a significantly new level of divine revelation: ulti-mately, the fulfillment of divine revelation. For this reason we are able to grasp the revelational meaning and importance of what Jesus is saying and doing. Moreover, we now perceive the deeper significance of Moses's origi-nal words and deeds. What God revealed in Moses was in anticipation of its being fulfilled in the new Moses, and thus its real significance, long hidden, can only be seen in the light of the new Moses. Jesus is only able to reveal who he truly is in the light of Moses, but in becoming the new Moses, Mo-ses himself takes on his true import.

Jesus: The New Moses

Within the opening sentence of the introduction to his first volume, Ben-edict notes insightfully that the Book of Deuteronomy "contains a promise that is completely different from the messianic hope expressed in other books of the Old Testament, yet it is of decisive importance for understanding the figure of Jesus" (1:1). Unlike other Old Testament books that look forward to a new David, a new king, Deuteronomy promises a new Moses. Moses is seen as a prophet, and it is upon this notion that God makes a promise. "The Lord your God will raise up for you a prophet like me from among you … him you shall heed" (Deut. 18:15). What makes Moses unique among the prophets, according to Benedict, is that he "conversed with the Lord 'face to face' as a man speaks to his friend, so he had spoken with God (cf. Ex. 33:11)" (1:4). Such speaking with God "face to face" is the basis of Moses whole ministry. Only within such an intimate relation could God have given the law to Moses, the basis of the covenant and thus for leading a godly life. While Moses can speak with God as a friend, he could not see God's actual countenance, for God placed his hand over Moses's eyes as he passed by. He could only see the back of God (see Ex. 33:18–23). For Benedict, the promise of a prophet like Moses contains a "greater expectation." The last prophet, "the new Moses, will be granted what was refused to the first—a real, immediate vision of the face of God, and thus the ability to speak from seeing, not just looking at God's back" (1:6). For Benedict, this implies that "the new Moses will be the mediator of a greater covenant than the one that Moses was able to bring down from Sinai (cf. Heb. 9:11–14)" (1:6).

It is because Jesus is the new Moses that the truth expressed in the Prologue of John's Gospel takes on its true meaning. "No one has ever seen God; it is the only Son, who is nearest to the Father's heart, who has made him known" (Jn. 1:18). It is because Jesus is the Son that he is able to fulfill, as man, the promise of a new prophet like Moses. He does not see and speak with the Father as a friend but as an only begotten Son.

What was true of Moses only in fragmentary form has been fully realized in the person of Jesus: He lives before the face of God, not just as a friend, but as a Son; he lives in the most intimate unity with the Father. (1:6)

Later in the same first volume, again when treating the Gospel of John, Benedict returns to this same understanding. Benedict argues that Bultmann is wrong in holding that the Gospel of John is rooted in Gnosticism; rather, it is thoroughly rooted in the Old Testament. This is confirmed in Jesus fulfilling the prophecy concerning the new Moses. He first quotes John.

And from his fullness have we all received, grace upon grace. For the law was given through Moses; grace and truth came through Jesus Christ. No one has ever seen God; it is the only Son, who is nearest to the Father's heart, who has made him known. (Jn. 1:16–18)

Benedict thus sees the promise made to Moses "fulfilled superabundantly" in Jesus. "The one who has come is more than Moses, more than a prophet. He is the Son. And that is why grace and truth now come to light, not in order to destroy the Law, but to fulfill it" (1:263).

The New Moses: Sermon on the Mount

The Sermon on the Mount Matthew, as has often been noted, portrays Jesus as the new Moses. The Pope notes this as well, but he provides a deeper, fresh understanding to this image. In the Sermon on the Mount, "Matthew puts together a picture of Jesus as the new Moses in precisely the profound sense that we saw earlier in connection with the promise of a new prophet given in the Book of Deuteronomy" (1:65). It is not simply that Jesus ascends a mountain similar to Moses ascending Mount Sinai, but rather he ascends a mountain, sits down, and teaches. Benedict comments: "Jesus sits down—the expression of the plenary authority of the teacher. He takes his seat on the *cathedra* of the mountain" (1:65). While the rabbis sit on the chair of Moses and have authority, Jesus sits on the mountain "as the greater Moses, who broadens the Covenant to include all nations" (1:66). The Sermon on the Mount is a dramatic lesson, in word and deed, wherein Jesus assumes the role of the new Moses, thus revealing that he is the author of the law of the new covenant. In so doing, Jesus also reveals the real significance of the first Moses. Moses's significance resides not solely in his role in establishing the first covenant, but in the establishment of the first covenant whereby he became the prefigurement of the new Moses, Jesus. We see the true importance of Moses only in the light of Jesus, for he provides the means by which Jesus is able to reveal who he is—the new and greater Moses who will establish a new and everlasting covenant for all nations.

Jesus, the new Moses, is on a new Sinai enacting a new covenantal law, and the atmosphere is far different from that of the first Sinai. Unlike the first Sinai, where the people were terrified by storm, fire, and earthquake and only Moses ascended the mountain in safety, on this new Sinai "God's power is now revealed in his mildness, his greatness in his simplicity and closeness" (1:67). While the scene is pastoral and serene, according to Benedict, Jesus's message is one of a deeper love, a love that embraces the Cross. "Now God speaks intimately, as one man to another. Now he descends into the depth of their human sufferings" (1:67). Benedict summarizes beautifully what is taking place, in word and deed, on the new Mount Sinai.

It should be clear by now that the Sermon on the Mount is the new Torah brought by Jesus. Moses could deliver his Torah only by entering into the divine darkness on the mountain. Jesus' Torah likewise presupposes his entering into communion with the Father, the inward ascents of his life, which are then prolonged in his descents into communion of life and suffering with men. (1:68)

Benedict's understanding of what is happening in the Sermon on the Mount is indeed theologically profound. He perceives that Jesus teaches us how to understand who he is in light of the Old Testament. He not only sees Jesus as the new Moses promulgating the new Torah, but he also perceives that Jesus is able to do so only because he (in a singular fashion, one that differs in kind from that of Moses) possesses a filial relationship with the Father. Because of this divine filial relationship, Jesus not only proclaims the Sermon on the Mount, but he also literally embodies the sermon that he preaches. Unlike Moses, Jesus is the new Torah incarnate, the law of love. Because Jesus embodies the new law of love—love for the Father and love for the whole of humankind—he as Son will embrace, in filial love, the will of the Father and so ascend the mountain of Golgotha and take possession of the new chair of Moses: the Cross. On the Cross, Jesus, as the new Moses, will establish the new and everlasting covenant with his Father, a covenant for all nations.

The New Moses and the Prayer of Jesus

Because of Jesus's unique filial relationship with his Father, Benedict emphasizes that Jesus's teaching is not the product of human learning. Again, fulfilling the experience of Moses: "It originates from immediate contact with the Father, from 'face-to-face' dialogue—from the vision of the one who rests close to the Father's heart" (1:7). This unity between Jesus and the Father is the source of Jesus's life of prayer. His prayer—within his human consciousness, intellect, and will—"becomes a participation in this filial communion with the Father" (1:7). This is at the heart of the Our Father. "We must also keep in mind that the Our Father originates from his own praying, from the Son's dialogue with the Father. This means that it reaches down into depths far beyond the words" (1:133).

Because of this unity, Jesus as the new Moses is able to make known the full name of God. Benedict sees this taking place within the Our Father where Jesus teaches us to pray "hallowed be thy name" (see 1:142–45). Also, in the Johannine high priestly prayer, Jesus prays to the Father: "I have manifested your name to the men that you gave me out of the world" (Jn. 17:6). Jesus also states: "I made know to them your name, and I will make it known, that the love with which you have loved me may be in them, and I in them" (Jn. 17:26). Benedict comments: "With these words Jesus clearly presents himself as the new Moses, who brings to completion what began with Moses at the burning bush" (2:90–91; see also 1:144). Knowing the name of God allows the Jewish people to invoke him and so make him present. The Jewish people also knew that God was made known in the temple for that was his dwelling (cf. Deut. 12:11). When Jesus says that he has made known the name of God, he is stating a truth that again is singularly different from the manner in which Moses made God's name known. In Jesus "the revelation of the name is in a new mode of God's presence among men, a radically new way in which God makes his home with them. In Jesus, God gives himself entirely into the world of mankind: whoever sees Jesus sees the Father (cf. Jn. 14:9)" (2:91–92). Jesus, as the new Moses, is able to make the Father fully known because, in accordance with Benedict's Christological hermeneutical key, he and the Father are ontologically one and the same God. The immanence of God, through the revelation of his name in the Old Testament, "has now become ontological: in Jesus, God has truly become man. God has entered our very being. In him God is truly 'God-with-us'" (2:92). We also see once again that his prayer illustrates how Jesus, in his words and actions, brings new depth to Moses speaking with God at the burning bush by expanding who can call upon his name. God the Son, in knowing the Father perfectly, makes his name known not simply to the Jews but to all nations.

Johannine Images of Jesus as the New Moses

Benedict examines two images of Jesus as the new Moses within the Gospel of John: Jesus as the bread of life and the living water. "I am the bread of life; he who comes to me shall not hunger, and he who believes in me shall never thirst" (Jn. 6:35). Jesus is the new Moses because he will truly give bread from heaven. "I am the living bread which came down from heaven; if any one eats of this bread, he will live forever; and the bread which I shall give for the life of the world is my flesh" (Jn. 6:51). For Benedict, "Moses gave manna, bread from heaven. But it was still just earthly 'bread.' The manna is a promise: The new Moses is also expected to give bread. Once again, however, something greater than manna has to be given" (1:241). The reason that Jesus's flesh gives eternal life is twofold. First, it is because of, once again, his intimate unity with the Father. "As the living Father sent me, and I live because of the Father, so he who eats me will live because of me" (Jn. 6:57). It is because Jesus possesses the very divine life of the Father that all who feast upon Jesus obtains communion with the Father, the author of all life. Second, the body and blood that the faithful receive in the Eucharist are not the earthly body and blood of Jesus but the real heavenly manna— the resurrected body and blood of the new Moses—Jesus the risen Lord.

On the Feast of Tabernacles, the Gospel of John informs us that "on the last day of the feast, the great day, Jesus stood up and proclaimed: 'If anyone thirst, let him come to me. He who believes in me, as the Scripture has said, "out of his heart shall flow rivers of living water"'" (Jn. 7:37–38). Benedict notes that on the last day of the feast there was a water ritual that commemorated "a piece of salvation history, of the water from the rock that, in spite of all their doubts and fears, God gave the Jews as they wandered in the desert (cf. Num. 20:1–13)" (1:244). For Benedict, not only would the new Moses provide living bread from heaven that would exceed the manna, but he would also provide living water that would quench one's spiritual thirst. Jesus "is the new Moses. He himself is the life-giving rock" (1:245). Commenting on John 7:38, "As the Scripture has said 'Out of his body shall flow rivers of living water,'" Benedict follows those Fathers of the Church who interpreted "his heart" as referring, not to the heart of the believers, but to the heart of Jesus. "'His body' is now applied to Christ: He is the source, the living rock, from which the new water comes" (1:246). As the new Moses, Jesus is the source of the life-giving waters because, as with being the bread of eternal life, he is in divine communion with his Father—the eternal spring of all life.

The Transfiguration: The New Moses

The typology of Jesus being the new Moses reaches its climax prior to his death and resurrection in the Transfiguration. Scripturally, the Transfiguration is also closely conjoined to the Feast of Tabernacles, culminating on the last day with the festival of light. It is likewise connected to Moses's ascent up Mount Sinai. There the glory of God covered the mountain for six days (cf. Ex. 24:16). Benedict points out that Mark simply states that Jesus was transfigured before them, noting that "his clothes became radiant, intensely white, as no one on earth could bleach them" (Mk. 9:2–3). Matthew more elegantly states: "His face shone like the sun, and his clothes became white as light" (Mt. 17:2). Only Luke, Benedict notes, indicates the purpose of the ascent. He "went up on the mountain to pray" (Lk. 9:28). It was while he was at prayer that "the appearance of his face was altered, and his clothing became dazzling white" (Lk. 9:29). Here, in the context of the Feast of Tabernacles, both Jesus's closeness to his Father and his being the New Moses become one. Benedict begins:

The Transfiguration is a prayer event; it displays visibly what happens when Jesus talks with his Father: the profound interpenetration of his being with God, which then becomes pure light. In his oneness with the Father, Jesus is himself "light from light." (1:310)

The Transfiguration manifests the prayerful unity of the Father and the Son—a unity that far exceeds the unity of friendship between God and Moses. Jesus's prayerful unity is ontological in that the Transfiguration illuminates the fact that Jesus and the Father share one and the same glorious divine being.

Benedict also perceives other similarities and differences between Jesus and Moses. When Moses finished speaking with God, "the skin of his face shone" (Ex. 34:29–35). Benedict comments:

Because Moses has been talking with God, God's light streams upon him and makes him radiant. But the light that causes him to shine comes upon him from

the outside, so to speak. Jesus, however, shines from within; he does not simply receive light, but he himself is light from light. (1:310)

The Transfiguration anticipates the Cross and Resurrection, for it is it
is through his salvific death that Jesus obtains the fullness of glory. His glorious humanity now completely manifests the ontological depth of his divine filial relationship to the Father. Through his death and resurrection,
Jesus absolutely becomes the new Moses, for now his full human intimacy
with the Father is established and manifested. This also points to his Second Coming, for when he comes again in all of his glory, Jesus will bring
his kingdom to completion, and all men and women as well as the whole of
creation will radiate from within the divine light of glory. The first Moses
will no longer reflect the glory of God as from the outside, but he will share
within his very humanity the inner divine life of the new Moses.

The New Moses: Obedience and Intercession

In examining the Last Supper, Benedict states that the first covenant was
founded on two elements: "first, on the 'blood of the covenant.' The blood
of sacrificed animals with which the altar—as the symbol of God—and the
people were sprinkled, and second, on God's word and Israel's promise of
obedience" (2:132). After the reading of the book of the covenant, the people promised obedience to all that God had told them, and Moses sprinkled them with the blood of the covenant. Immediately afterward, however,
while Moses was on the mountain, the Israelites broke the covenant by wor-
shiping the golden calf. Benedict states that, as the new Moses, Jesus would
need to forge a new covenant, one that was "founded on an obedience that
is irrevocable and inviolable. This obedience, now located at the very root
of human nature, is the obedience of the Son, who made himself a servant
and took all of human disobedience upon himself in his obedience even
unto death, suffered it right to the end, and conquered it" (2:132). As the incarnate Son of the Father and thus within that intimate relationship, a relationship that exceeded Moses's with God, Jesus, as man, was fully obedient
to the Father's will even unto death, a sacrificial death that established the
new and everlasting covenant.

In his sacrificial death, Jesus, as the intercessor for the whole of humankind, is also the new Moses, which he achieves through his vicarious atone-

ment. Having broken his covenant, God was angry and threatened to destroy the Israelites. Moses stepped into the breach. He cried out to God, "But now, if you will forgive their sin—and if not, blot me, I beg you, out of your book which you have written" (Ex. 32:32). Benedict comments that Moses is "the substitute, the one who bears the fate of the people and through pleading on their behalf is able to change it again and again" (2:173). As the new Moses, Jesus will stand in the place of humankind and offer himself to the Father on its behalf so that all nations may be reconciled to God. Jesus does what Moses could not do. Because he is the obedient incarnate Son, through the offering of himself in sacrifice, he is able to truly cleanse humankind of sin and transform it into a truly righteous and holy people.

A Personal Relationship with Jesus, the New Moses

Benedict observes that the apostles struggled to articulate who Jesus is, though they did grasp that, because of his relationship to the Father, he is the new Moses, the one who truly speaks to God face-to-face. They perceived him to be "God himself." Benedict sees this ever-growing clarity culminate in Thomas's confession, whereby the clarity "could arrive at its complete form only when Thomas, touching the wounds of the Risen Lord, cried out, in amazement: 'My Lord and my God' (Jn. 20:28)" (1:304–5). Only in his death and resurrection did Jesus manifest the full divine oneness that he shared with the Father. In the Paschal Mystery, Jesus accomplished his work as the new Moses, liberating humankind from sin and death and bringing it into the promised land of the heavenly kingdom.

Benedict emphasizes that as the apostles and followers of Jesus had a personal encounter with him while on earth, after his resurrection men and women of faith are able to encounter him even more personally now. Moses helped the Israelites to enter into the presence of God, so Jesus, as the new Moses, not only aids us in knowing the Father, but it is also in union with him that humankind is able to enter into the heavenly Holy of Holies, and in him see the Father face to face. At the beginning of volume one Benedict states that he hopes to "foster the growth of a living relationship with him (Jesus)" (1:xxiv). Likewise, at the beginning of volume two he writes:

I have attempted to develop a way of observing and listening to the Jesus of the Gospels that can indeed lead to personal encounter and that, through collective listening with Jesus' disciples across the ages, can indeed attain sure knowledge of the real historical figure of Jesus. (2:xvii)

I believe that Benedict has accomplished what he set out to do. In encountering Jesus, the Son, we encounter the new Moses who gives us, in the Holy Spirit, access to the Father.

CHAPTER 3

The Supremacy of Christ
Aquinas's *Commentary on the Epistle to the Hebrews*

Scripture, Hermeneutics, and Themes

Psalm 86:8 may take the reader by surprise, for its relationship to the book of Hebrews is not immediately evident: "There is none like you among the gods, O Lord, nor are there any works like yours."[1] Yet at the very onset of his *Commentary*, we find the first of numerous examples of Aquinas cre-

Originally published as "The Supremacy of Christ in the Letter to the Hebrews," in *Aquinas on Scripture: An Introduction to His Biblical Commentaries*, ed. Thomas G. Weinandy, Daniel A. Keating, and John Yocum (London: T&T Clark/Continuum, 2005), 223–44. Reprinted by permission of Continuum, an imprint of Bloomsbury Publishing, PLC.

1. In all probability, Aquinas taught his course on Hebrews in Rome sometime between 1265 and 1268, which would have been during the time he wrote the first part of his *Summa Theologiae* (*ST*). See J.-P. Torrell, *Saint Thomas Aquinas*, vol. 1, *The Person and His Work* (Washington, DC: Catholic University of America Press, 1996), 340. Throughout this chapter, all references to the Psalms are from the Vulgate.

Aquinas notes that even at the Council of Nicaea some doubted the Pauline authorship because "it does not follow the pattern of his other epistles"; its style is different in that "it is more elegant"; and it proceeds, more than any other work of Scripture, in "an orderly manner in the sequence of words and sentences." In refutation, Aquinas states that Paul did not write his name because he was the apostle to the Gentiles and not to the Jews and so did not want to prejudice his audience against him. This epistle is more elegant because Paul writes in his native tongue, Hebrew, and it was translated into Greek by the great Greek stylist, Luke (see *In Heb.* Prol. [5]). Because Aquinas refers to Paul as the author, I will use that designation in this essay as well. All translations of Aquinas's *Commentary on the Epistle to the Hebrews* are taken from an unpublished translation by Fabian Larcher.

atively drawing upon passages from the whole Bible to illustrate more fully, to develop more broadly, or to sanction more convincingly truths contained within Hebrews itself.[2] For Aquinas, the various biblical books, with their distinctive revelational content, help to clarify and complement one another, and so this interplay advances one's understanding of the individual books themselves. The variety and the scope of Scripture that Aquinas weaves within his *Commentary* on Hebrews are staggering in number and impressive in content. While he obviously recognizes that each book of the Bible possesses it own genre and its own unique revelational and theological focus, it clearly demonstrates that Aquinas perceives the whole biblical narrative, Old and New Testaments together, as proclaiming the one complete Gospel, and thus it is only in the interrelationship, and so the interweaving, of the whole biblical content that one is able to come to a full understanding of that Gospel.

Now Aquinas's employment of the above passage from the Psalms is not random. Rather, it highlights what he considers the central theme of Hebrews: that Christ, as the Son of God incarnate, is supreme among all others who might be called gods, significantly within the Letter—angels, prophets, and priests. "Christ, therefore, is the great God above all the gods, because he is the splendor [of God], the Word, and the Lord (*quia Splendor, quia Verbum, quia Dominus est*)."[3] Moreover, his supremacy is manifested in his works. He is above the angels because, unlike them, who are creatures, he is the Creator. While prophets are enlightened, Christ is the "enlightener." Priests do not justify, but, as the supreme High Priest, Christ does.[4] Aquinas states that Christ's transcendence, who he is and what he does, is what distinguishes this epistle from all of the others.[5] Paul wrote

2. Aquinas quotes from a variety of patristic sources as well: Augustine (forty-two times); Gregory the Great (twelve times); Dionysius (nine times); Jerome (eight times); Chrysostom (seven times); Bernard of Clairvaux (twice); and Basil, Boethius, and Lactantius each once.

3. *In Heb*. Prol. [2]. The Latin text is taken from *Sancti Thomae Aquinatis: Opera Omnia, Expositia in Omnes S. Pauli Epistolas, Tomus XIII* (New York: Masurgia, 1949).

4. See *In Heb*. Prol. [3].

5. Ibid., Prol. [4]. Aquinas considers some epistles teaching about grace insofar as it extends to the whole mystical body of the Church: Roman, Galatians, Corinthians, and so on. Others treat grace as it extends to individuals: Timothy, Titus, and Philemon. Hebrews "treats of this grace, in as it pertains to the head, namely, Christ" (*In Heb*. Prol. [4]). Because this letter treats of the centrality of Christ and his salvific work, Aquinas holds that "almost all of the mysteries of the New Testament are contained in this epistle" (13:17–25 [772]).

the Letter to correct the errors of those converts from Judaism who wanted to preserve the legal observations along with the Gospel, as though Christ's grace were not sufficient for salvation. It is hence divided into two parts: first, he extols Christ's grandeur to show the superiority of the New Testament over the Old; second, he discusses what unites the members to the head, namely, faith.[6]

For Aquinas, it is faith in the incarnate Son that is salvific. "For faith in the godhead is not enough without faith in the Incarnation."[7] How Aquinas therefore perceives the intention of the Letter is important, for he employs it as the hermeneutical guide to his commentary.

Failing to grasp this hermeneutical principal with its subsequent reading and understanding, a reader's initial impression of Aquinas's *Commentary* may be one of disappointment, for it might first appear that he is merely providing an even more logical and systematic presentation of a treatise that expounds already the most sustained and coherent argument of all the New Testament books. Unlike his treatment within the *Summa Theologiae*, Aquinas does not seem to develop the sacrificial nature of Christ's priesthood beyond the most rudimentary level. It must be remembered, however, that Aquinas's *Commentary* is principally a set of lectures presented to student theologians, and he wishes them not to speculate on or develop further theological issues that arise from the text, but rather to master the inherent logic and content of the Letter itself. As will be seen, what Aquinas does do is take seriously the inbuilt logical structure of the Letter to the Hebrews and in so commenting on the first part of the Letter (chapters 1–10), he clearly articulates two interrelated aspects that are essential to the Letter's argument: first, the fulfillment of Old Testament revelation as found in the supremacy of the Incarnation, and second, the ensuing fulfillment and supremacy of Christ's priestly sacrifice. To fully appreciate how Aquinas conceives the relationship between God's revelatory words and actions as narrated in the Old Testament and their fulfillment within the person

6. *In Heb.* 1:1–2 [6]. It should be noted that Aquinas uses the terms "Old Testament" and "New Testament" not simply to designate two groupings of biblical books, but more so to designate the two distinct, though interrelated, covenants, with their various revelational contents—the New Testament/Covenant fulfilling and so surpassing what is prefigured in the Old Testament/Covenant.

7. *In Heb.* 10:19–25 [502].

and work of the incarnate Christ, his *Commentary on the Epistle to the Hebrews* is essential reading.[8]

In keeping with the theme of the second part of the Letter (chapters 11–13), Aquinas maturely advances his understanding of faith as the only authentic and legitimate response to the finality of God's revelation made manifest in Christ, and that such faith gives rise to and is embodied within the Church. Contained within Aquinas's *Commentary*, as within the Letter itself, there resides the centrality of the Gospel message of the Incarnation and Jesus's redemptive death and life-giving resurrection as well as an ecclesiology—that is, the subjective response of faith by which one appropriates the salvific work of Christ and so becomes a member Christ's body, the Church.

Introducing the Supremacy of Christ in Hebrews 1:1–3

Aquinas recognizes that the first three verses of Hebrews provide a summary proclamation of the whole content and argument of the Letter, for it furnishes the foundation of Christ's supremacy both in who he is and in what he did. Moreover, as within the remainder of the Letter, there is in these initial verses an inherent and necessary bond between Christology and soteriology. Only because of who Christ is as the Son incarnate is he able to accomplish the work of salvation, but equally his work of salvation testifies to who he is, for he could only accomplish such mighty deeds if he were the Son incarnate. What distinguishes the New Covenant from the Old resides in the manner of God's revelation.[9]

As Hebrews begins, God—in various times past and in various ways—enlightened the minds of many prophets who in turn spoke God's many words. But God has now spoken to us through his Son (see Heb. 1:1–2). For Aquinas, God eternally speaks only one eternal Word, who is the Son. All other "words," spoken at various times, found either in the beginning within

8. For a study on the relationship between the Old and New Testaments as found in Aquinas's teaching on salvation, see Matthew Levering's excellent work, *Christ's Fulfillment of Torah and Temple: Salvation According to Thomas Aquinas* (Notre Dame, IN: Notre Dame University Press, 2002).

9. For Aquinas, "the greatest wonder was that God became man (*Praecipium vero portentum est quod Deus factus est homo*)" (*In Heb.* 2:1–4 [99]).

the wonders of the created order that manifest the truth of God or through the various prophets, are but manifestations of that one eternal Word. Thus the Son, as the one eternal Word of the Father, in becoming man now himself speaks the truth, and this manner of revelation far exceeds and is actually different in kind from all previous manner of revelation.[10]

Others are called sons inasmuch as they contain within themselves the Word of God … But he is the true Son who carries all things by the word of his power. Therefore, Christ's preeminence is clear from his unique origin and from his relationship to other sons of God. It is these things, which make the New Testament greater than the Old.[11]

For Aquinas, Christ's preeminence is twofold. First, it resides, not surprisingly, in his unique origin as the eternally begotten Son of the Father, which accounts for his full divinity. Second, Aquinas astutely observes, it resides also in his relationship to other sons in that they are sons only to the extent that they share in and are so conformed by the word of the Son, for sonship resides in one taking on the likeness and image of the God of truth; that is, the Father.

For Aquinas, the Letter, by way of introduction, professes why Christ is supreme and so heir of all things both as God and as man. He reflects the glory of God "because he is not only wise but is Wisdom itself (*ipsa sapientia*)." He is not only noble "but nobility itself because he bears the very stamp (figure) of his [the Father's] substance (*sed ipsa nobilitas: quia est figura substantiae ejus*)."[12] Aquinas, following Nicaea, perceives Hebrews as professing that the Son is the same substance as the Father and, while distinct subjects or persons, they are nonetheless the one God.[13] Christ is supreme

10. Aquinas states that "the apostles were instructed immediately by the Word of God, not according to his divinity, but according as he spoke in his human nature" (*ST* I, q. 117, a. 2, obj. 2, ad 2). Translation taken from *The Summa Theologica*, trans. Fathers of the English Dominican Province (New York: Benziger Brothers, 1947).

11. *In Heb.* 1:1–2 [18], 9–18. As stated above, Aquinas provides throughout his *Commentary* a wealth of supporting Scripture passages taken from both the Old and the New Testaments. I quote some of them here but, unfortunately because of limitations of space, all of these passages cannot be quoted. The reader is encouraged, however, to refer to the text itself in order to obtain the fullness of Aquinas's argument and so equally obtain the full flavor of his commentary.

12. *In Heb.* 1:3 [25].

13. Ibid., 1:3 [27–29]. Unlike many contemporary theologians and Scripture scholars,

by the power of his activity in that the Father created the world through him and upholds all things by his powerful word.[14] Aquinas summarizes Hebrews' testimony as follows:

Consequently, by those three characteristics he (Paul) shows three things of Christ: for by the fact that he is the brightness, he shows his co-eternity with the Father; for in creatures splendour is coeval, and the Word is co-eternal ... But when he says, the image of his substance, he shows the consubstantiality (*consubstantialitate*) of the Son with the Father. For since splendor is not of the same nature as the resplendent thing, then lest anyone suppose that it is not similar in nature, he says that it is the image or figure of his substance. But because the Son, even though he is of the same nature with the Father, would be lacking power, if he were weak, he adds, supporting all things by the word of his power. Therefore, the Apostle commends Christ on three points, namely, co-eternity, consubstantiality and equality of power (*a coaeternitate, a consubstantialitate, et ab aequalitate potestatis*).[15]

Now what is important for Aquinas is not simply that the Son or Word of God as truly divine is supreme, but equally that his supremacy resides within his incarnate glorified state as well. In fact, the whole Letter is an argument as to why Christ has achieved his supremacy as the risen, glorious, incarnate Lord and so is written from this perspective. In conformity with Hebrews itself, it was "indeed as man (*sed inquantum homo*), [that] he has been appointed heir of all things."[16] For Aquinas, Christ is also the worthy heir of all things because of the "strenuousness and industry in acting (*strenuitas et industria*)"; that is, by overcoming sin through his passion, death, and resurrection.[17] As the Letter to the Hebrews itself will argue, it is the glorious, risen Son of God incarnate, and not simply the Son as God, who is superior and so inherits everything. It is as incarnate that the Son accomplished the strenuous work of redemption—the fullness of revelation, the vanquishing of sin, and the providing of a new and perfect covenant through his priestly sacrificial death and glorious resurrection.

Aquinas sees the conciliar doctrines of the Trinity and the Incarnation as residing within Scripture itself. In a sense there is not even a development of doctrine, for Scripture proclaims the doctrine, and the Councils merely uphold, clarify, and so sanction the doctrine already contained within the sacred text. This is why Aquinas in his opening discussion on Sacred Doctrine in his *ST* equates Sacred Doctrine and Sacred Scripture in that Sacred Doctrine is contained within Sacred Scripture (see *ST* I, q. 1, a. 3; I, q. 1, a. 8).

14. See *In Heb.* 1:1–2 [22], 1:3 [32–33].   15. Ibid., 1:3 [36].
16. Ibid., 1:1–2 [20].   17. Ibid., 1:3 [37].

Aquinas, by way of introducing what will become the themes of the Letter's subsequent chapters, creatively links the attributes of the divine Son with his work of salvation as man and displays why it is appropriate for the Son to become man and, as man, accomplish the work of salvation. First, Aquinas, following Anselm, notes that sin is "a transgression of the eternal law and of God's rights." "Therefore, since the eternal law and divine right stem from the eternal Word (*sit a Verbo aeterno*), it is clear that cleansing from sins is Christ's prerogative, inasmuch as he is the Word." This is an insightful comment by Aquinas. The eternal law embodies all that is true, just, and good in relationship to God—that is, the law of love—and it is the Word himself who eternally embodies and so lives out this law. The divine right that demands that such a law be lived out equally stems from the Word, for only as others live in conformity to this law of truth, goodness, and justice—this law of love—do they conform themselves to the Word. When human beings transgress God's divine right by sinning against the eternal law, it appropriately falls to the Word to rectify this defective and unrighteous situation. Second, "sin involves a loss of the light of reason and consequently of God's wisdom in man, since such a light is a participation of divine wisdom." While employing multiple Scripture passages to sanction such claims, Aquinas also refers to "the Philosopher (Aristotle)," who confirms that "all evil is ignorance." "Therefore, to set aright according to divine wisdom belongs to the one who is divine wisdom." Third, since sin is "a deformity of the likeness of God in man ... it belongs to the Son to correct this deformity, because he is the image of the Father." It is because human beings were first created in his image that the Son possesses those attributes that authorize him to re-create human beings in his image, and he does so in becoming human himself. Fourth, since sin deprives humankind of eternal life, "it is obvious that it belongs to Christ to purge sins both by reason of his human nature and by reason of the divine (*et ratione humanae, et ratione divinae*)."[18] As God the Son possesses all righteousness and thus can purge away sin, equally and importantly for Hebrews, this is primarily accomplished through his humanity, for it was as man and out of love for humankind that the Son purged sin by the loving offering of his humanity to the Father as a sacrifice for sin. The manner in which all of this was accomplished was, for Aquinas, fourfold.

18. Ibid., 1:3 [39].

First, because sin is a "perversity of will by which man withdraws from the unchangeable good," Christ "bestowed sanctifying grace," by which the will would be healed and so empowered to do what is unchangeably good. Second, because the perversity of will leaves a stain upon the soul, Christ removes this stain by the shedding of his blood through which our souls are cleansed. Third, because sin incurs "debt of punishment," "to satisfy this debt he (Christ) offered himself as a victim on the altar of the cross." Fourth, because sin enslaves us to the devil, Christ redeemed us from such slavery.[19]

A focus on Aquinas's understanding of the first three verses of Hebrews allows us to understand what Aquinas did—establish the basic Christological and soteriological truths that govern the entire Letter.

Greater Than the Angels and Moses

Aquinas, having shown from Hebrews that Christ excels in a fourfold manner— (1) in origin, as the Son of God; (2) in dominion, as heir of all things; (3) in power, as the creator of all; and (4) in honor, as sitting gloriously at the right hand of the Father—proceeds now, along with the Letter, to apply this excellency so as to demonstrate his superiority to the angels.

---

19. *In Heb.* 1:3 [40]. Aquinas states that through the priesthood of Christ the stain of sin is blotted out by grace, "by which the sinner's heart is turned to God," and the debt of punishment is removed in that he "satisfied for us fully … Wherefore it is clear that the priesthood of Christ has full power to expiate sins" (*ST* III, q. 22, a. 3).

What Aquinas is doing here at the very onset of his *Commentary* is succinctly but systematically outlining the various causal effects of Christ's death on the Cross, which Hebrews itself will later delineate. Nonetheless, it is only within *ST* III, q. 48–49 that he will fully articulate them in a systematic manner. There he discusses the efficiency and the effects of Christ's passion. The latter of which, corresponding to various aspects of the passion—atonement, sacrifice, redemption, and so on—are: deliverance from sin, freedom from the power of Satan, freedom from punishment, reconciliation with God, obtaining of eternal life, and the meriting of Christ's own exaltation. All of these aspects ultimately find mention within his commentary on Hebrews. Aquinas beautifully summarizes the above when he states:

> Christ's passion, according as it is compared with his Godhead, operates in an efficient manner; but insofar as it is compared with the will of Christ's soul it acts in a meritorious manner; considered as being within Christ's very flesh, it acts by way of satisfaction, inasmuch as we are liberated by it from the debt of punishment; while inasmuch as we are freed from the servitude of guilt, it acts by way of redemption; but insofar as we are reconciled with God it acts by way of sacrifice. (*ST* III, q. 48, a. 6, ad 3)

Aquinas argues that Christ was made superior to the angels not insofar as he was God, because as Son he was not "made (*factus*)" but "begotten (*genitus*)." His superiority resides precisely within the Incarnation, "inasmuch as by effecting that union [of divine and human natures] he became better than the angels, and should be called and really be the Son of God."[20] Although the Son was eternally the Son, he retained this name as man since it is truly the Son who came to exist as man, and so it is as man that the Son is still superior to the angels. Thus the name Son, even when applied to the incarnate Christ, is superior to that of the angels.[21]

Aquinas interprets Hebrews' employment of Old Testament passages to affirm this twofold superiority of the Son, that of being God and man. For example, Psalm 2:7 speaks of the ever-present eternal day, as if the Father addresses the Son: "You are perfect, Son; and yet your generation is eternal and you are always being engendered by me, as light is perfect in the air and yet is always proceeding from the sun."[22] Yet the passage from 2 Samuel 7:14, "I will be a father to him and he a son to me," refers, for Aquinas, to the future Incarnation whereby the Father will be Father to his incarnate Son and his incarnate Son will be his son.[23] Moreover, this dual application is found in that the angels worship the Son not merely as God but equally as incarnate. Again, while the Son's throne as God is eternal, it equally belongs to him "as man ... as a result of his passion, victory and resurrection" and because, as the risen Lord, he rules over an everlasting kingdom in which everlasting life is bestowed.[24] Equally, Psalm 110:1, where God states, "Sit at my right hand and I will make your enemies a footstool for you," refers not only to the Son as God who eternally resides with the Father but also to the incarnate Son, especially insofar as he will reign in glory at the end of time.[25] Unlike Jesus, the angels are merely servants of the salvation inaugurated by him.[26]

---

20. *In Heb.* 1:4–7 [46]. See also *ST* III, q. 22, a. 1, ad 1.
21. See *In Heb.* 1:4–7 [47–48].   22. Ibid., 1:4–7 [49].
23. Ibid., 1:4–6 [50–54].   24. Ibid., 1:8–10 [60].
25. Ibid., 1:13–14 [79–84].
26. Ibid., 1:13–14 [86–88]. While Aquinas sees the risen incarnate Son as superior to the angels and risen human beings as equal to angels, I have argued, contra Aquinas and the tradition, that human beings as created in the image and likeness of the Son are superior to the angels by the mere fact that they are human beings. See my article "Of Men and Angels," *Nova et Vetera* 3, no. 2 (2005): 195–206.

Because of Christ's superiority to angels, Christians are called to an even greater commitment of faith and perseverance in response to Christ than the commitment and faith required in response to the promises made by the angels in the past (see Heb. 2:1–4). For Aquinas, the reason is three-fold: first, because of Jesus's divine authority as Creator and as Son of God; second, because Christ's words "are words of eternal life"; and third, "because of the sweetness of their observance, for they are sweet"; "His commands are not heavy" (1 Jn. 5:3); "My yoke is sweet and my burden light" (Mt. 11:30); "This is a yoke which neither we nor our fathers have been able to bear" (Acts 15:10)."[27] Here we see an example of how Aquinas employs various scriptural passages that augment the argument contained within Hebrews itself.

While it might appear that man is of no account and vile because of sin, "the cause of the Incarnation is God's care for man (*causa autem incarnationis est memoria Dei de homine*)."[28] It is the incarnate Son who was "the son of man" and so made a little less than the angels in that he would, unlike the angels, take upon himself our suffering and death. Nonetheless, it was because of his becoming less than the angels that he is exalted above the angels. "Christ won the crown by the struggle of his passion."[29] While as divine the Son was eternally perfect, as incarnate he was made perfect through his suffering (see Heb. 2:10) because "he had to be made perfect by the merit of the passion: 'Ought not Christ to have suffered these things and so to enter into his glory' (Lk. 24:26)."[30] In so perfecting himself through the Cross, he was able to bring many sons to glory.[31] Now Christ is crowned with the glory of his risen body and also with the brightness that "comes from the confession of all people: 'Every tongue should confess that the Lord Jesus Christ is in the glory of God the Father' (Phil. 2:11)".[32] Notice again that, for Aquinas, it is the incarnate risen Son who is crowned with splendor and glory that exceeds the splendor and glory of the angels.[33] Moreover, those who are members of his Church through faith recognize and proclaim his supreme glory and primacy.

27. *In Heb.* 2:1–4 [90].
28. Ibid., 2:5–8 [107].
29. Ibid., 2:5–8 [113].
30. Ibid., 2:9–13 [128].
31. Ibid., 2:9–13 [125–33].
32. Ibid., 2:5–8 [112].
33. While we will examine how Christ became one with those whom he saved, Aquinas, commenting on Hebrews' employment of Isaiah 8:17, "In him I hope," makes an important

The reason that Christ is not ashamed to call us his brothers is that, for Aquinas, "he that sanctifies and we who are sanctified have one origin, namely, of the Father."[34] If Christ and all of humankind are brethren, however, then it is appropriate that we not only come to participate in his divine nature through grace and so be like him, but also that he share in our human nature and so be like us—"because the children share in flesh and blood, he himself likewise partook of the same nature."[35] For Aquinas, this assuming of the same nature was not in the abstract, but "in an individual, and from the seed of Abraham."[36] Christ "assumed a nature without sin, but with the possibility of suffering, because he assumed a flesh similar to the sinner: 'In the likeness of sinful flesh' (Rom. 8:3)."[37] In the days of his flesh, the Son of God "wore flesh similar to the sinner, but not sinful (*idest in quibus gerebat carnem similem peccatrici, non peccatricem*)."[38] For Aquinas, this truth has soteriological significance. Following Anselm's argument that a sinful man under a debt because of his sinfulness was unable to settle that debt, "it was necessary that the one who satisfied be man and God, who alone has the power over the whole of the human race. By the death of God and man, therefore, he destroyed him [the devil] who had the empire of death."[39] Thus Christ was like unto his brethren "in all things, I say, in which they are brethren, not in guilt but in punishment (*non in culpa, sed in poena*). Therefore, it behooved him to have nature that could suffer."[40]

---

distinction. Aquinas notes that many have previously held that Christ did not have faith or hope but only charity; however, "I answer that hope is one thing and trust another: for hope is the expectation of future happiness; and this was not in Christ, because he was happy from the instant of his conception. But trust is the expectation of help, and in regard to this there was hope in Christ, inasmuch as he awaited help from the Father during his passion" (134).

34. *In Heb.* 2:9–13 [130].　　　　35. Ibid., 2:14–18 [137].
36. Ibid., 2:14–18 [148].
37. Ibid., 2:14–18 [138]; 2:139–41; 9:23–28 [478].
38. Ibid., 5:1–7 [254].　　　　39. Ibid., 2:14–18 [143].
40. Ibid., 2:14–18 [150]. In his *ST*, Aquinas would develop this understanding in that he clearly recognizes that the humanity of the Son assumes it is not some generic humanity but a humanity taken from the fallen race of Adam. First, because it would seem to belong to justice that he who sinned should make amends, and hence from the nature that he had corrupted should be assumed that whereby satisfaction was to be made for the whole nature. Second, it pertains to man's greater dignity that the conqueror of the devil should spring from the stock conquered by the devil. Third, God's power is thereby made more manifest because, from a corrupt and weakened nature, he assumed that which was raised to such might and glory (*ST* III, q. 4, a. 6). Christ ought to be separated from sinners with regard to sin, which he came

It is because the Son took upon himself our sin-scarred humanity that he could be tempted as we are and so become the compassionate High Priest. In this, "he [Paul] shows its utility. As if to say: I do not speak of Christ as God, but as man. Therefore, in that, i.e., in that nature which he assumed, in order to experience in himself that our cause is his own ... Or, another way: He became merciful and faithful, because in suffering and being tempted he has kinship to mercy."[41] While temptations could not arise within Christ himself since he did not possess concupiscence, Aquinas, because he was a member of Adam's race, could be tempted from without by earthly prosperity, vainglory, and adversity. In this way he was tempted like us, "for if he had existed without temptations he would not have experienced them, and then he could not have compassion. But if he had sinned, he would not have been able to help us, but would need help."[42]

Now Christ is not only superior to the angels but also to Moses in that he was faithful to God not merely as a servant within God's house as was Moses, but as a Son who was the actual builder of God's house. The Son as man was faithful to God in three ways: (1) "by not attributing to himself what he had, but to the Father"; (2) "he sought the Father's glory and not his own"; and (3) "he obeyed the Father perfectly."[43] What Aquinas has done here is define the authentic nature of sonship. A son always acknowledges, in gratitude, his dependence upon his father for his existence. He equally seeks the glory of the one upon whom he is dependent, and finally this gratitude and solicitousness is expressed in his perfect, loyal filial obedience.

Christ's sonship is witnessed in the fact that he is the builder of God's house. Thus what is also supremely important for Aquinas is that Christ's supremacy resides in his bringing into being the Church—God's house in which all the faithful dwell. As the Father created the world out of nothing

---

to overthrow, and not with regard to nature that he came to save, and in which "it behooved him in all things to be made like to his brethren," as the apostle says (Heb. 2:17). And in this is his innocence about the more wonderful, seeing that, though assumed from a mass tainted by sin, his nature was endowed with such purity (*ST* III, q. 4, a. 6, ad 1). See also *ScG* IV, ch. 30, 28. For a more comprehensive discussion of this issue in Aquinas, see my book *In the Likeness of Sinful Flesh: An Essay on the Humanity of Christ* (Edinburgh: T&T Clark, 1993), 47–53. It should be noted that Aquinas quotes the Letter to the Hebrews at least 208 times in his *ST*.

41. *In Heb.* 4:14–16 [40].   42. Ibid., 4:14–16 [237].
43. Ibid., 3:1–6 [159].

through his Son, through that same Son "God created that house, name-ly, the Church, from nothing, namely from the state of sin to the state of grace."[44] It is the members of the Church who assume the filial attributes of Christ, for they become children of the Father through the transforming work of the Holy Spirit.

Jesus: The Great High Priest

The Letter to the Hebrews, having established that Christ, as the glorious incarnate Son, is superior to the angels and to Moses, turns its attention to Jesus being the Great High Priest who is superior to Aaron and his priest-ly descendants because of the preeminence of his sacrifice and the everlast-ing covenant that it establishes. For Aquinas, the importance of Christ's priesthood lies in its "end and utility"; that is, its usefulness lies in the fact that human beings are now able to obtain eternal life.[45] Aquinas notes that it was the Son of God as man, and not as God, who was appointed High Priest by his Father.[46]

We perceive how important the humanity of Christ is for Aquinas in his comments on the phrase that, "although he was a Son, he learned obe-dience from what he suffered" (Heb. 5:8). While the Son as God was om-niscient, and for Aquinas, from the moment of his conception he as man possessed the beatific vision, "there is a knowledge gained by experience."[47] This learning of obedience was through suffering, and what the incarnate Son learned through his obediential suffering was compassion for his fellow human brothers and sisters who were enslaved by sin and death, a compas-sion that he did not literally possess as God prior to the Incarnation, since God is impassible, but that he now literally possessed in a human manner.[48]

---

44. Ibid., 3:1–6 [164]; 3:159–69.

45. Ibid., 5:1–7 [242]; 5:239–41. It is interesting that in respect of our own present-day concerns over defining the nature of the priesthood and its proper ministry, Aquinas states: "Therefore, just as the things which pertain to the worship of God transcend temporal things, so the pontifical dignity exceeds all other dignities. Therefore, high priests should not entangle themselves with secular business and neglect the things that pertain to God: 'No man being a soldier to Christ entangles himself with secular businesses' (2 Tim. 2:4)" (243).

46. See *In Heb.* 5:1–7 [252–57]. See also *ST* III, q. 22, a. 3, ad 1.

47. *In Heb.* 5:8–14 [259].

48. I am not comfortable with the attribution by Aquinas and the tradition of the beatific

Christ accepted our weakness voluntarily; consequently, he (Paul) says that "he learned obedience," i.e., how difficult it is to obey, because he obeyed in the most difficult matters, even to the death of the cross (Phil. 2:8). This shows how difficult the good of obedience is, because those who have not experienced obedience and have not learned it in difficult matters, believe that obedience is very easy. But in order to know what obedience is, one must learn to obey in difficult matters, and one who has not learned to subject himself by obeying does not know how to rule others well. Therefore, although Christ knew by simple recognition what obedience is, he nevertheless learned obedience from the things he suffered, i.e., from difficult things, by suffering and dying: "By the obedience of one many shall be made just" (Rom. 5:19).[49]

What is significant here is not merely that Aquinas recognizes the importance of Christ's human obedience for our salvation, but that he could not truly "learn" how to rule as our King and Lord, and so hold us to obedience, if he did not himself first "learn" how to obey. This is exactly, for Aquinas, what Hebrews continues to point out: "and being made perfect he became the source of eternal salvation to all who obey him" (Heb. 5:9). Christ was made perfect through his obedience, and being "altogether perfect, he could perfect others. For it is the nature of a perfect thing to be able to engender its like,"[50] and this engendering likeness is accomplished through his engendering in human beings the filial obedience of faith.

The heart of Aquinas's commentary on Hebrews 7–10 is to demonstrate, in accordance with the Letter itself, that Christ's priesthood and its salvific effects fulfill and so are superior to the Old Testament priesthood and its effects. The hermeneutical key to this interpretation, again in keeping with the Letter, is one of prefigurement and fulfillment. Thus both the priests of the Old Testament and Melchizedek's priesthood prefigure Christ's priesthood in different manners. Christ, too, like the priests of the Old Testament, will offer a sacrifice, but unlike them and like Melchizedek,

---

vision to the earthly Jesus. See my "Jesus' Filial Vision of the Father," *Pro Ecclesia* 13, no. 2 (2004): 189–201 (chap. 18 in this volume). For Aquinas, God as God is not literally compassionate in the sense that he suffers emotionally as do human beings. Nonetheless, Aquinas does argue that God is supremely compassionate in that he alleviates the causes of suffering—sin, evil, and death—and he does this primarily through the sending of his Son. See also my *Does God Suffer?* (Edinburgh: T&T Clark, 2000), chap. 6–8.

49. *In Heb.* 5:8–14 [259].
50. Ibid., 5:8–14 [260].

his priesthood is forever.[51] Because the sacrifices of the Old Testament were corruptible and thus imperfect, the priests were multiplied.

This was a sign that the priesthood was corruptible, because incorruptible things are not multiplied in the same species. But the priest who is Christ is immortal, for he remains forever as the eternal Word of the Father, from whose eternity redounds an eternity to his body, because "Christ rising from the dead, dies now no more" (Rom. 6:9). Therefore, because he continues forever, he holds his priesthood permanently. Therefore, Christ alone is the true priest, but others are his ministers: "Let a man so account of us as the ministers of Christ" (1 Cor. 4:1).[52]

The superiority of Christ's priesthood resides in the perfect nature of his sacrificial death on the Cross. Moreover, it is the perfect nature of Christ's sacrifice that will merit his resurrection as the glorious eternal High Priest.

For Aquinas, the Old Testament Law according to the Letter to the Hebrews sets forth four qualities of a priest that Christ fulfills perfectly and so surpasses and fulfills what has gone before. The first is that the priest must be holy. "But Christ had this perfectly. For holiness implies purity consecrated to God"; "Therefore, also the Holy which shall be born of you shall be called the Son of God" (Lk. 1:3); "That which is conceived in her is of the Holy Spirit" (Mt. 1:20); "The saint of saints will be anointed" (Dn. 9:34). The second is that the priest should be innocent, which is purity to one's neighbor. "But Christ was completely innocent, being one who did not sin." The third is that the priest should be unstained with regard to himself. "Of Christ it is said in a figure: 'It shall be a lamb without blemish.'" The third is that the priest must be separated from sinners. While Christ ate with sinners, he lived a perfectly holy life, "and to such a degree he was separated that he was made higher than the heavens, i.e., exalted above the heavens."[53] This exultation was again as man, for this "is more in keeping with the Apostle's intention, because he is speaking about the high priesthood of Christ, who is a high priest as man. So he is seated in that way, because the assumed humanity has a certain association to the godhead."[54]

---

51. Aquinas states that the sacrifice of Melchizedek better foreshadowed the participatory nature of Christ's sacrifice as well as its effects in that it consisted of bread and wine and so prefigured "ecclesiastical unity, which is established by our taking part in the sacrifice of Christ" (*ST* III, q. 22, a. 6, ad 2).

52. *In Heb.* 7:20–28 [368]. Aquinas argues in a similar manner in *ST* III, q. 22, a. 5.

53. *In Heb.* 7:20–28 [375].   54. Ibid., 8:1–5 [381].

We now recognize why Christ's priesthood is superior, and it first of all pertains to a threefold relationship that in turn effects his exaltation. First, it pertains to his relationship to the Father as the all-holy Son. Second, it pertains to his relationship with his fellow human beings in that being "innocent" he has never been found guilty of sin; that is, he has never sinned against anyone but instead, in his innocence, has consistently loved everyone. Third, it is in relationship to himself in that he is himself holy and without blemish within his own being. This threefold holiness in relationship to God, others, and himself has separated Christ from everyone else even though he associated himself with sinners, and therefore his priesthood has merited for him an everlasting superiority that exceeds all others. Christ not only merited his own risen glory, but as head of the Church he also merited humankind's risen glory.[55]

It is as man that Christ is "a minister of the holies" and of the "true tent/tabernacle" (Heb. 8:1–2), "for the humanity of Christ is an organ of the divinity (*humanitas enim Christi est sicut organum divinitatis*). Therefore, he is the minister of the holies, because he administers the sacraments of grace in the present life and of glory in the future."[56] Priests are mediators of holiness because they are ministers of the all-holy God. Jesus is the High Priest because he is the supreme mediator of holiness in that he is both the all-holy Son of God and through his humanity the supreme dispenser of grace through the sacraments.[57]

While every priest is appointed to offer gifts and sacrifices (see Heb. 8:3), so Christ, too, must offer something, and what he offered was himself. But it was a clean oblation, because his flesh had no stain of sin. Furthermore, it was suitable because it was fitting that man should satisfy for man: "He offered himself unspotted unto God" (Heb. 9:14). It was also fit to be immolated because his flesh was mortal: "God sending his own Son, in the likeness of sinful flesh and sin" (Rom. 8:3). Also, it was the same as the one to whom it was offered: "I and the Father are one" (Jn. 10:30). And it unites

---

55. Ibid., 13:17–25 [768].   56. Ibid., 8:1–5 [382].

57. Aquinas argues equally that Christ is the Supreme High Priest because he bestows upon those who believe his very divine nature (2 Pet. 1:4) and reconciles humankind to God (*ST* III, q. 22, a. 1). This is ultimately because Christ becomes the head of his body: "Christ, as being the head of all, has the perfection of all graces. Wherefore, [he is] ... the fount of all grace" (*ST* III, q. 22, a. 1, ad 3).

to God those for whom it is offered: "That they may one, as thou, Father, in me, and I in thee, that they also may be one in us" (Jn. 17:21).[58]

Here Aquinas brings together many of the points he has made previously within his *Commentary*. Christ's sacrifice was holy because he offered his own holy life. It was right for him to do so because he was of the same race of Adam, as were all. He offered himself to the Father, but equally, as man, he offered himself to himself because he himself is God. Lastly, the causal effect of such a supreme sacrifice is that it forms an everlasting and unbreakable communion with God for those for whom it was offered.

While Christ fulfilled in himself all that had gone before him—the Old Testament priesthood and its sacrifices—Aquinas does not want to disparage their earthly and material importance. The "sacraments of the Old Law," while inferior, "naturally tend to a likeness of superior things (*quia naturalites inferiora tendunt in similitudinem superiorum*). For the Lord wished to lead us by sensible things to intelligible and spiritual things."[59] The New Testament then "completes and perfects the Old" because the new Christ mediates a better covenant by which "we are made partakers of the divine nature."[60]

Aquinas states on a number of occasions that the difference between the Old and New Testaments is that between "fear" and "love."[61] The reason is that within the Old Testament, sin with its condemnation of death continued to reign and in so doing engendered fear. Following upon the prophecy of Jeremiah, chapter 31, however, the new covenant not only brought an interior knowledge of the law, but also, through the Holy Spirit, "inclines the will to act as well."[62] While "both the Old and New Testaments were instituted in order that by them the soul might come to God," and although

---

58. *In Heb.* 8:1–5 [384]. Aquinas argues that as priest Christ must offer a sacrifice first for the remission of sin; second for human beings, that they might be preserved in grace by adhering to God; and third so that human beings may be fully united to God. These three ends are accomplished through Christ, the priest, offering himself, the victim. "Now these effects were conferred on us by the humanity of Christ. For in the first place our sins were blotted out ... Secondly, through him we received the grace of salvation, according to Heb. 5:9 ... Thirdly, through him we have acquired the perfection of glory, according to Heb. 10:9 ... Therefore, Christ, as man, was not only priest, but also a perfect victim" (*ST* III, q. 22, a. 2).

59. *In Heb.* 8:1–5 [389].

60. Ibid., 8:6–10b [396, 392].

61. See, e.g., *In Heb.* 8:6–10b [401]; 10:1–18 [480]; 12:18–24 [696, 703].

62. Ibid., 8:6–10b [404].

both are bodily, only the New Testament "contains grace and is holy, and in it divine power works salvation under cover of visible things. This is not so in the Old Testament, because it contained no grace in itself: 'How turn you again to the weak and needy elements?' (Gal. 4:9)."[63] The point that Aquinas is making is that the purpose of the Old Testament was to prepare people for the new covenant in Christ, and thus whatever grace that pertains to it is not in itself, but only insofar as is related to and finds its fulfillment in the new salvific covenant made in Christ.

Again, in accordance with Hebrews, Aquinas recognizes the Old Testament tabernacle/tent as a prefigurement. But while the tabernacle of the first covenant prefigures the new, "in another way, by the first tabernacle the present Church [is prefigured], and by the second, heavenly glory. Therefore, inasmuch as it signifies the Old Testament, it is a figure of a figure; but inasmuch as it signifies the present Church, which in turn signifies future glory, it is a figure of the truth in regard to each."[64] For Aquinas, too, "the holies" signified the Old Testament, and the "the holy of holies" signified the New Testament, for through it one was able to enter into heaven itself.[65] As Hebrews professes, however, it was Christ who first entered into the heavenly holy of holies and with his own blood, by which he won for all humankind an eternal redemption. Here Aquinas stresses the efficacy of Christ's blood. First, Christ's blood cleanses us of sin; second, it has such power because Christ offered his life's blood "by the Holy Spirit, through whose movement and instinct, namely, by the love of God and neighbour he did this"; third, because Christ himself was "without blemish."[66] Thus, for Aquinas, Christ's sacrificial offering of his life's blood was no mere mechanical event. What made Christ's sacrifice efficacious was that, through the Spirit of love, he offered his all-holy life to the Father out of obediential love for the Father, and he did so out of love for all who were to be cleansed

63. Ibid., 9:1–5 [414, 415].

64. Ibid., 9:1–5 [418].

65. Aquinas makes a similar point toward the end of the *Commentary*: "Therefore, the doctrine of the Old Testament is the doctrine of Christ speaking on earth for two reasons: because there under the figure of earthly things he spoke of heavenly things; furthermore, he promised earthly things there. But the doctrine of the New Testament is that of Christ speaking from heaven, because we turn earthly things into signs of heavenly things by a mystical interpretation. Likewise, heavenly things are promised in it" (*In Heb.* 12:25–29 [717]).

66. *In Heb.* 9:11–14 [444].

of sin.[67] Love is the foundation of this new covenant in Christ's blood.[68] Equally, then, those who believe in Christ are cleansed of dead works, "which take God from the soul, whose life consists in union of charity."[69] By being cleansed of sin with its condemnation to death, the Christian casts off fear and is empowered to live in love and so serve the living God. "Therefore, he that would serve God worthily, should be living, as he is (*Quod ergo vult Deo digne servire, debet esse vivens et ipse*)."[70]

Although Christ offered a single sacrifice once for all, within the sacrifice of the Mass "we do not offer something different from what Christ offered for us, his blood; hence, it is not a distinct oblation, but a commemoration of that sacrifice which Christ offered."[71] By one offering, Christ has perfected for all times those who are sanctified because "Christ's sacrifice, since he is God and man, has power to sanctify forever ... For by him we are sanctified and united to God: 'By whom we have access to God' (Rom. 5:12)."[72]

Now the old covenant was confirmed when Moses, taking the blood of goats and calves and mixing it with water, sprinkled the book of the covenant and the people using scarlet wool and hyssop. Jesus fulfills this prefigurement:

For that blood was a figure of Christ's blood, by whom the New Testament was confirmed ... This is the blood of a goat because of its likeness to sinful flesh [Christ's humanity], and of a calf because of courage [Christ's courage]. But it is mixed with water, because baptism derives its efficacy from the blood of Christ. It is sprinkled with hyssop, which cleanses the breast, by which faith is signified: "By faith purifying their hearts" (Acts 15:9); and with purple wool, which is red to signify charity ... because the people are cleansed by faith and the love of Christ. The book of the Law is sprinkled, because the passion of Christ fulfilled the Law: "It is consummated" (Jn. 19:30); "I have not come to destroy the law, but to fulfill it" (Mt. 5:17).[73]

---

67. Aquinas emphasizes the importance of Christ's obedience when he comments on Hebrews quoting Psalm 40:6–8. The Father fitted his Son with a body for the purpose of his passion. "To what end? To do your will O God" (*In Heb.* 10:1–18 [492]).

68. "Christ obtained a result from his passion, not as by virtue of the sacrifice, which is offered by way of satisfaction, but by the very devotion with which out of charity he humbly endured the passion" (*ST* III, q. 22, a. 4, ad. 2).

69. *In Heb.* 9:11–14 [446].   70. Ibid.

71. Ibid., 10:1–18 [482].   72. Ibid., 10:1–18 [499].

73. Ibid., 9:15–22 [457].

Aquinas creatively links the blood of Christ with the efficacy of faith and baptism, for both are justifying responses to the sacrificial death of Christ, but the efficacy of such responses, by which one is cleansed of sin and made holy, resides solely within that efficacious sacrificial, and so salvific, death. Faith, then, is the unqualified response to Christ's supremacy— the fulfillment and perfection of the old covenant through the offering of his own blood as the new and eternal covenant. Commenting on Hebrews' use of Habakkuk that "the just man lives by faith," Aquinas states:

Not only is justice by faith, but the one justified lives by faith (*Nec solum per fidem justitia, sed etiam per fidem justificatus vivit*). For just as the body lives by the soul, so the soul of God. Hence, just as the body lives by that through which the soul is first united to the body, so by that through which God is first united to the soul, the soul lives. But this is faith, because it is the first thing in the spiritual life ... But faith not formed by charity is dead; therefore, it does not give life to the soul without charity.[74]

In his *Commentary*, Aquinas combines the teaching of both Romans and James. Yes, one is justified by faith, but if one is so justified, one must live out that faith in love. The reason is (and here Aquinas is most insightful) that faith unites us to God, and being united to the living God of love demands that one, like God, perform the living good deeds of love. But this is Aquinas's preliminary discussion of faith, which he will now address more fully when examining Hebrews, chapter 11.

Faith and the Church

Aquinas obviously believes that Scripture is inspired and that Paul is the inspired author of the Letter to the Hebrews. Yet surprisingly, as initiated in his commentary on Paul's famous definition in Hebrews 1:1, he writes that Paul "gives a definition of faith which is complete but obscure (*complete sed obscure*)."[75] Aquinas is probably correct in his assessment, and what he will now do is make clear this complete, though obscure, inspired definition of faith.

For Aquinas, in order to define virtues properly, as with all habits, one

---

74. Ibid., 10:32–39 [548]. Here Aquinas, probably without fully realizing it, is acknowledging that while the author of the Letter to the Hebrews is inspired, he is a *human* author and therefore what is said, while true, may not necessarily be the best way to say it.

75. *In Heb.* 11:1 [552].

must define its matter—that is, the area with which it deals—and its end—
that is, what good it is intended to achieve. Faith is a theological virtue in
that it has to do with our immediate relationship to God and thus "its object and end are the same, God."[76] Following Augustine, the act of faith "is
to believe, because it is an act of the intellect narrowed to one thing by the
command of the will. Hence, to believe is to cogitate with assent … Therefore, the object of faith and of the will must coincide." Now, the intellect is
ordered to the truth and the will is ordered to the good, for it is in truth and
in goodness that authentic happiness is obtained. Both the intellect and the
will seek God, who is the fullness of truth and goodness, and thus complete
happiness is found in God alone. The act of faith thus takes place in this
manner. The intellect lays hold of the truth of God and recognizes that such
truth is good. But it is the will, which desires the good, that moves the intellect to lay hold of that good. Thus the will commands the intellect to give
intellectual assent to the truth of God. The act of faith, then, is laying hold
of the supreme truth and ultimate goodness, which is God himself.[77]

Yet here on earth this fullness of the reality of God is not seen but
hoped for. "The end, therefore, of faith on earth is the attainment of the
thing hoped for, namely, of eternal happiness."[78] This act of faith does not
possess the certainty that arises out of natural knowledge (the seeing and
perceiving of things), nor is it doubt, as in holding a dubious opinion. Faith
"fixes on one side with certainty and firm adherence by a voluntary choice."
Faith holds what it believes to be absolutely certain. This choice "rests on
God's authority, and by it the intellect is fixed, so that it clings firmly to the
things of faith and assents to them with the greatest certainty. Therefore, to
believe is to know with assent." Faith is "a sure and certain apprehension of
things it does not see."[79] Although one does not know the truths of faith by
natural knowledge and thus with natural certainty, one does hold the truths
of faith with absolute certainty because of the authority of God, who cannot deceive and who is the author of all truth and goodness. Aquinas humbly concludes:

76. Ibid. See also *ST* II-II, q. 1, a. 1.

77. See *In Heb.* 1:1 [554]. Aquinas states that "the intellect of the believer is determined to
one object, not by the reason, but by the will, wherefore assent is taken here for an act of the intellect as determined to one object by the will" (*ST* II-II, q. 2, a. 1, ad 3).

78. *In Heb.* 11:1 [553]. See also *ST* II-II, q. 1, a. 4.

79. *In Heb.* 1:1 [558]. See also *ST* II-II, q. 2, a. 1.

Now, if someone were to reduce those words (Paul's definition of faith) to their correct form, he could say that faith is a habit of the mind by which eternal life is begun in us and makes the intellect assent to things that it does not see (*fides est habitus mentis, qua inchoatur vita aeterna in nobis, faciens intellectum assentiri non apparenibus*). Therefore, it is obvious that the Apostle has defined faith completely, but not clearly.[80]

While faith in the Christian mysteries allows one to begin to perceive and experience the truth and goodness of God, complete happiness "consists in the vision of God," which will only be achieved in heaven.[81] Moreover, while the act of faith is an act of an individual person, it is equally an ecclesial act, for the person, through faith, becomes a member of the body of Christ, the Church. In union with the whole earthly Church, individual believers come to perceive and are in communion with the heavenly realities they hope for. This again finds its completion in heaven. "In heavenly glory there are two things which will particularly gladden the just, namely, the enjoyment of the godhead and companionship with the saints. For no good is joyfully possessed without companions."[82] As the Trinity of persons is only able to enjoy the godhead in communion with one another, so the blessed in heaven are only able to enjoy that Trinitarian communion in communion with one another. True happiness, for Aquinas, always consists in the joy, founded upon truth and goodness, shared in communion with others, whether those others be the communion of the divine persons or the communion of the saints.

Conclusion

Aquinas's *Commentary on the Epistle to the Hebrews* is a sustained argument, in keeping with the Letter itself, for the supremacy of Christ. This supremacy resides in who he is as the Son of God incarnate and what he has done through his passion and death. These salvific actions have merited for him a place above all the angels, the prophets, and the priests. It is because of his supremacy that all are called to faith in him. It is through faith that one is united to Jesus and so comes to participate in the life of the Church, and thus equally comes to share in what Jesus himself has merited—eternal life with the Father in the heavenly temple.

80. *In Heb.* 1:1 [558].   81. Ibid., 1:1 [556].
82. Ibid., 12:18–24 [706].

While we have obviously not touched upon everything that Aquinas treats in his *Commentary*, we have examined the major themes,[83] demonstrating the insight and creativity of Aquinas as well as his love for Christ and his work of redemption. Aquinas, like the Letter itself, ultimately wishes that our response would be one of deeper faith, for it is faith that recognizes that Jesus is indeed the supreme and only Lord and Savior—"the Perfector of our faith" (Heb. 12.2).[84]

83. Merely to note that Aquinas did have a sense of humor, commenting on the fact that Paul had written "briefly" (Heb. 13:22), Aquinas states: "Short talks are most welcome; because if they are good, they will be heard eagerly. If they are bad, they are a little boring" (*In Heb.* 13:17–25 [772]).

84. It is surprising that the Franciscan tradition, which accentuates the primacy of Christ, does not employ the Letter to the Hebrews to authorize its theological endeavor. The most probable reason is that Jesus's primacy within Hebrews is too closely tied to his death on the Cross. The Franciscan tradition misguidedly wants to disengage his primacy from the Cross. For further discussion of this issue, see my works *In the Likeness of Sinful Flesh*, 135–48; "The Cosmic Christ," *Cord* 51 (2001): 27–38 (chap. 28 in this volume).

PART II

HISTORICAL
AND SYSTEMATIC
CHRISTOLOGY

CHAPTER 4

The Apostolic Christology of Ignatius of Antioch

The Road to Chalcedon

With which New Testament teachings Ignatius of Antioch (d. ca. 107–10 AD) was acquainted, either in their written form or through the oral apostolic traditions that gave rise to them, has caused a great deal of debate. Did Ignatius have access to some or all of the written Gospels of Matthew, Luke, and John, or was he merely acquainted with their various oral traditions or even traditions parallel to them? Which and how many of Paul's letters did he possess or had he read? There is no scholarly consensus concerning the answers to these questions. Some authors offer a more positive assessment, and so affirm that Ignatius did possess various apostolic writings, the most likely being the Gospels of Matthew and John as well as 1 Corinthians, along with being acquainted with other various oral traditions, the most likely being the Lukan and Pauline traditions. Others scholars are skeptical to varying degrees.[1]

Originally published as "The Apostolic Christology of Ignatius of Antioch: The Road to Chalcedon," in *Trajectories through the New Testament and the Apostolic Fathers*, ed. A. Gregory and C. Tuckett (Oxford: Oxford University Press, 2005), 71–84. By permission of Oxford University Press.

1. On this issue, see, for example, W. Burghart, "Did Saint Ignatius of Antioch Know the Fourth Gospel?," *Theological Studies* 1 (1940): 130–56; R. M. Grant, "Scripture and Tradition in St. Ignatius of Antioch," *Catholic Biblical Quarterly* 25 (1963): 322–35; *The Apostolic Fathers*, vol. 4, *Ignatius of Antioch* (London: Thomas Nelson and Sons, 1966), 1–24; C. Hill, "Ignatius and the Apostolate: The Witness of Ignatius to the Emergence of Christian Scripture,"

It is presently difficult, and in the end likely impossible, to ascertain exactly what apostolic writings Ignatius either had read or knew simply from the various oral accounts that made up the apostolic tradition. I would cautiously affirm that Ignatius did have access to the written Gospel of Matthew and 1 Corinthians, as well as much of the Pauline corpus or at least of the Pauline tradition, and that he was at least familiar with the Lukan and Johannine traditions, the latter of which he may have even known in written form.[2]

Nonetheless, what is most significant within this discussion, and often overlooked, is that whatever specific apostolic writings Ignatius did or did not have access to or whatever specific apostolic traditions he was aware of or not, Ignatius's seven letters are still very much within the parameters of the various apostolic traditions and within the boundaries of the writings that emerged from those traditions. To read Ignatius, then, is to be undoubtedly within the dominion or home of New Testament Christianity. While Ignatius obviously did not treat within his letters the whole of the apostolic proclamation and thus the whole of the New Testament teaching, and while, given his contemporary concerns, he molded the apostolic tra-

---

in *Studia Patristica*, vol. 36, ed. M. Wiles and E. Yarnold (Louvain: Peeters, 2001), 226–48; D. Hoffman, "The Authority of Scripture and Apostolic Doctrine in Ignatius of Antioch," *Journal of the Evangelical Theological Society* 28 (1985): 71–79; L. W. Hurtado, *Lord Jesus Christ: Devotion to Jesus in Earliest Christianity* (Grand Rapids, MI: Eerdmans, 2003), 235–40; H. Koester, "History and Cult in the Gospel of John and in Ignatius of Antioch," *Journal for Theology and the Church* 1 (1965): 111–23; S. Johnson, "Parallels between the Letters of Ignatius and the Johannine Epistles," in *Perspectives on Language and Text*, ed. E. Conrad and E. Newing (Winona Lake, IN: Eisenbrauns, 1987), 327–38; C. Richardson, *The Christianity of Ignatius of Antioch* (New York: AMS Press, 1967), 60–75; S. Smit, "Ignatius and Matthew," *Novum Testamentum* 8 (1966): 263–83; C. Trevett, "Approaching Matthew from the Second Century: The Under-Used Ignatian Correspondence," *Journal for the Study of the New Testament* 20 (1984): 59–67.

2. While this essay highlights some of the similarities between Ignatius's Christology and that of various New Testament writings, there are other elements of his writings that also bear a likeness to New Testament documents. For example, Ignatius's emphasis on Christians being Christ's "temples," and living "in Christ" and so composing "the body of Christ," is substantially Pauline (see *Eph.* 4, 10:3, 11:1, 12:2, 15:3; *Mag.* 12, 15; *Tral.* 7, 11, 1.2; *Poly.* 8.3). Richardson notes that there are at least five clear parallels between Ignatius's letters and 1 Corinthians: *Eph.* 16:1 / 1 Cor. 6:9; *Eph.* 18:1 / 1 Cor. 1:18–23; *Rom.* 5:1 / 1 Cor. 4:4, 9:2 / 1 Cor. 15:8–10; *Mag.* 10.3 / 1 Cor. 5:7. *Christianity of Ignatius of Antioch*, 61. Of the references in note 1 above, see especially Grant, "Scripture and Tradition in St. Ignatius of Antioch." He finds parallels between Ignatius's letters and the Pauline corpus, plus Matthew, Luke, and the Johannine tradition.

dition to address certain specific issues, the basic Christian Gospel that Ig- natius espoused and defended is recognizably the same Christian Gospel as that found within the New Testament. The various apostolic traditions that became embodied within the New Testament are the same apostolic tradi- tions (some more than others) that are found within Ignatius's seven brief letters. Ignatius, I argue, is by no means a doctrinal innovator, for it is this composite apostolic tradition, which he regarded as the already-given au- thoritative tradition, that he wanted to defend.[3] Ignatius endorsed and fos- tered such a high theology of the bishop, one that he believed to have arisen from within the apostolic tradition itself, because he was convinced that it is specifically the bishop who is now the appointed apostolic custodian and guardian of this apostolic Gospel.[4]

I have concerned myself with these preliminary issues because I believe that Ignatius's Christology is an apostolic Christology; that is, a Christolo- gy that originated from within and gave expression to the various apostolic traditions, some more than others, that comprised New Testament Chris- tianity. There is a necessarily entwined continuity between the apostolic Christology as recounted and proclaimed within New Testament Christi-

3. Throughout this essay I use the terms "apostolic traditions" and "apostolic writings" and argue that Ignatius espoused an "apostolic Christology." By "apostolic" I mean traditions that made up the kerygma of the first generation of Christians as it arose from within the proclama- tion of the apostles. These various oral "apostolic traditions" will ultimately find their written form in what would become the New Testament. The New Testament, then, is composed of the various apostolic traditions and in so being composed embodies the complete apostolic tra- dition. It is within these apostolic traditions both as distinct parts and as a composite whole, whether oral or written, that I situate Ignatius's seven letters and the Christology articulated within them.

W. Schoedel argues that there is not only evidence of Ignatius's employment of New Testa- ment material, but also the use of semicreedal patterns. *Ignatius of Antioch* (Philadelphia: For- tress Press, 1985), 7–8. R. M. Grant recognizes three creedal passages in Ignatius's letters: Eph. 18:2, *Tral.* 9.1–2, and *Smy.* 1.1–2. "Scripture and Tradition in St. Ignatius of Antioch," 10.

4. While it could be argued that Ignatius's understanding of the threefold ecclesial order of deacons, priests, and bishops was innovative since it does not appear as such within the New Testament, I would argue that even here he was not the originator of such an ecclesial notion. Ignatius stressed the centrality of the monarchical Bishop within the local Christian communi- ty, but he did so not as one attempting to establish an ecclesial order that was controversial or one that was yet to be fully recognized. Rather, he was merely clarifying and expounding what to him were the evident implications and consequences of an ecclesial order that was already recognized to be in place. How this ecclesial order, historically and theologically, derived from the various ministries found within the New Testament is another question.

anity and as found within Ignatius's letters. Some may think that this in itself is a rather dubious enterprise, but the more controversial aspect of this essay is that I demonstrate equally that Ignatius's apostolic Christology, and so New Testament Christology, is the first step taken down the road that leads, inevitably and necessarily, to Chalcedon. My thesis is that Ignatius of Antioch forged the first of many links that historically and doctrinally established the fundamental and obligatory continuity between the Christology of the New Testament and the Christology of the Council of Chalcedon.[5]

My argument is composed of four parts. The first examines how Ignatius conceived Jesus's relationship to the Father and in so doing established his apostolic foundation for discerning the Son's divine status. The second part examines Ignatius's understanding of Jesus's humanity in relation to the apostolic traditions. The third part articulates how Ignatius perceived the unity between the divinity and humanity within Jesus as primarily found within his use of the Communication of Idioms. Lastly, what has been garnered from all of the above is marshaled to demonstrate that Ignatius's apostolic or New Testament Christology is an initial step down the theological road that will ultimately arrive at the Council of Chalcedon.

---

5. In saying this I do not imply, as will become clear, that Ignatius already employed the technical theological concepts and vocabulary of Chalcedon. Rather, I merely want to demonstrate that for both it is one and the same Son who existed as God and as man, and so both divine and human attributes can properly be predicated of one and the same Son.

For other studies of Ignatius's Christology, see E. de Bhaldraithe, "The Christology of Ignatius of Antioch," in *Studia Patristica*, vol. 36, ed. M. Wiles and E. Yarnold (Leuven: Peeters, 2001), 200–206; W. F. Bunge, "The Christology of Ignatius of Antioch" (ThD diss., Harvard University, 1966); V. Corwin, *St. Ignatius and Christianity in Antioch* (New Haven, CT: Yale University Press, 196), 91–115; M. Goulder, "A Poor Man's Christology," *New Testament Studies* 45 (1999): 332–48; Hurtado, *Lord Jesus Christ*, 635–40; M. Rackl, *Die Christologie des heiligen Ignatius von Antiochien*, Freiburger Theologische Studien 14 (Freiburg im Breisgau: Herdersche Verlagshandlung, 1914); E. Robillard, "Christologie d'Ignace d'Antioche," in *Le Christ Hier, Aujourd'hui et Demain*, ed. R. Laflamme and M. Gervais (Quebec: Les Presses de L'Université, 1976), 479–87; I. Saliba, "The Bishop of Antioch and the Heretics: A Study of a Primitive Christology," *Evangelical Quarterly* 54 (1992): 65–76; G. F. Snyder, "The Historical Jesus in the Letters of Ignatius of Antioch," *Biblical Research* 8 (1963): 3–12; C. Story, "The Christology of Ignatius of Antioch," *Evangelical Quarterly* 56 (1984): 173–82; R. D. Young, "Ignatius of Antioch, 'Attaining the Father,'" *Communio* 26 (1999): 333–43.

The Divinity of Jesus Christ

Ignatius's whole Christology is conceived and articulated from within a so-teriological setting.[6] Correctly acknowledging who Jesus is and what he did bears upon the genuine effecting of human salvation, and to propose a coun-terfeit Christology completely nullifies, for Ignatius, the reality of that sal-vation. The nature of Jesus's divine status is articulated from within the his-torical and earthly economy, for it is the historical and earthly Jesus, and not some ethereal transcendent divinity, such as found within the Gnostics, who secures human salvation. "For our God, Jesus the Christ, was conceived by Mary according to God's plan (κατ᾽ οἰκονομίαν θεοῦ), both from the seed of David and of the Holy Spirit" (Eph. 18:2, 20:1).[7] Ignatius primarily articulat-ed his understanding of Jesus's divine status by descriptively elucidating what it means for him to be the Son of Father and the Word of God.[8]

In harmony with the Pauline corpus, Ignatius frequently aligned the Father and Jesus Christ together in such phrases as: "greetings in God the Father and in Jesus Christ" (*Mag.* Prol., see also *Mag.* 1.2) or "Farewell in God the Father and in Jesus Christ" (Eph. 21:2). This close configuration is founded upon their singular relationship. Throughout his letters, Igna-tius emphasized that the Father is uniquely the Father of Jesus Christ (see Eph. 2:1; *Mag.* 3.1; *Tral.* Prol., 9.2), and therefore he is the Father's "only Son (τοῦ μόνου υἱοῦ αὐτοῦ)" (*Rom.* Prol.).[9] As the only Son, he not only "came forth from the one Father (τὸν ἀφ᾽ ἑνὸς πατρὸς προελθόντα)," but he also "re-mained with the One and returned to the One (καὶ ἕνα ὄντα καὶ χωρήσα-ντα)" (*Mag.* 7.2). This is an eternal coming forth, for the Son is "before all

6. For some examples of the soteriological setting of Ignatius's Christology, see Eph. 3, 19, 20; *Mag.* 5.2, 9; *Tral.* Prol., 2, 13; *Phil.* 5, 11; *Smy.* 2, 4, 6.2; *Poly.* 3. For studies of Ignatius's soteriology, see, for example: Corwin, *St. Ignatius and Christianity in Antioch*, 154–88; D. F. Winslow, "The Idea of Redemption in the Epistles of St. Ignatius of Antioch," *Greek Orthodox Theological Review* 11 (1965): 119–31.

7. I am employing the Greek text as found in J. B. Lightfoot and J. R. Harmer, eds., *The Ap-ostolic Fathers: Greek Texts and English Translations of the Writing*, 2nd ed., rev. M. W. Holmes (Grand Rapids, MI: Baker Book House, 1992).

8. For an excellent study of Ignatius's "God language," see D. Trakatellis, "God Language in Ignatius of Antioch," in *The Future of Early Christianity: Essays in Honor of Helmut Koester*, ed. B. A. Pearson (Minneapolis: Fortress Press, 1991), 422–30.

9. This name "Jesus" conjoined with this title "Christ" is Ignatius's almost-universal man-ner of referral (112 times).

ages with the Father (ὅς πρὸ αἰώνων παρὰ πατρὶ ἦν) and appeared at the end of time" (*Mag.* 6.1). So it is not surprising that Ignatius highlighted, within his overarching theme of unity, the unity between the Father and Jesus Christ. Christians are to be united to the bishop as the church is united to Christ and "as Jesus Christ is with the Father (καὶ Ἰησοῦς Χριστὸς τῷ πατρί)" (Eph. 5:1; see *Smy.* 3.3). Therefore Christians must be subject to their bishop "as Jesus Christ in the flesh was to the Father" (*Mag.* 13.2).

For Ignatius, this intimate relation between the Father and Jesus Christ, in keeping with the Johannine tradition, finds its ultimate expression in his being subject to the Father within the economy of salvation. Jesus "as the Lord did nothing without the Father either by himself or through his apostles for he was united with him (ἡνωμένος ὤν)" (*Mag.* 7.1). Again, Christians are to be "imitators of Jesus Christ, just as he is of his Father" (Phil. 7:2) and all must follow the bishop, "as Jesus Christ followed the Father" (*Smy.* 8.1).

This doing of the Father's salvific will, for Ignatius, is chiefly witnessed in Jesus being the Word and Wisdom of the Father and so the Revealer and Teacher of the Father. Here Ignatius appears to be both following the Johannine tradition as well as creatively exploiting it. For Ignatius, there "is one God who revealed himself through Jesus Christ his Son, who is his Word which came forth from silence (ἀπὸ σιγῆς προελθών), who in every respect pleased him who sent him" (*Mag.* 8.2). Ignatius's notion is that silence would have prevailed within the world and so human beings would have been deprived of divine knowledge if the Word had not come forth from the Father and been sent by the Father into the world to reveal the Father; it is the Son's revelation of the Father that specifically pleased him. As the Word of the Father, "Jesus Christ [is] the unerring mouth (ὑμῖν ταῦτα φανερώσει ὅτι ἀληθῶς λέγω τὸ ἀψευδὲς στόμα) by whom the Father has spoken truly" (Rom. 8:2). Moreover, Jesus Christ "is the mind of the Father (τοῦ πατρὸς ἡ γνώμη)" (Eph. 3:2), and "all become wise by receiving God's knowledge, which is Jesus Christ" (Eph. 17:2). Jesus Christ is therefore "our only teacher" (*Mag.* 9.1), who is so powerful that he "spoke and it happened" and yet "even the things which he has done in silence are worthy of the Father" (Eph. 15:1). Echoing the Johannine tradition and in harmony with the Letter to the Hebrews, Ignatius stated that Jesus Christ is "the High Priest entrusted with the Holy of Holies" and to him "alone has been entrusted with the hidden things of God, for he himself is the door of the

Father (αὐτὸς ὢν θύρα τοῦ πατρός)," through whom all must enter (Phil. 9:1).

Ignatius's understanding of the relationship between the Father and Jesus Christ, his Son and Word, possesses the authentic ring of the apostolic tradition as found within New Testament Christianity. Even where he is articulating something that is particularly his own, he has not moved significantly from New Testament motifs, but rather his creativity arises specifically from within these various traditions, such as his notion of the Word coming forth from the silence of the Father and so becoming his mouthpiece.

While descriptive and functional, Ignatius's apostolic conception of the singular relationship between the Father and the Son/Word confirmed for him that the earthly and historical Jesus Christ as the Son and the Word, unlike other human beings, is truly divine.[10] Ignatius thus effortlessly and spontaneously weaved within his understanding of the relationship between the Father and the Son the simple and unequivocal proclamation that Jesus Christ is God. For Ignatius, Jesus Christ is "our God (τοῦ θεοῦ ἡμῶν)" (see Eph. Prol., 18:2; Rom. Prol., 3:3, 6:3; *Smy.* 1.1; *Poly.* 8.3). The Lord dwells within Christians, and therefore they are "his temples and he may be in us as our God (ἐν ἡμῖν θεὸς ἡμῶν)" (Eph. 15:3). Unlike the New Testament, for which ὁ θεός is used almost exclusively for the Father, Ignatius unhesitatingly (as the above references testify), effortlessly, and spontaneously applied this designation to Jesus Christ.[11] I would argue that Ig-

10. Grant states: "Ignatius is insisting upon the divine function, and also upon the divine nature, of the incarnate Lord, just as certain New Testament writers also insist upon it (John 1:1, 20:28; Heb. 1:8–9; Tit. 2:13; 2 Pet. 1:1)." "Scripture and Tradition in St. Ignatius of Antioch," 8.

11. Ignatius designates Jesus as "God" on at least eleven occasions. M. P. Brown states: "Ignatius does not make a theological issue of this usage; the epithet (i.e., God) is applied casually, for the most part, and apparently without fear of being misunderstood ... Thus, it is difficult to avoid the conclusion that the peculiar assignment ὁ θεός to Jesus Christ is unselfconscious." *The Authentic Writings of Ignatius* (Durham, NC: Duke University Press, 1963), 22. D. Trakatellis insists that Ignatius's designation of Jesus as God was not "unselfconscious"; rather, while "Ignatius 'does not make an issue of this usage,' he does make a clear statement." "God Language in Ignatius of Antioch," 426. Or, again, Trakatellis states: "Ignatius makes no effort to prove that Jesus Christ is God or to develop apologetic strategies in that direction. He simply issues his high christological statement as a matter of fact, as a truth taken for granted and fully shared by the recipients of his letters." Ibid., 427. While the New Testament almost always reserves the term ὁ θεός to designate the Father, there are a few instances where it could be argued that it refers to Jesus Christ. See Ti. 2:13 (τοῦ μεγάλου θεοῦ καὶ σωτῆρος ἡμῶν Χριστοῦ Ἰησοῦ); 1 Jn. 5:20 (ἐν τῷ υἱῷ αὐτοῦ Ἰησοῦ Χριστῷ. Οὗτός ἐστιν ὁ ἀληθινὸς θεός.); 2 Pt. 1.1 (τοῦ θεοῦ ἡμῶν καὶ

natius is both faithful to the apostolic tradition as witnessed within the New Testament as well as accentuating, intensifying, and exploiting what is often implicitly, though at times explicitly, contained within that tradition. Moreover, I argue, as I did at the onset, that he has done so not as an innovator, but that he was the first to do so. Rather, the very spontaneity with which Ignatius designated Jesus Christ as "our God," without strained argument or embarrassed defense, bears witness that Christianity, at least as Ignatius knew it, now embraced a fuller appreciation of the New Testament proclamation that Jesus Christ, as Son and Word, is indeed the God of Christians.[12] He has exploited this affirmation in order to refute clearly what he considered to be false perceptions of who Jesus Christ is. Contrary to the Jews, who wish to deny the divinity of Jesus; in contrast to the Gnostics, who acknowledge a whole host of deities; and in opposition to the Docetists, who refuse to acknowledge Jesus's authentic humanity, Ignatius, by designating this historical and earthly Jesus to be ὁ θεὸς of Christians has shrewdly countered them all.

By articulating his conception of Jesus Christ's divinity within the apostolic tradition as found within New Testament Christianity and by exploiting the present interpretation of that tradition by unequivocally affirming that "Jesus Christ is our God," Ignatius has both intrinsically linked his Christology to that apostolic tradition and simultaneously nudged it vigorously down the doctrinal road to Nicaea and, ultimately, to Chalcedon.

The Humanity of Jesus Christ

As stated above, the full soteriological significance of Jesus Christ being "our God" lies specifically, for Ignatius, within the economy—that is, in

---

σωτῆρος Ἰησοῦ Χριστοῦ); Heb. 1. 8 (τοῦ θρόνος σου ὁ θεὸς); and Jn. 20:28 (ὁ κύριός μου καὶ ὁ θεός μου). For a discussion of these and other similar passages, see: R. Brown, *An Introduction to New Testament Christology* (New York: Paulist Press, 1994), 171–89.

12. Ignatius frequently calls Jesus Christ "Lord," which could also be seen, given the New Testament evidence, as a divine title. See *Eph.* 6:1, 7:2, 10:3, 15:2, 17:2; *Mag.* 9.1, 13.1; *Tral.* 10; Rom. 4:2; Phil. 1:1, 11:1; *Smy.* 1.1, 4.2, 5.2; and *Poly.* Prol., 4.1, 5.1, 8.3. There are also a few passages within Ignatius's letters that are Trinitarian in nature and thus equally manifest his belief in the full divinity of Jesus Christ as the Son and the Word of the Father. See *Eph.* 9:1, *Mag.* 13.1, and Phil. 7. One might also argue that Ignatius's designation of both God the Father and Jesus Christ as Polycarp's bishop equally affirms Jesus's divine status: μᾶλλον ἐπισκοπημένῳ ὑπὸ θεοῦ πατρὸς καὶ κυρίου Ἰησοῦ Χριστοῦ, πλεῖστα χαίρειν (*Poly.* Prol., 1; see also Eph. 1:3 and *Mag.* 3.1).

the authentic reality of the Incarnation and thus in Jesus's genuine humanity—for it is what he actually underwent as man and the deeds he actually performed as man that are salvific. Our salvation was procured "when God appeared in human form (θεοῦ ἀνθρωπίνως φανεπουμένου) to bring the newness of eternal life" (Eph. 19:3). This is articulated primarily in response to the Docetists, who denied the genuineness of Jesus's humanity and also, to some extent, against the Gnostics, who separated Christ from Jesus the man.[13] In keeping with 1 John 2:22 and 4:2, Ignatius accused both parties of blasphemy "by not confessing that he (the Lord) was clothed in flesh (μὴ ὁμολογῶν αὐτὸν σαρκοφόρον). Anyone who does not acknowledge this thereby denies him completely and is clothed in a corpse" (*Smy.* 5.2). Ignatius, while never addressing theologically or philosophically the issue of how God could actually become truly man, consistently, in almost repetitious monotony, asserted the reality of Jesus's humanity, and so the reality of those human experiences undergone within that humanity and the reality of those human deeds performed within that humanity.

Ignatius affirmed Jesus's full humanity not by constructing an anthropology, but by insisting upon the historicity and physicality of his salvific experiences and actions. For Ignatius, as for Paul, while the Cross "is a stumbling block to unbelievers, [it is] salvation and eternal life to us" (Eph. 18:1). Ignatius himself has "taken refuge in the gospel as the flesh of Jesus (ὡς σαρκὶ Ἰησοῦ)" (Phil. 5:1). For Ignatius, "the 'archives' (ἀρχεῖά) are Jesus Christ, the inviolable archives are his cross and death and his resurrection and the faith that comes through him" (Phil. 8:2). The suffering and resurrection were but a part of "the divine plan with respect to the new man Jesus Christ" (Eph. 12:3; see *Smy.* 7).

Within these affirmations, the Magnesians were warned "not to get snagged by the hooks of worthless opinions." Rather, they must be fully "convinced about the birth and the suffering and the resurrection, which took place during the time of the governorship of Pontius Pilate. These things were truly and most assuredly done by Jesus Christ, our hope (πραχθέντα ἀληθῶς καὶ βεβαίως ὑπὸ Ἰησοῦ Χριστοῦ)" (*Mag.* 11). At the same time, the Trallians were to "keep away from every strange plant, which is

13. This is probably why Ignatius consistently joined the two. In speaking of "Jesus Christ," Ignatius was constantly designating that it was the earthly man Jesus who was the Christ and not some transcendent deity apart from him.

heresy," for such people "mix Jesus Christ with poison" (*Tral.* 6), and the Philadelphians were not to align themselves with schismatics because such "are not the Father's planting," for they have disassociated themselves "from the Passion" (*Phil.* 3; see *Tral.* 11). He exhorted the Trallians:

Be deaf, therefore, whenever anyone speaks to you apart of Jesus Christ, who was of the family of David, who was the son of Mary, who really (ἀληθῶς) was born, who both ate and drank, who really (ἀληθῶς) was persecuted under Pontius Pilate, who really (ἀληθῶς) was crucified and died while those in heaven and on earth and under the earth looked on; who, moreover, really (ἀληθῶς) was raised from the dead when his Father raised him up, who—his Father, that is, in the same way will likewise also raise us up in Christ Jesus who believe in him, apart from whom we have no true life. (*Tral.* 9)

For Ignatius, it was ludicrous for him to be in real chains and on the verge of actual death if "these things were done by our Lord in appearance only" (*Smy.* 4.2). It is actually the unbelievers, Ignatius believed, who "exist in appearance only," who assert that Jesus Christ "suffered in appearance only (τὸ δοκεῖν πεπονθέναι)" (*Tral.* 10; see also *Smy.* 2). Ignatius, as did Paul, glorified in "Jesus Christ, the God who made you [the Smyrnaeans] wise," for they, too, in faith, have been nailed to the Cross of their Lord Jesus Christ (*Smy.* 1.1). Ignatius was convinced that Jesus was not only in the flesh prior to his death, but that he was also "in the flesh even after the resurrection." In accordance with the Lukan and Johannine traditions, the risen Jesus "ate and drank" with his disciples "like one who is composed with flesh" and urged them to touch him (*Smy.* 3.3).

Ignatius's insistence upon the human flesh of Jesus found its termination in the Eucharist. Those who refuse to acknowledge Jesus's physical humanity "abstain from the Eucharist and prayer, because they refuse to acknowledge that the Eucharist is the flesh (σάρκα) of our Savior Jesus Christ, which suffered for our sins and which the Father by his goodness raised up" (*Smy.* 6 2). What Ignatius desired most is "the bread of God, which is the flesh of Christ (σὰρξ τοῦ Χριστοῦ) who is of the seed of David, and for drink I want his blood, which is incorruptible love" (Rom. 7:3).[14]

There are a couple of conclusions to be drawn. First, Ignatius's under-

---

14. For further references and allusions to the Eucharist and the physical reality of Jesus's presence, see Eph. 20:2, *Tral.* 8.1, *Smy.* 12.2, and *Phil.* 4.

standing of the historicity and physicality of Jesus's humanity is the same as that expressed within New Testament Christianity. One clearly perceives the echoes of the Gospels of Matthew, Luke, John, and 1 John, as well as phrases and ideas that bear the voice of Paul. Even if Ignatius was merely acquainted with their various apostolic traditions, the traditions that he was defending were theirs. Ignatius's Christology, when it bears upon Jesus's authentic physical reality and the actual historicity of his life, is thus genuinely apostolic in origin, content, and expression. Second, as with his understanding of the divinity of Jesus Christ, Ignatius did not merely repeat the apostolic tradition; rather, he also molded it so as to affirm it against erroneous tenets.[15] It is here, more than in his clear affirmation that Jesus Christ is "our God," that Ignatius has become, I believe, truly an innovator in that he has made an original contribution that is particularly his own. While the apostolic tradition did provide him with his faith in the historical and physical Jesus, it was Ignatius who now clearly articulated that the historical events (contrary to the Gnostics) of Jesus's fleshly birth, death, and resurrection (contrary to the Docetists) are salvific. The authenticity, genuineness, efficaciousness, and reality of humankind's salvation is predicated, for Ignatius, intrinsically and necessarily upon the authenticity, genuineness, efficaciousness, and historical reality of Jesus's incarnation, life, death, and resurrection. While this causal connection is embedded within the apostolic tradition of the New Testament—for example, within Romans, chapters 5–8, and the Letter to the Hebrews—it was Ignatius who unearthed it for all to see. Third, while he was clearly tethered to the Christology of the apostolic tradition as found within the New Testament, Ignatius has tugged it farther down the road to Chalcedon. Already within Ignatius's stress upon the reality and historicity of the Incarnation one finds some of the foundational principals and central arguments later employed by Irenaeus in his refutation of the Gnostics.[16] Moreover, the whole soteriological setting of Ignatius's Christology, whereby the human experiences and historical actions of "our God" effect a newness of life with the Father, foreshadows the

15. Trakatellis states that Ignatius "evidently did not invent his Christology ... What Ignatius did was to interpret the Johannine and the Pauline christological traditions or formulas in a way that could serve the immediate and pressing needs of the church." "God Language in Ignatius of Antioch," 430.

16. See, for example, Irenaeus, *Ad. Haer.* 3.18.6–7, 4.20.4.

Irenaean and Athanasian tenet that God came in the likeness of man, and that man might become the likeness of God.[17] Likewise, incubating within his Christology is the theological refutation of Apollinarius's denial of Christ's human soul and the prophetic clue to Gregory of Nazianzus's maxim that "what is not assumed is not healed/saved."[18]

The Oneness of Jesus Christ

Ignatius's Christology bears the indelible imprint of the apostolic tradition as witnessed within the New Testament in a twofold manner. (1) He affirmed that Jesus Christ, as the Son and the Word of the Father, is "our God." (2) He equally affirmed the reality of Jesus Christ's physical humanity and all that authentically pertains historically to such a humanity. Moreover, in confirming (and, most of all, in defending) these two Christological truths of apostolic origin against what he considered the counterfeit gospels of the Judaizers, Gnostics, and Docetists, Ignatius advanced the authentic understanding and interpretation of the apostolic Christological tradition. Where all this finds its cumulative effect, and in so doing proceeds to a new depth of meaning and insight, is in Ignatius's employment of what came to be termed the Communication of Idioms.[19] For Ignatius, it is one and the same Jesus Christ who *is* both "Son of God" and "Son of man," and thus he instinctively recognized that the authentic attributes of each are properly and necessarily predicated of that one and the same Jesus Christ (see Eph. 20:2). Moreover, these passages have the feel of being part of an already-existing tradition, for Ignatius employed them spontaneously and effortlessly without providing any intimation of their needing to be defended nor displaying any symptoms of embarrassment at their use. While he used them to address his immediate concerns, they are not entirely his own creations. In other words, Ignatius was not the originator of such theological linguistic expressions; rather, he was utilizing a manner of speaking that was readily available to him.[20]

17. See Irenaeus, *Adv. Haer.* 5. praef.; Athanasius, *De Incar.* 54.
18. See Gregory of Nazianzus, *Ep.* 101.4.
19. The term "communication of idiom" was first used in its Greek form in the sixth century by those who wanted to defend the definition of the Council of Chalcedon. The Latin form, taken from the Greek, was not in use until some time in the Middle Ages.
20. The scriptural basis for the Communication of Idioms might be found in such Pauline passages as Rom. 1:2–4, 2 Cor. 8:9, Gal. 4:4, Phil. 2:5–11, Col. 1:15–20. A. Grillmeier holds

Ignatius thus assured the Ephesian Christians that they had assumed new life "through the blood of God (ἐν αἵματι θεοῦ)" (Eph. 1:1). This is a striking and even scandalous phrase. First, God can only truly possess human blood if he has actually become a human being. What the Communication of Idioms does linguistically, then, is conjoin the two Christological truths of Jesus Christ's divinity and humanity so as to express the ontological oneness of who Jesus is as the Son or the Word of God existing as man. This phrase, like all instances of the Communication of Idioms, is an arresting alignment of seemingly clashing words with their seemly irreconcilable meanings ("blood" and "God") that accentuates the reality of the Incarnation; that is, only if the divine Son of God did actually become man and so exist as man does such an alignment make theological sense and possess any literal meaning. The Communication of Idioms testifies to the truth that the incarnational "becoming" actually terminates in an incarnational "is." Second, this particular phrase also alludes to the shedding of God's blood, which would scandalize the Docetists, but which, for Ignatius, would strikingly portray the grandeur of the Christian Gospel. Moreover, for Ignatius, Christians derive their true existence from Jesus's "divinely blessed suffering (θεομακαρίστου αὐτοῦ πάθους)" (Smy. 1.2). This phrase, too, equally attests that what makes Jesus's suffering blessed, and so salvific, is that it was the divine Son of God who endured it, but he could only endure such suffering if he had truly existed as a human being. Ignatius himself desired to imitate "the suffering of my God (τοῦ πάθους τοῦ θεοῦ μου)" (Rom. 6:3). Again, God could humanly suffer only if he actually became a man, and Ignatius desired to imitate "the suffering of my God" so as to achieve precisely what that human suffering endured by God attained—eternal life.

Besides these phrases that accentuate the reality of the Incarnation and so the ontological unity of the divinity and humanity in the one Jesus

---

that the Communication of Idioms became popular around the time when the Christian books (particularly book 6) were added to the Sibylline Oracles, which was some time during the second Century. In book 6 is found the proclamation: "O blessed tree, on which God was hung!" *Christ in Christian Tradition* (London: Mowbrays, 1975), 1:63.

I argued that "the whole of orthodox patristic Christology, including the conciliar affirmations, can be seen as an attempt to defend the practice and to clarify the use of the communication of idioms." *Does God Suffer?* (Edinburgh: T&T Clark, 2000), 175. See also my "Cyril and the Mystery of the Incarnation," in *The Theology of St. Cyril of Alexandria: A Critical Appreciation*, ed. T. G. Weinandy and D. Keating (London: T&T Clark/Continuum, 2003), 31.

Christ, Ignatius also employed a couple of what might be termed rhythmical or poetic semicreedal proclamations, the purpose of which is to accentuate this incarnational oneness. He exhorted Polycarp to "wait expectantly for him who is above time: the Eternal, the Invisible (τὸν ἄχρονον, τὸν ἀόρατον), who for our sake became visible (ὁρατόν); the Intangible, the Unsuffering (τὸν ἀψηλάφητον, τὸν ἀπαθῆ), who for our sake suffered (παθητόν), who for our sake endured in every way" (*Poly.* 3.2).[21] Here there is clearly present only one subject, one "who," who is eternal, invisible, intangible, and unsuffering but who equally, because of the Incarnation, became visible and suffered for our sake. Here divine and human attributes are predicated of one and the same subject, and such an attribution finds its legitimacy in the reality of the Incarnation.

For Ignatius, moreover, "there is only one physician, who is both flesh and spirit, born and unborn, God in man, true life in death, both from Mary and from God, first subject to suffering and then beyond it, Jesus Christ our Lord (εἷς ἰατρός ἐστιν, σαρκικὸς καὶ πνευματικός, γεννετὸς καὶ ἀγέννητος, ἐν ἀνθρώπῳ θεός, ἐν θανάτῳ ζωὴ ἀληθινή, καὶ ἐκ Μαρίας καὶ ἐκ θεοῦ, πρῶτον παθητὸς καὶ τότε ἀπαθής, Ἰησοῦς Χριστὸς ὁ κύριος ἡμῶν (Eph. 7:2). This is the most celebrated example of Ignatius's use of the Communication of Idioms.[22] There is one subject in that there is "one physician" who is "Jesus Christ our Lord." Yet the physician Jesus Christ possesses both "flesh" insofar as he actually is man and "spirit" insofar as he actually is God. He is actually "born" in that he is from Mary as man, and he is actually "unborn" in that he is eternally from God the Father. He is "true life" even "in death" because the one who died as man is the living God. While Jesus Christ was "first subject to suffering" as a human being like us, he has now passed beyond it as a risen man. Ignatius's ontological basis for this juxtaposition of divine and human attributes lies precisely in that Jesus is "God in man"— that is, in the authentic reality of the Incarnation.[23]

21. For scriptural, philosophical, and early patristic parallels to this passage, see Schoedel, *Ignatius of Antioch*, 267–68.

22. Ibid., 60. Schoedel sees once again some semicreedal formulae in this passage.

23. Significant for my thesis, Schoedel states: "In Ignatius ... flesh and spirit represent two spheres or two dimensions that refer to human and divine reality respectively. We have here the kernel of the later two-nature christologies." *Ignatius of Antioch*, 60. He also writes in relationship to this passage: "When Ignatius refers to Christ as 'both fleshly and spiritual,' he has in mind the union of the divine and human in the God-Man and thus anticipates the classical

Ignatius and the Council of Chalcedon

The above demonstrates that Ignatius employed the Communication of Idioms, as would his descendants, to ensure the reality of the Incarnation and in so doing ensure the reality of the salvific events associated with the Incarnation. The fact that Ignatius had descendants is of the utmost significance for my thesis. He has anticipated and even embodied within his own Christology later controversies and doctrinal development. In light of the subsequent Christological history, Ignatius lifted the apostolic Christological tradition of the New Testament upon his shoulders and carried it, being joined along the way by many Fathers, especially Athanasius and Cyril of Alexandria, to the doorstep of the Council of Ephesus, and then by way of Ephesus into the inner sanctum of the Council of Chalcedon.

On one level, the above statement may be an anachronistic exaggeration. Ignatius did not display, philosophically and theologically, the Christological refinements of the later Fathers and Councils. Nowhere did he speak of one *prospon* or of one *hypostasis*, nor did he employ the concepts of *ousia* and *phusis*. Nonetheless, I am convinced that Ignatius would not have felt out of place or out of his depth at either Nicaea, Ephesus, or Chalcedon. His understanding of the singular relationship between the Father and the Son, which found its most concise formulation in the simple truth that "Jesus Christ is our God," would have allowed him to give his immediate assent to the Nicene Creed's declaration that the Son is "God from God, Light from Light, true God from true God, begotten and not made, one in being with the Father," even if he, along with many others, might struggle to explain the exact meaning the term *homoousios*. His adamant defense of the historical and physical humanity of Jesus would have easily allowed him to champion the constituency that condemned Apollinarius. Moreover, he would have had no doubt that Mary was *Theotokos*, for he himself had as-

---

two-nature-christology." Ibid., 20. Likewise, Hurtado states that Ignatius's "letters are also noteworthy for expressions of faith that anticipate, and perhaps influenced, subsequent developments in formative orthodox doctrine about Jesus.'" *Lord Jesus Christ*, 635. Or, again, he writes: "it is fairly clear that he [Ignatius] represents the profound commitment to Jesus' divinity and real human existence that demanded those efforts toward the distinctive Christian idea of God, and especially toward the idea of Jesus' 'two natures,' doctrinal efforts that heavily occupied the developing orthodox/catholic tradition well through the fourth century." Ibid., 640.

serted that the Son, who was eternally with the Father and so unborn, was the same Son who was born of Mary. Ignatius would have eagerly taken up arms over the issue surrounding the Christological legitimacy of the Communication of Idioms, for he was present on the field of battle long before Nestorius and Cyril had sounded the trumpets of war. Lastly, while I am sure that he would have been awed by the Christological sophistication of the Creed of Chalcedon, Ignatius would have felt comfortable professing it, for it bears the imprint of his own faith—one and the same Son is truly God and truly man, and thus both divine and human attributes can properly be predicated of that one and the same Son. Equally, as Ignatius's employment of the Communication of Idioms demonstrates, while the attributes pertaining to God and man are united in the one and the same subject of Jesus Christ, and so are not separated and divided, neither the divinity nor the humanity is changed or confused.

Now the one and the same Ignatius of Antioch, who I believe concluded his journey by way of the Christological tradition at the Council of Chalcedon, began his journey within the apostolic Christological tradition of the New Testament, and thus it is this same Ignatius, along with many subsequent Fathers, who pioneered the unalterable and unswerving route between the faith of the Apostles and the faith of the Fathers at Chalcedon.

While a significant milestone in the history of Christology, Chalcedon is not lands' end. The history of Christological development continues through the centuries to the present and beyond, and with it the same continuity of faith continues its apostolic journey as well. And so Ignatius, whose Christology finds its departure within the earliest apostolic tradition, continues to be a fellow apostolic pilgrim.

CHAPTER 5

Athanasius
The Incarnation and the Soul of Christ

To read the literature, one would think that the single most decisive issue concerning Athanasius's Christology is whether he affirmed that Christ possessed a human soul. Any other aspect of Athanasius's Christology appears at best to be secondary and even inconsequential. While some have admirably defended Athanasius, the common perceived consensus is that his understanding of the Incarnation makes no provision for a soul, or, if it does (especially after the Synod of Antioch in 362), that soul has no Christological or soteriological significance. The soul is merely acknowledged, along with the body, as a constitutive factor within Christ's human composition.[1]

Originally published as "Athanasius: The Incarnation and the Soul of Christ," in *Studia Patristica XLI*, ed. M. J. Edwards, F. M. Young, and P. Parvis (Leuven: Peeters, 2006), 265–69. Reprinted by permission.

1. It is not possible to provide a complete bibliography pertaining to this issue. G. D. Dragas notes that F. C. Baur raised the issue of whether Athanasius believed that Christ had a human soul for the first time (*Die christliche Lehre von der Dreieinigkelt und Menschwerdung Gottes*, 1841). But it was K. Hoss and A. Stülcken who popularized the issue within patristic Christology. K. Hoss, *Studien über das Schriftum und die Theologie des Athanasius auf Grund* (Freiburg: 1899); A. Stülcken, *Athansiana, Literar-und dogmengeschichtliche Untersuchungen* (Leipzig: 1899). See *St. Athanasius Contra Apollinarem*, Church and Theology 6 (Athens: 1985), 289.
  Some critics of Athanasius include: A. Grillmeier, *Christ in Christian Tradition*, rev. ed. (London: Mowbrays, 1975), 6:308–28; R. P. C. Hanson, *The Search for the Christian Doctrine of God* (Edinburgh: T&T Clark, 1988), 446–58, 645–51; J. N. D. Kelly, *Early Christian Doctrines*,

While the issue of Christ's soul is indeed crucial for an adequate under-standing of the Incarnation, I believe that Athanasius would be perplexed as to why the issue ever arose in the first place, and bemused that it has become such a *cause célèbre*. His bewilderment would not arise out of his own am-bivalence or indifferent attitude toward the issue of Christ's soul, for I be-lieve that, from the very onset of his theological work, Athanasius took the presence of a soul as a given, and even a soteriologically significant given. Rather, he would readily perceive that for one to raise the issue of whether his Christology allowed for and sanctioned a soul within Christ manifested that one completely failed to grasp, and so was completely ignorant of, his incarnational and soteriological concerns. Focusing exclusively on his *Con-tra Arianos III*, I present succinctly Athanasius's understanding of the Incar-nation and in so doing liberate him from the charge of being an Apollinari-an before Apollinarius.

Within *Contra Arianos III* Athanasius worked out his understanding of the Incarnation in response to the Arian assertion that the weaknesses as-cribed to Christ in the Gospels, such as growth, fear, and ignorance, con-firm their judgment that the Son must be a creature (26–27). They "deny the Eternity and Godhead of the Word in consequence of those human attributes (ἀνθρωπίνων) which the Saviour took on him by reason of that flesh (σάρκα) which he bore" (27).[2]

While it is common knowledge that he never denied that Christ pos-sessed a soul, it is in his refutation of the Arian charge that Athanasius is sternly reprimanded for not employing it when it would appear to be the most obvious Christological explanation to exploit. In contrast to the ab-sence of a soul within Arian Christology, Athanasius, by arguing that Christ did possess a human soul, could then have emphasized that all of the hu-

---

4th ed. (London: Adam and Charles Black, 1968), 284–89; M. Richard, "Saint Athanase et la psychologie du Christ selon les ariens," *Méanges de Science Religieuse* 4 (1947): 7–49.

Besides Dragas (*Die christliche Lehre*, 289–399), some others who have defended Atha-nasius include: K. Anatolios, *Athanasius: The Coherence of His Thought* (London: Routledge, 1998), 70–73, 78–84, 140–55, 201–2, 226n116, 226n121; A. Pettersen, *Athanasius* (London: Geoffrey Chapman, 1995), 130–32; T. E. Pollard, *Johannine Christology and the Early Church* (Cambridge: Cambridge University Press, 1970), 232–44; T. F. Torrance, *Theology in Reconcili-ation* (London: Geoffrey Chapman, 1975), 224–31.

2. Translations are taken from P. Schaff and H. Wace, eds., *Nicene and Post-Nicene Fathers*, vol. 4 (Edinburgh: T&T Clark/Eerdmans, 1987).

man attributes resided within it so as to protect, and so endorse, the full divinity of the Word. In so censuring Athanasius, however, his critics neglect his deeper and more fundamental incarnational and soteriological concerns. While the human attributes such as ignorance and fear do reside in a human intellect or soul, of which Athanasius was well aware, his strategy was not to protect the divinity by using the soul as a shield against all that pertains to being authentically human. For Athanasius, if the soul became the primary center and so subject of the human experiences, then, while the divinity of the Logos may be preserved, the truth of the Incarnation would be abandoned. Athanasius was not about to become a Nestorian before Nestorius![3]

Athanasius's primary concern was to establish the proper incarnational principle for interpreting the manner in which the human attributes are predicated of Christ. For Athanasius, this hermeneutical tool lay within the appropriate understanding of the *skopos* of the Gospels or the economy. The story being told is of the one and the same Son, who "is God's Son, for being Son, he is inseparable from the Father, and never was there when he was not, but he was always" (28), and who "afterwards for us he took flesh of the Virgin, Mary Bearer of God, and was made man. And this *skopos* is to be found throughout inspired Scripture" (29; see also 28). Thus "let us, retaining the general *skopos* of the faith (τόν σκπὸν τῆς πίστεως) acknowledge that what they (the Arians) interpret ill, has a right interpretation" (35). While Athanasius ardently defended the full divinity of the Son, he refused to allow such a defense to undermine the integrity of the Incarnation, for it is to this purpose that the divinity must be upheld—so that it is truly the same divine Son who actually exists as an authentic man. Thus, as the *skopos* of the economy demands, the Son who is God must be the same Son who is man.

By insisting that it is one and the same Son, Athanasius was insisting that the incarnational "becoming" terminates in an incarnational "is." In accordance with John's Gospel, the Word who was eternally God "became man, and did not come into man," and it is equally here then as well that Athanasius insists that the biblical word "flesh" means "man" in his completeness (30). For Athanasius, neither Adoptionism nor merely the assum-

3. Some critics seem to want Athanasius to espouse a Nestorian position, thus giving the impression that they themselves tend toward Nestorianism. See Grillmeier, *Christ in Christian Tradition*, 314–15; Hanson, *Search for the Christian Doctrine of God*, 449; Kelly, *Early Christian Doctrines*, 287.

ing of a material body will do. "To become flesh" demands both that the Son *truly exists* as man and that it is *truly as man*, assuming all that pertains to being authentically human, that the Son exists. Athanasius noted that when the Logos came to the saints of old and hallowed them, it was never said that "he had become man (γεγένηται ἄνθρωπος), nor, when they suffered was it said that he himself suffered" (31). It is only right, thought Athanasius, that the Son "in putting on human flesh, to put it on whole with the affections (πάθη) proper to it" (32). Note that Athanasius insisted that the Son assumed the whole of what it means to be human and thus the *pathe*, those passible affections proper to it—possible affections that bear not merely upon the body as such but upon the whole of the humanity, body and soul. Athanasius's entire concern was to establish this incarnational principle that "when the flesh suffered the Word was not external to it (ὅθεν τῆς σαρκὸς πασχούσης οὐκ ἧς ἐκτὸς ταύτης ὁ λόγος) ... and when he did divinely his Father's works, the flesh was not external to him, but in the body itself did the Lord do them (οὐκ ἦν ἔξωθεν αὐτοῦ ἡ σάρξ, ἀλλ᾽ ἐν αὐτῷς τῷ σώματι ταῦτα πάλιν ὁ κύριος ἐποίει)" (32).[4] In light of, and in accordance with, the above understanding of the Incarnation, Athanasius proceeded to interpret, in an almost monotonous fashion, the various Gospel passages that the Arians believed demonstrated the Logos's createdness. Here I focus on only the most problematic passage—that on Jesus's ignorance.

The Arians accusingly asked, if the Son is truly divine, why did Jesus need to ask questions, such as where Lazarus was buried, and why did he admit his ignorance of the last day? While the Word as God is omniscient, and so he has no need to ask questions nor was he then ignorant of the last day, in accordance with the *skopos* of the economy and thus in keeping with the incarnational principle, Athanasius insisted that this very same Word

4. Athanasius argued that not only must the human affections and passions be predicated of the Son, but also that the Son's "divine" deeds must equally be done as man. As incarnate the Son did not do divine deeds in a man, but he performed divine deeds as a man, for that is the manner in which the Son existed (32). It is in this sense that Athanasius's understanding of the Son using his humanity as an instrument (organon) must be understood. It is not an instrument external to him, but an instrument that is integral to the manner and mode of his very being and so acting—as man (31, 35). Such an understanding of the Incarnation refutes any notion that Athanasius underplays or disregards the humanity of Christ. It also makes mockery of Hanson's own derision that Athanasius espouses a "space-suit Christology" where the Son's "relation to this body is no closer than of an astronaut to his space-suit" (448).

did actually exist as man, and so as is only proper was genuinely ignorant as man (37, 38).

The Word, though as man he was ignorant of it (the last day), for ignorance is proper to man, and especially ignorance of these things. Moreover, this is proper to the Saviour's love of man; for since he was made man, he is not ashamed, because of the flesh, which is ignorant, to say "I know not." That he may show that knowing as God, he is but ignorant according to the flesh. (43)

This is the incarnational paradigm that Athanasius employed throughout his interpretation of those scriptural passages that the Arians proffered as confirmation of the Word's nondivinity.[5] The real matter at hand for Athanasius was not the issue of Christ's soul, but the proper incarnational understanding of how divine and human attributes are predicated of one and the same Son. For Athanasius, the proper employment of this hermeneutical principle did not merely illustrate but actually authenticated the truth of the Incarnation (35, 57).

Critics have faulted Athanasius's interpretation on a number of points. First, critics contend that because Athanasius insisted that it was the Son who was the subject of the ignorance and yet he, as God, is omniscient, the ignorance was merely feigned. Such a criticism misses entirely Athanasius's incarnational concern. The ignorance is not feigned in the slightest, because Athanasius's entire concern was to ensure, since the Son had actually become man, that all that pertains to being man—including ignorance—was properly his own. It was an authentic, and not a bogus, human life that the Son lived. Second, the fact that Athanasius did not have recourse to the soul or human intellect by way of situating the ignorance does not in any manner undermine his Christology. Although Athanasius did not state that ignorance resided in the human soul or intellect, these were undoubtedly present within his stress on the authenticity of the Son's ignorance, which

5. While the Son as divine is impassible, fearless, immortal, and in no need of increase, as man the Son was passible, fearful, dies, and increases (31, 34, 52–57). All of these human weaknesses, as with ignorance, imply the presence of a human soul and intellect. Moreover, while Athanasius describes the death of Jesus as the separation of the Son from his body, this does not imply, as the critics assume, the absence of a soul. It is again the insistence that it is actually the Son who dies as man. That Athanasius sees death as the departure of the soul from the body is witnessed in his twice noting that Jesus calls back Lazarus's soul when raising him from the dead (38, 46).

resided not in a body but within a human intellect. The reason the soul or intellect is not mentioned is because Athanasius's primary incarnational concern was to confirm that what is truly human—in this case, genuine human ignorance—was rightly predicated of the Son of God, for it was he who existed as man. The Son, for Athanasius, is the primary and immediate bearer of the ignorance and not the soul. While the soul is present, it is not present, for Athanasius, as an intermediate "subject" shielding the divine Son from authentic human weakness. Third, that Athanasius stressed that it was the Son who was the true subject of all the human attributes does not betoken, as some critics avow, a Logos/Sarx rather than a Logos/Anthropos Christology. Rather, this again illustrates Athanasius's true incarnational concern that it must be the Son who actually lived a human life. The criticism itself bears no relationship to his actual Christology; rather, it is the mere imposing of a flawed and erroneous template by which to interpret (in the end falsely) his Christology. Actually, the whole issue and the ultimate censure of Athanasius's Christology for not subscribing to a human soul would never have arisen if these misconceived and artificial templates had not been capriciously imposed upon the whole of patristic Christology.

By way of conclusion, Athanasius employed, for soteriological reasons, this incarnational hermeneutical principle. All human attributes, attributes that imply a union of body and soul, such as suffering, ignorance, fear, and the like, must be predicated of the Son, for it is only in the Son assuming our human weaknesses in becoming man that we have been "thoroughly delivered from them" (33). Being deified through baptism only became possible because "the Lord, putting on the body, became man, so we men are deified by the Word as being taken to him through his flesh, and henceforward inherit life everlasting (ὡς γὰρ ὁ κύριος ἐνδυσάμενος τὸ σῶμα γέγονεν ἄνθρωπος, οὕτως ἡμεῖς οἱ ἄνθρωποι παρὰ τοῦ λόγου τὲ θεοποιούμεθα προσληφθέντες διὰ τῆς σαρκὸς αὐτοῦ καὶ λοιπὸν ζωὴν αἰώνιον κληρονομοῦμεν)" (34; see also 56, 58). For Athanasius, it is only because the Son became an authentic human being so as to experience all that is thoroughly human, and thus undertook experiences which by their very nature imply both a body and a soul, that he was able to save us from sin and death so as to share with us his incorruptible life.

CHAPTER 6

The Soul/Body Analogy and the Incarnation

Cyril of Alexandria

Once patristic theologians undertook a systematic enquiry into the relationship between the humanity and the divinity of Christ, they almost universally employed, by way of analogy, the relationship between the soul and the body. Not clearly distinguished at that time (nor even today) were the two aspects inherent within this analogy. (1) As the soul and body form one ontological reality or entity (man), the divinity and the humanity are united so as to form one ontological entity (Jesus). There is a substantial union between the divinity and the humanity analogous to that of the soul/body.[1] But there is simultaneously (and almost necessarily) a second aspect. (2) The soul/body union illustrates not only the ontological and substantial oneness of the divinity and the humanity in Jesus, but also the type of relationship or the manner of the oneness that exists between the divinity and the humanity. As the soul is united and relates to the body, the divinity is united and relates to the humanity.

Originally published as "The Soul/Body Analogy and the Incarnation: Cyril of Alexandria," *Coptic Church Review* 17, no. 3 (1996): 59–66. Reprinted by permission.

1. While most patristic authors will use the soul/body analogy to illustrate the substantial union, bringing about an ontological oneness between the divinity and humanity in Christ, some (notably the Antiochenes) will use the analogy to demonstrate how the divinity and humanity can be united without losing their full integrity and thus not form a substantial union according to their understanding; that is, where such a union would imply change and mutation on the part of the divinity and humanity.

In this essay I briefly examine Cyril of Alexandria's use of the soul/body analogy, for I believe he is the first (and maybe only) patristic theologian to use the analogy properly. I demonstrate that while the first aspect of the analogy is legitimate, the second is not. That is, in the Incarnation the eternal Son of God becomes man so as to form the one ontological reality of Jesus (as the soul/body constitute the one reality of man), but the divinity and the humanity are not united to one another, nor do they interact with one another, nor are they related to one another as the soul and the body unite, interact, and relate.[2] The incarnational union is therefore not what I would label a compositional union—that is, a union of different "natures" or "parts" so as to form some third kind of being—as the union of the distinct soul and body gives rise to man. Cyril of Alexandria uses the analogy only to illustrate the ontological oneness of Christ, but not to illustrate the type of relationship between them.

Logos/Sarx Christology

The full implications (and dangers) of the soul/body analogy are first found within the extreme forms of Logos/Sarx Christology. As the soul is united to the body, the divinity is united to the flesh (only). The human soul of Christ is denied to make the analogy work, to ensure the substantial oneness between the divinity and the *sarx*, and in turn to explain the manner of their relationship.

Within Arian Christology, for example, the Incarnation consists in the Logos uniting to himself flesh (without soul) so as to form one reality.[3] Because the Logos is united to flesh as the soul is to the body, he becomes the life principle within this substantial union or *systasis*. The Logos also direct-

---

2. Different Fathers conceive the union of the divinity and the humanity in Christ in different ways depending on whether they understand the soul/body union in a Stoic, Platonic, or Aristotelian manner.

3. For example, Eudoxius, Bishop of Antioch (357–59), and Constantinople (360–69) in an Arian confession of faith stated: "We believe in … the one Lord, the Son, … who became flesh, but not man. For he took no human soul, but became flesh so that God was revealed to us men through the flesh as through a curtain; not two natures, since he was no complete man, but God in the flesh instead of a soul; the whole is one nature by composition (μία τό ὅλον κατά σύνθεσιν φυ'σις)." As quoted by A. Grillmeier, *Christ in Christian Tradition* (London: Mowbrays, 1975), 244. Lucian, Bishop of Alexandria (373–78), said that Christ is "one person, one composite nature (ἕν προ'σωπον, μία σύνετος φύσις), like a man, of body and soul." Ibid., 245.

ly assumes the experiences of the flesh. Therefore Arius and his followers are forced to conclude that the Logos cannot be God since God cannot enter into such a compositional union. He would be changed in the process of becoming "flesh," and the human experiences would be located within his very nature as the Logos. Thus the question posed to the Nicenes: "How dare you say that the Logos shares in the Father's existence, if he had a body so as to experience all this?"[4]

We find the same problem within Apollinarianism, but now in the other extreme. Like the Arians, the Apollinarians' governing analogy is the soul/body. For Apollinarius the Incarnation is not by way of indwelling or adoption. The Son actually has to *become* "man" and thus Christ must be ontologically one, a σύνθεσις ἀνθρωποειδής.[5] If Christ had a soul, however, there would be two complete wholes, and two wholes cannot form a third whole.[6] "A *physis* is made up of the two parts, as the Logos with his divine perfection contributes a partial energy to the whole. This is also the case with the ordinary man, who is made up of two incomplete parts which produce one *physis* and display it under one name."[7] Jesus, then, is a "Heavenly man" because of the flesh's substantial union with the Logos. Christ is μία φύσις because the Logos and flesh form one organic whole, with the Logos being the vivifying and governing (ἡγεμονικόν) principle just as the soul is to body. Within Apollinarianism it is the humanity that is now jeopardized precisely because the Incarnation is modeled after the soul/body relationship.

All Logos/Sarx Christology fails because it is patterned after the soul/body analogy. The unity of the divinity and the humanity is seen as a compositional union of natures. Unlike Apollinarius, Arius comprehends, in denying the divinity of the Logos, the full implications of such a union.

Logos/Anthropos Christology

Since the soul/body analogy was employed, to disastrous effect, within Logos/Sarx Christology as the basic model for the incarnational union, one might be surprised to find the analogy being used by the Antiochene Christologists. That they use it demonstrates just how entrenched it was within

4. Athanasius, *Contra Arianos* 3:27.
6. See Ps. Athanasius, *C. Apollin.* I, 2.
5. Apollinarius, *Ep. ad Dionys.* A 9.
7. Apollinarius, *De Unione* 5.

the Christological tradition. What is not so surprising is that they used it to illustrate not the oneness of the divinity and the humanity, but to justify how two "natures" can be united and yet remain what they are.[8] But it is precisely because the Antiochenes have not only not liberated themselves from the soul/body framework but have also actually modeled their own Christology upon it that they themselves offer a defective view of the Incarnation. Having separated the divinity and the humanity, they cannot find a way to substantially unite them because to do so, they believe, would jeopardize the integrity of each.

Cyril of Alexandria

The problem, to this point, is that the soul/body analogy has been used not only to illustrate the oneness of the divinity and the humanity, but also the type, manner, and nature of the union. What has not been grasped is that the incarnational act or "becoming" is not the compositional or organic union of natures, and thus it is not like the union between the soul/body. Christ is one ontological being or entity, but he is ontologically one in a different kind of way than that of the soul/body.

Cyril of Alexandria is the first to grasp adequately the true nature of the incarnational union. He begins to make, not without ambiguity, a distinction between person (the who) and nature (the manner of person's existence). He proposes what I have come to call a "personal/existential" understanding of the Incarnation. One and the same person of the Son comes to exist as man. It is not a compositional union of natures similar to the soul/body, but rather the person of the Son taking on a new mode or manner of existence. Thus Cyril never uses the soul/body analogy to illustrate the relationship between divinity and humanity, but only to illustrate that they form one ontological reality—the Son existing as man. The manner of the union is quite different from that of the soul/body.

The novelty and insight of Cyril's Christology is easily missed, however. Because he was bred within the Logos/Sarx tradition, it can too easily be assumed, as the Antiochenes did, that he conceived the incarnational union

---

8. See Theodore of Mopsuestia, *Ad. Apollinarem* 4; *De Incarnatione*. See also Nestorius, *Nestoriana* 197ff., 330–31; Theodoret of Cyrus, *Eranistes* 2.

in a manner similar to Apollinarius. His ambiguous use of such terms as φύσις, μία φύσις, and ἐκ δύο contributed to this misunderstanding. Moreover, since he continues to employ the traditional soul/body analogy in relationship to his μία φύσις formula, it can again be too easily presumed that he conceives the incarnational union as a compositional union of natures forming some *tertium quid*. To elucidate Cyril's Christology, I first examine his use of the soul/body analogy and then discuss, in this light, how he conceives the incarnational act.

Cyril rightly upholds, against what he considers the Antiochene dualism, the ontological oneness of Christ. But what is the nature of the oneness that Cyril insists upon? Cyril, for example, writes to Nestorius:

As for our Saviour's statements in the Gospels, we do not divide them out to two subjects (ὑποστάσεοι) or persons (προσώποις). The one, unique Christ has no duality though he is seen as compounded in inseparable unity out of two (ἐκ δύο) differing elements in the way that a human being, for example, is seen to have no duality but to be one, consisting of the pair of elements, body and soul.[9]

This quotation contains a number of ambiguities as to the manner of Christ's oneness. It is all too obvious to Nestorius and his supporters that since the one Christ is formed *out of* two natures just as the body and soul forms one man, Cyril could only mean that the divinity and the humanity form some *tertium quid*. But the point Cyril is making is not that the divinity and the humanity form one nature in the sense of one quiddity, but rather that they form one reality or entity. As one human being is formed *out of* soul/body, the one Christ is "formed" *out of* the divinity and the humanity. The analogy is used to illustrate the one ontological entity of Christ and not the one quiddity of Christ.[10]

What Cyril has not adequately distinguished is the one person (ὑπόστασις or πρόσωπον) of Christ (the eternal Son) and the one reality

9. *Ad Nest.* 3, 8; see also 4. Translation from L. R. Wickham, ed. and trans., *Select Letters* (Oxford: Clarendon Press, 1983).

10. This is equally the point that Cyril wishes to make by calling the incarnational union "natural" (ἕνωσιν φυσικήν or κατά φύσιν). The union is "natural" in the sense that it results in one ontological being or entity. As the union of body and soul is "natural," forming the one reality of man, so the union of divinity and humanity is "natural," forming the one reality of Christ. For examples, see *Ad Nest.* 3, 5, and appended third Anathema; *C. Nest.* 2, 1, 13; *Ad Successus* 1; *Apol. c. Theodore.*

(φύσις") of Christ (the Son of God existing as man). While Cyril begins speaking in the above quote, about the necessity of one subject or person, his whole argument addresses the question of the need for Christ to be ontologically one reality. Cyril realizes instinctively, despite his lack of clarity, that Christ can possess only one subject or person if the humanity is substantially united to the person forming one ontological entity. He concludes the above paragraph by stating: "Accordingly all the sayings contained in the Gospels must be referred to a single person (προσώπῳ), to the one incarnate subject of the Word (ὑποστάσει μιᾷ τῇ τοῦ λόγου σεσαρκω-μένῃ)."[11]

Significantly, Cyril uses the soul/body analogy almost exclusively (the above quote being somewhat the exception) as a hermeneutical tool for understanding his μία φύσις formula. The analogy normally comes immediately before or after the formula. Thus the meaning of the formula not only becomes clear in light of the analogy, but also, and equally, Cyril's use of the analogy can be clearly seen in relation to the formula. Cyril writes:

The same holds good of Nestorius if he says "two natures" to indicate the difference between the flesh and God the Word—the point being that the nature of the Word is other than that of the flesh. However, he fails to affirm the union along with us. We unite these, acknowledging one Christ, one Son, the same one Lord and, further, one incarnate nature of the Son (μίαν τὴν τοῦ υἱοῦ φύσιν σεσαρκωμένην) in the same way that the phrase can be used of ordinary man. The point is that man results from two natures—body and soul, I mean—and intellectual perception recognises the difference; but we unite them and then get one nature of man. So, recognising the difference of natures is not dividing the one Christ into two.[12]

Μίαν φύσιν could mean that the unity of the divinity and the humanity form one nature in the sense of quiddity, which would imply that Jesus is neither fully God nor fully man, but a *tertium quid*. This is how the Antiochenes would interpret it. The soul/body analogy, however, as the interpretative tool for understanding the μία φύσις, makes clear that for Cyril, φύσις here means not one quiddity but one reality or one entity. The rest of the formula designates what the one Christ is—the one φύσις is the Son incarnate.

Part of the difficulty is that Cyril uses the word φύσις equivocally, mean-

11. *Ad Nest.* 3, 8.
12. *Ad Eulogius.*

ing both quiddity (as in the nature of the soul and the nature of the body and as the nature of man) and also as designating one ontological being or entity (as in the one reality of man and the one reality of Christ). But in his *Letters to Successus*, while the equivocation still remains, his meaning becomes even clearer.

May we illustrate the case from the composition which renders us human beings? We are composed out of soul and body and observe two different natures, the body's and the soul's; yet the pair yields a single united human being, and composition out of two natures does not turn the one man into two men but, as I said, produces a single man, a composite of soul and body.[13]

Moreover, in his *Second Book against Nestorius* he writes:

The nature (φύσις) of the Incarnate Word himself (ν9 αὐτοῦ λόγου σεσαρκωμέου) is after the union now conceived as one (μιςα), just as will reasonably be conceived in regard to ourselves too, for man is one, compounded of unlike things, soul I mean and body.[14]

In both quotations the soul/body analogy illustrates only the ontological oneness that is obtained between the divinity and the humanity and not the manner or mode of that oneness. In answering the criticism that to say that Jesus is μία φύσις τοῦ λόγου σεσαρκωμένη means that there is a mixture and merger of natures, Cyril responds:

If we call the Only-begotten Son of God become incarnate and made man "one," that does not mean he has been "mingled," as they suppose; the Word's nature has not transferred to the nature of flesh or that of the flesh to that of the Word—no,

---

13. *Ad Successus*, 1, 7.

14. *C. Nest.* 2: proema. Translation taken from *Cyril of Alexandria, Library of the Fathers* (Oxford: James Parker, 1881). Cyril employs two versions of the μία φύσιν formula. The most common uses σεσααρκωμένη, which would modify the μία φύσιν and thus be translated: "The one incarnate nature/person of the Word." The second, as in the above quote, uses σεσαρκωμένου, which would modify the τοῦ λόγου and thus be translated: "The one nature of the Incarnate Word." In a previous work I argued that the first version stresses that it is the one nature/ person of the Word who is incarnate. Nature here verges on the meaning of person, and so Cyril is defining who Christ is—he is the one person of the Word incarnate. The second variation highlights the being/reality of Christ as one. Christ is one ontological reality. The one reality of Christ is the Word incarnate. While I think there is still some validity to this interpretation, I argue that because Cyril uses the soul/body analogy to interpret both formulas, both formulas tend to stress that Christ is ontologically one reality. See T. G. Weinandy, *Does God Change? The Word's Becoming in the Incarnation* (Petersham, MA: St. Bede's Press, 1985), 47–50.

while each element was seen to persist in its particular natural character for the reason just given, mysteriously and inexpressibly unified he displayed to us one nature (μίαν φύσιν), (but as I said, *incarnate* [σεσαρκωμένην] nature) of the Son. "One" is a term applied properly not only to basic single elements but to such composite entities as man compounded of soul and body. Soul and body are different kinds of thing and are not mutually consubstantial; yet united they constitute man's single nature despite the fact that the difference in nature of the elements brought into unity is present in the composite condition. It is therefore idle for them to claim that if there is one incarnate nature of the Word (μία φύσις τοῦ λόγου σεσαρκωμένη) it follows there must have been a mingling and merger … for to state that he is incarnate gives completely adequate expression to the fact that he has become man.[15]

Again the soul/body analogy is employed to illustrate not the manner of the relationship between the divinity and the humanity in Christ, but only to assert that as the soul/body form one being (man), so the incarnational union forms the one entity or reality of Christ. The one reality or being (φύσις) of Christ is the incarnate Word. Again Cyril writes:

Take the normal human being. We perceive in him two natures: one that of the soul, a second that of the body. We divide them, though, merely in thought, accepting the difference as simply residing in fine drawn insight or mental intuition; we do not separate the natures out or attribute a capacity for radical severance to them, but see that they belong to one man so that the two are two no more and the single living being is constituted complete by the pair of them. So though one attributes the nature of manhood and of Godhead to Emmanuel, the manhood has become the Word's own and together with it is seen one Son.[16]

What is now also becoming clearer is Cyril's use of the term μία. I have emphasized that for Cyril this oneness consists in the one ontological reality of Christ. This one Christ is also defined by Cyril as the *one* person of the Son existing as man. Here we see the significance of Cyril's understanding of the incarnational union as καθ' ὑπόστασιν. It is by conceiving the incarnational union as καθ' ὑπόστασιν that Cyril is able to break free of the detrimental effects of the traditional soul/body analogy. While the union forms the one ontological reality of Christ, it is not a union of natures similar to

15. *Ad Succensus* 2, 3.
16. Ibid., 5. For a couple of other examples of Cyril's use of the soul/body analogy, see *Scholia de Incarn. Unigen.* 8, 27.

that of the soul/body, which would bring about change and mutation, but a union according to the hypostasis.

We do not mean that the nature of the Word was changed (ἡ τοῦ λόγου θύσις μεταποιηθεῖσα) and made flesh or, on the other hand, that he was transformed into a complete man consisting of soul and body, but instead we affirm this: that the Word personally (καθ' ὑπόστασιν) united to himself flesh.[17]

Thus the manner of the relationship between the Son and his humanity is not similar to that of soul/body, but a completely unique kind of relationship. The relationship being καθ' ὑπόστασιν means that the humanity is united to the person of the Word so that the Word actually comes to exist as man. It is, as noted above, a personal/existential notion. No longer is the incarnational union the compositional or organic union of natures (similar to the soul/body), but rather the incarnational act is seen as the one person of the Son taking on a new manner or mode of existence—that is, as man. This is why Cyril could legitimately stress, against Antiochene accusations, that the natures are not merged or mixed and thus not changed. They are not transformed because the manner of the union is no longer on the level of natures, as is the soul/body, but rather on the level of the person of the Son assuming a new existence as man. Thus what the Son eternally is (God) and what he has become (man) are in no way jeopardized. Actually, conceiving the incarnational act as personal/existential establishes, and so guarantees, that it is truly the one person of the Son who is man, and that it is truly as man that the Son exists. It is this insight that the Council of Chalcedon will sanction.

17. *Ad Nest.* 2, 3; see also 4. I disagree with Wickham's translation. He translates καθ' ὑπόστασιν as "substantially." While it does designate a substantial union, Cyril sees it as a substantial union of a special type. The incarnational act does not bring about a union of natures, but rather it is the act by which the humanity is united substantially to the person (ὑπόστασις) of the Word. See L. R. Wickham, ed. and trans., *Cyril of Alexandria Selected Letters* (Oxford: Clarendon Press, 1983), 4n6.

CHAPTER 7

Cyril and the Mystery
of the Incarnation

Cyril of Alexandria is undoubtedly most often identified with his understanding of the Incarnation, an understanding that was forged within the Christological firestorm of the Nestorian controversy. His understanding, as articulated in his *Second Letter to Nestorius*, was accepted by the Council of Ephesus (431) as a true expression of orthodox belief. Moreover, although Cyril died (444) before the Council of Chalcedon (451), the Chalcedonian Creed can be interpreted properly only if it is read, I believe, through his eyes. Cyril's Christology has been to the present the foundational expression of the Christian tradition's doctrinal understanding of who Jesus is. Within contemporary Christology, however, Cyril's understanding of the Incarnation has provoked immense criticism, and with it thrown into question the whole doctrinal Christological tradition. In this essay, I not only examine carefully and express clearly Cyril's Christology, but also, in so doing, clear it of many current misconceptions and thus liberate it from many fashionable misinterpretations.

Originally published as "Cyril and the Mystery of the Incarnation," in *The Theology of Cyril of Alexandria: A Critical Appreciation*, ed. T. G. Weinandy and Daniel A. Keating (London: T&T Clark/Continuum, 2003), 49–85. Reprinted by permission of Continuum, an imprint of Bloomsbury Publishing, PLC.

The Christology of Cyril's Early Commentaries

While Cyril's conception and expression of the incarnational mystery developed and matured during the course of the Nestorian controversy, his prior Christological thinking, contained within his earlier biblical commentaries, especially within his *Commentary on the Gospel of John*, is often overlooked or even ignored.[1] In addressing Christological questions and concerns already within his commentaries, Cyril began to make incarnational distinctions, to develop incarnational concepts, and to employ incarnational language that he would draw upon during the Nestorian debate, acquiring deeper insight and clearer articulation as the controversy evolved that can be seen in a sixfold interrelated manner.

Cyril's Christological thought principally and consistently emerged from his soteriological concerns.

It was therefore necessary that the only-begotten Word of God who brought himself down to the level of self-emptying, should not repudiate the low estate arising from that self-emptying, but should accept what is full by nature on account of the humanity, not for his own sake, but for ours, who lack every good thing.[2]

Echoing his predecessors Irenaeus and Athanasius, Cyril argued that the Son of God must become man so that humankind might become divine.[3]

It was not otherwise possible for man, being of a nature which perishes, to escape death, unless he recovered that ancient grace, and partook once more of God who holds all things together in being and preserves them in life through the Son in the Spirit. Therefore his Only-begotten Word has become a partaker of flesh and blood (Heb. 2:14), that is, he has become man, though being Life by nature, and begotten of the life that is by nature, that is, of God the Father, so that, having united himself with the flesh which perishes according to the law of its own nature ... he might restore it to his own Life and render it through himself a partaker of God the Father ... And he wears our nature, refashioning it to his own Life. And he himself is also in us, for we have all become partakers of him, and have him in ourselves through

---

1. One notable exception is the work by J. Liébaert, *La doctrine christologique de S. Cyrille d'Alexandrie avant la querelle nestorienne* (Lilles: Facultés Catholiques, 1951).

2. *In Is.* 11:1–3; N. Russell, trans., *Cyril of Alexandria* (London: Routledge, 2000), 83.

3. Irenaeus stated that the Word of God "became what we are that he might make us what he himself is" (*Ad Haer.* 5, praef.). Athanasius stated that "he was humanized (ἐνανθρώπησεν) that we might be deified (θεοποιηθῶμεν)" (*De Incarn.* 54)

the Spirit. For this reason we have become "partakers of the divine nature" (2 Pet. 1:4), and are reckoned as sons, and so too we have in ourselves the Father himself through the Son.[4]

This divinizing incentive for the Incarnation was, for Cyril, closely aligned to the Cross. The cause of the Incarnation was "that being by nature God and of God, the Only-begotten has become man; namely with intent to condemn sin in the flesh, and by his own death to slay death, and to make us sons of God, regenerating in the Spirit them that are on earth unto supernatural dignity."[5] Again, Cyril states:

For this cause, though he is Life by nature, he became as one dead; that, having destroyed the power of death in us, he might mould us anew into his own life; and being himself the righteousness of God the Father, he became sin for us.[6]

Inherent within his overarching soteriological concerns, as witnessed in the above quotations, is Cyril's conviction that Jesus must be truly God. He inherited from his predecessors, especially from Athanasius, the soteriological principle that the Son must be truly God, *homoousion* (one in being) with the Father, for only he who is truly God is able to save humankind and so allow it to partake of the divine nature.

He that is God by nature became, and is in truth, a man from heaven; not inspired merely, as some of those who do not rightly understand the depth of the mystery imagine, but being at the same time God and man, in order that, uniting as it were in himself things widely opposed by nature, and averse to fusion with each other, he might enable man to share and partake of the nature of God.[7]

He likewise argued, as seen within the above quotations, that the Son must be truly and fully human, for it is our humanity that is in need of salvation, and it is our humanity that is in need of divinization. Commenting on the Johannine term that the Word became "flesh" rather than "man," Cyril held that John proclaimed that the Son of God did assume a whole man, body and soul, but that he was here designating and so emphasizing

---

4. *In Jo.* 14:20. Translation mine.

5. Ibid. E. T. T. Randell, *Commentary on the Gospel According to John by S. Cyril Archbishop of Alexandria* (London: Walter Smith, 1885), 2:316.

6. *In Jo.* 17:19; Randell, *Commentary on the Gospel*, 539.

7. *In Jo.* 14:20; Randell, *Commentary on the Gospel*, 549.

the weakness, vulnerability, and woundedness of fallen humanity, and that
it was such a "fallen" humanity that the Son of God needed to assume so as
to redeem and heal it and so give it life.

That, in my opinion, is the most probable reason why the holy Evangelist, indicating the whole living being by the part affected, says that the Word of God became
flesh. It is so that we might see side by side the wound together with the remedy,
the patient together with the physician, that which had sunk towards death together with him who raised it up towards life, that which had been overcome by corruption together with him who drove out corruption, that which had been mastered
by death together with him who was superior to death, that which was bereft of life
together with him who is the provider of life.[8]

As seen above, Cyril consistently employed the principle that what is not
assumed is not saved. This meant for Cyril not only that the Son did assume
a full humanity, body and soul, but also that the humanity he did assume was
of the fallen race of Adam. He became, as stated above, "sin for us." In accord
with Romans 8:3, the Son thus assumed "sinful flesh" (ἁμαρτία σάρκα) and
so was "subject to corruption."[9] Moreover, the humanity that was affected by
sin and corruptibility must be restored by "having the fallen body united in
an ineffable manner with the Word that endows all things with life. And it is
necessary that when the flesh had become his own flesh it should partake of
his own immortality."[10] The Son did not merely appear to be man, nor was
his life a mere fiction, but being truly born of a woman, he experienced "every human characteristic except sin alone. Now fear and timidity, being natural emotions in us, are not to be classified among the sins.... Just as he experienced hunger and weariness as a man, so too he accepts the disturbance
that come from the emotions as a human characteristic."[11] This means then
that even the Son's humanity needed to be saved and sanctified. Cyril can
speak of the real sanctification of Christ's humanity at his baptism.[12] The ris-

8. *In Jo.* 1:14a; Russell, *Cyril of Alexandria*, 105–6.

9. *In Jo.* 14:20; Randell, *Commentary on the Gospel*, 315. See also *In Jo.* 17:18. For a fuller
argument on the importance of this incarnational truth, see T. G. Weinandy, *In the Likeness of
Sinful Flesh: An Essay on the Humanity of Christ* (Edinburgh: T&T Clark, 1993).

10. *In Jo.* 1:14a; Russell, *Cyril of Alexandria*, 105.

11. *In Jo.* 12:27; Russell, *Cyril of Alexandria*, 120. For further examples, see *C. Nest.* 1, 1; 3, 2;
Ad Nest. 2; *Exp. XII Cap.* 2, 10; *Scholia* 2, 12; *Quod Unus.*

12. For example, see *In Jo.* 3:5.

en Jesus himself, as the Son incarnate, experienced "the first fruits" of salvation and "newness of life."[13]

The above exposition also testifies to the soteriological necessity that, for Cyril, the Son of God must actually *come to exist* as man. No form of Adoptionism, which allows a merely moral union between the divine Son and the man Jesus, would suffice. For Cyril, the incarnational concept of "become" must convey an ontological union between the Son of God and his humanity, for only within such a union could the Son truly save and so divinize his and our own humanity. Thus he insisted that the Evangelist "does not say that the Word came into flesh; he says that he became flesh in order to exclude any idea of a relative indwelling, as in the case of the prophets and the other saints. He truly did become flesh, that is to say, a human being, as I have just explained."[14]

This did not mean to Cyril that the Word was changed into flesh. Already in his *Commentary on the Gospel of John*, Cyril made a distinction that would allow him to ward off the later Antiochene accusations that he mixed and confused the natures whereby they were changed and mutated. Arguing that "become" demands a real ontological union, Cyril nevertheless adamantly maintained that "we do not, of course, say that God the Word who is from the Father was transformed into the nature of flesh, or that the flesh changed into the Word. For each remains what it is by nature and Christ is one from both."[15]

Cyril realized that the incarnational "becoming" was not like the caterpillar changing into the butterfly, where the caterpillar ceases to exist in the metamorphic change. For him the Johannine phrase "and dwelt among us" indicated that although the Son did actually become man, he did not change into man, for it was the unchanged Son himself who now dwelt among us as man. "The Theologian" was distinguishing "the subject of the

13. *In Jo.* 12:27; Russell, *Cyril of Alexandria,* 120. See also *In Jo.* 17:20. For a fuller exposition of this theme, see D. Keating, "Divinization in Cyril: The Appropriation of Divine Life," in *The Theology of Cyril of Alexandria: A Critical Appreciation,* ed. Thomas G. Weinandy and Daniel A. Keating (London: Continuum/T&T Clark, 2003), 149–85.

14. *In Jo.* 1:14a; Russell, *Cyril of Alexandria,* 106.

15. *In Jo.* 6:54; Russell, *Cyril of Alexandria,* 117. Note that Cyril nonetheless used the ambiguous phrase "one from both," which will cause confusion in the later controversy and which will in turn have to be clarified and ultimately dropped.

dwelling and that in which the dwelling was taking place."[16] The "indwelling" did not denote merely a moral union, but rather the "becoming" established an ontological union that did not involve any change in the Word, for the Word can actually be said, after the "becoming," to dwell among us as a man.

Within his early commentaries, Cyril already upheld the Communication of Idioms, which in his view manifested a true understanding of the Incarnation. Since it was truly the eternal Son of God who became and is man, then all those attributes that pertain to his divinity or humanity are predicated of one and the same Son. "Observe how in order to show that he was truly God as well as man, the prophet [Isaiah] assigned to him attributes that were both divine and human."[17] While human attributes can truly be predicated of the Son, because the Son actually exists as a humble man, the Son—as Cyril would argue at length in the later controversy—remained impassible as God.[18]

Although I will examine this issue again later, we must pause briefly to address a common criticism of Cyril's Christology. Because Cyril was an Alexandrian, his Christology, especially within its early form, is often simplistically labeled as an example of Logos/Sarx Christology, as if he reluctantly attributed a soul to Christ, and then only perfunctorily. This designation is not only utterly misleading, but also entirely artificial.[19]

Similarly, Cyril is often accused of being solely concerned with upholding the divinity of Jesus and so only showed a superficial interest in his humanity.[20] The above exposition of Cyril's actual thought concerning the humanity of Christ, a humanity that is one with "sinful" humanity and thus physically and emotionally vulnerable, needing itself to be sanctified, man-

---

16. *In Jo.* 1:14b; Russell, *Cyril of Alexandria,* 106, 107–8.

17. *In Is.* 7:14–16; Russell, *Cyril of Alexandria,* 79.

18. See *In Jo.* 11:9; Russell, *Cyril of Alexandria,* 125–27.

19. A. Grillmeier in his classic work popularized the rather unaccommodating and often simplistic classification that patristic Christologies tended toward or actually were either Logos/Sarx or Logos/Anthropos. *Christ in Christian Tradition* (London: Mowbrays, 1975), 414–17. Sadly, Cyril, especially the early Cyril, was chucked into the Logos/Sarx paradigm. For a defense of Cyril, see L. Welch, "Logos-Sarx? Sarx and the Soul of Christ in the Early Thought of Cyril of Alexandria," *St. Vladimir's Theological Quarterly,* 38 (1994): 271–92.

20. Examples of such a criticism are given below in a fuller examination of the heart of this issue.

ifestly contradicts such a facile allegation. While Cyril might not have fully appreciated certain authentic contemporary concerns, such as Christ's historically and culturally conditioned human ignorance, the Son's humanity was more than a peripheral or external tool that he artificially employed as an impersonal instrument to manifest his all-powerful divinity. Because for Cyril the Son actually existed as man, all that he did he did as a man. In addition to what has already been observed, this view is also illustrated in Cyril's understanding of Christ's miracles.

Addressing the life-giving effects of Christ's Eucharistic flesh, Cyril commented on his ability to raise the dead. When Jesus raised the dead, he "is seen to be operating not by word alone, nor by commands such as befit God, but he firmly insisted on using his holy flesh as a kind of co-worker, that he might show it to be capable of giving life and already one with him. For it really was his own body and not that of another." Being "his own body," he not only commanded the daughter of the synagogue ruler to arise, but he also "took her by the hand." Thus, "while giving life as God by his all-powerful command, he also gives life by the touch of his holy flesh, demonstrating through both that the operation was a single and cognate one."[21] The operation was one act, for it was the Son of God acting as man, and within this one act both his divinity and humanity were equally engaged.

Already in the first half of his theological career, Cyril realized significantly (though he did not state it so succinctly) that a proper conception and articulation of the Incarnation, for soteriological reasons, demanded that the three following truths must simultaneously be upheld. In addition, he instinctively realized that the Communication of Idioms concisely embodies and expresses these three truths.

21. *In Jo.* 6:53; Russell, *Cyril of Alexandria,* 115. Prior to discovering this text, I created a scenario of Jesus raising Lazarus from the dead that I thought would illustrate how Cyril would have understood the manner in which the Son worked as incarnate. While I did not emphasize, because of my own incarnational concerns, the life-giving nature of the Son's humanity as did Cyril, my example is in accord with his understanding. It was indeed the Son of God who raised Lazarus from the dead, but he did so as man through the power of the Holy Spirit. The action was not the Son of God performing a divine action *in* a man, but the Son of God performing a divine action *as* a man, and thus the action was the one action of the incarnate Son. See T. G. Weinandy, *Does God Suffer?* (Edinburgh: T&T Clark, 2000), 205. For an excellent discussion of how Cyril understands Jesus performing divine acts as a man, see S. A. McKinion, *Words, Imagery, and the Mystery of Christ: A Reconstruction of Cyril of Alexandria's Christology* (Leiden: Brill, 2000), 212–24.

1. It is *truly God* the Son who is man. Here the emphasis is on the full divinity of the Son.
2. It is *truly man* that the Son of God is. Here the emphasis is on the full and complete humanity.
3. The Son of God *truly is* man. Here the emphasis is on the ontological union between the person of the Son and his humanity.

These three statements can be incorporated in the following declaration, which summarizes, even before the Nestorian controversy, Cyril's Christology: Jesus is one ontological entity, and the one ontological entity that Jesus is is the one person of the divine Son of God existing as a complete and authentic man. Thus we find already in his commentaries Cyril articulating a conception of the Incarnation that will form the basis of his critique of Nestorius and the foundation upon which he will conceive and convey his own mature Christology.[22]

The Communication of Idioms as a Hermeneutical Principle

The Communication of Idioms is the hermeneutical key for unlocking Cyril's Christology as he progressively articulated it during the course of the Nestorian controversy. In light of his earlier Christological convictions, it is not surprising that Cyril would adamantly oppose Nestorius's denial of the propriety of the title, *Theotokos*. Such a rejection, with its inherent denunciation of the Communication of Idioms, for Cyril negated an authentic understanding of the Incarnation and the efficacy of Christ's salvific work. It was, as stated above, the inner Christological logic embedded within the Communication of Idioms that propelled Cyril to grasp, conceptu-

22. J. J. O'Keefe argues (rightly I believe) that Cyril was more faithful to the New Testament proclamation than were the Antiochenes. Unlike the Antiochenes, he fashioned his philosophical concepts to be in conformity with the biblical narrative. "The Antiochene position interprets the text in the light of philosophy, the Alexandrian position interprets the philosophy in the light of the text." "Kenosis or Impassibility: Cyril of Alexandria and Theodoret of Cyrus on the Problem of Divine Pathos," *Studia Patristica* 32 (1997): 365. In the end Cyril was not only the better theologian but, contrary to common scholarly opinion, he was equally the better exegete. See also J. J. O'Keefe, "Impassible Suffering? Divine Passion and Fifth-Century Christology," *Theological Studies* 58 (1997): 41–45, 55–58; "'A Letter That Killeth': Toward a Reassessment of Antiochene Exegesis, or Diodore, Theodore, and Theodoret on the Psalms," *Journal of Early Christian Studies* 8 (2000): 83–104.

alize, and articulate the three incarnational truths that he realized must be maintained for a proper understanding of the Incarnation. In the process of clarifying the mystery of the Incarnation through his defense of the Communication of Idioms, the proper use and rendering of it were themselves corroborated and so sanctioned.

Cyril founded his defense of the Communication of Idioms upon the Creed of Nicaea, which illustrated and so demanded its legitimacy. The Son who was *homoousion* with the Father was the same Son who "became incarnate of the Virgin Mary." Having articulated his understanding of the Creed's Christology, Cyril continued:

> This is what it means to say that he was also born of woman in the flesh though owning his existence before the ages and begotten of the Father: not that his divine nature originated in the holy Virgin ... (to say that ... is idle and stupid)— no, it means that he had fleshly birth because he issued from woman for us and for our salvation having personally united the humanity to himself (ἐνώσας ἑαυτῷ καθ' ὑπόστασιν τὸ ἀνθρώπινον). The point is that it was not the case that initially an ordinary man was born of the holy Virgin and then the Word simply settled on him—no, what is said is that he underwent fleshly birth united from the very womb, making the birth of his flesh his very own.[23]

For Cyril, the Communication of Idioms demanded that Christ be one in two ways. First, it demanded that Jesus be one existing reality, being, or entity, for if he were not one, then we could not authentically predicate of him divine and human attributes. Second, the one existential reality that Jesus is must be the one and same divine Son of God existing as incarnate, for if it were not the one and same Son existing as man, then it would not be the one and same Son who was *homoousion* with the Father and who was born, suffered, died, and rose as man. It is simply this double conception of Jesus's oneness that Cyril found embedded within the heart of the Communication of Idioms and that he continually attempted to conceptualize and articulate.

We already observed these incarnational notions concerning Christ's oneness within Cyril's pre-Nestorian commentaries, and they are also readily apparent at the onset of the controversy. This is most evident in his championing the *mia physis* formula—that is, that Jesus is "the one nature of the

23. *Ad Nest.* 2, 4; L. R. Wickham, ed. and trans., *Cyril of Alexandria: Selected Letters* (Oxford: Clarendon Press, 1983), 7. The translation is slightly altered.

yes

Word incarnate" (μία φύσις τοῦ λόγου σεσαρκωμένη)—for it, too, contains his dual concern about the oneness of Christ. That is why Cyril clung to it with such tenacity. Nonetheless, since the formula was and is still so contentious, having originated with Apollinarius but thought by Cyril to be from Athanasius, his use of it must be carefully examined.[24]

What does Cyril mean by *mia physis*? Nestorius and the Antiochenes were convinced that by *mia physis* Cyril meant that Christ is one nature or essence (*physis*) in the sense of one quiddity in which the divine and the human natures were compositionally united, through mixture and confusion, so as to form a common third nature (quiddity), which would be neither fully divine nor fully human. Nestorius wrote:

> You [Cyril] do not confess that he is God in *ousia* in that you have changed him into the *ousia* of the flesh, and he is no more a man naturally in that you have made him the *ousia* of God; and he is not God truly or God by nature, nor yet man truly or man by nature.[25]

I have argued elsewhere that Cyril did not employ the *mia physis* formula to espouse one nature in the sense of one quiddity, but rather he primarily used it to emphasize that Christ is one being or reality—one entity.[26] The clue to this interpretation, which I have more recently perceived, is found within the comparison Cyril made between the soul/body union and that found within the Incarnation.[27] He principally and almost exclusively drew on the soul/body union, which normally appears immediately either before or after the *mia physis* formula, to illustrate that as the soul and the body of a human being are ontologically united to form one reality or entity—the human being—so the Son of God is ontologically united to the humanity to form the one reality of Jesus.[28]

24. See Apollinarius, *Ad Jovinianum* 1.

25. *Liber Heraclidis*. C. R. Driver and L. Hodgson, eds., *The Bazaar of Heracleides* (Oxford: Clarendon Press, 1925), 16, 26–27.

26. See T. G. Weinandy, *Does God Change? The Word's Becoming in the Incarnation* (Petersham, MA: St. Bede's Press, 1985), 46–58.

27. See T. G. Weinandy, "The Soul/Body Analogy and the Incarnation: Cyril of Alexandria," *Coptic Church Review* 17 (1996): 59–66 (chap. 6 in this volume).

28. The soul/body relationship was employed by patristic authors in two ways with regard to the Incarnation. First, they used it so as to allow them to affirm the ontological union between the divinity and the humanity. As the soul and body form the one ontological reality of a human being, so the divinity and the humanity similarly formed the one ontological reality of Jesus. The

As for our Saviour's statements in the Gospels, we do not divide them out to two subjects (ὑποστασεσι) or persons (προσώποις). The one, unique Christ has no duality though he is seen as compounded in inseparable unity out of two (ἐκ δύο) differing elements in the way that a human being, for example, is seen to have no duality but to be one (εἷς) consisting of the pair of elements, body and soul.[29]

The Antiochenes believed that, because Cyril spoke of Christ being one nature (*mia physis*) formed out of two (*ek duo*), in a manner similar to the union between body and soul, he could only mean that the divinity and humanity were united so as to form a *tertium quid*, in which the divine nature itself became passible.

With his eye on Cyril, Nestorius wrote against the Arians:

They confuse his divine and his human (qualities), saying that the union with flesh resulted in one nature ... even as the soul and the body are bound (together) in one nature in the body, suffering of necessity, whether he will or not, the sufferings of the nature which he took upon himself, as though he was not of the nature of the Father impassible and without needs ... He hungered and thirsted and grew weary and feared and fled and died; and in short they say that he naturally endured whatever appertained to the sensible nature which he assumed.[30]

---

soul/body union merely illustrated how two diverse and distinct "things" could become one. In this sense the soul/body relationship was used merely by way of analogy or comparison. Second, the soul/body relationship was also used, often simultaneously with the first, as an exact model for designing the type and manner of the relationship between the divinity and the humanity, and so how the ontological oneness of Christ was achieved. As the soul is united and relates to the body, the divinity is united and relates to the humanity. I have argued at length elsewhere that it is legitimate to use the soul/body relationship as an illustrative analogy or comparison for the oneness of Christ, but that it is not legitimate to use it as an exact model for designing the type and manner of the relationship between the divinity and the humanity in Christ. While both the soul/body relationship and the divinity/humanity relationship are ontological in nature, they are different kinds of ontological relationships. When the soul/body relationship is used as a model for the incarnational union, both the divinity and the humanity are always jeopardized, for a *tertium quid* being is always lurking close at hand. The tendency is either to have the divinity wash into the humanity and so transform it, or to have the humanity wash into the divinity and so transform it, both resulting in a *tertium quid* being who is neither fully God nor fully man. Nonetheless, with the exception of Cyril (and probably Athanasius), the soul/body relationship became, almost universally within the patristic era, the normative model for conceiving and articulating the Incarnation. Thus its use as a model gave rise not only to all the Christological heresies, but also to many of the Christological problems, conundrums, and confusions within the orthodox Fathers as well. See Weinandy, *Does God Suffer?*, 182–92.

29. *Ad Nest.* 3, 8; Wickham, *Cyril of Alexandria*, 23.

30. Driver and Hodgson, *Bazaar of Heracleides*, 8–9.

While the "out of two" is ambiguous and will be clarified by Chalcedon, it is nonetheless evident that Cyril did not mean what the Antiochenes thought he meant. First, for Cyril, the Gospels bear witness that there is one subject or person in Christ. Second, the reason there is one subject or person is that the divinity and the humanity are united in the one person so as to form the one nature of Jesus in the sense of one entity (not quiddity), similar to the way the soul and body form the one entity of a human being. The comparison is used only to denote the oneness and not the manner in which the oneness is achieved. As Cyril states:

For the nature (φύσις) of the Incarnate Word himself (ἡ αὐτοῦ λόγου σεσαρκωμένου) is immediately, after the union, conceived as one (μία). It is not unreasonable to see something similar in our own case too. For a human being is truly one compounded of dissimilar elements, by which I mean soul and body.[31]

Or again, in defending his use of the *mia physis* formula, Cyril writes:

May we illustrate the case from the composition which renders us human beings? We are composed out of (ἐκ) soul and body and observe two different natures (δύο φύσεις), body's and soul's; yet the pair yields a single united human being, and a composition out of two natures does not turn the one man into two men but, as I said, produces a single man, a composite of soul and body.[32]

Or again:

Take the normal human being. We perceive in him two natures (δύο φύσεις): one that of the soul, a second that of the body. We divide them, though, merely in thought accepting the difference as simply residing in the fine drawn insight or mental intuition; we do not separate the natures out or attribute a capacity for radical severance to them, but see that they belong to one man so that the two are two no more and the single living being is constituted complete by the pair of them. So though one attributes the nature of manhood and of Godhead to Emmanuel, the manhood has become the Word's own and together with it is seen as one Son.[33]

31. *C. Nest.* 2, proema; Russell, *Cyril of Alexandria,* 142. The translation is slightly altered.

32. *Ad Succ.* 1, 7; Wickham, *Cyril of Alexandria,* 77.

33. *Ad Succ.* 2, 5; Wickham, *Cyril of Alexandria,* 93. Similar citations, demonstrating the same point, can be found in *Ad Nest.* 3, 4; *Ad Succ.* 2, 2; 3; *Ad Eul.*; *Ad Mon.* 12; *Scholia* 27; *C. Diod.* 9, 22; *C. Theod.* 2:4; *Quod Unus*; J. A. McGuckin, *On the Unity of Christ* (Crestwood: St. Vladimir's Press, 1995), 78.

The sole point Cyril wished to make within the above quotations is that as a human being is one entity so Christ is one entity. In no way did he use the manner of the relationship between the soul/body or the mode of union established between the soul/body as a model for the manner of the relationship between the divinity/humanity or for the mode of the union established between the divinity/humanity. He is merely making a comparison in order to draw a conclusion—Christ is one.[34] To insist that Christ is *mia physis* simply affirms that he is one entity and not that he is one quiddity.[35]

34. B. Meunier equally argues that Cyril used the soul/body union as a "simple illustration pédagogique" and not as an exact model for the incarnational union. *Le Christ de Cyrille D'Alexandrie: L'Humanité, Le Salut et La Question Monophysite* (Paris: Beauchesne, 1997), 235. McKinion also states that Cyril "is using this image to illustrate his christological statement that Emmanuel is one individual." *Words, Imagery, and the Mystery of Christ*, 190; see also 188–96.

35. As I have stated, it must be noted that on one occasion Cyril did use the manner of the relationship between the soul/body not merely to illustrate that Christ is one entity, but to portray the workings of the Communication of Idioms. *Does God Suffer?*, 194, 195n43. Cyril speaks of the relationship between the two natures as ineffable, and adds that even the relationship between the soul/body is beyond our comprehension. He then states:

> I should say (although the description altogether falls short of the truth) that it is fitting to understand the union of Emmanuel to be such as the soul of a man might be thought to have with its own body. For the soul appropriates the things of the body even though in its proper nature it is apart from the body's natural passions, as well as those which impinge on it from without. For the body is moved to physical desires, and the soul which is within it feels these things too, because of the union, but in no way does it participate in these things, except insofar as it takes the fulfillment of desire as its own gratification. If the body was struck by a sword, or tortured on an iron grid, the soul would share in its grief, because it is its own body which is suffering. But in its own nature the soul does not suffer anything of these things.
>
> This indeed is how we attribute the union to Emmanuel. For it was necessary that the soul united to it should share in the grief of its own body, so that rising above these sufferings it could submit itself as obedient to God. But it is foolish to say that God the Word shared in feeling the sufferings. For the Godhead is impassible and is not in our condition. Yet [the Word] was united to the flesh endowed with a rational soul, and when the flesh suffered, even though he was impassible, he was aware of what was happening within it, and thus as God, even though he did away with the weaknesses of the flesh, still he appropriated those weaknesses of his own body. This is how he is said to have hungered, and to have been tired, and to have suffered for our sake.

Scholia 8; J. A. McGuckin, *St. Cyril of Alexandria: The Christological Controversy: Its History, Theology and Texts* (Leiden: Brill, 1994), 300–301.

I have quoted Cyril at length so as to leave no doubt that, while he employs the soul/body relationship, he does so not as a model for the Incarnation, but solely as an illustrative comparison for understanding the Communication of Idioms. As the soul can appropriate the

Similarly, when Cyril states that the union is "natural" (ἕνωσις φυσική) or "according to nature" (κατὰ φύσιν), he is expressing the same point. The union is "natural" or "according to nature" not in the sense that the divine and the human natures are compositionally united, forming a third nature in the sense of quiddity, but in the sense that it brings about the one ontological entity of Christ. Just as the union of soul and body is "natural," forming the one entity of man, so the union of the divinity and the humanity is natural bringing about the one Christ.[36]

While these quotations confirm that Cyril employed *mia physis* to de-

---

sufferings of the body and make them its own, so the Word, in becoming man, can make the weaknesses of his humanity his own. While I am not particularly pleased with the illustration, the reason Cyril could make such a comparison is because Christ, like a human being, is one, and the one that he is is the person of the Son of God existing as man. "Accordingly, the union of the Word with humanity can reasonably be compared with our condition. Just as the body is of a different nature to the soul, still from both we say that one man results, so too from the perfect hypostasis of God the Word and form a humanity perfect in his own right there is one Christ, and the selfsame is at once God and man" (*Scholia* 8; McGuckin, *St. Cyril of Alexandria*, 301).

While McGuckin provides a good explanation of Cyril's use of the soul/body relationship, and rightly sees it as central to his thought, he does not appreciate Cyril's singular and proper use of it. He assumes that the above use is Cyril's primary and sole understanding. See J. A. McGuckin, *St. Cyril of Alexandria and the Christological History* (Crestwood: St. Vladimir's Press, 2004), 198–207, and his introduction to *On the Unity of Christ*, 38, 40. For a similar understanding of the above passage, see H. Chadwick, "Eucharist and Christology in the Nestorian Controversy," *Journal of Theological Studies*, n.s., 2 (1951): 159–62. B. Meunier interprets the above passages in a manner similar to my own. *Le Christ de Cyrille D'Alexandrie*, 243–53. F. Young not only has an equal understanding of the above passages, but she also grasps that Cyril's primary use of the soul/body analogy is to illustrate that Christ is one being, and therefore should "not be taken as an analysis of the relationship" between the divinity and the humanity. "A Reconsideration of Alexandrian Christology," *Journal of Ecclesiastical History*, 22 (1971): 106. See also her *From Nicaea to Chalcedon* (London: SCM, 1983), 260–63. G. Gould has also given a clear account of Cyril on this point. "Cyril of Alexandria and the Formula of Reunion," *Downside Review* 106 (1988): 238–43. While R. A. Norris believes that Cyril's primary Christological model is that of the subject-attribute model, he nonetheless interprets (wrongly, I believe) Cyril's use of the soul/body union as a way for him to espouse, in a confused and contradictory manner, a compositional model of the Incarnation whereby the divinity and humanity form one nature. "Christological Models in Cyril of Alexandria," *Studia Patristica* 13 (1975): 261–67. See also his "Toward a Contemporary Interpretation of the Chalcedonian *Definition*," in *Lux in Lumine*, ed. R. A. Norris (New York: Seabury Press, 1966), 68.

36. For examples of Cyril speaking of the union of the divinity and the humanity as "natural" (ἕνωσις φυσική) or "according to nature" (κατὰ φύσιν), see *C. Nest.* 2, 1; 13; *Ad Nest.* 3, 4–5; Anathema 3; *Expl. XII Cap.* 3.

clare Christ to be one entity and not one quiddity, it is equally clear that he used the term *physis* in two different senses. He speaks simultaneously of the soul and body, and the divinity and the humanity as each being a *physis* in the sense of nature or quiddity. This equivocal, and so ambiguous, use of the term *physis* obviously caused, and still causes, confusion and misunderstanding.

Assuming that for Cyril *mia physis* designated Jesus as one entity, and that he affirmed this in order to confirm the Communication of Idioms—for only if the Son of God *truly is* man, and so one with his humanity can the attributes of each nature be predicated of him—what does the remainder of the formula tell us? The answer to this question bears upon Cyril's second concern about Christ's oneness and the manner of that oneness. The remainder of the formula designates who/what the one reality of Jesus is. The one reality or entity (μία φύσις) is that of the Word incarnate (τοῦ λόγου σεσαρκωμένη). Contained within the *mia physis* formula, something Cyril instinctively realized and appreciated but that others found too subtle to grasp, was the notion of one subject or person and the manner of the one subject's existence. The subject (the who) of the *mia physis* (of the one entity) is the Word. The manner or mode of the Word's existence as *mia physis* (as one entity) is as man. This is why Cyril could write: "Accordingly all the sayings contained in the Gospel's must be referred to a single person (ἑνὶ προσώπῳ), to the one incarnate subject of the Word (ὑποστάσει μιᾷ τοῦ λόγου σεσαρκωμένη)."[37] Here the customary term *physis* has been substituted by the terms *prosopon* and *hypostasis*, which acquire the more Chalcedonian sense of person or subject. The reason Cyril can make such a substitution is that, for him, the one entity of Christ (*physis*) is none other than the one divine person/subject (*prosopon/hypostasis*) of the Son existing as incarnate.

Bearing on this point, Cyril actually has two readings of the *mia physis* formula. The more prevalent one is: μία φύσις τοῦ λόγου σεσαρκωμένη. The other, less common rendering ends in σεσαρκωμέου. Is there a difference of meaning between the two? In the light of the soul/body comparison, which accompanies both, I believe that the two versions of the *mia physis* formula denote that Christ is one entity. But this distinction is most clearly seen within the σεσαρκωμένου rendering where it modifies the τοῦ λόγου. The

37. *Ad Nest.* 3, 8; Wickham, *Cyril of Alexandria*, 25.

translation would be: "The one nature (entity) of the incarnate Word." The one entity of Jesus is the Word existing as man. Where the σεσαρκωμένη modifies the μία φύσις, the formula is translated: "The one incarnate nature of the Word." This translation also specifies that Christ is one entity—one incarnate entity—but now the one incarnate *physis* is that of the Word, and so hidden within the use of the term *physis* is the notion of one subject or person as well. Thus this rendering of the formula could be translated: "The one incarnate nature/person of the Word." This translation, it seems to me, best articulates Cyril's meaning and one that is closest to Chalcedon's understanding. The whole problem could have been solved if Cyril had consistently used πρόσωπον or ὑπόστασις instead of φύσις.

While I have attempted to clearly distinguish the dual oneness that Cyril wanted to uphold, that of the one entity of Christ and the one subject of the Son, he frequently conflates these two concerns within the same fluid argument. In arguing against Nestorius's notion of a conjunctive union between the divinity and the humanity of Christ, for example, Cyril insisted that the union is hypostatic (καθ᾽ ὑπόστασιν). Although I will discuss the significance of this formula, he then proceeded to argue both that Christ is one entity, as is the unity of the body and soul, and equally that Christ is one subject. As the body and soul form the one human being, "we should think about Christ in the same way. For he is certainly not twofold. On the contrary, the Word of God the Father, together with his flesh, is the one and only Lord and Son." Notice the dual oneness: Christ is "not twofold" but one entity, and Christ is equally "the one and only Lord and Son." Cyril concluded that, while he is not confusing and mixing the natures, he refused to uphold "two Christs, or [to say] that there are two Sons." The reason there are not two Christs is that Christ is one entity, and the reason there are not two Sons is because the one entity that is the one Christ is the one Son existing as man, "because the Word of God, having partaken of flesh and blood, is still thought of as a single Son and is called such."[38]

While I have been arguing that Cyril stressed the oneness of Christ in a twofold manner, R. A. Norris holds that Cyril actually articulated two different Christological models.[39] The first, which Norris believes is

---

38. *C. Nest.* 2, 6; Russell, *Cyril of Alexandria,* 149–50, 182. See also *Expl. XII. Cap.* 4.
39. See Norris, "Christological Models in Cyril of Alexandria," 255–68.

Cyril's primary model, is what he calls "a subject-attribute model." Within this model Cyril can attribute divine and human predicates of one and the same subject—the Son. But Norris also sees within Cyril's Christology "a compositional model." Here the Incarnation is seen as the act of "putting together" two different realities (divinity and humanity), similar to the union of soul and body. Thus Christ is one composite entity. Norris believes that it is Cyril's use of this second model that causes "such a remarkable conceptual chaos" within his Christology. Norris is correct in that Cyril did speak of the Incarnation in two different manners, but these do not denote different models. What Norris fails to grasp is that Cyril used two different sets of language or concepts not to articulate two different conceptions of the Incarnation, but to state two different truths about his one conception of the Incarnation. He used the soul/body language to confirm the truth that Christ is one ontological being or entity (Norris's compositional model), and he used the subject-attribute "model" in order to designate who and what the one Christ is—the one person of the Son existing as man. While Cyril was aware that he was attempting to articulate these two truths, I would agree with Norris that he seemed unaware at times that he was not distinguishing them in a manner that was unambiguous.

Nonetheless, for Cyril the *mia physis* formula embodied all three truths needed for a proper understanding of the Incarnation, and this is why he loved it. It said it all. As the above exposition probably demonstrates, however, it may try to do too much. It requires a "Cyrillian insight," something his detractors, past and present, lack.

"Becoming" as Personal/Existential

In the course of expounding, and so clarifying, the meaning of the *mia physis* formula, Cyril conceived and formulated a major Christological innovation concerning the true character of the incarnational "becoming" and the ensuing union between the Son/Word of God and his humanity. This is why he was willing, in the end, to set the formula aside. Cyril's insight was in designating that the union of the natures takes place within the person of the Word. The incarnational "becoming" and ensuing union is "according to the person" (καθ᾽ ὑπόστασιν). "We affirm this: that the Word personally [according to the person] united to himself flesh (σάρκα ... ἑνώσας ὁ λόγος ἑαυτῷ καθ᾽ ὑπόστασιν)."[40] This was the heart of his beloved formula, but now stated more explicitly and more accurately. Here we witness a true Christological breakthrough, one that springs from the Communication of Idioms and, simultaneously, precisely defines it.

I have noted in a number of instances that I have slightly altered Wick-ham's translation of Cyril. In light of my above interpretation, I believe my alteration is nonetheless significant. Wickham makes an equivalence be-tween Cyril's saying that the union is "natural" (ἕνωσις φυσική) and that the union is καθ᾽ ὑπόστασιν, giving the meaning "substantial union" to both. While both do designate a substantial union, Cyril used "natural" to em-phasize that the union establishes Christ as one entity, and he used καθ᾽ ὑπόστασιν ("according to person" or "personally") to designate the distinc-tive and singular type of substantial union it is. The incarnational act does not bring about a union of natures, but it is rather the act by which the humanity is united substantially to the person (ὑπόστασις) of the Word. Moreover, when Cyril spoke, as quoted above, of "the one incarnate subject (ὑποστάσει μιᾷ σεσαρκωμένε) of the Word," Wickham interprets ὑποστάσει μιᾷ as equivalent to μία φύσις. While the ὑποστάσει μιᾷ is contained within the μία φύσις, the nuance is significant. The μία φύσις is emphasizing the one entity of Christ. The ὑποστάσε μιᾷ is highlighting who the one subject is within the one entity of Christ—the one Word/Son.[41]

In designating the incarnational "becoming" as *kath' hypostasin*, Cyril clarified and established three points concurrently.

1. He distinguished between the person (the who) and the person's na-ture (the manner of the who's existence). It is one and the same per-son, who existed eternally as God, who now exists as man.

2. He clarified the exact nature of the incarnational "becoming." The Incarnation does not involve the changing, mixing, or confusing of natures (as in the soul/body model), but rather the person of the Word taking on a new mode or manner of existence (that is, as man). There is a change or newness in the mode of the existence of the Son, though not a change or newness within the natures. The Son now

---

40. *Ad Nest.* 2, 3; Wickham, *Cyril of Alexandria*, 5. Translation altered slightly. See also *Ad Nest.* 2, 4; 3, 11.

41. See Wickham, *Cyril of Alexandria*, 4n6, 25n16.

exists newly as man. Commenting on the meaning of "manifested in the flesh," Cyril wrote:

> It means that the Word of God the Father became flesh, not by a change or alteration of his own nature, as we have already said, but because having made the flesh taken from the holy Virgin his own, one and the same subject is called Son, before the Incarnation as Word still incorporeal and after the Incarnation as the same Word now embodied. That is why we say that the same subject is simultaneously both God and man, not dividing him conceptually into a human being with a separate individual identity and God the Word also with a separate identity, that we may exclude any idea of two Sons, but acknowledging that one and the same subject is Christ and Son and Lord.[42]

3. By correctly conceiving and articulating that it is the one person of the Son who exists as man, Cyril, as examined below, has equally validated the Communication of Idioms.

Cyril's understanding of the Incarnation is what I have come to refer to as a personal/existential conception. Jesus is the *person* of the Son *existing* as a man.[43] While the Incarnation remains a mystery, Cyril, in accordance with authentic doctrinal development, has clarified more exactly what the mystery is—it is truly the person of the divine Son who truly exists as a true man.

Cyril and the Council of Chalcedon

Because of both Antiochene concerns and Leo's Tome written in response to Eutyches's Monophysitism, the Council of Chalcedon (451) decreed that the Son was "made known in two natures" (ἐκ δύο φύσεσιν) as opposed to stating that the Son was composed "out of" (ἐκ δύο) two natures. This clarified the lingering ambiguities within Cyril's Christology. Nonetheless, Cyril's stamp on the Council's creed is unmistakable, and it is his understanding of the Incarnation that bears its *imprimatur*. To read the Chalcedonian Creed other than through the eyes of Cyril is to misread it.

---

42. *Expl. XII Cap.* 2; Russell, *Cyril of Alexandria*, 179–80.

43. On the personal/existential understanding of the Incarnation, see Weinandy, *Does God Change?*, 53–55.

Three times the Council employs the Cyrillian phrase "one and the same" (ἕνα καὶ τὸ αὐτὸν) and five times speaks of "the same" (τὸν αὐτὸν). Who is "one and the same" and "the same" is none other the person of the Son. It is one and the same Son who is "perfect in Godhead" and "perfect in manhood, truly God and truly man … consubstantial (ὁμοούσιον) with the Father in Godhead, and the same consubstantial (ὁμοούσιον) with us in manhood." It is the same Son, who existed eternally with the Father, who came to exist as man. In so speaking the Council thoroughly endorsed Cyril's personal, existential understanding of the Incarnation.

The Council also declared that the two natures were united "without confusion, without change, without division, without separation" (ἀσυγχύτως, ἀτρέπτως, ἀδιαιρέτως, ἀχωρίστως). Why are the natures not confused and changed? Why are they undivided and unseparated? Is the Council making negative statements merely to ward off various heresies, or does it also have a positive, theologically informed conception of the Incarnation that authorized it to do so? I believe it is the latter. The Council grasped, in agreement with Cyril, that the natures are not confused and changed because the incarnational act, the "becoming," is not the compositional union of natures that would demand change and confusion. Rather, the incarnational act, the "becoming," equally in agreement with Cyril, is the person of the Son uniting to himself a human nature so as to exist personally as man. Thus the natures are not divided or separated, but find their unity in the one person of the Son. As the Council states, "the difference of the natures being by no means removed because of the union [the reason being that the union is not a union of natures], but the property of each nature being preserved and harmonized (συντρεχούσης) in one *prosopon* and one *hypostasis*." This, too, testifies to the Council's personal/existential understanding of the Incarnation.

It is this understanding of the Incarnation that provided, at last, the Christological justification for and a proper reading of the Communication of Idioms. As I argue, however, it was not a proper understanding of the Incarnation that gave rise to the Communication of Idioms, for it was used long before a proper understanding was fully articulated, but rather it was the Communication of Idioms, as preeminently exemplified within Cyril's Christology, that gave rise to a proper understanding of the Incarnation.

Before concluding with an examination of Cyril's understanding of the Communication of Idioms, here I briefly address a further criticism leveled against Cyril's (and thus Chalcedon's) understanding of the Incarnation. The critics argue, in keeping with their accusation that Cyril minimizes the significance of Christ's humanity, that if Christ is a divine person and not a human person, then he is not fully human, for something that is essential to being fully human—that is, human personhood—has now been discarded. According to John Macquarrie, Cyril's Christology is "surely to be rejected as undermining the true humanity of Christ," and in the end "is repeating in a slightly different form the heresy of Apollinarius."[44] Under the pretense of attempting to assure the full humanity of Jesus, however, what the critics are most anxious to refute and so deny—which they always do—is his full divinity, that it is actually the divine Son of God who exists as man. To state this more bluntly, the actual source of disquiet among Cyril's critics, it seems to me, is not so much that they fear the demise of Christ's full humanity, but that they frantically want to dismiss his full divinity. In their misguided criticism of Cyril, they are in fact exploiting, for the sake of their own denial, the legitimate contemporary concern that Christ be indeed fully human. Nonetheless, to such a criticism and denial a twofold response can be made.

First, in defining that Jesus is the Son of God existing as man, nothing is denied as to the manner of his human existence. As the subsequent doctrinal history will clarify and confirm, the Son of God possesses a human intellect and will and, in more recent scholarship, a human self-consciousness. Whatever pertains to being a human being pertains to Christ.[45] What Cyril and the Chalcedonian tradition demand is that who this man is—that is, his identity—is the Son of God. The term "person" is not to be understood as some kind of distinct component or part that when absent or separated

---

44. J. Macquarrie, *Christology Revisited* (London: SCM, 1998), 50, 51. Macquarrie totally misconceives and misrepresents Cyril's Christology (43–60). See also his *Jesus Christ in Modern Thought* (London: SCM, 1990), 162–63. For a sampling of others who make the same criticism, see D. M. Baillie, *God Was in Christ* (London: Faber and Faber, 1956), 85–93; R. Haight, *Jesus Symbol of God* (Maryknoll: Orbis Books, 1999), 263–66, 285–92; J. Knox, *The Humanity and Divinity of Christ* (Cambridge: Cambridge University Press, 1967), 63–65; J. A. T. Robinson, *The Human Face of God* (London: SCM, 1973), 40, 102–16.

45. I have argued, in what I believe to be accordance with Cyril and Chalcedon, that as incarnate the Son of God even possesses a human "I." The identity of this human "I," who it is who is this "I," is the person or subject of the Son. See T. G. Weinandy, "The Human 'I' of Jesus," *Irish Theological Quarterly* 62, no. 4 (1996/97): 259–68 (chap. 17 in this volume).

renders the humanity less that what it would be if the component called "person" were attached. The term "person" is merely, but significantly, identifying who the subject is, who this man is—his identity as the Son of God. Only if the identity of the man Jesus—that is, who this man is, and in this sense the "subject" or "person"—is the divine Son of God can one speak of an authentic and true Incarnation.

Second, in denying that Jesus is truly the divine Son of God, *homoousion* with the Father, the critics of Cyril and the Christological tradition depreciate the significance of the very thing they want to enhance—the humanity. One never enhances the import of Jesus's full humanity, in all its authentic historicity, by denying that it is truly the divine Son who is man. His wholly otherness as God gives significance to the Son's incarnate existence. If it were not truly the Son, *homoousion* with the Father, who became man, then the whole impact of his being man, *homoousion* with all men, is forfeited.

Similarly, one could argue and Cyril would passionately agree, it would be incongruous to uphold that Jesus is truly the divine Son of God at the expense of his full humanity, for within the Incarnation the only reason one does want to uphold the full divinity is to assure that it is truly the Son of God who is actually an authentic man. Within the Incarnation, if the Son of God is not fully and truly man, then the whole point of Jesus being the Son of God vanishes. For Cyril, the Communication of Idioms accentuates and intensifies these truths.

Cyril and the Communication of Idioms

The patristic tradition had long employed and the Creed of Nicaea sanctioned, as Cyril grasped, the Communication of Idioms. What neither had ever clearly achieved, as witnessed in the Antiochene rejection, was a proper theological rationale for its use, and thus a precise understanding of the manner in which these attributes were predicated of the Son. In providing the Christological basis for its use, Cyril equally clarified the manner in which it was used, and he did so in two ways.

Negatively, Cyril perceived that the human attributes were not predicated of the divine nature, nor, in turn, that the divine attributes were predicated of the human nature. To understand the Communication of Idioms in such a manner would require that the natures be confused and mixed and so changed within the incarnational "becoming." This was how Nestorius interpreted its use, and if it had been the correct interpretation, his rejection would have been justified.

Positively, Cyril comprehended and explicitly stated, for the first time, that the attributes were predicated not of the natures, but of the person, for the Incarnation is not the compositional union of natures but the person of the Son taking on a new manner or mode of existence.[46] Because the incarnational "becoming" is *kath' hypostasin*, according to the person, it can actually be said that the person of the Son of God is truly born, grieves, suffers, and dies, not as God but as man, for that is now the new manner in which the Son of God actually exists.

R. A. Norris, in his interpretation of Cyril, misses the significance of this crucial point. He rightly argues that Cyril's primary Christological model is that of the subject-attribute model (though I take issue with the term "model"), but he interprets such an understanding not as a metaphysical statement about the ontological constitution of Christ but merely as a linguistic or grammatical tool to govern Christological language.[47] What Norris fails to appreciate is that Cyril's (and Chalcedon's) insistence that the divine and human attributes be predicated of the one and same subject of the Son is founded upon their metaphysical understanding of how Christ is ontologically constituted. While the Communication of Idioms was the catalyst that gave rise to such an understanding (that Christ is the one person/subject of the Son *existing* as God and as man), it was this same understanding that in turn provided the metaphysical warrant for the use of such language (that divine and human attributes must therefore be predicated of the one Son). Christological grammar and logic, as Cyril well knew, is dependent upon Christological ontology.

R. Siddals also interprets Cyril's use of the Communication of Idioms from within a faulty understanding of his Christology. She argues that un-

---

46. In fairness, it should be noted that Athanasius grasped that the divine and human attributes were predicated of one and the same Son. What Athanasius failed to achieve, however, although his understanding of the Communication of Idioms placed him on the brink, was the precise and comprehensive conceptual understanding of the Incarnation that could properly justify such predication.

47. See Norris, "Toward a Contemporary Interpretation of the Chalcedonian *Definition*," 71–79.

derlying Cyril's use of the Communication of Idioms is a subject-accident Christological model; that is, that while the Son, being by nature God, actually does possess the divine attributes as part of his being, he acquires, within the Incarnation, the human attributes as "virtual accidents." Cyril "treats humanity etc. as mysteriously inhering within the Word as an *accident* inheres within a subject."[48] But for Cyril, being a man is what the Son of God *is*, and thus the use of the Communications of Idioms is not the mere espousal of accidental predicates to the Son, but statements about his actual mode of being or manner of existing.[49]

For Cyril, to call Mary *Theotokos* does not mean that she gave birth to God as God: "no, it means that he [the Son] had fleshly birth because he issued from woman for us and for our salvation having united humanity to himself personally (ἐνώσας ἑαυτῷ καθ᾽ ὑπόστασιν τὸ ἀνθρώπινον)." Equally, when it is said that the Son of God suffered and died, it is not meant

that God the Word suffered blows, nail-piercings or other wounds in his own nature (the divine is impassible because it is incorporeal) but what is said is that since his own created body suffered these things he himself "suffered" for our sake, the point being that within the suffering body was the Impassible (ὁ ἀπαθὴς ἐν τῷ πάσχοντι σώματι). We interpret his dying along exactly comparable lines.[50]

In the twelfth of his infamous anathemas, Cyril provocatively declared, "Whoever does not acknowledge God's Word as having suffered in flesh, being crucified in flesh, tasted death in flesh and been made first-born from the dead because as God he is Life and life-giving shall be anathema."[51]

Here again scholars are frequently critical of Cyril, especially those who wish to espouse a passible and so suffering God. R. Haight, commenting on traditional Christology, which is exemplified by Cyril, writes that "the problem in this tradition is that it is a christology of only one subject, and,

48. R. Siddals, "Logic and Christology in Cyril of Alexandria," *Journal of Theological Studies*, n.s., 38 (1987): 342–67; "Oneness and Difference in the Christology of Cyril of Alexandria," *Studia Patristica* 18 (1985): 207–11.

49. For a similar criticism of Siddals, see Meunier, *Le Christ de Cyrille D'Alexandrie*, 276–79.

50. *Ad Nest.* 2, 4, 5; Wickham, *Cyril of Alexandria*, 7. For Cyril, "all the sayings contained in the Gospels must be referred to single person (ἑνὶ προσώπῳ), to the one incarnate subject of the Word (ὑποστάσει μιᾷ τῇ τοῦ λόγου σεσαρκωμένῃ)" (*Ad Nest.* 3, 8; Wickham, *Cyril of Alexandria*, 23). See also *Ad Nest.* 3, 9–11.

51. *Ad Nest.* 3, Anathema 12.

that subject being impassible, it leaves no other subject who can suffer."[52] Initially it may seem that what Cyril was attempting to articulate is indeed contradictory and thus meaningless. If the Impassible is truly impassible, how can the Impassible truly and authentically suffer and die? For Cyril, however, the entire point of ensuring a proper understanding of the mystery of the Incarnation is not only to allow but more so to warrant, for soteriological reasons, the truth that the Impassible did indeed suffer and die. What Cyril was articulating within his understanding of the Communication of Idioms therefore must be clearly understood.

First, who, for Cyril, truly experiences the authentic, genuine, and undiminished reality of human suffering? None other than the divine Son of God! It is he who is one in being (*homoousion*) with the Father. Second, what is the manner in which he experiences the whole reality of human suffering? As man! It is actually the Son of God who lives a comprehensive human life, and so it is the Son who, as man, experiences all facets of this human life, including suffering and death. The Son is the exclusive active subject in what he experiences and in what he does, and the manner or mode under which he experiences and acts is as man.

But this is the problem the critics protest. After all is said and done, Cyril's understanding of the Incarnation and the Communication of Idioms that ensues from it forbids that suffering be experienced by the Son of God within his divinity, and so falls short of allowing God truly to suffer. Here again many scholars miss the logic of Cyril's Christology. For example, J. Hallman judges that, because Cyril insisted that the Son of God remains impassible as God and yet truly suffers as man, he is simply illogical.[53] For Cyril, what is truly at issue is not that the Son of God suffers as God in a divine manner, but that the Son of God suffers as man in a human manner. Moreover, behind Hallman's accusation that Cyril was illogical lies the erroneous premise that the incarnational process is a compositional union of natures modeled after the soul/body union. This is how Hallman ultimately wants to conceive the incarnational union, for it then would allow God to suffer as God. Because Cyril's understanding of the Incarnation is radically

52. Haight, *Jesus Symbol of God*, 265. For similar criticisms, see my discussion in *Does God Suffer?*, 14–19.

53. See J. Hallman, "The Seed of Fire: Divine Suffering in the Christology of Cyril of Alexandria and Nestorius of Constantinople," *Journal of Early Christian Studies* 5 (1997): 384, 391.

different, however—being a personal/existential understanding—he is not illogical at all. The person of the Son, within his existence as God, is impassible. Within his existence as man, the Son is passible. While not fully comprehensible, this is the rational, intelligible, and coherent logic that the mystery of the Incarnation demands. As Cyril explicitly stated, almost as if he had Hallman in mind:

He (the Son) suffered without suffering … If we should say that through conversion or mutation of his own nature into flesh, it would be in all ways necessary for us even against our will to confess that the hidden and divine nature was passible [Hallman's wish]. But if he has remained unchanged albeit he has been made man as we, and it be a property of the heavenly nature that it cannot suffer, and the passible body has become his own through the union: He suffers when the body suffers, in that it is said to be his own body, he remains impassible in that it is truly his property to be unable to suffer.[54]

Such criticisms are postulated upon the false premise that the Son of God must suffer within his divine nature in order for the suffering to be theologically and soteriologically significant. But because of such mistaken assumptions, this criticism actually ignores the inner Christological and soteriological logic contained within Cyril's understanding of the Communication of Idioms, and so neglects its true import.

The Communications of Idioms, as understood by Cyril, wishes to uphold that the fully divine Son of God did indeed suffer and die. This is just what Nestorius wanted to deny and Cyril wanted to vindicate. This is exactly why Cyril asserts that he who is impassible as God actually is passible as man. The Impasssible suffered.[55] To say, in accordance with Cyril, that "the Impassible suffers" is not to be incoherent, but to state the very heart of the

54. *Scholia* 37. Cyril earlier states: "He suffers humanly in the flesh as man, he remains impassible divinely as God" (*Scholia* 36). See also *Scholia* 33–35. In *Quod Unus*, he writes: "So, even if he [the Son] is said to suffer in the flesh, even so he retains his impassibility insofar as he is understood as God." See McGuckin, *On the Unity of Christ*, 117. References to Cyril speaking of the Son being impassible as God and passible as man could be multiplied, but see especially *Ad Succ.* 2, 2, and his three defenses of the twelve anathemas: *Adv. Orient. Epis.*, *C. Theodoret.*, and *Expl. XII Cap.*

55. I concur with Hallman that, as far as I can also ascertain, this exact phrase (ἀπαθῶς ἔπαθεν) is not found in Cyril's Greek. "The Seed of Fire," 383n57. Nonetheless, it is Cyrillian in tone and meaning. Cyril did state "that within the suffering body was the Impassible (ἡ γὰρ ὁ ἀπαθὴς ἐν τῳ πάσχοντι σώματι)" (*Ad Nest.* 2, 5), and that "he [the Son] was in the crucified body

incarnational mystery. First, the term "the Impassible" guarantees that it is actually God, in all his wholly transcendent otherness as God, who suffers, and not "God" in some mitigated or semidivine state. The fact that God does not lose his wholly transcendent impassible otherness in so suffering enhances to the extreme, as Cyril well knew, the import of the suffering, for it means that the Son who is incapable of suffering as the wholly other God is the same one who is actually suffering as man. Second, we perceive here, in contrast to Nestorius and the Antiochenes, just how important the humanity of Christ was for Cyril. While Cyril was concerned with upholding the impassible divinity of the Son as God, his interest in this was primarily for incarnational and soteriological reasons. He wished to assure that it was actually the divine Son who lived a full human life, and so the Son who was impassible as God is the same Son who could truly experience human suffering and death. The Communication of Idioms ensures that it is truly human suffering that the Son of God experiences and endures, and thus the Son's authentic and genuine humanity is the absolute prerequisite for establishing the truth of the Communication of Idioms.

Even if one did allow the Son of God to suffer in his divine nature, as some critics of Cyril wish to do, this would negate the very thing Cyril wanted to preserve and cultivate. For if the Son of God experienced suffering in his divine nature, he would no longer be experiencing human suffering in an authentic and genuine human manner, but instead he would be experiencing "human suffering" in a divine manner, which would then be neither genuinely nor authentically human. If the Son of God experienced suffering in his divine nature, then it would be God suffering as God *in a man*. But the Incarnation, as Cyril well understood, which demands that the Son of God actually exists as a man and not just dwells in a man, equally demands that the Son of God suffer *as a man* and not just suffer divinely in a man. If one wishes to say in truth, as Cyril did, that the Son of God actually experienced and knew what it was like to be born, eat, sleep, cry, fear, grieve, groan, rejoice, suffer, die, and most of all love *as a man*, then the experience and knowledge of being born, eating, sleeping, crying, fearing, grieving, groaning, rejoicing, suffering, dying, and again most of all loving

---

claiming the sufferings of his flesh as his own impassibly (ἣν ἐν τῷ σταυρωθέντι σώματι, τὰ τῆς ἰδίας σαρκὸς οἰκειούμενος πάθη)" (*Ad Nest.* 3, 6).

must be predicated of the Son of God solely and exclusively *as a man*. Because Cyril gloried in the biblical drama of the Incarnation—that is, that it truly was the impassible Son of God who did actually suffer as man—he was not afraid to use language that appeared to be incoherent but was logically coherent in the light of his Christological ontology.[56]

Nonetheless, if the Son of God suffers as man, why does this suffering not affect his divinity given that the Son of God is equally God? While Cyril did not explicitly address this issue, we delve more deeply into the heart of the incarnational mystery. The answer lies (and I believe Cyril would agree, for his Christology implicitly contained it) in the fact that, as God, the Son was not deprived of any good that would have caused him to suffer as God. As man, however, the Son of God was deprived of human goods, which did cause him to suffer humanly. Cyril instinctively realized that one must maintain the unchangeable impassibility of the Son of God as God so as to guarantee that it is actually the divine Son of God who truly suffers as man. Only if the Son remains immutably God in becoming man can one guarantee that it is actually the divine Son who exists as man, and, equally, only if the Son remains impassible and so truly God within his incarnate state can one guarantee that it is actually that same impassible divine Son who passible as man.

For Cyril, this is the marvelous truth of the Incarnation. God from all eternity may have known, within his divine knowledge, what it is like for human beings to suffer and die, and he may have known this perfectly and comprehensively. But until the Son of God actually became man and existed as a man, the Son of God, who is impassible in himself as God, never experienced and knew suffering and death as man *in a human manner*. In an unqualified manner one can say that, as man, the Son of God had experiences he never had before because he never existed as man before—not the least of which are suffering and death. This is what, for Cyril, a proper understanding of the Incarnation requires and affirms, and this is what the Communication of Idioms so remarkably, clearly, and even scandalously safeguards, advocates, and confesses. The eternal, almighty, all-perfect, unchangeable, and impassible divine Son—he who is equal to the Father in

---

56. For similar views, see McKinion, *Words, Imagery, and the Mystery of Christ*, 212–24; Meunier, *Le Christ de Cyrille D'Alexandrie*, 243–75; O'Keefe, "Impassible Suffering?," 46–51.

all ways—actually experienced, as a weak human being, the full reality of human suffering and death. What was an infamy to the Docetists, to Arius, and to Nestorius was for Cyril and the subsequent Christian tradition the glory and grandeur of the Gospel. Even among those today who advocate a suffering God, the Incarnation is still a scandal, for, while with the best of intentions, having locked suffering within God's divine nature, they have in so doing locked God out of human suffering.

Conclusion

I trust that this essay offers readers a greater understanding and apprecia-tion of the scope and depth of Cyril's Christology. While he may at times be difficult to read and understand, I hope it has become evident that Cyril possessed profound insight into the mystery of the Incarnation, insight that the Church has continually contemplated to this day. Through an exam-ination of his writings, the reader can glimpse inside Cyril's mind, so that in coming to think as Cyril thought, we might not only grasp what he was thinking and saying, but also perhaps think it and say it more clearly than even he himself thought it and said it, and so ultimately be truly faithful to Cyril himself. In expounding and clarifying Cyril's Christological thought, we can seen that his pre-Nestorian biblical commentaries already expressed an understanding of the Incarnation that he would subsequently develop during the course of the Nestorian controversy. Even in the midst of his am-biguity and sometimes-infelicitous expressions, Cyril never deviated from the central truths that he thought necessary for upholding an authentic un-derstanding of the Incarnation, maturing in his Christological conception and improving in his articulation of these truths. I hope that my rendering of Cyril's Christology has been clear, accurate, and fair to his multifaceted thought and versatile expression. By expressing, explaining, and clarifying Cyril's Christological thought in a logical and comprehensible manner, I, as my secondary aim, have sought to defend his work against what I believe to be often unwarranted attacks. I have made such a defense not merely for the sake of defending Cyril but more so for the sake of defending what Cyril himself defended—the truth of the Incarnation.

CHAPTER 8

Aquinas
God *IS* Man and the Marvel
of the Incarnation

The Trinity is the central mystery of the Christian faith. As the foundational mystery, the fountain from which all subsequent Christian mysteries flow, the Trinity is acknowledged, correctly, to be the most incomprehensible. Because the persons of the Trinity exist in a manner that is ontologically unique, their existence differs in kind from that of the finite created order, and thus the mystery that they are as the one God infinitely exceeds our human ability to comprehend. But I argue that the Incarnation is an even greater mystery in one way at least, and thus an even more difficult mystery to envisage.

While the Trinity exists in an entirely different ontological order from that of finite creation, all three persons, as the one God, exist in communion with one another and so share that same divine ontological order. When human beings attempt to gain greater clarity as to the precise nature of this Trinitarian mystery, they have the ever so slight advantage of having to deal with only one ontological order, even if that order is completely other than their own. What adds greater mystery to the Incarnation is that the Son of God exists not only as God (within the divine ontological order), but also as man (within the finite and created ontological order). It is the

Originally published as "Aquinas: God IS Man: The Marvel of the Incarnation," in *Aquinas on Doctrine: A Critical Introduction*, ed. T. G. Weinandy, Daniel A. Keating, and John Yocum (London: T&T Clark/Continuum, 2004), 67–89. Reprinted by permission of Continuum, an imprint of Bloomsbury Publishing, PLC.

twofold existence, this twofold "IS," that makes for the Incarnation's mystery and so equally for the sheer wonder of it all.[1]

Aquinas was very much aware of this:

Indeed, among divine works, this most especially exceeds the reason; for nothing can be thought of which is more marvellous than this divine accomplishment: that the true God, the Son of God, should become true man.[2]

For nothing more marvellous could be done than that God become man and that Christ's humanity should become a partaker of divine immortality after his resurrection.[3]

But nothing is more a source of wonder than the Son of God made man, so that everyone can fittingly ask, "What is this?" That is, how can the Son of God be the Son of Man? How can Christ be one person with two natures? "His name will be called Wonderful" (Is. 9:6).[4]

In this essay I examine the marvel of the Incarnation as grasped and articulated by Aquinas.[5] The aim is not merely to expound and clarify what Aquinas taught, but to come to a clearer understanding of the Incarnation ourselves, and in turn to be able to address more adequately contemporary Christological concerns.[6]

1. In doing theology for many years now, I have found that I am happier with my grasp and articulation of the mystery of the Trinity than I am with my grasp and articulation of the mystery of the Incarnation. I have found the Incarnation and all its implications a far more difficult mystery to conceive and express.

2. *ScG* IV, ch. 27, 1. The translation is taken from C. J. O'Neil, trans., *On the Truth of the Catholic Faith*, vol. 4 (Garden City, NJ: Image Books, 1957).

3. *In Io.* 2:19 [398]; James Weisheipl, *Commentary on the Gospel of St. John: Thomas Aquinas*, vol. 1 (Albany, NY: Magi, 1980), 170.

4. *In Io.* 6:35 [914]; Weisheipl, *Commentary on the Gospel of St. John*, 364.

5. Aquinas has substantial treatments on the Incarnation in seven of his works: III *Sent.*, 1–32; *ScG* IV, ch. 27–55; *De Ver.* 29; *Comp. Theol.* 199–245; *In Io.* 1:14 [165–90]; *De Unione* 1–5; *ST* III, q. 1–59.

6. For expositions of Aquinas's Christology, see B. Bro, "La notion métaphysique de tout et son application au problème théologique de l'union hypostatique I," *Revue Thomiste* 68, no. 2 (1968): 181–97; "La notion métaphysique de tout et son application au problème théologique de l'union hypostatique II," *Revue Thomiste* 68, no. 3 (1968): 357–80; B. Davies, *The Thought of Thomas Aquinas* (Oxford: Clarendon Press, 1992), 297–319; M. Gorman, "Christ as Composite according to Aquinas," *Traditio* 55 (2000): 143–57; M. Gorman, "Uses of the Person-Nature Distinction in Thomas' Christology," *Recherches de Théologie et Philosophie Médiévales* 67 (2000): 58–70; M.-V. Leroy, "L'union selon l'hypostase d'après saint Thomas d'Aquin," *Revue Thomiste* 74, no. 2 (1974): 205–41; F. Ruello, *La Christologie de Thomas D'Aquin* (Paris: Beauchesne, 1987);

The Faith of the Church: Three Incarnational Truths

The Church's teaching on the Incarnation, as proclaimed and understood within the Scriptures and as defined by the conciliar tradition, formed the basis of Aquinas's Christology.[7] When treating the question of whether it is true to say "God is man," Aquinas answered simply:

Supposing the truth of the Catholic belief, that the true divine nature is united with true human nature not only in person, but also in suppositum or hypostasis; we say that this proposition is true and proper; *God is man*—not only by the truth of its terms, i.e. because Christ is true God and true man, but by the truth of the predication.[8]

Embedded within Aquinas's entire treatment of the Incarnation is a "Christological logic"; that is, the very nature of the Incarnation demands that certain indispensable truths be preserved and that the consequences flowing from these truths also be assured. By embracing as his own through faith this "truth of the Catholic belief," Aquinas, throughout his writings, realized that to conceive and to articulate the Incarnation properly, one's conception and articulation must simultaneously comprise, and so ensure,

---

H. J. M. Schoot, *Christ the "Name" of God: Thomas Aquinas on Naming Christ* (Leuven: Peeters, 1993); É.-H. Wéber, *Le Christ selon Saint Thomas D'Aquin* (Paris: Desclée, 1988).

7. The scriptural foundation of Aquinas's theology is becoming more appreciated. This is very much the case within his Christology. Not only does Aquinas quote Scripture in most of the articles of the *Summa Theologiae* and the *Summa contra Gentiles*, but he is also concerned about ensuring that his doctrinal explication is in accord with its traditional Christological interpretation. See T. Hibbs, *Dialectic and Narrative in Aquinas* (Notre Dame, IN: University of Notre Dame Press, 1995); Schoot, *Christ the "Name" of God*; J. P. Torrell, *St. Thomas Aquinas: The Person and His Work*, vol. 2 (Washington, DC: Catholic University of America Press, 2003); W. G. B. M. Valkenberg, *Words of the Living God: Place and Function of Holy Scripture in the Theology of St. Thomas Aquinas* (Leuven: Peeters, 2000).

It is also fascinating that, while many contemporary Eastern theologians perceive Aquinas as the quintessential Western Scholastic, his Christology was very much influenced by the Eastern fathers—Cyril of Alexandria and especially by John Damascene—through whom he obtained knowledge of the ecumenical councils. He obtained this knowledge because the Pope had asked him to study the Greek Fathers owing to the contemporary endeavor to obtain a reunion between the East and West. He was also the first scholastic to quote directly from Chalcedon. See I. Backes, *Die Christologie des hl. Thomas von Aquin und die griechishen Kirchenväter* (Paderborn: Ferdinand Schöningh, 1931).

8. *ST* III, q. 16, a. 1. Translation taken from Fathers of the English Dominican Province, trans., *Summa Theologica* (New York: Benziger Brothers, 1947).

three absolutely essential truths, the absence of any one of which would nullify its truth. These three truths are simply put.

1. It must be *truly the divine Son of God* who is man. The full divinity of the Son must be maintained within the incarnational becoming and subsequent union. Within the Incarnation, to compromise the divinity of the Son in any way for whatever reason nullifies the whole import of the Incarnation; it is *the Son of God* who exists as man.

2. It must be *truly man* that the Son of God is. Equally, if the Son of God is not truly and fully human, living an authentic and complete human life, then the whole point of his being the true Son of God vanishes. The significance of the divinity and humanity of Christ lies in their reciprocal relationship. There is no point in upholding the divinity of the Son if that divine Son is not man. Nor is there any point in upholding the full humanity if the one who is fully man is not the divine Son of God.[9]

3. The Son of God must *truly be* man. As implied above, it is no use upholding either the full divinity or the full humanity if the divine Son of God does not *actually exist* as an authentic man. The incarnational "becoming" must terminate in the extraordinary fact that the Son of God now simply *is* man, and it is this "*is*" and only this "*is*" that impregnates the terms of predication—that is, "the Son of God" and "man"—with their full incarnational significance and meaning, for it is this "*is*" that establishes their shared ontological unity or oneness. This incarnational "to be," this incarnational "to exist," this incarna-

---

9. Those contemporary authors who deny the divinity of Jesus in order to accentuate and so ensure his humanity miss the entire point of why Jesus must be fully human; that is, in order to ensure that this is what *the Son is*—man. For example, see J. Macquarrie, *Christology Revisited* (London: SCM, 1998), 43–60; *Jesus Christ in Modern Thought* (London: SCM, 1990).

While it cannot be treated in this essay because of space restraints, I have emphasized elsewhere, in accordance with Aquinas, that the Son of God assumed a humanity from the fallen race of Adam. See *ST* III, q. 4, a. 6; III q. 14, 15; *ScG* IV, ch. 29, 7; *In Phil.* 2:7–8 (59–61). Only if he assumed a humanity tainted by sin, though not sinning himself, could he save sinful humankind. See T. G. Weinandy, *In the Likeness of Sinful Flesh: An Essay on the Humanity of Christ* (Edinburgh: T&T Clark, 1993). See also P. Gondreau, *The Passions of Christ's Soul in the Theology of St. Thomas Aquinas* (Münster: Aschendorff Verlag, 2002), 166–89; M. McCool Adams, *What Sort of Nature? Medieval Philosophy and the Systematics of Christology* (Milwaukee, WI: Marquette University Press, 1999).

tional "is," is the cornerstone to Aquinas's whole Christological enterprise. His Christology is a Christology of "is" whereby the Son who
is God is also the same Son who *is* man. As the opening quotations
exemplify, it is this incarnational "is" that makes the Incarnation, for
Aquinas, the most marvelous of all mysteries.[10]

Denial of These Christological Truths

Both within his positive Christological exposition and within his refutation of Christological errors we see Aquinas attempting to maintain, with
their own inborn incarnational logic, these three Christological truths. In
so doing, Aquinas endeavored to clarify the exact ontological configuration of the Incarnation and so produce a greater depth of theological understanding. We first examine his refutation of Christological errors, especially
as found within the *Summa contra Gentiles*.[11]

Aquinas realized that every Christological error denies, in some fashion, one or more of these three incarnational truths. Aquinas therefore argued against Adoptionism in all its forms, whether that of the Ebionites,
Paul of Samosata, or Photinus, by noting that "this position destroys the
Incarnation's mystery. For according to this position, God would not have
assumed flesh to become man."[12] For Aquinas, the incarnational "becoming" must terminate in the Son of God actually existing as man. This is what
Adoptionism always denies, for it only allows a moral or accidental union
between the Son of God and the man Jesus. Adoptionism's denial of an ontological union thus nullifies the mystery of the Incarnation; that is, that
the Son actually *is* man.

---

10. Aquinas's Christology must never be seen in isolation from his soteriology. The reason
that the Incarnation is fitting is that through it, humankind's salvation is assured; see *ST* III, q.
1–4; *In Io.* 1:14a [169]. Aquinas repeatedly emphasizes in his *Summa contra Gentiles* that the
goal of the Incarnation and the redemptive acts of Jesus is our obtaining the beatific vision (see
ScG IV, ch. 29, 13; IV, ch. 42, 1). J. F. Boyle notes that there is a twofold structure in the *tertium
pars* of the *Summa Theologiae*. The first delineates who Christ is as the Son of God incarnate
and the second specifies what he accomplished for our salvation, precisely because of who he is
as the incarnate Son. "The Twofold Division of St. Thomas's Christology in the *Tertium Pars*,"
Thomist, 60 (1996): 439–47.

11. Aquinas treated a similar list of Christological errors in his *Compendium Theologiae*,
202–8.

12. *ScG* IV, ch. 28, 3 and 4.

Having argued for the full divinity of the Son within the context of the Trinity, Aquinas, within the context of the Incarnation and while noting the errors of those who deny the Son's divinity, such as Arius, focused his defense on Christ's full and authentic humanity. Aquinas thus opposed the Manicheans and Valentinus. In denying the reality of Christ's humanity and professing it to be only phantasmal, Aquinas argued that "they reduce the whole mystery of the Incarnation to a fiction."[13] Arius's and Apollinarius's denial of Christ's human soul equally makes nonsense of the Incarnation. For Aquinas, Christ must possess a "sensitive soul" in order for him to experience bodily hunger, thirst, anger, and the like. Moreover, he must possess a rational soul in order to be of the same species as ourselves. In an interesting argument, Aquinas observed that because Christ "marveled" (Mt. 8:10), in addition to his divinity, there must be "that which can make wonder seemly in him; namely a human mind."[14]

In ardently defending the full divinity of the Son and the genuineness of his humanity, Aquinas was but securing the authenticity of the terms of which the incarnational "is" could now be predicated, for the incarnational "is" makes the Incarnation. Grasping the Incarnation's inherent logic, it is not surprising that Aquinas perceived both Nestorianism and Monophysitism to be the most dangerous of all Christological heresies. Nestorianism, in its attempt to preserve the integrity of the natures, denied the incarnational "is," and Monophysitism, while it attempted to preserve the incarnational "is," conceived it in a manner that annihilated the natures. Thus Aquinas's whole refutation of Nestorianism and Monophysitism concentrates on properly conceiving and appropriately expressing the true nature of the incarnational "is."

When Aquinas turned to Theodore of Mopsuestia and Nestorius, he realized that the Communication of Idioms was their ultimate concern, for they believed that it nullified the integrity of the natures.

---

13. Ibid., ch. 29, 1. See also the whole of ch. 29 and 30. What should be noted, too, is that Aquinas, contrary to the Manicheans and Valentinus, wanted to ensure the integrity of Scripture and thus the authenticity of Christ's being born, eating, drinking, walking, suffering, dying, and being buried. Moreover, it is upon these human events, especially his passion and death, that salvation is predicated for Aquinas.

14. *ScG* IV, ch. 33, 5. See also the whole of ch. 31–33. See also *In Io.* 1:14a [168].

Therefore in the union of the Word and that man they think this must be observed: the things proper to that man and pertinent to the human nature cannot be said becomingly of God's Word, or of God. Just so it becomes that man that he was born of a virgin, that he suffered ... and all of these, they assert ought not be said of God, or of the Word of God.[15]

In attempting, rightfully, to protect the authenticity of the natures, Theodore and Nestorius were nonetheless unable to conceive the incarnational "is" in a manner that would simultaneously confirm its true existential and ontological character and equally confirm the integrity of the natures. Failing in this, they were forced to deprive the incarnational "is" of its true existential quality, and so reduced it to designating merely a moral or accidental union.

For Aquinas, such a stance is incompatible with a true understanding of the Incarnation. "The indwelling of God's Word in man is not for God's Word to be made flesh ... this ... indwelling ... cannot be called incarnation."[16] Aquinas is concerned with maintaining the true meaning of Scripture. God in the past may have dwelt with the prophets and other holy men and women, yet in none of these instances is God's Word ever said to have become flesh.[17] Moreover, Jesus's manner of speaking, especially within John's Gospel—"I and the Father are one" (Jn. 10:30) for example—reveals "necessarily, then, the person and hypostasis of that man speaking is the person and hypostasis of the Word of God."[18] Equally, that same Word of God also spoke of his own suffering and death. Now "every change or passion, furthermore, proper to one's body can be ascribed to him whose body it is ... Therefore, every suffering that took place in the body of that man can be ascribed to the Word of God."[19] What this manner of speaking reveals is that the Word of God *is* both truly God and truly man, and as such Jesus, according to Aquinas, is one supposit; that is, one entity or reality. The one entity or reality that Jesus is, in accordance with the incarnational "is," is the Son of God existing as man. Aquinas concluded his refutation of Nestorius by stating: "Therefore, God's Word and the man Christ are one supposit and, consequently, one person; and whatever is said of that man must be said of the Word of God, and conversely."[20]

These same Christological concerns are found in Aquinas's refutation

15. *ScG* IV, ch. 34, 2.
16. Ibid., ch. 34, 3.
17. Ibid., ch. 34, 4; ch. 25.
18. Ibid., ch. 34, 9. See also ch. 34, 7.
19. Ibid., ch. 34, 10.
20. Ibid., ch. 34, 29.

of two contemporary incarnational theories, what came to be known as the "*assumptus-homo* theory" and the "*habitus* theory." These two theories, along with a third, the "*subsistence* theory," formed part of Peter Lombard's *Sentences*.[21]

Peter Abelard first espoused the *assumptus-homo* theory. While Abelard affirmed that there was one person in Christ, he wanted also to assert that there were two hypostases, which would ensure the full reality of the humanity. But Aquinas was convinced that in so doing Abelard and others had made the humanity of Christ not merely a distinct substance different from that of the divinity, but a separate substance/reality that existed independently of the divinity. Aquinas held that the distinction between person and hypostasis is merely verbal; more importantly, to maintain that manhood was a supposit/ reality of its own apart from the divine Son demanded that Christ be two beings or realities. The union between them would then be only moral or accidental and so similar to the position espoused by Nestorius.

Things that are many in supposit are many simply, and they are but incidentally one. If in Christ there are two supposits, it follows that he is two simply, and this is "to dissolve Jesus" (1 Jn. 4:3), for everything, insofar as it is, is one.[22]

Some of Abelard's followers, in an attempt to avoid such a criticism, proposed that the soul and the body were not united, thus disallowing any human person or supposit. The soul and body were separately united to the Son of God, "just as a man puts on his clothes."[23] While the *habitus* theory may alleviate the problem of suggesting that Christ is a human person/supposit, for Aquinas it is still Nestorian or even something worse. "For there is no difference in saying that the Word of God is united to the Man Christ by indwelling, as in a temple [as Nestorius said] or by putting on man, as a garment ... rather it is something worse than Nestorius—to wit, that the soul and body are not united."[24] In denying that the soul and body are united, the proponents of the *habitus* theory ultimately gainsay the reality and authenticity of the humanity.[25]

21. See Peter Lombard, *Sentences*, Book III, questions 6, 7, 10, 21, and 22.
22. *ScG* IV, ch. 38, 11. See also *In Io.* 1:14a [171].
23. *ScG* IV, ch. 37, 1. See also *De Unione* 1.
24. *ST* III, q. 2, a. 6. See also *ScG* IV, ch. 37, 6.
25. See *ScG* IV, ch. 37, 10. For fuller studies of Aquinas's treatment of these theories, see

Aquinas's critique of these two Christological theories illustrates again his insistence on the ontological nature of the incarnational union. "If the Word was united to the soul and body accidentally ... the human nature was not the nature of the Word."[26] For Aquinas it is the incarnational "is" that ensures that the Son is *actually man*, and so this, too, testifies to his concern for Christ's true humanity. "One will not be able to say that the Word assumed human nature if he did not assume a body united to a soul."[27]

While his refutation of those Christological theories that allow only a moral or accidental union underscores Aquinas's insistence on the ontological nature of the incarnational "is," he realizes that such an "is," in establishing and upholding the ontological union, must neither substantially alter nor entirely eliminate either the divinity of the Son of God or the authenticity of his humanity. To do so, in so constituting their ontological oneness, would nullify the whole point of their being one; that is, to ensure that it is *truly God* who is man and *truly man* that God is. Thus, against Eutyches, Aquinas protests:

[One cannot] say that the form of God in Christ is corrupted by this union, because thus after the union Christ would not be God. Nor again, can one say that the form of the servant was corrupted in the union, because thus they would not have received the form of the servant. But neither can one say that the form of the servant is mixed thoroughly with the form of God, for things mixed thoroughly do not retain their integrity ... If a mixture were to come into being, neither nature would be preserved ... but some third.[28]

Aquinas realized that the incarnational "becoming" cannot be the ontological or substantial union of natures, for such a union would suppress the distinctiveness of each nature, giving rise to a *tertium quid*, a being who would be neither truly God nor truly man.[29]

W. H. Principe, "St. Thomas on the *Habitus*-Theory of the Incarnation," in *St. Thomas Aquinas (1274–1974) Commemorative Studies,* ed. A. A. Maurer (Toronto: Pontifical Institute of Mediaeval Studies, 1974), 1:381–418; Schoot, *Christ the "Name" of God,* 124–27; J. L. A. West, "Aquinas' Use of Metaphysics: Natura, Suppositum and Esse" (diss., University of Waterloo, 2003).

26. *ScG* IV, ch. 37, 6.

27. Ibid., ch. 37, 4. See also *ST* III, q. 2, a. 5.

28. *ScG* IV, ch. 35, 4. See also ch. 35, 8.

29. See *ST* III, q. 2, a. 1; q. 2, a. 6. Aquinas noted that John the Evangelist excluded a compositional union of natures, which would have given rise to a *tertium quid* by adding "and made his dwelling among us"; that is, "in our nature, yet so as to remain distinct in his own" and thus

While he was aware that the Athanasian Creed stated that as the body and soul form the one reality of man, so the divinity and humanity form the one reality of Jesus, Aquinas was also well aware that this analogy (and it is only an analogy within the Creed) must be properly interpreted. Although the body/soul union may illustrate how two "things" are able to give rise to one ontological reality, the incarnational "becoming" and subsequent union nonetheless cannot be modeled after the relational union that gives rise to a human being.[30] While both the incarnational union and the body/soul union are ontological, giving rise to one supposit or entity, the manner of their so doing is entirely different. For Aquinas, as a model there is no similarity (*quantum ad hoc non attenditur similitudo*), for the body/soul union gives rise to a new kind of being, that of a man, whereas in the Incarnation the union of divinity and humanity does not give rise to a new kind of being (a *tertium quid*).[31] Rather, the incarnational union establishes that God is man. If the divinity related to the humanity as the soul related to the body, the divinity would always tend to wash into the humanity, undermining its true authenticity.[32]

"we would not think there was a mingling or transformation of natures in Christ because he had said, 'the Word was made flesh'" (*In Io.* 1:14a [173–74]). Also, in his *Commentary on Philippians*, Aquinas held that the Son did not deprive himself of his divinity in becoming man. "No, because he remained what he was; and what he was not, he assumed … So he also emptied himself, not by putting off his divine nature, but by assuming a human nature" (*In Phil.* 2:7 [57]; F. R. Larcher and Michael Duffy, *Commentary on Saint Paul's First Letter to the Thessalonians and the Letter to the Philippians* [Albany, NY: Magi, 1969], 80).

30. Many of the Fathers of the Church used the soul/body union not only as an analogy for illustrating the ontological oneness of Christ, but also as an exact model for conceiving how the divinity and the humanity were united in Christ. Such modeling always gave rise to Christological heresy, such as in Apollinarius. See T. G. Weinandy, "The Soul/Body Analogy and the Incarnation: Cyril of Alexandria," *Coptic Church Review* 17 (1996): 59–66 (chap. 6 in this volume); *Does God Suffer?* (Edinburgh: T&T Clark, 2000), 182–90.

31. *ST* III, q. 2, a. 1, ad 2. See also *ScG* IV, ch. 41, 10. Here Aquinas states that, while the soul/body cannot be used as a model for the Incarnation because it gives rise to a new nature, he kindly interprets the "ancient Doctors, who held that the human nature in Christ was 'a kind of organ of the divinity,' just as the body is held to be an organ of the soul." Nonetheless, in *De Unione Verbi Incarnati* 1, he noted that such an interpretation cannot be taken literally "because the union of an instrument is accidental." Translation taken from J. L. A. West, "The Aquinas Translation Project," DeSales University, http://www4.desales.edu/~philtheo/loughlin/ATP/, accessed August 30, 2013. For Aquinas's understanding of the soul/body model in relation to the Incarnation, see M.-V. Leroy, "L'union selon l'hypostase d'après saint Thomas d'Aquin," *Revue Thomiste* 74, no. 2 (1974): 220–24.

32. See the whole of *ST* III, q. 2, q. 1, as well as III *Sent.* 5, 1, 2; *ScG* IV, ch. 35, 9; ch. 41, 2 and 4; *De Unione* 1 and ad 1.

If the above refutation of Christological errors demonstrates how the incarnational "becoming" and its ensuing incarnational "is" is not to be understood, how are they to be understood? This takes us to an examination of Aquinas's positive exposition of the Incarnation.

The Truth of the Catholic Faith: The Son Subsists as Man

Believing it not to be an opinion but "an article of the Catholic faith," Aquinas endorsed the "subsistence theory" of the Incarnation.[33] This conception maintains that "in Christ there is a perfect divine nature and a perfect human nature, ... and that these two natures are united in Christ not by indwelling only, nor in an accidental mode, ... but in one hypostasis and one supposit."[34] While he is here upholding the authenticity of each nature, Aquinas is also designating a twofold oneness in Christ. He is confirming that Christ is one ontological reality/supposit, and the one ontological reality/supposit that Christ is is the one person/hypostasis of the Son existing as man.[35] Aquinas declares that "only in this way can we save what the Scriptures hand on about the Incarnation." Significantly, Aquinas grasped that subsistence theory alone ensures the scriptural employment of the Communication of Idioms; that is, that divine and human attributes are predicated of one and the same person.[36]

The Communication of Idioms, as witnessed from Ignatius of Antioch to Cyril of Alexandria and the Council of Chalcedon, was traditionally both the litmus test for Christological orthodoxy and the catalyst for properly conceiving and articulating that orthodoxy.[37] For Aquinas, the Communication of Idioms is at the heart of the scriptural proclamation because it embodies and expresses all three incarnational truths, especially in accen-

33. *ST* III, q. 2, a. 6. See also *Comp. Theol.* 209.
34. *ScG* IV, ch. 39, 1.
35. Aquinas stated that Christ is two "in the neuter," in that he exists in two natures, but that he is only one in the masculine, in that he is the one Son (see III *Sent.* 6, 2, 1 and *De Unione* 3). In his *Quodlibetal* questions, Aquinas stated that while the two natures must be maintained and even that the "human nature in Christ is a certain individual or singular or particular," it is nonetheless "necessary to posit one person, so also one hypostasis, one suppositum and one thing of two natures" (*Quodl.* 9, 2, 1[2]). Translation taken from West, "The Aquinas Translation Project." See also *Comp. Theol.* 210–12.
36. See *ScG* IV, ch. 39, 1.
37. See Weinandy, *Does God Suffer?*, 172–77.

tuating the incarnational "is." Only if the Son of God *is* man can divine and human attributes be predicated of the one and the same person of the Son. While the Catholic faith demands this understanding of the Incarnation, and Aquinas wished to endorse such an understanding, how did he conceive and articulate such an understanding?

In harmony with the church's Christological tradition, Aquinas understood that the incarnational "becoming" was the uniting of the humanity to the person or hypostasis of the Word.

The Word of God from all eternity had complete being (*esse completum*) in hypostasis or person; while in time the human nature accrued to it, not as if it were assumed unto one being (inasmuch as this is of the nature [*non quasi assumpta ad unum esse prout est naturae*] even as the body is assumed to the being of the soul), but to one being inasmuch as this is of the hypostasis or person [*sed ad unum esse prout est hypostasis vel personae*]). Hence the human nature is not accidentally united to the Son of God.[38]

While the incarnational union was not a compositional union of natures, which would suppress them, the union does bring about "one being" in that the human nature is ontologically united to the person of the Son, so that the one reality of the Son incarnate comes to be.

Since the human nature is united to the Son of God, hypostatically or personally . . . and not accidentally, it follows that by the human nature there accrued to him no new personal being (*esse personale*), but only a new relationship of the pre-existing personal being (*esse personale*) to the human nature, in such a way that the Person is said to subsist not merely in the divine but also in the human nature.[39]

---

38. *ST* III, q. 2, a. 6, ad 2.

39. Ibid., q. 17, a. 2. See also *ScG* IV, ch. 49, 16; III *Sent.* 5, 1, 3; *In Phil.* 2:7–8 [57–61]; Larcher and Duffy, *Commentary on Saint Paul's First Letter*, 80–81. As the above quotations exemplify, Aquinas insisted that the union between the divine and human natures was not accidental—that is, a moral union such as through indwelling. Some medieval Scholastics wanted to see the human nature as an accident within the divinity of the Son. As whiteness would inhere in the substance of a man, so the humanity would inhere and so exist within the divinity of the Son. But for the humanity to be an accident in this sense would be a form of Monophysitism, for the humanity is now not united to the person of the Son but actually subsumed within the divine nature itself. Aquinas clearly recognized this distinction when he wrote: "Now, the things which accrue to one having a nature, but do not belong to the integrity of that nature, seem either to be accidents—say whiteness and music; or to stand in an accidental relation—say, a ring, a garment, a house, and the like." Neither are in accord with the Incarnation, for "God is not susceptible to an accident; and because human nature, being in the genus of

In uniting the human nature to the person of the Son, the Son did not become a different person ("there accrued to him no new personal being"), for if he did, then it would no longer be the person of Son who existed as man. Rather, the human nature was ontologically united to the Son such that the Son now actually existed as man.

> The mystery of the Incarnation was not completed through God being changed in any way from the immutable state in which he had been from all eternity, but through his having united himself to the creature in a new way or rather through his having united it to himself.[40]

To grasp Aquinas's incarnational notion of "become" with its ensuing incarnational "is," it is necessary to perceive the significance of his use of *esse personale* and his emphasis that the human nature is united to the Son rather than vice versa. Relationships are established between human beings by some mediating act that unites them—hugs, kisses, sexual relations. The incarnational act, the "becoming," is not the uniting of the human nature to the very person of the Son by some mediating act. Instead, the incarnational act, the "becoming," is the uniting of the human nature immediately, and so unmediatedly, to the Son as the Son actually personally exists in his *esse personale*. While the Son does not accrue any new personal being, any new *esse personale* that would establish him as a different person, he does acquire a new mode of existing—that is, as man—which is achieved only because the humanity is ontologically united to him as he actually exists personally as God. Aquinas's use of the *esse personale* thus accentuates and establishes the three incarnational truths.

First, uniting human nature to the Son as the Son is in his *esse personale* and establishes the singular ontological depth of the incarnational "becom-

---

substance, cannot be the accident of anything," and an accidental union cannot account for the Son actually existing as man (*ScG* IV, ch. 41, 5). R. Cross makes much of some of the scholastics seeing the humanity as an accident within the divinity. *The Metaphysics of the Incarnation: Thomas Aquinas to Duns Scotus* (Oxford: Oxford University Press, 2002). See also M.-V. Leroy, "L'union selon l'hypostase d'après saint Thomas d'Aquin," *Revue Thomiste* 74, no. 2 (1974): 218–19.

40. *ST* III, q. 1, a. 1, ad 1. I have argued at length that historically, both within the Fathers and Aquinas, that the immutability of the Son as divine was defended not merely to protect the divinity of the Son insofar as he is God, but also for the sake of the Incarnation. If he changes in becoming man, then it is no longer the Son who is man. *Does God Change? The Word's Becoming in the Incarnation* (Petersham, MA: St. Bede's Press, 1985), 33–100.

ing," so that it terminates in the truth that the Son *is* man.[41] Second, such a union guarantees that it is actually *the Son* who is man, since the humanity is ontologically united to the Son as the Son actually exists personally as God, without any change in his *esse personale*. Third, such a union equally guarantees that it is actually *man* that the Son is, since human nature is ontologically united to the Son as the Son exists in his *esse personale*. To state this all succinctly: the human nature in being ontologically united to the person of the Son in his *esse personale* confirms simultaneously that the Son *truly is* man—it is *truly the Son* who is man and *truly man* that the Son is.[42]

The Incarnation: A Mixed Relation

Aquinas gives his understanding of the incarnational "becoming" with its terminating incarnational "is" greater depth, though at times not without some ambiguity, when he places these within the context of a "relationship." While "become" normally implies change in the one who "becomes," Aquinas believes that this is not the case within the Incarnation.

The union of which we are speaking is a relation that we consider between the divine and the human nature, inasmuch as they come together in one person of the Son of God. As mentioned above, every relation that we consider between God and the creature is really in the creature, by whose change the relation is brought into being, whereas it is not really in God, but only in our way of thinking, since it does not arise from any change in God. And hence we must say that the union of which we are speaking is not really in God, except only in our way of thinking, but in the human nature, which is a creature, it is really.[43]

41. Aquinas grasped the difference between what I am referring to as the incarnational "becoming" and the incarnational "is" when he differentiates between "assumption" and "union." "Union implies the relation; whereas assumption implies the action, whereby someone is said to assume, or the passion, whereby something is said to be assumed" (*ST* III, q. 2, a. 8). Aquinas argues that the union between the Son and his humanity is the greatest of all unions, even greater than that between the body and soul within human beings. It is even in one sense greater than that between the divine persons within the one nature of God. While the divine persons are the one God, the Son is not the Father or vice versa; in the Incarnation the Son simply is man and so one supposit. See *ST* III, q. 2, a. 9. See also Ruello, *La Christologie de Thomas D'Aquin*, 202–3.

42. See *ST* III, q. 2, a. 2.

43. Ibid., q. 2, a. 7.

Aquinas further attempts to clarify this understanding in his first reply: "The Union is not really in God, but in our way of thinking, for God is said to be united to a creature inasmuch as the creature is really united to God without any change in him."[44] Later in the *Summa Theologiae* Aquinas again states:

Whatever is predicated relatively (by way of relation) can be newly predicated of something without its being changed, as a man may be made to be on the right side without being changed, and merely by the change of him on whose left side he was. Hence in such uses, not all that is said to be made is changed, since it may happen by the change of something else ... Now to be man belongs to God by reason of union, which is a relation. And hence to be man is newly predicated of God without any change in him, but by a change in the human nature, which is assumed to a divine person. And hence when it is said, "God was made man," we understand no change on the part of God, but only on the part of the human nature.[45]

While I have written extensively already on Aquinas's notion of "relation" with regard to the Incarnation, it is necessary that I summarize my understanding here not only because it is pertinent to the present discussion, but also because it has been the subject of much misunderstanding and criticism from within the theological community.[46]

The common criticism leveled against Aquinas's position is that such an understanding of relations denies that God is actually related to the world at all, and specifically, within the Incarnation, denies that the Son is related to his humanity and so is not actually incarnate. He may seem to be related to our way of thinking, but in actuality he is not. Is this criticism valid?

For Aquinas, relations are of three types. The terms of a relationship can be related logically or really, or their relationship can be logical in one term and real in the other. This latter type of relationship is often referred to as a mixed relation. Logical relations (*rationis relatio*) or relations according to reason (*secundum rationem*) are relations "in idea only, as when mutual order or habitude can only be between things in the apprehension of reason."[47] Logical relations then are established by the mind and its under-

44. Ibid., q. 2, a. 7, ad 1. See also III *Sent.* 2, 2, 2, 3, ad 2 and 5, 1, 1, 1.

45. *ST* III, q. 16, a. 6, ad 2. See also *In Io.* 1:14a [172].

46. See Weinandy, *Does God Change?*, 88–98; *Does God Suffer?*, 127–43, 206–8.

47. *ST* I, q. 13, a. 7. See A. Krempel, *La Doctrine de la Relation chez Saint Thomas* (Paris: Vrin, 1952); M. Henninger, *Relations: Medieval Theories 1250–1325* (Oxford: Clarendon Press,

standing of the terms, such as the relating of "Fido" to the "canine species." When such terms are related by the mind, there is obviously no change within either of the terms related. Real relations are those in which there is something in the terms themselves that causes the relationship. One person can be relatively taller than another because they have height in common. Or, more commonly understood, some action between the terms causes them to be related. A man becomes a husband because he marries a woman (and so becomes related to her), who in turn becomes his wife. Real relations established by actions on the part of both of the terms bring about a change within the terms related.[48]

Besides these mutually logical and real relations, there can be relations that are real in one term and logical in the other, and "this happens whenever two extremes are not in the same order."[49] By "order" Aquinas means ontological order, and so mixed relations would be those between Creator and creature, knower and known, and the divinity and humanity within the Incarnation. In this type of relationship the Creator, the known, and the divinity are the logical terms of the relationship and as such they do not change. The creature, the knower, and the humanity are the real terms of the relationship and so do change. On a number of occasions Aquinas gives the example of being on the right or the left of a column. For a man to move from the right to the left of the column brings about only a change in himself, and so the relationship is real in him. But the column is only related to the man logically and so remains unchanged by the man's movement. This example has caused a great deal of confusion and misunderstanding, since it implies that God as Creator and the Son within the Incarnation are like the column, which has no actual relationship to the man. This example merely portrays an illustrative similarity to a real mixed relation, since such a relation only truly exists between terms of different ontological orders. Aquinas wished merely to illustrate how one term (the "logical" term) can be related to the real term only because the latter is related to the former, which is thus how and why the logical term remains unchanged. In an authentic

---

1989), 13–39; E. Muller, "Real Relations and the Divine Issues in Thomas's Understanding of God's Relation to the World," *Theological Studies* 56 (1995): 673–95; Schoot, *Christ the "Name" of God*, 133–44.

48. See *ST* I, q. 13, a. 7.

49. Ibid.

mixed relation the logical term (God as Creator and the Son as man) is in an entirely different situation.

How does Aquinas conceive the Incarnation as a mixed relation? I emphasized above that Aquinas saw the incarnational "becoming" as the uniting of the humanity to the Son of God in such a manner that it terminated in the incarnational "is"; that is, the Son actually came to subsist as man. Placed now within the context of a mixed relation, we can grasp more clearly the exact nature of that incarnational "becoming" with its resulting incarnational "is." The real effect in the humanity is both that it comes to be and is ontologically united, simultaneous to its coming to be, to the Son of God, so that the humanity only is/exists as united ontologically to the Son. "From the moment of conception the human nature was united to the Word of God."[50] For Aquinas the actual effect of the humanity coming to be and being really related to the Son is a created effect, and thus the union itself is a created union.[51]

It is here as well that we see why, for Aquinas, the humanity is a real substance, but not a separate supposit that would constitute a distinct human person, a human "who." The humanity comes to be and so there is a true man, but since that humanity is simultaneously united to the person of the Son when it comes to be, it is the person of the Son who is this man.[52] "The human nature in Christ, although it is a particular substance, nevertheless cannot be called a hypostasis or suppositum, seeing that it is in union with a completed thing, viz. the whole Christ, as he is God and man. But the completed being with which it concurs is said to be a hypostasis or suppositum."[53] For Aquinas this in no way undermines the integrity of the humanity. "The human nature of Christ has a greater dignity than ours, from this very fact that in us, being existent by itself, it has its own personality, but in Christ it exists in the person of the Word."[54] This does not mean that Christ does not have his own personality in the sense of his own human distinctiveness and singularity. "Its proper personality is not wanting to the nature assumed through the loss of anything pertaining to the perfection of the human nature but through the addition of something which is above

50. *ScG* IV, ch. 43, 4.   51. See *ST* III, q. 2, a. 7; q. 2, a. 10.
52. Ibid., q. 2, a. 5.
53. Ibid., q. 2, a. 3, ad 2; see also *ScG* IV, ch. 49, 11.
54. *ST* III, q. 2, a. 2, ad 2.

human nature, viz. the union with a divine person."[55] This is all well summarized:

since the human nature in Christ does not subsist separately through itself but exists in another, i.e. in the hypostasis of the Word (indeed not as an accident in a subject, nor properly as a part in a whole, but through an ineffable assumption), thus the human nature in Christ can indeed be called some individual or particular or singular, yet it cannot be called a hypostasis or suppositum, just as it cannot be called a person. Hence, it remains that in Christ there is only one hypostasis or suppositum, namely the divine Word.[56]

By conceiving the Son as the logical term of the incarnational relation, Aquinas specifies the ontological intimacy of the union and the depth of the real effect in the Son's humanity. The humanity is ontologically united to the Son as the Son actually exists as God in his *esse personale* and not by some mediating act. This ensures that it is truly the Son *as God* who is man. Equally, the created relational effect in the humanity is not "ordained to (another) act, but to the personal being (*ad esse personale*)" of the Word.[57] The created relational effect within the humanity is that it comes to be and is ontologically united ("ordered") to the Son as the Son exists as God in his *esse personale*, which ensures that it is *as man* that the Son actually now exists. "The grace of union is the personal being itself (*ipsum esse personale*) that is given gratis from above to the human nature in the person of the Word, and is the term of the assumption."[58] The Son of God gave himself as he is in himself (in his *esse personale*) to his humanity by uniting the humanity to himself as he is in himself (in his *esse personale*). The terminal, created effect of such a relationship is that the Son now exists as man.[59]

55. Ibid., q. 4, a. 2, ad 2.   56. *De Unione* 2.
57. *ST* III, q. 8, a. 5, ad 3.   58. Ibid., q. 6, a. 6.
59. Ibid., q. 3, a. 1. I have argued elsewhere that, because both the one God is conceived as pure act and the persons of the Trinity are conceived as subsistent relations fully in act, they must be placed within the rubric not of nouns but of verbs. It is only because God is pure act (*actus purus*) and equally the persons of the Trinity as subsistent relations fully in act (and so verbs) that they are able to unite something to themselves as they are in themselves. Because the Son as God in his *esse personale* is a subsistent relation fully in act, he does not have any self-constituting relational potential to enact in order to establish further relations. Being fully relational in himself when, in the Incarnation, the humanity is ontologically united/related to him, by the power of the Holy Spirit, it is united to him as he actually is as Son and so he is able actually to exist as man. Thus it is the Son's immutable and unchangeable actuality as a person

We are now in a position to grasp clearly what Aquinas means when he says that the Son is the logical term of the incarnational relationship. Equally, it is now clear what he means when he states that "union is not really in God, but only in our way of thinking, for God is said to be united to a creature inasmuch as the creature is really united to God without any change in him."[60] Aquinas means neither that the Son is not actually related to the humanity and thus is not actually man, nor that he is only conceived to be related by our way of thinking but actually is not. With such a criticism in mind Aquinas states, "It cannot be said, however, that these relations exist as realities outside God."[61] What Aquinas does mean is that the Son is understood to be related, and is actually and authentically related, not by some effect or change in him, but because the humanity is really related to him as he actually exists as God. It is because the humanity is really related to the Son, as the Son is, that the Son becomes and is man, and we thus understand him in a new way—as man.[62]

It should also be noted that in placing the incarnational union within the context of a mixed relation, Aquinas has allowed us to perceive more clearly the astounding implications of the Communication of Idioms. Since human nature is really related ontologically to the Son as the Son exists in

---

(a subsistent relation) fully in act that enables him to establish an incarnational relationship. Far from being a detriment to the Incarnation, immutability, as Aquinas well knew, is an absolute prerequisite for allowing, empowering, and warranting the incarnational "becoming" with its consequent incarnational "is." See Weinandy, *Does God Change?*, 88–96; *Does God Suffer?*, 113–46, 206–8.

60. *ST* III, q. 2, a. 7, ad 1.

61. *ScG* II, ch. 13, 1. See also *ST* I, q. 13, a. 7, obj. 5, where Aquinas gives this interpretation as an objection to his own position. See also *De Ver.* 3, 2, obj. 8. Part of the difficulty lies in Aquinas's ambiguous use of the expressions "logical term" and "logical relation." I have dealt with this issue elsewhere. See *Does God Change?*, 94–95.

62. Aquinas confirms this in his understanding of the term "Lord" when applied to God. "Since God is related to the creature for the reason that the creature is related to him; and since the relation is real in the creature, it follows that God is Lord (and thus Creator also) not in idea only, but in reality, for he is called Lord according to the manner in which the creature is subject to him" (*ST* I, q. 13, a. 7, ad 5). See also *ScG* II, ch. 11, 2. For a similar explanation, see D. Burrell, *Aquinas: God and Action* (Notre Dame, IN: Notre Dame University Press, 1979), 84–87. What Aquinas forgot in his use of Aristotelian terminology is that Aristotle never had to deal with the Creator/creature relationship nor with the Incarnation, and so he seems unaware of how radically he had altered Aristotle's understanding of relations. For a discussion of this in relation to Mary being truly the Son of God's mother, see P. J. Bearsley, "Jesus the Son of Mary According to St Thomas Aquinas," *Angelicum* 55 (1978): 104–23.

his *esse personale*, it was truly the Son, in the fullness of his divinity, who was born, suffered, died, and rose from the dead. In addition, because it is an authentic human nature that is ontologically united to the Son, it is truly human birth, suffering, death, and resurrection that the Son experienced. This, for Aquinas, is what Christological logic demands when confronted with the marvelous and awesome mystery of the Incarnation.[63]

The Son's Uncreated *Esse* and Created *Esse*

Having clarified Aquinas's conception of the Incarnation as a mixed relation and demonstrated its importance, I turn to the controversial question of how many *esses* Aquinas envisaged in Christ. Does Aquinas hold that in

---

63. For a good discussion of Aquinas's understanding of the Communication of Idioms, see Schoot, *Christ the "Name" of God*, 147–52. A number authors have been critical of Aquinas's understanding of the Communication of Idioms. See A. Bäck, "Aquinas on the Incarnation," *New Scholasticism* 56, no. 2 (1982): 127–47; R. Cross, "A Recent Contribution on the Distinction between Monophysitism and Chalcedonianism," *Thomist* 65, no. 3 (2001): 361–83; *Metaphysics of the Incarnation*, 184–205; T. V. Morris, "St. Thomas on the Identity and Unity of the Person of Christ: A Problem of Reference in Christological Discourse," *Scottish Journal of Theology* 35 (1982): 419–30. I do not believe that the authors of these critiques properly grasp the ontological nature of the incarnational "is." For my critique of Cross, see my review of his book in *Thomist* 66, no. 4 (2002): 637–43.

While the traditional understanding of the Communication of Idioms has been severely criticized by many contemporary theologians because it does not allow for the Son to suffer as God, I have argued that what is soteriologically essential is not that the Son suffer as God, and so experience human suffering and even death in a divine manner, but rather that the Son experience suffering and death in a human manner as man. *Does God Suffer?*, 199–208.

While E. Stump wishes to defend Aquinas's understanding of the Communication of Idioms, she does not do so in a satisfactory manner. She speaks of Christ "borrowing properties" from each of his natures. "So, for example, Christ is limited in power and not limited in power, but he borrows the first attribute from his human nature and the second from his divine nature … Because the incompatible properties are borrowed properties, Christ does not have them in the same respect." "Aquinas' Metaphysics of the Incarnation," in *The Incarnation*, ed. S. Davis, D. Kendall, and G. O'Collins (Oxford: Oxford University Press, 2002), 214. As with the above authors, Stump does not grasp the nature of the incarnational "is." The term "Christ" (in a manner reminiscent of Nestorius) does not denote a "someone" apart from his divine and human natures and from which he "borrows" various divine and human attributes. Christ *is* the divine Son of God *existing* as man, and therefore to speak of various divine and human attributes as "borrowed" makes no sense. One does not "borrow" what one *is*. The Son of God *is* omniscient as God and the Son of God *is* ignorant as man. The omniscience and ignorance are intrinsic to what the Son of God *is*, that is, God and man.

Christ there is only one *esse*, the divine *esse personale* of the Son, or does he also allow that there is a created *esse*?

In four works Aquinas stated that there is only one *esse* in Christ. In his *Commentary on the Sentences* he wrote: "Of one thing there is only one being (*esse*). But Christ is one thing (*unum*), as was said. Therefore, he has only one being (*Ergo habet unum esse tantum*)."[64] In his *Quodlibetal Questions* Aquinas also stated:

Since we only posit one subsisting thing (*unam rem subsistentem tantum*), to whose completeness his humanity accompanies, since there is one suppositum of both natures, thus we must say that the substantial being (*esse substantiale*) which is properly attributed to the suppositum, is only one in Christ.[65]

In his *Compendium Theologiae*, Aquinas equally argued: "If we therefore consider Christ himself as a certain integral suppositum of two natures (*ut quoddam integrum suppositum duarum naturarum*), then there was only one *esse*, just as there is one suppositum."[66] Finally, in his *Summa Theologiae*, Aquinas also stated: "The being (*esse*) which belongs to the very hypostasis or person in itself cannot possibly be multiplied in one hypostasis or person, since it is impossible that there should not be one being for one thing (*quia impossibile est quod unius rei non sit unum esse*)."[67]

In his work *De Unione Verbi Incarnati* Aquinas, in considering once again whether "there is only one being (*esse*) in Christ," argued in a similar manner that because Christ "is one simply (*unum simpliciter*) … therefore, there is only one being in him (*ergo in eo est unum esse*)." He also stated, however, in what may appear to be a contradiction to the above, that

there is also another being (*aliud esse*) of this suppositum, not insofar as it is eternal, but insofar as it became a man in time. That being (*esse*), even if it is not an accidental being, because man is not accidentally predicated of the Son of God, … nevertheless, it is not the principle being of its suppositum, but [its] secondary [being] (*non tamen est esse principale sui suppositi, sed secundarium*).[68]

64. III *Sent.* 6, 2, 3. Translation taken from West, "The Aquinas Translation Project."

65. *Quodl.* 9, 2, 2(3).

66. *Comp. Theol.* I, 212.

67. *ST* III, q. 17, a. 2.

68. *De Unione* 4. There is some debate over the dating of *De Unione Verbi Incarnati*. Most scholars place it between 1271 and 1272 and thus just prior to Aquinas's writing of the *tertium pars* of the *Summa Theologiae*. See B. Davies, *Aquinas* (London: Continuum, 2002), 193–95;

As to what Aquinas actually held, scholars fall on both sides of the divide with some opting for one *esse* and others for two.[69] Those opting for one *esse* either believe that Aquinas forgot himself for a moment and so formulated an error, or that he flirted with an idea that he ultimately (and swiftly) abandoned in favor of his first held position, which is more in conformity with his metaphysics in general and his overall Christology in particular. But I believe that if Aquinas did hold that Christ possessed only one *esse* and that uncreated, he was a Monophysite.[70]

Those who advocate for two *esses* believe Aquinas stated something new that is compatible with his previous position of one *esse*. But they are not sure why he did not articulate it before, or why he did not continue to acknowledge it later in his *Summa Theologiae*. I believe that Aquinas implicitly held two *esses* from the start (and so was never a Monophysite), but only explicitly stated this position on the one occasion in the *De Unione Verbi Incarnati*. I am not absolutely certain as to why, but I think there are two factors. First, he was more concerned with ensuring the ontological oneness of Christ as the Son of God incarnate (in opposition to the Nestorian theories of his day), and therefore accentuated the one *esse* (the incarnational "is") that accounted for this ontological oneness. Second, I think he only gradually came to the realization that his own Christological position de-

---

Torrell, *St. Thomas Aquinas*, 1:205–7, 336–37; West, "Dating the *De Unione*," in "The Aquinas Translation Project."

69. For various historical overviews and positions taken on this issue, see B. Bro, "La notion métaphysique II," 373–74; R. Cross, "Aquinas on Nature, Hypostasis, and the Metaphysics of the Incarnation," *Thomist* 60, no. 2 (1996): 198–202; Cross, *Metaphysics of the Incarnation*, 51–64; H. M. Diepen, "L'existence humaine du Christ," *Revue Thomiste* 58 (1958): 197–213; É. Gilson, "L'*esse* du Verbe Incarné selon Saint Thomas d'Aquin," *Archives d'Histoire Doctrinale et Littéraire du Moyen Age* 35 (1968): 23–37; M.-V. Leroy, "L'union selon l'hypostase d'après saint Thomas d'Aquin," *Revue Thomiste* 74, no. 2 (1974): 231–39; A. Patfoort, *L'unité d'être dans le Christ d'après s. Thomas* (Tournai: Desclée, 1964); Ruello, *La Christologie de Thomas d'Aquin*, 115–19, 317–20, 352–55, 391; Schoot, *Christ the "Name" of God*, 160–64; J.-P. Torrell, "Le thomisme dans le débat christologique contemporain," in *Saint Thomas au XXe siècle: Colloque du centenaire de la "Revue Thomiste"* (Paris: Éditions Saint-Paul, 1994), 382–87; Wéber, *Le Christ selon saint Thomas d'Aquin*, 229–35; J. L. A. West, "Aquinas on the Metaphysics of the *Esse* in Christ," *Thomist,* 66 (2002): 231–50.

70. R. Cross argues that Aquinas is Monophysite because he only allows for one *esse* in Christ and that divine. Cross would be correct if in fact that is what Aquinas held, but he did not. "Aquinas on Nature, Hypostasis and the Metaphysics of the Incarnation," 171–202; *Metaphysics of the Incarnation*, 57–58, 60, 67–69, 80–81.

manded a second created *esse*. Below I demonstrate the validity of these two probabilities.

My position on this issue only becomes clear if it is placed within the context of Aquinas's entire Christology. I have emphasized that Aquinas's Christology is fundamentally a Christology of the incarnational "is." This is clearly witnessed in Aquinas's insistence that the incarnational "becoming" is the bringing into existence and the simultaneous uniting of the humanity to the Son of God as he exists in his divine *esse personale* in such a manner that the Son actually comes *to exist* as man. The termination of the incarnational "becoming" is the truth that the Son of God now *is* man. The placing of this incarnational "is" within the context of a mixed relation was precisely to articulate and so to ensure this. It is this position that Aquinas principally held throughout his theological career. This is why he insisted in all of the above quotations, including the one from *De Unione Verbi Incarnati*, that there is only one *esse* in Christ—that of the *esse personale* of the Son. Jesus is one being/reality and the one being/reality he is is the Son of God incarnate. What establishes the one being/reality of Jesus is *the esse personale* of the Son, for it is by ontologically uniting the humanity to the Son's *esse personale* that the Son actually comes to exists as man and so is man. This position, I believe, demands that Christ also possess a created *esse*.

Aquinas categorically stated that "the being of the human nature is not the being of the divine nature (*esse humanae naturae non est esse divinae*)."[71] If the *esse* of the humanity's existence were the divine uncreated *esse* of the Son, then the humanity would be divinized in an entirely unacceptable and wholly inappropriate manner. The humanity would not be divinized in the sense of it becoming perfectly human within its relationship with the Son and so acquiring divine qualities and virtues in a human manner.[72] Rather, such divinization would demand that the humanity actually be subsumed and so exist within the very divine *esse*, similar to an accident (whiteness) existing within a substance (cat), which would nullify its authentic human genuineness as a distinct substance/nature. We would once more be within the realm of a Monophysite *tertium quid*. Aquinas himself ruled out this

71. *De Unione* 4, ad 1.

72. Aquinas stated: "The flesh is called deified not because it was made the Godhead, but because it was made the flesh of God, and also because it shares more abundantly the gifts of the Godhead from the fact that it was united to the Godhead" (III *Sent.* 5, 1, 2, ad 6).

position: "To be sure, it [human nature] clearly cannot be in the Word as an accident: both because God is not susceptible to an accident; and because human nature, being in the genus of substance, cannot be the accident of anything."[73]

If the Son of God actually did assume the substantial nature of manhood and so come to exist as an authentic man, then the authenticity of that substantial manhood demands a human created esse. As far back as his *Commentary on the Sentences*, Aquinas stated: "The divine nature and the human nature are each a being in act (*divina autem natura et humana est ens actu*)."[74] While the humanity only exists within its ontological union with the Son, thus making Jesus one reality, that humanity's existence is a created act of existence in that it has come to be. The humanity is in act (exists) as a man and thus its act is human. If it did not have a finite created human *esse*, it would simply not be because it, obviously, exists only because it has been created.

I stated above, in the context of the Incarnation being a mixed relation, that the created relational effect within the humanity (what makes it the real term within the relationship) is that it comes to be and simultaneously is ontologically united to the Son as the Son is in his *esse personale* (what makes him the logical term within the relationship). This "created relational effect within the humanity" is the created *esse*, for the created *esse* is simply that the humanity comes to be and is ontologically related/united to the Son, so that the Son actually exists as man. Having articulated the above position within the *Summa Theologiae*, Aquinas himself stated that "since this union has its being nowhere save in a created nature … it follows that it has a created being (*Et quia unio talis non habet esse reale nisi in natura creata, ut dictum est, consequens est quod habeat esse creatum*)."[75] The human nature has a created being because the Son of God unites this created human nature to himself so as to exist as man. This is in complete conformity with what Aquinas states in his *De Unione Verbi Incarnati*.

---

73. *ScG* IV, ch. 41, 5. If the human nature was subsumed into the divine nature, this would also imply that the divine nature became the form of the humanity, similar to the soul being the form of the body. As seen above, however, Aquinas has completely ruled out such a union as incompatible with an authentic understanding of the Incarnation.

74. III *Sent.* 5, 1, 2.

75. *ST* III, q. 2, a. 7, ad 2.

Being (*esse*) belongs to both the subsisting person and to the nature in which the person subsists; in the sense that the person has being (*esse*) according to that nature. Therefore, the being (*esse*) of the person of the incarnate Word is one on the part of the subsisting person, but not on the part of the natures.[76]

Again, what Aquinas is noting is that the Son of God exists as man and therefore, while he is one reality through his one divine *esse personale*, his existence as man demands a human created *esse* because that is the manner in which the Son now also exists. As stated above, "The person has *esse* [that is, the manner of the person's existence] according to the nature." Therefore it is the *esse*/existence of the human nature that determines that the Son of God *is man*.

This is why in *De Unione Verbi Incarnati* Aquinas insisted that the created *esse* is neither an "accidental being (*esse accidentale*)" nor a "principle being (*esse principale*)," but a secondary being (*secundarium esse*). The created *esse* is more than accidental because the humanity is an authentic substance in its own right (manhood), and thus it possesses its own integral created human *esse*. But the created human *esse* is not the principle *esse* because the humanity does not exist independently of the Son as a separate supposit/reality. Aquinas's use of *secundarium* in reference to the created *esse* is an attempt at saying both what it is not—neither an accidental *esse* nor a principal *esse*, and also positively what it is—a substantial *esse* that is such only in that it is in ontological union with the Son. What should now be obvious is that Aquinas is ardently striving to conceive and to articulate a specific type of *esse* that is unique—a "one-off"—for the Incarnation is a singular event that demands metaphysical distinctions that apply solely to this one particular occurrence. For Aquinas it is all part of the marvel of the incarnational mystery, the marvel of the incarnational "is."

The above argument can even be discerned within the *Summa Theologiae*. On the one hand, Aquinas states: "The eternal being (*esse aeternum*) of the Son of God, which is the divine nature, becomes the being of man (*fit esse hominis*), inasmuch as the human nature is assumed by the Son of God to unity of person."[77] This passage might appear to contradict what Aquinas said above in *De Unione Verbi Incarnati*, that the being of the human nature

76. *De Unione* 1, ad 10. See also III *Sent.* 6, 2, 3.
77. *ST* III, q. 17, a. 2, ad 2.

is not the being of the divine nature. What Aquinas is saying here, on the other hand, is that the human nature exists only because it is assumed by the Son of God, and in this sense its created being (*esse*) is dependent upon the eternal being of the Son. In his fourth reply in the same article, Aquinas is clear:

> In Christ the soul gives being to the body (*anima in Christo dat esse corpori*), inasmuch as it makes it actually animated, which is to give it the complement of its nature and species. But if we consider the body perfected by the soul, without the hypostasis having both—this whole, composed of soul and body, as signified by the word *humanity*, does not signify *what is*, but *whereby it is*. Hence being belongs to the subsisting person, inasmuch as it has a relation to such a nature, and of this relation the soul is the cause, inasmuch as it perfects human nature by informing it.[78]

While the soul and body only exist in relation to the Son, the soul is the human animating principle, for without this "created soul/*esse*" the Son would not be authentically human. It is only this authentic humanity, to which the soul gives being, *whereby* the Son actually exists as man and so is one supposit or reality—that of the Son incarnate.[79]

Conclusion

In concluding this essay I want to end as I began. For Aquinas, the Incarnation is the most marvelous of all mysteries precisely because of the incar-

---

78. Ibid., q. 17, a. 2, ad 4. See also III *Sent.* 6, 2, 3, ad 1.

79. A similar form of the argument can be established with regard to the grace of union. The grace of union is the free bestowal of the Son's self/person upon the humanity so that the Son comes to exist as man. Thus it is the grace of union by which Christ is one reality/supposit—the Son incarnate. But there needs be an authentic humanity upon which the Son is able to freely bestow himself in such an intimate and personal manner so as to exist as man. The grace of union, that bestowal by which the Son freely becomes ontologically united to the humanity so as to exist as man, is accomplished by bringing the humanity into existence as an authentic existing humanity with its own human act of existence and simultaneously uniting it to the Son so that he now truly is a man. See *ST* III, q. 2, a. 10, ad 2; III, q. 6, a. 6, ad 1; *De Ver.* 29, 2; *Quodl.* 9, 2, ad 3.

I believe that my above position is similar to M. de la Taille's notion of "created actuation by uncreated act." The humanity comes into existence and so is actuated, possessing then a created act, because of its incarnational relation to the Son's uncreated act. "Actuation créée par Acte incréé, lumière de gloire, grâce sanctifiante, union hypostatique," *Revue des Sciences Religieuses* 18 (1928): 253–68.

national "is." Jesus is the Son of God existing as man. We have examined Aquinas's understanding of the incarnational "becoming" with its resulting incarnational "is," bringing some clarity and insight into Aquinas's Christology. While we have examined closely Aquinas's notion of the incarnational "is" as it pertains to his understanding of the hypostatic union, the Incarnation as a mixed relation, and the relationship between the Son's divine *esse* and his human created *esse*, we still do not actually know the "essence" of that incarnational "is."

It is not surprising that, when reading Aquinas on the Incarnation, one constantly stumbles across phrases such as the human nature was united to the Son *"in such a way* that person is said to subsist" as man.[80] Or he can speak of "the *uniqueness* of the union in Christ."[81] The humanity is united to the Son "in an *ineffable* way"[82] (emphasis mine in all the above quotations). Finally, for Aquinas, there is no adequate example found among creatures to compare with the Incarnation.[83] While we can say to some extent what the incarnational "is" is and is not, it remains a unique and ineffable mystery. The best we can do is state in faith that the Son of God is united to his humanity "in such a way" that he actually did come to exist as man, even though we do not fully grasp what "in such a way" means. For Aquinas, the Incarnation will always remain a mystery and so a marvel. The mystery and the marvel of the Son of God incarnate will even be the heart of our heavenly life, for only in union with the risen incarnate Christ, having been conformed into his perfect likeness by the indwelling Spirit, will we behold the glory of the Father.

80. *ST* III, q. 17, a. 2.
82. *De Unione* 2, ad 15.

81. *In Io.* 1:14a [169].
83. See *De Unione* 1.

9
Walter Cardinal Kasper
The Mystery of Jesus Christ

I first read Walter Cardinal Kasper's book *Jesus the Christ* when it was published in English in 1976.[1] Since then I have had occasion to refer to it in the course of my teaching and writing. It was not until being asked to contribute to his *Festschriften* in 2013 that I read it in its entirety once again. While it shows signs of the theological age in which it was first written, it has lost little of its original Christological importance. Being a systematic and historical theologian, I want to discuss part III of *Jesus the Christ*, where Kasper takes up the systematic and doctrinal concerns of "The Mystery of Jesus Christ." I do this in light of my own work in Christology and also in light of contemporary Christological issues.

Three Incarnational Truths

Part III of *Jesus the Christ* is divided into three chapters. Each chapter focuses on one of the three incarnational or Christological truths that arise out of Scripture and are enshrined in the subsequent conciliar and dogmatic tradition. These three truths must be clearly understood and properly articulated if

Originally published as "Das Geheimnis Jesu Christi: Gedanken zur Christologie Walter Kaspers" [Walter Cardinal Kasper: The Mystery of Jesus Christ], in *Mein Herr und mein Gott: Christus bekennen und verkünden*, ed. G. Augustin, K. Krämer, and M. Schulze (Freiburg: Herder, 2013), 294–303. © Verlag Herder GmbH, Freiburg im Breisgau 2013.

1. Walter Kasper, *Jesus the Christ* (New York: Paulist Press, 1976). Hereafter references to this volume will be placed within the body of this text.

one is to give authentic expression to the truth of the Incarnation; that is, who Jesus genuinely is. The first chapter, "Jesus Christ: Son of God," examines the incarnational truth that Jesus is *truly God*. The second chapter, "Jesus Christ: Son of Man," considers the incarnational truth that Jesus must be *truly man*. The third chapter, "Jesus Christ: Mediator between God and Man," addresses the incarnational truth that Jesus as the Son of God must *truly be* man.

Kasper realizes that only if Jesus is truly the divine Son of God, *homoousion* with the Father, is his genuine self-revelation as portrayed in the Gospels and faithfully professed by the apostolic Church authentically preserved. Moreover, Kasper recognizes that there is no value in maintaining the full divinity of the Son of God if that divine Son did not actually become truly and fully man. From a biblical and theological perspective, the Christological significance of Jesus's divinity is founded upon his full humanity, and the Christological significance of his humanity is founded upon his full divinity. It is of no Christological value for Jesus to be fully divine if he is not equally fully human, and it is of no Christological significance for Jesus to be fully man if he is not equally fully divine.

In keeping with the three incarnational truths, Kasper lastly affirms that the Son of God must *truly be* man. To be faithful to revelation and the received Christological tradition no form of Adoptionism will suffice, for such an understanding denies that Jesus is ontologically one being or reality. The one being or reality that Jesus must be is the Son of God ontologically existing as man. The incarnational "becoming" must terminate in an incarnational "is." Likewise, the incarnational "becoming" cannot be such that it would destroy or jeopardize the full divinity or the authentic humanity of Jesus. The divinity and humanity cannot be ontologically united, as in Monophysitism, in such a manner so as to form some *tertium quid* being that is neither fully God nor fully man. The incarnational becoming must be such that it not only terminates with the Son of God actually existing as man, but it also must do so in a manner that confirms that the person of the Son authentically exists both as God and as man. For Kasper, to perceive correctly in faith and to articulate that faith in an authentic manner Christology must ultimately ensure that it is truly *the Son of God* who truly *is* truly *man*.[2]

---

2. I treat these three incarnational truths at greater length in *Jesus the Christ* (Huntington, IN: Our Sunday Visitor Press, 2003), 54–79, and "Aquinas: God *IS* Man, The Marvel of the

Each of the three chapters in part III of Kasper's book affirms, defends, and fosters these three incarnational truths.

Jesus Christ: Son of God

In the first chapter of part III of his book, Kasper argues for the full divinity of Jesus, and he rightly does so within a soteriological context. He notes that the New Testament, while attributing to Jesus many titles, accentuates one—Jesus is the Son of God. Kasper claims that this designation is "the distinguishing mark of Christianity" (163). Other religions may speak of sons of gods and incarnations; however, the ultimate soteriological significance of such a title for Christianity is that, in proclaiming Jesus to be the Son of God, it is making an eschatological claim. It is professing "that in Jesus of Nazareth God revealed and communicated himself once and for all, uniquely, unmistakably, definitively and unsurpassably ... Christian faith stands or falls with the confession of Jesus as the Son of God" (163).[3]

Kasper perceives insightfully that Jesus reveals himself to be the divine Son of God not so much by affirming what others say of him or by attributing this title to himself. Nor does Jesus reveal his divine identity within some self-conscious understanding of who is as an autonomous and independent self. Jesus realized that he could reveal himself as the divine Son only through his unique relationship to God the Father.[4] Only by speaking and acting in such a manner as to reveal that God is his Father in a singular manner could Jesus reveal to others that he is the unique divine Son of the Father. Kasper sees this in the filial obedience of Jesus to his Father, especially as portrayed in the Gospel of John (see also, e.g., Mk. 14:36; Heb. 5:7–10). Actually, his "filial obedience" becomes, for Kasper, the hermeneutical principle for discerning Jesus's divine Sonship.

While the Gospel of John "speaks of the divine Sonship of Jesus as ontologically understood," such statements "provide an intrinsic substantiation of

---

Incarnation," in *Aquinas on Doctrine: A Critical Introduction,* ed. T. G. Weinandy, D. Keating, and J. Yocum (London: T&T Clark, 2004), 68–75 (chap. 8 in this volume).

3. When examining the third chapter of part III, I examine more closely how Kasper understands the definitive and universality of Jesus.

4. Actually, as seen below, for Kasper, Jesus could only come to know humanly who he is as the Son through his human relationship with the Father.

the soteriological statements" (166). If statements professing Jesus's ontological status as the Son of God ground the singular significance of his soteriological mission, his absolute soteriological obedience to the Father discloses the ontological status of his divine Sonship. "Thus the Son submits himself completely in obedience to the will of the Father (Jn. 8:29, 14:31). This obedience is the very nature of the Son" (166). This same pattern is also found in the Christological hymn in Philippians. While ontologically the Son was in the form of God, he humbled himself and ontologically came to exist as man. As man, the Son became obedient to his Father and even to death on the Cross (Phil. 2:6–8). It is within this filial obedience that Jesus reveals that he is the divine Son, and the Father confirms this by raising him up and making him Lord of all. For Kasper, it is this unity of Sonship and soteriological mission that founds and so confirms the Christian bestowal of the divine title "Lord" upon Jesus to the glory of God the Father (168–69).[5]

Jesus: Son of Man

In the second chapter of part III, Kasper addresses the issue of Jesus's complete and full humanity. He begins by noting that the Word became flesh in a particular man—Jesus of Nazareth. Thus the truth of the Incarnation "must not be taken to mean that God's Word has made human existence generally a sign and sacrament of salvation, still less entered into the structure of our concrete world, its power and its wealth, endorsing and even

5. When Kasper wrote *Jesus the Christ*, there was much debate and discussion over the distinction between "functional Christology" and "ontological Christology." Often these Christologies were seen in opposition to one another. The Christology of the New Testament was "functional" in that it was more concerned about Jesus's saving mission and his functional relationship to the Father and saving relationship to humanity. Ontological Christology was a later Christological formulization that arose not from the soil of the New Testament but from the pagan soil of Greek philosophy and thus could be seen as distorting the pristine functional Christology of the New Testament. Kasper rightly recognizes this to be a false understanding between what one does and what one is.

Although Kasper agrees that the New Testament Christology is more functional than ontological, he argues (and he might do so more strongly now) that it is Jesus's activity (his functions) that reveals who he is ontologically as the Son of God. How one acts reveals who one is. "The choice between an ontological and a functional Christology is therefore, theologically speaking, illusory and a position into which theology must not allow itself to be manoeuvered" (24). For Kasper there is an intrinsic unity be Jesus's mission and his divine identity and thus an intrinsic unity between soteriology and Christology (166).

transfiguring them. It has in fact an exclusive-critical sense: in this one man God is permanently in our midst" (198).

In discussing contemporary anthropology, Kasper emphasizes that human beings are not minds or souls residing in a body as in Cartesianism. "Man is wholly body and he is wholly soul and both are at all times the whole man" (201). All that human beings do is simultaneously done in an intellectual and bodily manner—speaking, laughing, crying, dancing, singing, and so on. "The body is expression, symbol, excarnation, essential medium of man. In the body the whole man is 'there,' that is why the body can be practically understood as man's 'being there' and his presence" (201).[6]

Within this context of human beings being intellectual and bodily creatures, with intellect and will Kasper takes up the issue of sin, for sin entails the whole of what human beings are—mind, will, and body. Sin alienates us, the whole of who we are, from God, others, and even ourselves. Sin is part of who we are in all that we are—our intellect, will, and body.

This shared sinfulness therefore is not merely something external to man, not merely a bad example, evil influence, seductive atmosphere: it characterizes each man inwardly in what he *is* in the sight of others and himself. (203)

This sinful situation, Kasper emphasizes, is founded upon human free will and not upon some evil inherent within matter and thus not upon God, the good Creator. It is at this juncture—who man is ontologically and what he has become historically—that the concrete, historical character of the Incarnation finds its importance.

In light of sin, Kasper holds that there needs to be a new beginning.

Against this background, it is understandable that Jesus Christ is proclaimed in Scripture as the New Adam (Rom. 5:12–21). In fact, by entering into the world in person as the Son of God he changes the situation of everyone. With Christ's coming a new *kairos*, a new opportunity of salvation, is opened to the whole world and to all men. With him the situation of all has become new, because in the one humanity the existence of each and every one is determined by the existence of all. It is precisely in the body of Christ that salvation is personally exemplified and offered to us (205).

6. For Kasper, "to become this man" means then that the Word assumed, contrary to Docetism, Gnosticism, Manichaeism, Apollinarianism, and Albigensianism, a complete humanity—body and soul (198–201, 209–13).

For Kasper, it is the Son's taking on our humanity and it is within and through that concrete, historical humanity that salvation of the whole person is achieved. "Salvation means the salvation of the one and entire human being: it is a question of the new man who is liberated from the alienations of his former existence to a new freedom, not *from* the body and *from* the world, but *in* the body and *in* the world" (207).[7]

While Kasper insists that it is truly the Son of God who enters time and history, he equally insists that he does so as man, and it is through that humanity that the Son obtains humankind's redemption. Both the divinity and the humanity of Christ are essential, and, for Kasper, neither dominates the other. Rather, it is through his humanity, and not simply through his divinity, that the divine Son of God achieves our reconciliation with God, with others, and with ourselves.[8] This is important because within some contemporary Christologies it appears that if Jesus is fully divine, he cannot be fully human and vice versa. These vie with one another about which is the most soteriologically significant.[9] Kasper rightly recognizes that each is in need of the other if humankind's salvation is to be attained.

Once again, Kasper returns to the centrality of Jesus's human obedience. Within the New Testament, Jesus's human obedience manifests and verifies that he possesses a human intellect and soul (208–9), and it is within that human intellect and will that the Son so loves humankind that, in loving obedience, he offers his human life to the Father for the sake of all.

The question of the full humanity of Jesus in body and soul is involved in that of the voluntariness of his obedience and thus the human character of salvation. It is concerned with the fact that God, even in his own cause, does not act by passing over or going beyond man, but always through man and by means of his freedom.

7. Kasper could have strengthened his argument if he had developed the notion that the Son of God in becoming man did not assume a generic humanity but a humanity inherited from the sinful Adam. Jesus bore the birthmark of sin. It is only if the Son of God assumed a humanity from the fallen race of Adam could he heal and save it. See T. G. Weinandy, *In the Likeness of Sinful Flesh: An Essay on the Humanity of Christ* (Edinburgh: T&T Clark, 1995). Kasper comes close when he writes, "Hence, according to Philippians, Jesus does not assume human nature in the abstract, but the form of a servant, *morphe doulou*; he submits voluntarily to the powers of fate which enslave man. In that too he becomes our brother" (218).

8. For my development of this important Christological and soteriological truth, see *Does God Suffer?* (London: T&T Clark, 2000), 214–42.

9. Some authors argue that if Jesus is a divine person, then he cannot be fully human. See, for example, J. Macquarrie, *Christology Revisited* (London: SCM, 1998), 43–60).

Jesus therefore is not a mere means of salvation in God's hand, but the personal mediator of salvation. (209)[10]

Thus far we have examined Kasper's upholding the first two Christological truths that must be present if a proper understanding of the Incarnation is to be conceived and articulated—that it is *truly* the Son of God who is man and that it is *truly* man that the Son of God is.

Jesus: Mediator between God and Man

Having treated the divinity and humanity of Jesus, Kasper lastly turns to the third incarnational truth—"the unity of the Godhead and humanity in the one person or hypostasis" (230). The classic biblical text is John 1:14: "The Word became flesh." As stated at the onset, Kasper understands that this incarnational "becoming" is neither some form of Adoptionism—a dwelling in a man, a metamorphosis—a changing into man; nor an ontological fusion of natures such that a third type of being arises that is neither fully God nor fully man. For the Word to become flesh means that the Son of God ontologically assumes a human nature such that he actually comes to exist as a man. It is one and the same subject, one and the same "who"— the Son/Word—who exists as God and as man (231–33).[11] Kasper concludes that in the Doctrine of Chalcedon "Jesus Christ in one person is true God and true man, must therefore be regarded as a valid and permanently binding interpretation of Scripture" (238).

Having established that Jesus is the one person of the Son God incar-

---

10. Later Kasper writes, "Jesus takes on himself our guilt-entangled history, but, through his voluntary obedience and his vicarious service, give it a new quality and establishes a new beginning. The history of disobedience, of hatred and lying is brought to a hold in his obedience and service. Even more: in his suffering and dying on the cross, where his obedience and service reach their supreme perfection" (218).

11. In his summary (234–40) of early Christological development—the controversies and the councils—Kasper closely follows A. Grillmeier, *Christ in Christian Tradition*, vol. 1 (London: Mowbrays, 1975). This view was common at the time. While Grillmeier offers many insights, his categorizing of early Christology into two camps—Logos/Sarx and Logos/Anthropos—confuses many issues and distorts many positions. This is especially true of his treatment of Athanasius and Cyril, which Kasper reproduces. See T. G. Weinandy, "Cyril and the Mystery of the Incarnation," in *The Theology of St. Cyril of Alexandria: A Critical Appreciation*, ed. T. G. Weinandy and D. Keating (London: T&T Clark, 2003), 23–54 (chap. 7 in this volume); *Athanasius: A Theological Introduction* (Aldershot: Ashgate, 2007), 46, 91–96.

nate, Kasper provides a rather lengthy historical and theological discussion of the term "person." He believes that the inherited understanding of "person" as "an individual in the intellectual order," while correct, is too abstract (245, 246; see also 240–45). He argues that "in the concrete, a person is only actually realized in relation." This relationship is threefold: "to himself, to the world, to his fellow men" and thus the essence of personhood "is love" (246). Moreover, there is a transcendent element within the notion of personhood that points to God. "The human person can therefore only ultimately be defined from God as the ground and in relation to God; God himself has to be included in the definition of the human person. In this sense, Scripture speaks of man as the 'image and likeness of God' (Gen. 1:27)" (246). Kasper now wishes to apply this understanding of the concept of person to Jesus.

Jesus's identity, who he is as a person, is constituted by his relation to the Father. Jesus never understands himself "from below" but always "from above" (247). Jesus's divine identity is founded upon his human free obedience to the Father. This not only makes him distinct from the Father in that his human obedience is the obedience of the divine Son, but it also establishes his unity with the Father in that his perfect filial human obedience makes the fullness of the Father's love known (248). Once again, we observe how important Jesus's filial obedience is for Kasper—it attests and confirms that he truly is the Son of the Father and so ontologically one with him.

Because the person of the Son actually exists as a man, Kasper argues that he, as man, is in one sense a human person. It is not that Jesus is not the divine person of the Son, but that he now experiences and manifests his divine personhood in a human manner.

The assumption of Jesus' humanity, the act of highest possible union, at the same time posits this in its own creaturely reality. Jesus' humanity is therefore hypostatically united with the *Logos* in a human way, and this means in a way which includes human freedom and a human self-consciousness. (248)

Kasper affirmatively quotes Alfaro: "Christ experienced himself in a human way as an 'I' who really is the Son of God" (248).[12]

This is an important point for confirming a genuine understanding of the Incarnation. While Kasper does not state it in this manner, I have ar-

12. See J. Alfaro, "Gott IV. Gott Vater," in HThG 1, 603.

gued for a similar position.[13] Within the Incarnation the Son of God possesses a human "I," and the ontological identity of that human "I," the "who" of that human "I," is the divine Son. When Jesus says "I," he is humanly, self-consciously aware in an authentically human manner, and who is authentically aware of himself in a human manner is the divine Son of God. Within the Incarnation there is a human "I" of a divine "who"—the Son of God.

How did the Son of God come to be self-consciously aware in a human manner? For Kasper, it was through his relationship to the Father.

Precisely because (and not despite the fact that) Jesus knew himself wholly one with the Father, he had at the same time a completely human consciousness, asked human questions, grew in age and wisdom (cf. Lk. 2:52). His consciousness of being one with the Father was therefore not a representational conceptual knowledge, but a sort of fundamental disposition and basic attitude which found concrete realization in the surprising situations in which Jesus became aware in the concrete of what God's will is. (248)

Not surprisingly for Kasper, filial obedience is at the heart of Jesus's human self-consciousness, and that human filial obedience allowed Jesus to become humanly self-conscious as the divine Son of the Father.[14]

Since Kasper first wrote this book, there has been an ever-increasing interest in religious pluralism. The question is frequently raised as to whether Jesus is truly the universal and definitive Savior. Kasper leaves no doubt that such is indeed the case. Because Jesus is the Son of God incarnate, who died for our sin and rose to give us new life, he is truly the Lord of all. He provides a number of reasons for this conclusion.

First, in Jesus the fullness of the Spirit is made operative in the world. "According to the New Testament, the universal historical operation of God's Spirit finds its goal and measure in Jesus Christ. He is different from

13. See T. G. Weinandy, "The Human 'I' of Jesus," *Irish Theological Quarterly* 62, no. 4 (1996/97): 259–68 (chap. 17 in this volume); *Jesus the Christ*, 88–95.

14. Given the fact that the Son of God became man, Kasper rightly concludes that neither the Father nor the Holy Spirit could have done so even though such a position has been argued as a possibility. Kasper states: "This is a complete disjunction of sacred history and theological metaphysics, to the detriment of both; sacred history is ultimately evacuated of its theological reality, while theological metaphysics becomes historically meaningless and of no consequence. At the very least it should be said that the various divine persons are involved in the Incarnation each according to his personal distinctive character" (250).

other bearers of the Spirit not only in degree but in kind; he is not simply moved by the Spirit but conceived and formed by the Spirit" (256). The coming down of the Holy Spirit at his baptism is the source and power of his public ministry. He breathes out the Spirit when he dies on the Cross and is raised by the Spirit to new life.

Second, not only is Jesus "the goal and culmination of the presence and operation of the Spirit of God," but he is also "the starting-point for the sending, the mission, of the Spirit. In Christ the Spirit has, as it were, finally attained his goal, the new creation. His further task now consists in integrating all other reality into that of Jesus Christ, or in other words, to universalize the reality of Jesus Christ" (256). The Spirit is now present within the Church and the world through Jesus Christ, who is the New Adam and the Lord of all. This being the case, "the abiding presence and significance of Jesus Christ in history can now be concretely described under three aspect by means of the traditional doctrine of the three offices. Jesus Christ through his Spirit is the way (pastor and king), the truth (prophet and teacher) and the life (priest) of the world (cf. Jn. 14:6)" (259).

Third, for Kasper, the above means that through Jesus and his Spirit the final age has been inaugurated. "The eschatological finality of the coming of truth includes two things, the historical impossibility of surpassing its revelation in Christ, and the abiding presence of Christ's truth in the world through the Spirit" (260). No revelation, no salvific act can surpass that of Jesus, for in him, in his very person, is the fullness of truth and the fullness of salvation (267).

Conclusion

Contemporary Christology may have taken up new questions and developed further insights, but Kasper's clarity and insight concerning the incarnational and soteriological significance of Jesus have not been overshadowed by what has been advanced since he authored *Jesus the Christ*. Given some of the rather shallow, more recent Christologies, it would be wise for scholars to return to Kasper's study. His study is first of all grounded in Scripture and the Church's authentic Christological tradition. This ecclesial faith is the basis upon which he founds his scholarship and intellectual skill. Kasper reveals in *Jesus the Christ* that he is an authentic and devoted Catholic theologian.

CHAPTER 10

Trinitarian Christology
The Eternal Son

Doctrinal Foundation: The Nicene Creed

The ancient Christian creeds are the foundation for a contemporary doctrinal or systematic study of God the Son. These creeds provide an authoritative organic synthesis of scriptural revelation—the faith that all members of the Church profess. They were often formulated to refute erroneous interpretations of Scripture and false expressions of the faith, and so they clarify what the Church believes and teaches. Here we begin our doctrinal study of God the Son by briefly examining the Nicene Creed (325 AD).

Arius, a priest from Alexandria, held that it was impossible for God to be one if the Son is truly God. If the Son were God, there would be two divine beings brought about by change and division, all of which is incompatible with the divine nature. Arius concluded that the Son must be created as the first and highest of all creatures and so the most divine like of all beings. Thus God is not eternally the Father, and there was, according to Arius, "a time/when when the Son was not."

In response to Arius, the Council of Nicea declared that the Son of God is "the only-begotten begotten from the Father, that is from the substance of the Father, God from God, light from light, true God from true God, be-

Originally published as "Trinitarian Christology: The Eternal Son," in *The Oxford Handbook of the Trinity*, ed. G. Emery and M. Levering (Oxford: Oxford University Press, 2011), 387–99. By permission of Oxford University Press.

gotten not made, consubstantial ('ομοούσιον) with the Father."[1] The Council expressed seven dogmatic truths that are essential for all subsequent systematic theology concerning the Son.

First, the Council specified that the Son is "the only-begotten begotten from the Father"; that is, as "only begotten," he is singular in his manner of existence from the Father. Authentic doctrinal development and theological speculation must uphold this unique existence and specific relationship with the Father.

Second, the Council clarified the difference between "begotten" and "made." What is made is necessarily different in kind from the maker. What is begotten is always of the same nature as the begetter. Ants make anthills but beget other ants. Human beings make houses but beget other human beings. God made the world but begot his Son. It is because the Son is begotten and not made that he is "from the substance of the Father" and so "God from God, light from light, true God from true God." The Son is God, then, as the Father is God. The Son's existence differs in kind and not just in degree from all else that exists and all theological enquiry must acknowledge this radical difference.

Third, in declaring that the Son is consubstantial (of the same substance or being) with the Father, the Council professed that God is one not in the sense of being a solitary being, but rather that the Father's begetting of the Son is of the very nature of what the one God is, and so the one God is the Father and the Son (and the Holy Spirit). The Council, in clarifying the mystery of God's nature, refuted Arius's claim that God could not be one if the Son is God for the one God is not simply the Father, but rather the one God is the Father and the Son, for from all eternity the Father begets his consubstantial Son. The consubstantiality of the Son affirms the equality and oneness of the divine persons, thus voiding any future attempt to subordinate the Son to the Father or to conceive them as different beings in their own right.

Fourth, while the Council specified that both the Father and the Son are equally the one God, it also acknowledged them to be distinct persons or subjects—each with his own unique identity. This demands, doctrinally,

---

1. N. Tanner, ed., *Decrees of the Ecumenical Councils, Nicaea I to Lateran V* (Washington, DC: Georgetown University Press, 1990), 1:5.

that while all actions of God are done as one, each person nonetheless acts in a manner that is in keeping with who he is. This is theologically important when addressing the Son's mission within the economy of salvation as the incarnate Son (as well as that of the Holy Spirit).

Fifth, their personal designations as "Father" and "Son" specify both their irreducible identities and their oneness of being. God the Father is distinct from God the Son, and yet God the Father is the Father only because he eternally begets God the Son as he who is one in being with him, and God the Son is the Son only because he is eternally begotten of the Father as he who is one in being with the Father. The Father and Son are then ontologically and intrinsically related to one another as the one God. This will be of the utmost significance in subsequent doctrinal development concerning the divine persons being subsistent relations.

Lastly, in employing the biblical designations of "Father" and "Son," the Council of Nicea implicitly affirmed that such names are dogmatically authoritative in that they define God's immanent being. Other names or titles attributed to the Father, such as Creator, or to the Son, such as Redeemer, specify actions that are within the economy, and as such these names or titles do not intrinsically define their eternal being as do the names "Father" and "Son" (and "Holy Spirit").

Having dogmatically defined the full divinity of the Son, the Council immediately professes that the divine Son "for us men and for our salvation came down and became incarnate, became man, suffered and rose on the third day."[2] The Nicene Creed thus intrinsically and doctrinally unites the proclamation of the Son's divinity with his incarnate humanity. Nicea establishes, as the Council of Chalcedon (451 AD) will confirm, that the Son who is fully divine is the same Son who is fully human.

There are a number of theological topics that flow from the foundational dogmatic truths concerning the Son's existence as God and as man.

The Son: A Subsistent Relation Fully in Act

Because the Father and the Son are ontologically related to one another in that the Father is only the Father in relation to the Son and the Son is only

2. Ibid.; quotation slightly altered.

the Son in relation to the Father, Augustine and Aquinas, building upon the Greek Fathers, conceived the persons of the Trinity as subsistent relations; that is, they subsist or exist as who they are only in relation to one another. In articulating this concept of subsistent relation, I offer an active role to the Holy Spirit—something Augustine, Aquinas, and the subsequent tradition did not do—for it bears upon the identity of the Son within the Trinity as well as his activity within the economy of salvation.

The Father only subsists eternally as Father by giving himself wholly in the begetting of his Son. Moreover, and significantly, the Father simultaneously spirates or breathes forth the Spirit in the begetting of the Son, for it is in the love of the Holy Spirit that the Father begets the Son, thus conforming him to be the loving Father of the Son. In this begetting of the Son in the love of the Holy Spirit, the Father actualizes his identity as Father. The Son subsists eternally as Son only in relation to the Father and to the Holy Spirit, for his identity is predicated upon his being begotten of the Father in the love of the Holy Spirit who conforms him to be the loving Son of the Father. Thus there is within the Trinity a *spirituque* in that the Son is begotten by the Father in the love of the Spirit. The Holy Spirit subsists eternally as the Holy Spirit only in relation to the Father and to the Son, for his identity as the Holy Spirit is predicated upon his coming forth from the Father as the one in whom the Father begets the Son in love and as the one in whom the Son, having been begotten in the love of the Spirit, in turn completely gives himself, in the Spirit of love, to the Father as his Son. This is ultimately the basis of the *filioque*. Not only does the Holy Spirit proceed from the Father as the one in whom the Father loving begets the Son in love, but the Holy Spirit also proceeds from the Son as the one in whom the Son loves the Father who has begotten him. In proceeding from the Father and the Son, the Holy Spirit reciprocally conforms them to love one another in the Spirit of love that he is.

Here we perceive the dynamic ontological nature of the persons of the Trinity being subsistent relations. Not only do the persons of the Trinity acquire their unique personal identities in relation to one another, but these relations also specify the very act that identifies each person. The Father is Father because he is the act that begets the Son in the love of the Spirit. The Father is the act of loving paternity, fatherhood fully in act. The Son is the Son because, being begotten by the Father in the Spirit of love, he is the act of giving himself to the Father as Son in the Spirit of love. The Son is the act of filial love, sonship fully in act. The Holy Spirit proceeds from the Father and the Son as the act by which they give themselves lovingly to one another. The Holy Spirit is love fully in act. While the terms "Father," "Son," and "Holy Spirit," are nouns, they are employed to specify the act by which each person is defined. The persons of the Trinity are not nouns; they subsist as verbs, as acts, and the names that designate them—Father, Son, and Holy Spirit—designate the acts by which they subsist in relation to one another.

The relations among the persons of the Trinity specify not only their singular ontological personal identity, what makes them three distinct subjects, but also their ontological unity as the one God. As a man and a woman are mutually defined as husband and wife by their relationship, so this same relationship makes them one married couple. Similarly, the relationships that define the singular identities of the three divine persons are the very relationships that ontologically constitute their unity. The one God is the persons of the Trinity ontologically subsisting in relationship to one another.

While the above may appear to focus more on the Trinity as such rather than specifically on the Son, it is only in conceiving the Trinity properly that one is able to articulate clearly and accurately the person of the Son not only within the immanent Trinity but also his role within the economy of salvation.

The Son as Word and Image

Since the Son is truly God, how are the New Testament designations "Word" and "Image" of the Father interpreted and understood? Do these names likewise bear the same dynamism as that of "Son"?

Thomas Aquinas, following Augustine, teaches that the two processions within God are by way of intellection (the generation of the Son) and by way of will (the spiration of the Holy Spirit). As the human intellect first conceives within itself an inner word prior to speaking that word, so the Father eternally conceives the Word. Thus the Word "is to be understood by way of an intelligible emanation, for example, of the intelligible word which proceeds from the speaker, yet remains in him" (*ST* I, q. 27, a. 1; I, q. 34, a. 1). Furthermore, while human inner words do contain the truth known, no one human word embraces the truth of all possible knowledge. In contrast, the Son, being consubstantial with Father, is designated Word in that he does possess and express fully the entire truth of who the Father is. Because the Word is the full truth of the Father, this Word is designated the Son of the Father, for he replicates as Son all the truth that the Father is.

Since the Father is fully in act as Father, the Word that emanates from within him is also fully in act; that is, the Son as Word is the Father's knowledge and truth fully in act—the fullness of the Father's knowledge of himself and all that is and could be. It is as the dynamic Word of the Father that the Son is then the creative and life-giving bearer of all truth.

Moreover, because the Son, as Word, contains the entire living truth of the Father, all that the Father is, he is the perfect image of the Father. Aquinas states that the term "image" has to do with similitude and that the greatest similitude is to proceed "from another like to it in species" (*ST* I, q. 35, a. 1). Human beings, for example, are of the same image, possessing the greatest similitude, for they belong to the same species. While God is not contained within a species, since the Son is begotten of the Father and consubstantial with him, possessing the entire truth of the Father as Word, he is the perfect image of the Father. But for the Son to be the image of the Father is not to be static or inert as a statue or portrait is a static and inert image of a king. Rather, the Son is the image of the Father fully in act for the Father is fully in act, and so the Son perfectly reflects the fullness of the Father's life and truth.

The Son is designated by these various names because no one name contains the totality of who the Son is. "To show that he is of the same nature as the Father, he is called Son; to show that he is co-eternal, he is called Splendour; to show that he is altogether like, he is called image; to show that he is begotten immaterially, he is called the Word" (*ST* I, q. 34, a. 2, ad 3).

While all of these names are proper to the being of the Son, do they have an inherent relationship to the created order? Again, following Augustine, Aquinas teaches that the Word "implies relation to creatures. For God by knowing himself, knows every creature." Unlike human beings who must use multiple words to express multiple truths, "God by one act understands himself and all things, his one only Word is expressive not only of the Father, but of all creatures" (*ST* I, q. 34, a. 3). It is precisely because the Word expresses the truth of all creatures that the Father creates though his

Word (Gn. 1:3; Jn. 1:3, 1:10; Ps. 33:6; 1 Cor. 8:6; Col. 1:16; Heb. 1:2). Thus the whole of creation is deemed to be good because it conforms to the truth contained within the Word and so, in some manner, bears the image of the Word (Ps. 19; Rom. 1:19–20). This is especially the case with human beings, who are created in the image and likeness of God.

Created and Re-Created in the Image and Likeness of the Son

On the basis of Genesis 1:27, Aquinas teaches that human beings, as "intellectual creatures alone, properly speaking, are made to God's image" (*ST* I, q. 93, a. 2). He further sees this image in that man's "intellectual nature imitates God chiefly in this, that God understands and loves himself." This imaging of God is threefold: (1) man's "aptitude for understanding and loving God;" (2) man's "actually and habitually knows and loves God, though imperfectly" through "conformity to grace"; and (3) man "knows and loves God perfectly" in "the likeness of glory" (*ST* I, q. 93, a. 4). Although Aquinas acknowledges that there are traces of God's image in the human body, strictly speaking the true image of God lies solely within man's intellect. Only in rational creatures do "we find a procession of the word in the intellect, and a procession of the love in the will," which mirrors "an image of the uncreated Trinity" (*ST* I, q. 93, a. 6). Thus the image of the Trinity "is found in the acts of the soul, that is, inasmuch as from the knowledge which we possess, by actual thought we form an internal word; and thence break forth into love" (*ST* I, q. 93, a.7).

What Aquinas teaches is insightful, but I argue, in keeping with the Patristic tradition exemplified in Irenaeus (*Adversus Haeresis* 5.6.1) and Athanasius (*Contra Gentes* 2.2), that human beings are created in the image and likeness of the God in that they are created in the image and likeness of the Son. The Father creates through the Son, and, in creating man in his own image, the Father creates him in the likeness of the Son, for the Son is his perfect image and likeness. To be created in the image of the Son means that the Father intended that human beings, like the Son, would be able to know and live the truth and so reflect the Son as Word of the Father. So, as Aquinas stated above, human beings have the natural aptitude for knowing and loving God as well as other human persons and all else that is good, but now this is particularly true because they are modeled after the Son.

I argue, contrary to Augustine and Aquinas and the received Christian theological tradition, that it is not only man's intellectual ability (his soul) that bears the image of God, but rather the whole of who he is as a human being. The Son is the perfect image of the Father because, as Son, he is fully in act as the Father is fully in act. For human beings to be the image of the Son demands that they be fully in act as well, but human beings are only fully in act when both their souls and bodies are fully in act and not simply their intellects and wills. The human act of intellection requires that the bodily senses and brain as well as the immaterial intellect be in act. Moreover, human beings can only speak the truth and act lovingly upon the truth through bodily spoken words and by bodily human actions—bodily actions of love, justice, courage, and so on. The whole human person, body and soul, is in the likeness of the Son, for only when the whole human person is fully in act does he or she properly reflect the image of the Son who is fully in act.

Now, in light of sin, which disfigured the image of the Son within human beings by undermining their ability to know and love the truth as does the Son, especially in knowing and loving God, the Father sent his Son into the world as man in order to re-create human beings in his image; that is, in the Son who is his perfect image. Does this imply that only the Son could have become man and as man re-create human beings in his image?

We observed above that Aquinas held that the Son as Word implies a relationship to creation in that the Father knows himself and all else through the Word. Nonetheless, Aquinas argued that, while it is most fitting for the Son to become man, any one of the three divine persons could have become incarnate (*ST* III, q. 3, a. 5). I argue, however, again in keeping with the Irenaeus (*Adversus Haeresis* 3.23.1, 5.16.1) and Athanasus (*De Incarnatione* 13.7, 13.9, 14.2), that it was right and proper that only the Son could become man.

Karl Rahner, in arguing that the economic Trinity is the immanent Trinity—that is, the manner in which the Trinity reveals itself within the economy of salvation is the manner in which it actually exists in itself—gives as his primary example the Incarnation of the Son. "In one way this statement [the economic Trinity is the immanent Trinity] is a defined doctrine of the faith. Jesus is not simply God in general, but the Son. The second divine person, God's Logos, is man, and only he is man. Hence there is a least *one* 'mission,' *one* presence in the world, *one* reality of salvation history which is not merely appropriated to some divine person, but which is proper to him."[3] Long before Rahner articulated his now-famous axiom, the Fathers of the Church as well as the Scholastics always argued that God revealed himself to be a Trinity of persons through the specific individual missions of the Son and the Holy Spirit. These missions within the economy provide a window through which the immanent Trinity can be properly discerned. The fact that only the Son could become man is significant not only for the sake of obtaining a proper understanding of the Son within the Trinity and his salvific work within the economy, but also of conceiving and articulating a proper understanding of the Father and the Holy Spirit—as they, too, exist within the Trinity and act within the economy.

Aquinas gives as an objection to the premise that any one of the divine persons other than the Son could have become man that such an actuality "would tend to confusion of the divine persons" (*ST* III, q. 3, a. 5, obj. 1). He should have taken this objection more seriously, for this objection is crucial for obtaining a proper understanding not only of the Trinity but also of the Son. If the Father or the Holy Spirit became man, this would not be in keeping with who they are as divine persons and would undermine the very identity of the Son as Word and Image of the Father. Moreover, it would render unintelligible the fact that the work of redemption was precisely that of re-creating human beings in the likeness of the Son. For any person other than the Son to become man would destroy the ontological order within the Trinity; that is, that the Father is Father because he begets the Son in his Spirit of love as his singular Word of truth and perfect Image. Equally, the work of redemption would not truly reveal the Trinity as the Trinity is. This is ultimately how Aquinas argues when he taught that it is "more fitting" for the Son to become man rather than the Father or the Holy Spirit.

First, Aquinas argues that the Son, as Word of the Father, possesses an inherent affinity with the created order since as Word he contains, as exemplar, the whole of the created order. Thus it would only be proper that the one through whom the universe was created and in whom the created order finds its exemplar be the one who restores creation—freeing it from evil and

---

3. Karl Rahner, *The Trinity* (New York: Crossroads, 1970), 23.

making it new (*ST* III, q. 3, a. 8). "The first creation of things was made by the power of God the Father through the Word; hence the second creation ought to have been brought about through the Word, by the power of God the Father, in order that the restoration should correspond to creation" (*ST* III, q. 3, a. 8, ad 2).

Second, Aquinas provides two further arguments, both pertaining to human beings, as to why it is proper for the Son, specifically as Word of the Father, to become man. The Word has "a particular agreement with human nature" in that the Word embraces the fullness of divine Wisdom. Since human beings are perfected through the obtaining of such wisdom, it is only proper and fitting that such wisdom be obtained through the Word incarnate, the fount of all wisdom. Moreover, since sin entered the world through a misconceived desire to obtain knowledge, precipitated through the lies of Satan, "it is only fitting that by the Word of true knowledge man might be led back to God, having wandered from God through an inordinate thirst for knowledge" (*ST* III, q. 4, a. 8). But it would seem more than fitting because the Son, as Word of the Father, should, as man, be the bearer of wisdom and truth since ontologically within the Trinity he is the divine person whose very divine identity, who he is as a divine person, is defined as the Word of wisdom and truth. While the Father begets his Son as the Word and Wisdom of truth and while the Holy Spirit is the Spirit of truth in that the Spirit fosters and confirms the truth of the Word within believers, only the Son, as Word, bears the wisdom and truth of the Father that the Spirit will engender and affirm within believers.

Lastly, Aquinas argues that since the end of human beings is to be adopted children of the Father, "it was fitting that by him who is the natural Son, men should share this likeness of sonship by adoption" (*ST* III, q. 8, a. 8). This is the heart of the issue. It would appear that for such sonship to be obtained through and in the Father or the Holy Spirit would not only be inappropriate but also ontologically impossible given that only the divine Son is ontologically the Son of the Father, and thus only he could obtain humankind's adopted sonship. As the Father created man through his Son and in the image of his Son, so the Father re-creates man in the image of his Son through the salvific work of his Son.

Given that only the Son is able to become man, how did the Son as man restore human beings to the wisdom and truth of the Father and re-create them in his divine image so that, in him and through the Holy Spirit, they become adopted children of the Father?

The Salvific Work of the Son Incarnate

As the Father eternally begets his Son in the love of the Spirit, so the Father in time sent his Son into the world and he becomes incarnate, Son of God as man, of the virgin Mary by that same power and love of the Holy Spirit. The Son, in whose image man was first created, assumed his own image so as to restore and elevate that image to his own divine likeness. But the image that the Son assumed in becoming man was the sin-scarred humanity of the fallen race of Adam. He is a son of Adam born in the likeness of sinful flesh (Lk. 3:38; Rom. 8:3; 2 Cor. 5:21). Only by assuming humankind's fallen humanity could he, within that humanity, re-create it and make it new.

In becoming one with humankind, the Son, as the divine Word, revealed as man the truth of his Father as well as providing the wisdom to live an authentic human life. In accordance with the Council of Chalcedon (451 AD), which professed that the Son of God actually existed as man, the manner in which he taught was as man. To hear the human voice of Jesus was literally to hear the human voice of the Son—the word of the Word. Moreover, the actions that Jesus performed, whether they were the routine human actions of eating, walking, and sleeping, or the divine actions of healing the sick, raising the dead, casting out demons, or performing other miracles, all such actions were done by the Son in a human manner. These latter actions are termed theandric actions—divine acts done humanly for the divine Son performed them as man. As the Son revealed his divine identity through his human words, so he equally revealed his divine identity through his human actions. Thus, in the Incarnation, the Son actively interrelated and was personally engaged, on an equal human level, with other human beings and with his environment. The singular difference being, for example, that when Jesus touched someone or when someone touched him, who was doing the human touching and who was being humanly touched was none other than the eternal divine Son equal to the Father. What is significant here is that the healing, restoration, and elevation of humankind was accomplished by the divine Son not in a divine manner, but in a human manner, for the Son of God existed and acted as man.

From a Trinitarian perspective, one must also acknowledge that, while the Son as man taught, healed, and so on, he did so through the power of the Holy Spirit who dwelt within his humanity. This follows the established Trinitarian paradigm. The Father begets the Son in the love of the Spirit, who conforms him to be the loving Son of the Father. Moreover, the Son of the Father is conceived in the womb of Mary through the same Spirit in whom he was eternally begotten. Similarly, at Jesus's baptism the Father declares, in the descent of the Holy Spirit, that this truly is his Son. The overshadowing of the Holy Spirit manifested that the incarnate Son is indeed the loving Son of the Father on earth and that as the loving Son existing as man, he will now lovingly, in the Holy Spirit, teach and restore humankind. The interior life of the immanent Trinity is now played out on earth through the visible, historical life of Jesus, the Son of God incarnate.

Ultimately, it was through his life of obedience to the Father that, as a member of the fallen race of Adam, the Son brought about humankind's salvation. As the Son was eternally the loyal and faithful Son of the Father in the love of the Holy Spirit, so now, as man the Son is the obedient Son, in the love of the Holy Spirit, and in so doing he reverses the disobedience of Adam and his posterity (Rom. 5:12–21). While the Son's whole earthly life was marked by obedience, this obedience finds its culmination in the Cross (Phil. 2:8). The Cross becomes the definitive revelation that Jesus is truly the faithful and loyal Son of the Father begotten by him in the love of the Spirit (Mk. 15:39; Jn. 8:28). And it is in this definitive revelation that the Son also humanly achieved humankind's salvation.

Jesus's death on the Cross contains many facets. First, his sacrificial death was a twofold act of love. It was an act of filial obedient sacrificial love offered to the Father, for, in the love of the Spirit, the Son freely offered his own human life to the Father to atone for and so offset (or literally counteract) all humankind's ungodly sinful acts. It was an act of sacrificial love performed out of love for humankind, for the incarnate Son did, out of love for those who had been created in his own image, what they could not do on their own behalf, having been rendered spiritually impotent due to sin. It was this twofold human act of free sacrificial love, rendered in the Spirit, that made the Son's sacrifice meritorious and efficacious.

Second, in offering himself out of love for humankind, the incarnate Son freely offered a sinless, perfect, and holy sacrifice to the Father, one that would fully and adequately express humankind's reparational or atoning love in the face of sin, thus reconciling humankind to the Father. It is in the Son's human blood, suffused with the love and holiness of the Spirit, that this perfect, all-loving, sinless, and all-holy sacrifice established the new and everlasting covenant with the Father.

Third, as evident above, while it was truly the person of the Son who offered the sacrifice, he did so, in accordance with the truth of the Incarnation, as man. The merit of the sacrifice, which expiated humankind's guilt and condemnation thus reconciling it to the Father, was located in the Son's human love for the Father and for the whole of humankind—again, a love born of the Spirit.

Fourth, while Jesus experienced our condemnation on the Cross, in the same act of assuming our condemnation, he simultaneously and equally offered in love, his human life to the Father as an atoning sacrifice on humankind's behalf. The Son's loving, sacrificial offering of his life to the Father on humankind's behalf transformed the suffering of humankind's condemnation into an act of freeing humankind from such condemnation.

Fifth, on the Cross the Son of God put to death humankind's sinful humanity. Because the Son of God lived a pure and holy life of obedience to the Father as a member of the sinful race of Adam, within his own sin-marred humanity, the loving offering of that humanity on the Cross brought about its demise. Our sinful human nature was put to death because the Son transformed it into a pure, holy, and loving sacrifice to the Father on behalf of all.

The drama of the Cross mirrors the life within the Trinity. The Father eternally begets his Son in the Spirit of love, and the Son loves the Father in the same Spirit of love. On earth, as man, in the Spirit of love, the Son, by his filial obedience to the Father, offered his human life to the Father on behalf of humankind. As the Father is eternally pleased with his Son so now he is equally pleased with his Son on earth, and as the Father eternally begot the Son in the love of the Spirit so now he exalts his Son, in the Spirit of love, as the risen and glorious Son incarnate.

The Resurrected Incarnate Son

The bodily resurrection of Jesus is of the utmost significance both for himself and for the whole of humankind. First, as pertains to Jesus himself, by raising him from the dead by the power of the Holy Spirit, the Father confirmed that he was indeed his eternal Son. If the Father had not raised him from the dead, it would have corroborated the accusations leveled against him that he had falsely made himself out to be the Son of God.

Second, in the Resurrection the Father validated and manifested the efficacy of his Son's sacrifice on the Cross. Actually, the Resurrection is the direct fruit of the Cross, and the Father ensured that Jesus, his Son, was the first to experience the inherent worth of his own salvific work. The Son of God, who had assumed in the Incarnation humankind's fallen nature, the sin-marred image of himself, now in the Resurrection is the first, through the Holy Spirit, to assume the restored and re-created image of himself. The Son, who as God is the perfect image of the Father, and in whose image man was first created, now bears the perfect likeness of himself, and so of the Father, as a risen man. The Son is now the perfect image of the Perfect Image.

Lastly, as the risen Lord and Savior, the glorious incarnate Son rightly possesses the authority to send forth the new life of the Holy Spirit, the divine endowment of his sacrificial death. Through this Spirit humankind can once more be re-created in the Son's own divine image and likeness. Thus Jesus became, as the risen incarnate Son, the new Adam—the father of a new human race (Rom. 5:14; 1 Cor. 15:45).

A New Creation in Christ

How do human beings appropriate the saving work of Jesus and so be re-created in his divine image? First, by dying and rising with Christ. The Son of God assumed the fallen nature of Adam, his own sin-marred image, and through his death and resurrection acquired a new glorious humanity, the perfect image of his own image. Through faith and baptism, Christians likewise shed their fallen humanity and become a new creation in him, sharing in his newly risen humanity (Rom. 6:1–11; 2 Cor. 5:17). Humankind's fallen humanity is not only restored in Christ, but it is also elevated to share in divine risen image—the image that it was to possess from the foundation of the world.

Second, because Christians are a new creation in Christ, they are freed from sin and its condemnation. As in the bondage of Adam's sin, bearing his enslaved image, Christians now share in the freedom of the children of the new Adam, bearing his unfettered image.

Third, more positively, Christians, through the Holy Spirit, are made righteous and holy, sharing in the righteousness and holiness of the risen Son. No longer do Christians do the deeds of the flesh after the manner of the old Adam, but they now do the deeds of the Spirit after the manner of the new Adam (Rom. 8). These virtuous deeds of the Spirit are not merely mental deeds, but rather they are done bodily—done by the entire Spirit-filled person. Jesus, as the Son incarnate, performed his holy human salvific deeds through power of the Spirit to the glory of his Father, so Christians, re-created in the Spirit, now reflect his image through their holy deeds and so, too, glorify the Father.

Fourth, having been re-created in the likeness of the Son, Christians, as adopted children, share in a new intimacy with the Father after the manner of Jesus the Son. This transformation once again follows the Trinitarian paradigm and so corroborates the necessity for the Son to be the incarnate means of humankind's salvation. The Father eternally begets his Son in the Spirit, so in that Spirit the Father and Son eternally love one another. Likewise, the Holy Spirit transforms Christians into the likeness of Jesus the Son so that they, too, can experience the love of the Father through the same Spirit and in turn love the Father in their newly acquired Spirit of sonship. In Christ, through the Spirit, Christians possess a new kind of relationship with the Father; that is, being his adopted children, a relationship that those who are not Christian do not share.

Fifth, not only do Christians, as his children, possess a unique relationship with the Father, they equally possess, as brothers and sisters in Christ, a unique relationship with one another, a relationship that they do not share with those who are not Christians, for they become one in him through the bond and love of the Spirit. By sharing in the common life of the Spirit, Christians become members of the living body of Christ, the Church, of which he is the head.

Sixth, in light of becoming a new creation in Christ through the indwelling Spirit, Christians live in anticipation both of Jesus's return in glory and of their own bodily resurrection. At present, Christians and the whole of creation are groaning to share in the fullness of Jesus's divine sonship (Rom. 8:18–25). Yet it is the Holy Spirit, the Spirit that dwells within them, who is the guarantee and first down payment assuring Christians that they will assume fully the divine likeness of risen incarnate Son (2 Cor. 1:22; Eph. 1:14, 4:30). At the coming of the Son of God, bearing his glorious humanity, every Christian will rejoice in the Spirit. This gladness is not simply because of their own resurrection, but in participating and witnessing the supreme event of all history, when every knee will bend and every tongue proclaim, to the glory of God the Father, that Jesus the incarnate Son is indeed Lord of heaven and earth (Phil. 2:11).

All of the above has been predicated on one truth that may have already become obvious. This truth finds its origin within the Trinity itself. The Father, the Son, and the Holy Spirit share their one common life because they are all ontologically united to one another. Christians come to share the very likeness of the Trinity because they are, in the Holy Spirit, united to Jesus the Son and so become children of the Father. This personal relationship with Jesus the Son, both on earth and in heaven, gives Christians access to and allows them to live within the life of the Trinity itself. This makes Christianity radically distinct from all other religions (excepting Judaism) where the religious founder merely imparts "saving" knowledge that is to be followed by his adherents. Within Christianity, it is the person of the Son, who took on our flesh, who is himself of the utmost importance, for in order to share in the fruit of his redemption—forgiveness of sins and the new life in the Spirit—one must be personally united to him. At the end of time, all of the just will be one in Jesus, the incarnate Son, and so share fully in the life of the Holy Spirit and the love of the Father (Eph. 1:10).

The Annunciation and Nativity
Undoing the Sinful Act of Eve

Employing the writings of Bernard of Clairvaux (1090–1153) and Bonaventure (1217–1274), I first examine the theology of the Annunciation. I argue, in collaboration with the above medieval theologians, that the Annunciation is the fundamental mystery in Mary's life and the mystery that founds all of the other mysteries she embodies—her immaculate conception, her perpetual virginity, her divine motherhood, her cooperation with her Son's salvific work, her bodily assumption, and her heavenly queenship. I examine the Annunciation through the specific hermeneutical lens employed by Bernard and Bonaventure; that is, the mystery of the Annunciation can only be clearly perceived and properly understood when it is viewed as the undoing of the sinful work of Eve. Moreover, because the Annunciation is the foundational Marian mystery, I argue that all other mysteries pertaining to Mary must be viewed equally as the undoing of Eve's sinful act. With this principle in mind, I conclude by advancing the thought of Bernard and Bonaventure, in a manner that they did not, that the Nativity must also be seen as the undoing of the sinful action of Eve.

Irenaeus on Mary and Eve

By way of introduction, I first lay a patristic foundation. Taking his cue from Paul, Irenaeus (ca. 130 to ca. 200 AD) chose as his organizing theological

Originally published as "The Annunciation and Nativity: Undoing the Sinful Act of Eve," *International Journal of Systematic Theology* 14, no. 2 (2012): 217–32. Reprinted by permission.

theme the recapitulation of all things in Christ (Eph. 1:9–10). The Son of God assumed, took to himself, and so recapitulated the sinful flesh of Adam, and in so doing he equally assumed, took to himself, and so recapitulated the whole of humanity's sinful history. Having united himself to the sinful race of Adam with its subsequent sinful history, Jesus reversed this sinful order by being, unlike Adam and his descendants, the obedient Son of his Father, the culmination of which was his obedient death on the Cross.[1] Having recapitulated the whole of human sinfulness and nailing it to the Cross through his own obedient death, Jesus, through his resurrection, becomes the Second Adam, re-creating all men and women by newly drawing them to himself (se Rom. 5:12–21; 1 Cor. 15:20–50). As the earthly Jesus assumed and so recapitulated the sinful order so as to vanquish it through his death, so now, as the risen Christ, he creates the new order by uniting and recapitulating the whole of creation to himself through the Holy Spirit.

Having employed the Pauline parallelism between Adam and Jesus so as to establish the order of sin and the order of salvation, Irenaeus creatively and insightfully expands this parallel to include Eve and Mary.[2] Just as

---

1. Irenaeus rightly perceived that the Son of God must assume a human nature taken from the fallen race of Adam.

> Unless he [the Son] had himself been made flesh and blood after the way of the original formation [of man], saving in his own person at the end that which had in the beginning perished in Adam ... He had himself, therefore, flesh and blood, recapitulating in himself not a certain other, but that original handiwork of the Father, seeking out that thing which had perished. (Irenaeus, *Ad. Haer.* 5.14.1, 5.14.2)

The Son of God could not redeem us by his blood "if he did not really become man, restoring to his own handiwork what was said [of it] in the beginning, that man was made after the image and likeness of God" (Ibid., 5.2.1). For Irenaeus, the Son of God must assume a humanity of the very race of fallen Adam, for "if the Lord had taken flesh from another substance, he would not, by so doing, have reconciled that one to God which had become inimical through transgression" (Ibid., 5.14.3). In assuming our Adamic humanity, the Son "sets forth the recapitulation of the same man, who was at the beginning made after the likeness of God" (Ibid., 5.12.4). Translations from A. Roberts and J. Donaldson, eds., *The Ante-Nicene Fathers*, vol. 1 (reprint, Grand Rapids, MI: Eerdmans, 1989).

For further study on the need for the Son of God to take upon himself a humanity of the fallen race of Adam, see T. G. Weinandy, *In the Likeness of Sinful Flesh: An Essay on the Humanity of Christ* (Edinburgh: T&T Clark, 1993). For a study of Irenaeus's anthropology, see M. C. Steenberg, *Of God and Man: Theology as Anthropology from Irenaeus to Athanasius* (London: T&T Clark, 2009), 16–54; T. G. Weinandy, "St. Irenaeus and the *Imago Dei*: The Importance of Being Human," *Logos: A Journal of Catholic Thought and Culture* 6, no. 6 (2003): 15–34.

2. For the development of the Eve/Mary parallelism within the Church Fathers, see S. J.

the incarnate Son of God, through his obedience, reversed Adam's sinful disobedience and so re-created humankind anew, so did Mary, by her obedience, reverse for Irenaeus Eve's sinful disobedience. In so doing Mary, by becoming the Mother of the Second Adam, becomes the Second Eve, the new mother of all who will come to life through and in her Son. This is how Irenaeus expresses his thoughts.

The Son of God came into his own and was making a recapitulation of that disobedience which had occurred in connection with a tree, through the obedience which was upon a tree, the deception also being done away with ... For just as the former [Eve] was led astray by the word of an angel, so that she fled from God when she had transgressed his word; so did the latter [Mary], by an angelic communication, receive the glad tidings that she should sustain God, being obedient to his word. And if the former did disobey God, yet the latter was persuaded to be obedient to God, in order that the Virgin Mary might become the patroness (*advocate*) of the virgin Eve. And thus, as the human race fell into bondage to death by means of a virgin so is it rescued by a virgin; virginal disobedience having been balanced in the opposite scale by virginal obedience.[3]

Mary, being obedient to the word of the angel and so consenting to becoming the Mother of Jesus, can even be said, for Irenaeus, to be "the cause of salvation, both to herself and to the entire human race." As Jesus's genealogy is traced back to Adam and so is regenerated in him, so "also it was that the knot of Eve's disobedience was loosed by the obedience of Mary. For what the virgin Eve had bound fast through unbelief, this did the virgin Mary set free through faith."[4]

Boss, ed., *Mary: The Complete Resource* (Oxford: Oxford University Press, 2007), multiple references in the index; M. O'Carroll, "Eve and Mary," in *Theotokos: A Theological Encyclopedia of the Blessed Virgin Mary* (Wilmington, DE: Michael Glazier, 1983), 139–41; L. Gambero, *Mary and the Fathers of the Church* (San Francisco: Ignatius Press, 1999), multiple references in the index; H. Graef, *Mary: A History of Doctrine and Devotion*, vol. 1 (New York: Sheed and Ward, 1963), multiple references in the index; J. Pelikan, *Mary through the Ages: Her Place in the History of Culture* (New Haven, CT: Yale University Press, 1996); 39–52; and an old but thorough study providing relevant patristic texts, T. Livius, *The Blessed Virgin in the Fathers of the First Six Centuries* (London: Burns and Oates, 1893), 35–59.

3. Irenaeus, *Ad. Haer.* 5.19.1. Translation slightly altered.

4. Ibid., 3.22.4. In his *Demonstratio Apostolica*, Irenaeus also articulated the Adam/Christ and Eve/Mary parallelisms.

And just as it was through a virgin who disobeyed that man was stricken and fell and died, so too it was through the Virgin, who obeyed the word of God, that man resuscitated by

We find in Irenaeus a number of points that our medieval theologians will adopt and expand upon. First, there is the importance of virginity and motherhood. Eve as a virgin sinfully disobeyed God and so became the mother of the sinful race that derives from Adam. Mary was a virgin who virtuously obeyed God and so became the mother of the incarnate Son of God through whom Adam's race will be re-created. But Mary's virginity is placed within the context of the Annunciation and consequent divine motherhood and so enhances the theological significance of this event. Second, we find not only the contrast between Eve's disobedience and Mary's obedience, but also the contrast between Eve's unbelief and Mary's faith. This is important because it establishes Mary's subsequent cooperative fidelity even to the foot of the Cross as well as becomes the pattern for all of her future "children" of faith and for the fidelity of the Church herself, of which Mary is the primordial symbol. The Church and her members can only be obedient to the Father if they have faith in his Word—Jesus, the incarnate Son.

Bernard and Bonaventure

A thousand years later, Bernard of Clairvaux appropriated and advanced Irenaeus's insight that Mary, in the Annunciation, undid what Eve had done and so became the new Eve.[5] He states, in the preface to his four *Homilies in Praise of the Blessed Virgin Mary*, that he will praise Mary "based on the gospel reading in which Luke tells the story of the Lord's annunciation."[6]

---

life received life. For the Lord came to seek back the lost sheep, and it was man who was lost; and therefore he did not become some other formation, but he likewise of her that was descended from Adam, preserved the likeness of formation; for Adam had necessarily to be restored in Christ, that mortality be absorbed in immortality, and Eve in Mary, that a virgin, become the advocate of a virgin, should undo and destroy virginal disobedience by virginal obedience.

Translation from J. P. Smith, *Ancient Christian Writers, St. Irenaeus, Proof of the Apostolic Preaching* (Westminster, MD: Newman Press, 1952), 1:33.

5. While Bernard advances the same Marian themes as Irenaeus, often in similar words, it is unclear if he actually read his works. If he did not, his knowledge of Irenaeus may have come from readings in the Divine Office or from a received theological tradition. See Francisco De P. Solá, "Fuentes Patristicas de la Mariologia de San Bernardo," *Estudios Eclessiásticos* 23 (1949): 223n68.

6. Bernard, *Homilies in Praise of the Blessed Virgin Mary*, trans. Marie-Bernard Saïd with an introduction by Chrysogonus Waddell (Kalamazoo, MI: Cistercian, 1993), 3.

Bonaventure, who was well acquainted with these homilies and quoted them extensively, confirmed Bernard's understanding of the Annunciation as Mary's undoing of the sin of Eve.[7] For both Bernard and Bonaventure, the Annunciation is the central praiseworthy event in Mary's life, for all of the other mysteries she embodies find their focus and source in this event.[8]

Mary's Undoing of the Sin of Eve

Bernard exhorts Adam, "our Father," to rejoice "and you more especially mother Eve, exult." While both Adam and Eve were "the destroyers of mankind," both are to find "consolation in your daughter ... especially you, woman, from whom evil had its beginning, you whose reproach has been handed down to all womankind."[9] No longer can men reproach women for the curse of sin; rather, Eve is to run to Mary, who will hear her plea. Mary will reconcile her mother Eve with the Father. "For, if man fell on account of woman, surely he will rise only through another woman." Divine Wisdom now prevails against Adam's shameful accusations against his wife.

Yes, he [the Father] gave woman for woman: a wise one for a foolish one; a humble one for an arrogant one. Instead of the tree of death, she offers you [Adam] a taste of life; in place of the poisonous fruit of bitterness she holds out to you the sweetness of eternity's fruit. [Adam must now exclaim:] "Lord, the woman whom you gave to be with me, she gave me the fruit of the tree of life, and I ate; and it was sweeter than honey to my mouth, for by it have you given me life."

For Bernard, it was for all of the above reasons that the angel was sent to a virgin, "admirable and worthy of all honor ... O fairest among all women! You have repaired your parents' weakness and restored life to all their offspring."[10] Moreover, God was anticipating Mary when he spoke of the enmity between the seed of the serpent and "her seed." "It is obvious that it

7. Bonaventure Bernard ninety times throughout his corpus quotes when discussing Mary. Interestingly, in his *Summa Theologiae*, Aquinas does not refer to or quote from Bernard when discussing Mary.

8. G. Tavard designates "the primacy" of the Annunciation as the central organizing event and theme around which Bonaventure constructs the whole of his Mariology. *The Forthbringer of God* (Chicago: Franciscan Herald Press, 1988), viii, 47, 49, 185.

9. For the Eve/Mary parallel within medieval theology, see L. Gambero, *Mary in the Middle Ages* (San Francisco: Ignatius Press, 2000), multiple references in the index.

10. The above quotations are from Bernard, *Homilies in Praise of the Blessed Virgin Mary*, Homily 2.3, 16–17.

was she [Mary] who bruised this venomous head, for she brought to nothing all suggestions of the evil one, those of carnal lust as well as those of spiritual pride."[11] Thus the manner in which God accomplished humankind's salvation was not only, for Bernard, an expression of his power, but also a demonstration of his wisdom. "It pleased him [God] to reconcile man to himself in the same way and by the same means that had caused him to fall ... Just as the devil deceived the woman first and then overcome man through the woman, so now he was going to be lead astray by a virgin woman and later be vanquished openly by the man Christ."[12]

Bonaventure took up this theme from Bernard, employing almost his very words, though he does so in a more systematic fashion as befits a Scholastic. In his initial notes (entitled *Dubia circa litteram*) that would form the basis for his *Commentary on the Sentences of Peter Lombard*, Bonaventure states:

the order of reparation would correspond to the order of prevarication. Hence, as the devil tempted a woman to bring her into doubt, and through doubt to consent and through consent to the fall; so the angel announced to the Virgin, that by this Annunciation she would be brought to faith, and by faith to consent, and by consent to the conception of the Son of God through the Holy Spirit.[13]

Later in his *Breviloquium,* Bonaventure argues that God, as the first Principle of humankind's salvation, acts in a manner that is in keeping with his divine wisdom, and thus he acts in a manner that is "most congruous" as when "medicine specifically corresponds to the disease, the restoration to the fall, and the remedy to the injury."[14]

The human race had fallen through the suggestion of the devil, through the consent of a deceived woman, and through a begetting become lustful that handed down original sin to the offspring. Conversely, and most fittingly, there was here [at the Annunciation] a good angel persuading to what was good, a Virgin believing him and consenting to the proposed good, and the love of the Holy Spirit making her both holy and fruitful for a virginal conception. Thus, "evils were healed by their opposites."[15]

---

11. Ibid., Homily 2.4, 18.   12. Ibid., Homily 2.13, 25.

13. Bonaventure, *Dubia circa litteram* III, d. 2, dub. IV. Translation taken from Tavard, *Forthbringer of God*, 8.

14. Bonaventure, *Breviloquium* 4.3.1. From José de Vinck, trans., *The Works of Bonaventure* (Paterson, NJ: St. Anthony's Guild Press, 1963), 2:150.

15. Bonaventure, *Breviloquium* 4.3.3, 151. Bonaventure quotes Gregory the Great, *Homiliae*

As Bernard and Bonaventure note, Mary contributed to the reversal of the sin of Eve because Mary possessed the virtues that Eve lacked. Eve, the foolish virgin, arrogantly did not believe the word that God spoke to her. She thoughtlessly listened to the lies of Satan and so recklessly disobeyed God. She offered to her husband, and through him to her progeny, the poisonous fruit of death. In contrast, Mary, the wise virgin, humbly believed the word that God spoke to her though the angel Gabriel. In accepting, in faith, the truth spoken to her, she conceived the fruit of new life—the incarnate Son of God. Mary, in reversing the words and actions of the first Eve, thus became, through her son, the new and true Eve—the mother of all the living.

What is crucial for Bernard and Bonaventure's understanding of the Annunciation as Mary's undoing of the sin of Eve is to recognize her humble station before God, her faith in the truth of his word, and her wholehearted obedience to his will. These virtues, counterpoised to Eve's vices, compelled Mary, in the Holy Spirit, to pronounce her *fiat* and so assume her supreme title, the foundation of all her other titles—Mother of God.

Mary's Humble Obedient Faith

Bernard never tires of praising Mary's humility, for from it springs her faith and obedience. So great is Mary's humility that, in the moving passage where he speaks of Gabriel anxiously awaiting Mary's positive response— along with Adam, Abraham, David, all of fallen humankind, and even the Lord himself—Bernard fears that she will think herself so unworthy of becoming the Mother of God that she will reply in the negative. Bernard impatiently presses Mary, saying "Let humility take courage and shyness confidence. This is not a moment for virginal simplicity to forget prudence." After Mary finally gives her *fiat* to the relief of all, Bernard exclaims:

Humility is always found in company with divine grace … To prepare the throne of grace, therefore, humility replied. "Behold," she said, "I am the handmaiden of the Lord." What is this humility so sublime that it resists honor and refuses to vaunt itself in glory? She is chosen to be the mother of God, and she calls herself a hand-

---

in Evangeliae II, from Homily 32:1. See also Aristotle, *Nicomachean Ethics* 2:3; Robert C. Bartlett and Susan D. Collins, *Aristotle's Nicomachean Ethics: A New Translation* (Chicago: University of Chicago Press, 2011).

maid. Surely this is a not insignificant sign of humility, when glory is proposed not to forget humility. It is no great thing to be humble when cast down, but honored humility is a great and rare virtue.[16]

Moreover, it was Mary's humility, in contrast to Eve's arrogant disobedience, that gave voice to her obedient faith. In that humble, obedient faith she conceived and gave birth to the Son of God incarnate. Interpreting the Gospel parable of the leaven, Bernard exclaims:

Happy the woman, blessed among women, in whose chaste womb this bread was baked when the fire of the Holy Spirit overshadowed her! Happy, I tell you, the woman who stirred the leaven of her faith into three measures. Indeed, she conceived in faith, she gave birth in faith, and as Elizabeth said, "*Blessed is she who believed, because what was spoken to her by the Lord has come to pass.*"[17]

Mary was able in the Annunciation to undo the sin of Eve because she, unlike prideful Eve, was humble. It was this humility that allowed her to acknowledge the truth that God spoke to her and obediently submit to it in faith. A similar configuration of virtues can also be found in Bonaventure where he quotes Bernard extensively.

Commenting on Mary's *fiat*, Bonaventure states that it was "done fittingly and in order, because *it proceeds from a humble predisposition, is performed out of love*, and *pronounced out of faith*." With regard to faith, Bonaventure perceives that it was only because Mary first conceived the word of truth in her heart through faith that she was able to conceive the Son of God in her womb. Mary is most blessed of all women "because in believing you have conceived, and in conceiving you have brought forth blessings sufficient for all nations."[18] With regard to humility, Bonaventure gives Abigail and Ruth as examples of Old Testament women who prefigured Mary's humility and then is content with merely quoting twice from Bernard's fourth sermon on *The Praises of the Blessed Virgin Mary*. In commenting on her *Magnificat*, Bonaventure states that because Mary "humbled herself beyond all others, [she] magnified the

---

16. The above quotations are from Bernard, *Homilies in Praise of the Blessed Virgin Mary*, Homily 4.9, 54–55.

17. "On the Lord's Birthday," Sermon 2.4 in I. Edmonds, W. B. Beckett, and C. Greenia, trans., with an introduction by W. Verball, *Bernard of Clairvaux: Sermons for Advent and the Christmas Season* (Kalamazoo, MI: Cistercian, 2007), 110.

18. Quotations are from Bonaventure's *Commentary on the Gospel of Luke*, 1.85 in R. J. Karris, trans., *The Works of St. Bonaventure* (St. Bonaventure, NY: Franciscan Institute, 2001).

Lord beyond others."[19] Finally, Mary gave her consent with perfect love, desiring communion with God above all else, for to conceive the Son of God within her own womb would be a singular grace of divine communion.[20]

Humility likewise gives distinction to virginity. For Bernard, Eve was a virgin when she sinned, and so virginity is no guarantor of virtue. For this reason, Bernard insists that Mary's humility gives splendor to her virginity. "Virginity is a praiseworthy virtue, but humility is by far the more necessary. The one is only counseled; the other is demanded." While Mary was the purest of virgins, "yet I [Bernard] say that without humility not even Mary's virginity would have been acceptable ... And even if it was because of her virginity that she found favor, she conceived nevertheless on account of her humility. Thus there is no doubt that her virginity was found pleasing because her humility made it so."[21]

Bernard and Bonaventure identify the Annunciation as the central mystery in Mary's life, because through this event the Son of God became man and was born of her. This conferred upon her the matchless title of Mother of God. They thus perceive that all privileged graces given to Mary either prepare for or are a consequence of the Nativity.

The Mysteries of Mary

Unlike unholy Eve, who conceived her children with the sinful mark of death, holy Mary conceived her Son as the author of new life. While Bernard and Bonaventure adamantly denied her immaculate conception, both were equally convinced that Mary was full of grace at the time of the Annunciation.[22] This was necessary in order to provide a worthy holy dwelling for the all-holy Son of God. Bernard professed, "So that she might conceive and give birth to the Holy of Holies, she was made holy in her body by the gift of virginity and she accepted that gift of humility to become holy in

19. Bonaventure, *Commentary on the Gospel of Luke* 1.87, 92–93.

20. Ibid., 1.67–69, 77–80.

21. Quotations are from Bernard's *Homilies in Praise of the Blessed Virgin Mary*, Homily 1.5, 9–10. See also Homily 1.7, 10–11; Homily 2.2, 16.

22. For Bernard, while Mary was conceived with the stain of Original Sin, prior to her birth she was filled with grace. "And so, although it has been given to very few to of the sons of men to be born holy [Bernard has in mind Jeremiah, John the Baptist and Mary], it has not been given to any to be conceived holy, so that the prerogative of a holy conception might be reserved for him [Jesus] alone who sanctified all of us." Translation from B. S. James, *The Letters of St. Bernard of Clairvaux* (Stroud: Sutton, 1998), Letter 215.8, 293.

spirit too."[23] Bernard asks: How could Mary be "full of grace" as Gabriel proclaimed, and yet have the Holy Spirit further overshadow her? "Could it be that the first grace had filled only her soul, and that the second was now to be showered in her womb because the fullness of divinity which already dwelt within her spiritually, as it does in many a saint, will now begin to dwell within her corporally as it had done in no other saint?"[24]

Bonaventure expresses similar sentiments:

Thus, the Blessed Virgin became a Mother in the most complete sense, for, without man, she conceived the Son of God through the action of the Holy Spirit. Because the love of the Holy Spirit burned so intensely in her soul, the power of the Holy Spirit wrought marvels in her flesh, by means of grace prompting, assisting, and elevating her nature as required for this wondrous conception.[25]

In undoing the sinful work of Eve, Mary, as the all-holy virgin, not only conceived, undefiled, by the overshadowing of the Holy Spirit, the Son of God within her womb, but she also, unlike mother Eve, gave birth without pain or loss of her virginity.[26] Bernard exclaims: "O truly new wonder! He was conceived without shame, born without pain! Eve's curse was transformed in our Virgin, for she bore a child without pain." While Christ took upon himself the shame of our ancestral sin and the pain of our hereditary death, he gave Mary as a sign of the new creation. "To give us confidence that he would take these things away from us, he first kept his mother immune from both, so that his conception was without shame, and his birth was without pain." Moreover, Mary maintained her virginity even in her motherhood. "This is truly new and unheard of! A virgin gave birth and remained inviolate after the birth; she possessed the fecundity of offspring with the integrity of her flesh, and had the joy of being a mother with the honor of being a virgin." In the preservation of her virginity, Mary broke the hold of Eve's sinful spell. "The mother is without corruption of her virginity, the Son is without any spot of sin. Eve's curse does not befall the mother, nor on her child has fallen the universal condition" of sin.[27]

23. Bernard, *Homilies in Praise of the Blessed Virgin Mary*, Homily 2.2, 16.

24. Ibid., Homily 4.3, 49.

25. Bonaventure, *Breviloquium* 4.3.5, 153.

26. See Bernard, *Homilies in Praise of the Blessed Virgin Mary*, Homily 2.1, 15.

27. Quotations are from Bernard, "On the Eve of the Lord's Birth," Sermon 4.3–5 in Edmonds, Beckett, and Greenia, trans., *Bernard of Clairvaux*, 72–74.

Speaking on behalf of Gabriel, Bonaventure concurs with Bernard:

You asked: How will I conceive? And to this I respond that you will be fruitful without corruption, you will conceive without sexual desire, you shall bring forth without labor, because this is not from male seed, but from the power of the Holy Spirit.[28]

Bonaventure even echoes Bernard's own words: "And therefore, this birthing was new, just as his conception was, because just as he was conceived without shame, so he was born without pain."[29]

The special and particular graces that were bestowed upon Mary empowering her to be the humble and obedient Virgin Mother of God and so undoing the sinful work of prideful and disobedient Eve, ultimately leads, for Bernard, to her glorious assumption into heaven as its Queen. Bernard explicitly joins together the mystery of the Annunciation with the mystery of the Assumption.

We ought to rejoice with her [Mary], because today she is received at her entrance into the holy city by him who was received by her at his entrance into the citadel (*castellum*) of this world. And oh! With how much honour is she received and welcomed! With what exultation! With what glory! There was not upon earth a worthier place than the temple of her own most blessed womb, into which Mary might receive the Son of God; nor is there in heaven a more honourable seat than the royal throne upon which today Mary has been exalted by Mary's Son.[30]

Finally, for Bernard, heavenly Mary is contrasted with earthbound Eve as our intercessor and mediator. While a man and woman caused humankind grievous harm, "by another man and another woman all that was lost has been restored to us, not without abundant grace." Not only has God provided humankind with a new Adam in Jesus Christ, but he also gave "Mary, a second Eve." While Christ could have accomplished the work of salvation on his own, "It seemed more congruous that as both sexes contributed to the ruin of our race, so should both have a part in the work of reparation." But so great and majestic is Christ our mediator that

---

28. Bonaventure, *Commentary on the Gospel of Luke* 1.62, 73. See also 1.55, 70.

29. Ibid., 2.10, 144.

30. Bernard, "First Sermon for the Feast of the Assumption of the Blessed Virgin," in A Priest of Mount Melleray, trans., *St. Bernard's Sermons on the Blessed Virgin Mary* (Chulmleigh: Augustine, 1987), 168–69.

we have need of another to mediate between him and us, and for this we can find none so well qualified as Mary. A most cruel mediatrix was our mother Eve, through whom the "old serpent" communicated the mortal poison of sin even to the man; but Mary is faithful, Mary offers the remedy of salvation both to men and women. The former [Eve] became the means of our seduction, the latter [Mary] co-operated in our reconciliation; the former was made the instrument of temptation, the latter the channel of redemption.[31]

While the above would rightly be unacceptable as an authentic understanding and expression of Mary's mediation between humankind and Jesus, Bernard gives a better, though still not entirely satisfactory, rendering of Mary's role as our intercessor.

May your integrity plead before him for the guilt of our corruption, and may the humility which pleases God procure pardon for our vainglory. May your abundant divine love cover the multitude of our sins, and your glorious fruitfulness confer on us a fruitfulness of merit. Our Lady, our Mediatrix, and our Advocate, reconcile us to your Son, commend us to your Son and represent us before your Son. O blessed Lady, through the grace which you have found, through the mercy to which you gave birth, bring it about that he who by your mediation—deigned to share our weakness and wretchedness may by your intercession—make us sharers of his glory and blessedness.[32]

Bonaventure also ascribes to Mary the role of heavenly advocate and mediator. Upon Gabriel's departure, Bonaventure remarks that not only did Mary conceive the Son of God as man within her womb, but also that multitudes of angels stood guard over her and reverenced her dignity as the Mother of God.

Thus, she [Mary] had been designated by that *ladder*, upon which the Lord had rested, and the angels were ascending. It was the ladder Jacob saw as we find in Genesis 28:12–13 and concerning which we read in Genesis 28:17: "This is nothing other than *the house* of God and the *gate* of heaven." Because no one can now enter heaven, unless he passes through her, so we must return to God through her. And therefore, she is said to be *house, gate,* and *ladder. House* because of the conception of Christ; *gate* because of the birth of Christ; *ladder* because of ascent to God.—

31. Bernard, "Sermon for the Sunday within the Octave of the Assumption," in A Priest of Mount Melleray, trans., *St. Bernard's Sermons on the Blessed Virgin Mary*, 206–7.

32. Bernard, "On the Lord's Advent," Sermon 2.5 in Edmonds, Beckett, and Greenia, trans., *Bernard of Clairvaux*, 17–18.

Thus, let us never depart from her, but having cast ourselves at her feet, let us always greet her with: *Hail, full of grace*, so that through her who found grace and mercy beyond all women in the sight of that great king, we might "find grace and obtain mercy through timely aid" (Hebrews 4:16).[33]

Bonaventure professes that God has given humankind three advocates—Jesus, the Holy Spirit, and Mary. Like Bernard, however, Bonaventure's expression is equally colored by the fact that Mary must soften the severity of her Son as the Judge.

She is the advocate of intercession, who, in order better to move the judge, shows her female sex. She is the Esther at whose sight the king's heart was changed into kindness, as is prefigured in Esther 15:11. She is the one to whom the Church sings, *Eia ergo, advocate nostra* [Oh, our Advocate].[34]

For both Bernard and Bonaventure the Annunciation is the event that so binds Mary to the life of her Son that she will follow him not only to his cross, but she will also follow him into his resurrected glory where, as Queen of heaven, she will be, along with him, our unfailing advocate. Likewise, in union with her Son, the new Adam, as the new Eve, she will dispense the new life of the Holy Spirit upon all of her children who are reborn in her Son. The undoing of Eve's sin is now fully complete. Eve brought sin and death into the world and so she and her children were expelled from the earthly Paradise. Mary brought forth the one who dispels sin and conquers death and so opens the gates to the new and heavenly Paradise.

A Theological Conclusion: The Active Role of Mary

To conclude, I highlight one point that gives rise to a theological concern. By making the juxtaposition of Eve and Mary central to their understanding of the Annunciation, Bernard and Bonaventure have allowed Mary to assume a distinctive and unique active role in the foundational mystery of our salvation—the Incarnation. As Eve was "coresponsible," through her words and deeds, for the sinful race of Adam, so Mary is now coresponsible,

33. Bonaventure, *Commentary on the Gospel of Luke* 1.70, 81–82.
34. Bonaventure, *Collationes* [Sermons on the Gospel of John] 53. Translation from Tavard, *Forthbringer of God*, 88. For further discussions of Mary as our Advocate in Bonaventure, see Ibid., 25, 149.

through her words and deeds, for the re-creation of Adam's sinful race. By casting her as the new Eve, it is impossible for Mary to be a merely passive character within the drama of the Incarnation. Only Mary's *fiat* allowed the Holy Spirit to overshadow her, and through this joint action of Mary and the Spirit did the Son of God take flesh within her womb and so become the new Adam. As Eve, through her arrogant words of disbelief and shameful deed of disobedience, actively conceived sin and gave birth to death, so Mary, through her humble words of faith and virtuous deed of obedience, actively conceived goodness incarnate and so gave birth to life.[35]

Moreover, Bernard and Bonaventure, through the counterpoising of Eve and Mary, have firmly situated their respective dynamic Mariologies within Christology. Mary is significant only in that she actively cooperated with the Holy Spirit in the conception of the Son of God incarnate, and in so doing she actively took her place at the side of her Son throughout his whole work of redemption. It is upon this theological basis—Mary's active role in the coming to be of the Son of God incarnate—that any valid notion of her joining herself to and cooperating with her Son in the work of salvation, both while on earth and now in heaven, must be founded.

The Nativity: The Eve/Mary Parallelism

There is one theological query concerning the Eve/Mary parallelism that flows directly from what has been stated above. While Bernard and Bonaventure's understanding that Mary gave birth without pain was an already ancient tradition, one still present today, I wonder whether this un-

---

35. The Second Vatican Council highlighted this very point. It stated:

Thus the daughter of Adam, Mary consenting to the word of God, became the Mother of Jesus. Committing herself whole-heartedly and impeded by no sin to God's saving will, she devoted herself totally, as a handmaid of the Lord, to the person and work of her Son, under and with him, serving the mystery of redemption, by the grace of Almighty God. Rightly, therefore, the Fathers see Mary not merely as passively engaged by God, but as freely cooperating in the work of man's salvation through faith and obedience. (*Lumen Gentium* 56)

Translation from Austin Flannery, ed., *Vatican Council II: The Conciliar and Post Conciliar Documents* (Wilmington, DE: Scholarly Resources, 1975). The Council Fathers proceed to quote from Irenaeus and Jerome as well as reference many other Fathers. Bernard and Bonaventure would approve wholeheartedly.

derstanding is genuinely in keeping with the Eve/Mary parallelism, particularly in light of the active role that Mary assumes within it. Bernard and Bonaventure argue that Jesus, in being miraculously born of Mary in a painless manner, was already revealing in her the heavenly future—the painless dispensation of the heavenly new creation. But if Jesus undoes the penalty of Adam's sin by taking upon himself Adam's sin-marred nature, putting it to death through his suffering on the Cross and so re-creating it in his resurrection, why should Mary not undo the curse of Eve by giving birth in pain, in so doing contributing to humankind's re-creation in union with her Son? If Mary cosuffers with her Son as she stands beneath the Cross, why should she not suffer when she gives birth to her Son? This is particularly fitting, as it was from her own passible flesh that he received a human nature capable of suffering. This is totally in keeping with the whole thrust of this essay; that is, that the Eve/Mary parallelism provides the theological foundation for Mary's active and sustained role in the entire work of salvation. By allowing her to suffer in giving birth, one preserves Mary's active role in the undoing of Eve's sin. As Christ, in becoming man, assumed the penalty of Adam's sin, and so on the Cross transformed it into an act of loving salvation, so Mary assumed the curse of Eve, giving birth in pain, and so transformed it into a loving act of giving birth to the one who would free humankind from all pain and suffering.

To assert that Mary gave birth in pain raises the obvious question concerning the integrity of Mary's perpetual virginity, however. There is no doubt that Mary was a virgin prior to her conception of Jesus; that the conception itself was virginal in that she conceived not by the seed of man but by the overshadowing of the Holy Spirit; and that she remained a virgin subsequent to giving birth to Jesus. But if she gave birth in pain, does this not imply that the integrity of Mary's virginity was jeopardized?[36] This is, it appears to me, not necessarily the case.

In order to preserve the virginal integrity of Mary, Bernard and Bonaven-

36. For short historical studies on the question of Mary's preserving her virginity in giving birth to Jesus, see M. O'Carroll, "Virginity *in Partu*," in *Theotokos*, 361–62; L. G. Owens and F. M. Jelly, "Virgin Birth," in *The New Catholic Encyclopedia*, 2nd ed. (Washington, DC: Catholic University of America Press, 2002), 14:532–36; Graef, *Mary*, 1:34–100; T. Beattie, "Mary in Patristic Theology," and E. De Visscher, "Marian Devotion in the Latin West in the Later Middle Ages," in Boss, ed., *Mary*, 96–99, 189–92, respectively.

ture (and Aquinas and many others) have argued that Jesus was miraculously born of her without pain, lest a normal physical birth in pain would nullify her virginity. What is miraculous here is the manner of the birth in order to guarantee the physical integrity of the virginity.[37] I think this mode of thinking and arguing is misconceived, however, for it erroneously rotates the hierarchy of mysteries embodied in Mary's life. Since the title "Mother of God" holds primacy, the principal concern should not be that of reconciling Mary's motherhood with her virginity, but that of reconciling Mary's virginity with her motherhood.[38]

While the ancient, and even authoritative, tradition desired to preserve the virginity of Mary, which I also wish to uphold, it must be remembered that Mary's virginity is affirmed only in order to enhance the singularity of her Motherhood and not vice versa. Mary is the "Virgin Mother," and while this title is a compound noun, the noun "virgin" also acts as an adjectival qualifier to the noun "mother," and does so in a manner that is not reciprocal for the noun "mother." It would be improper, as its absence in the tradition bears witness, to speak of Mary as a "Mother Virgin." It is precisely as an adjectival qualifier that the term "virgin" infinitely enhances the nature of Mary's motherhood. It is because "virgin" specifically accentuates the marvel of Mary's motherhood that it would erroneous to undermine her authentic motherhood for the sake of her virginity, because to do so would deprive Mary of the supreme title that one wishes to enhance—that of being the Mother of God.

In light of the above, if physical integrity is absolutely essential for preserving Mary's virginity, then I argue that even though she gave birth in a natural manner and so in pain, it was her virginity that was miraculously

37. Aquinas expresses the argument precisely: "The pains of childbirth are caused by the infant opening the passage from the womb. Now it has been said above that Christ came forth from the closed womb of his mother, and, consequently, without opening the passage. Consequently there was no pain in that birth, as neither was there any corruption" (*ST* III, q. 35, a. 6). Translation from Fathers of the English Dominican Province, trans., *Summa Theologica* (New York: Benziger Brothers, 1946). For recent discussions of this issue, especially among those who have argued that Jesus in his birth opened the womb of Mary (e.g., A. Mitterer, K. Rahner, O. Semmelroth, D. Ryan, and J. Galot), see Graef, *Mary*, 1:12–19. She provides bibliographical references.

38. J. McHugh exemplifies the false reversal of this hierarchy of mysteries. He states, "When we are considering Mary, then, the title 'ever-virgin' takes precedence over 'virgin-mother.'" *The Mother of Jesus in the New Testament* (New York: Doubleday, 1975), 346.

preserved in the very act of natural childbirth. What was miraculous was not the manner in which Mary gave birth, but the manner in which her virginity was preserved while giving birth naturally. In the act of giving birth, Mary was *by nature* a mother while miraculously remaining a virgin. In the act of giving birth, she was not naturally a virgin while miraculously becoming a mother. If Mary merely passively and miraculously "gave birth" to Jesus in that he simply came forth from her without her being actively involved (that is, physically active in giving birth to him in pain), then it is difficult to conclude that she is truly the Mother of God.[39]

Although the theological tradition, from quite early on, and the subsequent magisterial pronouncements have maintained the truth that Mary remained a virgin in giving birth to Jesus, both simply presumed that this could only be asserted if a miraculous painless birth were posited. But it must be remembered that one miracle is as easy for God to perform as another. It is a question of discerning, as the Scholastics would argue, what is and is not appropriate and fitting. Since Mary's supreme title is "Mother of God," I believe that it is theologically more fitting for Mary to give birth to Jesus in a natural physical manner rather than for him to be born miraculously. Because theological priority ought to be given to Mary's genuine

---

39. It is extremely fascinating that, to my knowledge, no patristic or medieval theologian ever commented on how one should interpret Revelation 12:1–2 in light of Mary giving birth to Jesus. There it states, "And a great portent appeared in heaven, a woman clothed with the sun, with the moon under her feet, and on her head a crown of twelve stars; she was with child and she cried out in her pangs of birth, in anguish for delivery." The woman in this passage is traditionally interpreted as a symbol of the Church anguishing to give birth in pain to newborn Christians. A. Feuillet writes:

> The ancient commentators differed widely in their explanation of the difficult chapter 12 of the Apocalypse. An ecclesial exegesis is by far the best attested: it is that of most of the ancient interpreters. The Marian exegesis, so obvious at first reading inasmuch as the text speaks of the Messiah's mother, was impeded both by the reference to pangs of childbirth in verse 2, and by the false conception then operative concerning the literary genre of the Apocalypse: could a prophecy like the Apocalypse be recounting past events like the birth of Jesus in Bethlehem?

Jesus and His Mother: The Role of the Virgin Mary in Salvation History and the Place of Woman in the Church (Still River, MA: St. Bede's Press, 1984), 27–28. While the ecclesial interpretation is an accurate understanding, it is only valid for the Church, I would argue, if it is equally valid for Mary, who is literally in this case the supreme type of what the Church is. Only if Mary, having assumed the curse of Eve, gave birth to Jesus, in pain and anguish, does she represent and so be the perfect icon of the Church.

motherhood, it is more fitting for Mary's virginity to be miraculously preserved in the course of her giving birth naturally, since the miraculous preservation of her virginity accentuates the absolute purity of the conception and birth of her divine Son.[40] This also better grounds the two truths that the Church wishes to affirm—first that Mary is indeed the true and authentic Mother of God, and second that she became so while miraculously preserving her virginity.

Conclusion

The writings of Bernard and Bonaventure demonstrate the centrality of the Annunciation within the life of Mary and, more specifically within this mystery, that Mary undoes the work of Eve. The Annunciation also sets the template for all the other mysteries in Mary's life, for, as she actively undid Eve's sin in the Annunciation, so she continued to undo Eve's sin in actively giving birth to her Son and subsequently accompanying her Son not only to the Cross but also into heaven. There, as Queen of heaven and earth, she continues, in union with her glorious Son, to intercede on behalf of all of humankind.

40. *Catechism of the Catholic Church,* 2nd ed. (Washington, DC: United States Catholic Conference, 1997) states that "the deepening of faith in the virginal motherhood led the Church to confess Mary's real and perpetual virginity even in the act of giving birth to the Son of God made man. In fact, Christ's birth 'did not diminish his mother's virginal integrity but sanctified it'" (n499).

The catechism quotes *Lumen Gentium* n57 and gives multiple references to other magisterial documents. While the catechism teaches, in accordance with the authoritative tradition, that Mary in giving birth remained a virgin, it does not specify in what manner this preservation was accomplished. Also, it should be noted that the catechism speaks clearly of "even in the act of giving birth" and not of its miraculous nature.

CHAPTER 12

The Human Acts of Christ and the Acts That Are the Sacraments

In their constitution on the sacred liturgy, *Sacrosanctum Concilium*, the Fathers of the Second Vatican Council stated:

> The liturgy, then, is rightly seen as an exercise of the priestly office of Jesus Christ. It involves the presentation of man's sanctification under the guise of signs perceptible by the senses and its accomplishment in ways appropriate to each of these signs. In it full public worship is performed by the Mystical Body of Jesus Christ, that is, by the Head and his members.

It follows that every liturgical celebration, because it is an action of Christ the Priest and of his Body, which is the Church, is a sacred action surpassing all others. No other action of the Church can equal its efficacy by the same title and to the same degree.[1]

In this essay I address, from within a Thomistic context, what is here professed by the Council Fathers. As the Council emphasizes the primacy of the "sacred action" within the sacramental liturgy, there is also a primacy of "act" that makes "action" possible within Aquinas's thought, which I

Originally published as "The Human Acts of Christ and the Acts That Are the Sacraments," in *Ressourcement Thomism: Sacred Doctrine, the Sacraments, and the Moral Life*, ed. R. Hütter and M. Levering. (Washington, DC: Catholic University of America Press, 2010), 150–68. Reprinted by permission.

1. *Sacrosanctum Concilium* § 7. Translation from A. Flannery, ed., *Vatican Council II: The Conciliar and Post Conciliar Documents* (Wilmington, DE: Scholarly Resources, 1975).

believe extends to his understanding of the sacraments.[2] It is this conciliar and Thomistic focus on the sacraments as the personal "acts" of Christ and of his Body that gives them their inherent dynamism and vitality, and thus their unequalled efficacy.

In order to conceive rightly and to articulate adequately this primacy of act within Aquinas's sacramental theology, I demonstrate that the sacraments are founded upon Jesus's historic priestly human actions, which he now, as its risen Head, actively makes sacramentally present within his Body through those ministers who act *in persona Christi*. I also consider how all believers are empowered to participate actively in these dynamic sacramental acts and so actively lay hold of the salvific events that they make efficaciously present. While I do not always agree fully with Aquinas's presentation, my hope is that this essay will not only further our appreciation of his understanding of the sacraments, but also enhance our contemporary appreciation of these marvelous acts that are the sacraments.[3]

2. We find this already within Aquinas's early work, *De ente et essentia*, where he detects this primacy of act within the metaphysical composition of finite beings. Because there is nothing within the definition of any finite being, what it is (*essentia*) demands that it be, that it must be given being (*esse*) in order to be and so be in act. Aquinas further concludes that, since finite beings do exist and cannot, by their own nature, account for their own existence, there must be a being whose very nature, *essentia*, is being itself, *ipsum esse*, and so *actus purus*, pure act, who is thus capable of bestowing being, *esse*, upon all other beings. This being is called God. The act of creation God, by the pure act that he is, bestows the act of existence upon finite reality, thus allowing it not only to exist, but also to act in accordance with the potential inherent within its essence. The Thomistic principle is that a being can act, perform actions, only insofar is it is in act; that is, only to the degree that it possess the perfection of "being."

For example, I have argued that the persons of the Trinity, because they possess the fullness of being, are subsistent relations fully in act. Although the terms "Father," "Son," and "Holy Spirit" are nouns, what they designate are the fully relational acts by which they are the one God. The term "Father" is that act by which he begets the Son and spirates the Holy Spirit, and so is the Father eternally subsisting only in relation to them. The term "Son" is that act of being Son of the Father and cospirator of the Holy Spirit, and so is the Son eternally subsisting only in relation to them. The term "Holy Spirit" is that act of conforming the Father to be the loving Father of the Son and conforming the Son to be the loving Son of the Father, and so is the Holy Spirit eternally subsisting only in relation to them. See T. G. Weinandy, *The Father's Spirit of Sonship: Reconceiving the Trinity* (Edinburgh: T&T Clark, 1994); *Does God Suffer?* (Notre Dame, IN: University of Notre Dame Press, 2000).

3. There are a number of excellent introductory studies and articles on Aquinas's understanding of the sacraments. For example, see, E. Schillebeeckx, *L'économie sacramentelle du salut* (Fribourg: Academic Press, 2004), 107–53; L. G. Walsh, "The Divine and the Human in St. Thomas's Theology of Sacraments," in *Ordo sapientiae et amoris: Image et message doctrina-*

The Human Acts of the Son: The Foundation of Sacramental Acts

To understand how the incarnate Son of God is the foundation of sacramental acts, it is necessary to grasp the metaphysics of the Incarnation and the kind of acts that necessarily flow from it. Within his incarnate state, the Son of God is always the principal actor, but the manner in which he acts is always *as man*, for that is the manner in which he now exists. For Aquinas, the assumed humanity is thus a personal instrument of Son. "The humanity of Christ is the instrument of the Godhead—not, indeed, an inanimate instrument, which nowise acts, but is merely acted upon; but an instrument animated by a rational soul, which is so acted upon as to act."[4] The Son of God does not employ his humanity as an external or separate instrument, as a man employs a pen to write. Rather, the Son of God personally acts through his humanity as a man acts through his own arms and hands. The Son of God is acting, and the manner in which he is acting is in accordance with his manner of existing—as man.[5]

---

les, ed. C.-J. Pinto de Oliveira (Fribourg: Editions Universitaires, 1993), 321–52; "Sacraments," in *The Theology of Thomas Aquinas*, ed. R. Van Nieuwenhove and J. Wawrykow (Notre Dame, IN: University of Notre Dame Press, 2005), 326–64; J. Yocum, "Sacraments in Aquinas," in *Aquinas on Doctrine: A Critical Introduction*, ed. T. G. Weinandy, D. Keating, and J. Yocum (London: T&T Clark/Continuum, 2004), 159–81.

4. *ST* III, q. 7, a. 2, ad 3. All translations are from Fathers of the English Dominican Province, trans., *Summa Theologica* (New York: Benziger Brothers, 1947). For an excellent study of this topic, see T. Tschipke, *L'humanité du Christ comme instrument de salut de la divinité* (Fribourg: Academic Press, 2003). See also P. G. Crowley, "*Instrumentum Divinitatis* in Thomas Aquinas: Recovering the Divinity of Christ," *Theological Studies* 52 (1991): 451–75.

5. This becomes clear when Aquinas speaks of the one operation within Christ. While the Son of God exists as God and so possesses a divine operation, such as sustaining the universe, he also possesses a human operation in that he exists as man. Miracles exemplify this unity of operation perfectly. Following Dionysius's understanding of a "theandric" act, Aquinas perceives such an "operation not by any confusion of the operations or powers of both natures, but inasmuch as his divine operation employs the human, and his human operation shares in the power of the divine," and thus "he [the Son] wrought divine things humanly, as when he healed the leper with a touch" (*ST* III, q. 19, a. 1, ad 1). Thus, for Aquinas, "to heal a leper is a proper work of the divine operation, but to touch him is the proper work of the human operation. Now both these operations concur in one work, inasmuch as one nature acts in union with the other" (*ST* III, q. 19, a. 1, ad 5). These operations concur in the one act of healing the leper because the divine Son of God performed the miracle through the instrumentality of his humanity. "If we speak of the soul of Christ as it is the instrument of the Word united to him, it

Most importantly for our study, the acts by which humankind is saved are, for Aquinas, the human acts of the divine Son. While only God could achieve our salvation, the Son of God accomplished such work through his human actions.

The instrument is said to act through being moved by the principle agent; and yet, besides this, it can have its proper operation through its own form ... And hence the action of the instrument as instrument is not distinct from the action of the principle agent; yet it may have another operation, inasmuch as it is a thing. Hence the operation of Christ's human nature, as an instrument of the Godhead, is not distinct from the operation of the Godhead; for the salvation wherewith the manhood of Christ saves us and that wherewith the Godhead saves us are not distinct.[6]

I now argue that there is in place a dynamic causal sequence beginning with the Son's priestly human salvific acts, which find their efficacious end in being made present through the sacraments.[7] The dynamic causal link is the risen High Priest Jesus Christ, who is now Head of his Body. As Head of his Body, he acts so as to make sacramentally present these saving mysteries within his Body. Thus the one who enacted these saving mysteries on earth is the same one who now makes these saving mysteries sacramentally present—the one Lord Jesus Christ. To this end, I first examine the sacramental significance of Christ's priestly acts and only then consider the acts of the risen Christ as Head of the Church. In so doing, I am purposely reversing the order of Aquinas's treatment. He first treats in question 8 of part III the grace of Christ's headship, which he possesses because of the incarnational union of the humanity to the divinity, and only addresses Christ's

---

had an instrumental power to effect all the miraculous transmutations ordainable to the end of the Incarnation, which is 'to re-establish all things that are in heaven and on earth' (Eph. 1:10)" (*ST* III, q. 13, a. 2). What should also be noted here is that, unlike within the Old Testament, where the touching of a leper contaminates the person, the touch of Jesus does not contaminate him but actually brings healing. The touching is thus essential to the healing. Because of their "matter," the sacraments will literally keep us in touch with Jesus so that we can be healed and sanctified.

6. *ST* III, q. 19, a. 1, ad 2.

7. Aquinas states: "Since, however, the death of Christ is, so to say, the universal cause of human salvation, and since a universal cause must be applied singly to each of its effects, it was necessary to show men some remedies through which the benefit of Christ's death could somehow be conjoined to them. It is of this sort, of course, that the sacraments of the Church are said to be" (*ScG* IV, ch. 56, 1). Translation from C. O'Neil, *On the Truth of the Catholic Faith* (Garden City, NJ: Image Books, 1957).

priesthood in question 22. I believe that because Aquinas founds, in question 8, the grace of headship upon the incarnational union, this will conflict with what he will say about Christ's priestly acts in question 22, and his acts as Head of his Body the Church. While Christ, throughout his life, acts as priest and as Head of the Church, his priestly actions culminate in the offering of his own life to the Father on the Cross, and it is only in his resurrection that he is fully empowered to be the Head of the Church. My concern throughout is to keep the dynamic bond between Christ's salvific acts and his sacramental acts.

The Human Acts of Christ as Priest and as Head of the Church

For Aquinas, a priest is a mediator between God and man, and as such his office is twofold. A priest "bestows divine things on the people" and "offers up the people's prayers to God, and, in a manner, makes satisfaction for their sins."[8] Christ fulfilled this priestly function in a preeminent manner, for he made it possible for humankind to share in the divine nature by reconciling it to God. Christ accomplished such a great work because, as priest, the act that he performed was to offer his own sacred humanity as a loving sacrifice.

Aquinas developed this understanding further. Human beings are required to offer sacrifice to God for three reasons: first, for the remission of sins; second, for the preservation of grace; and third, for perfect union with God. Again, Aquinas stresses here the singular importance of Christ's human acts.

Now these effects were conferred on us by the humanity of Christ. For, in the first place our sins were blotted out ... Secondly, through him we received the grace of salvation ... Thirdly, through him we have acquired the perfection of glory ... Therefore Christ himself, as man, was not only priest but also a perfect victim, being at the same time victim for sin, victim for peace-making, and a holocaust.[9]

8. *ST* III, q. 22, a. 1.
9. Ibid., q. 22, a. 2. A similar argument is found within the notion that Christ is the Mediator. Christ is Mediator between God and man not insofar as he is God, but insofar as he is man. "It belongs to him as man, to unite men to God, by communicating to men both precepts and gifts, and by offering satisfaction and prayers to for men. And therefore he is most truly called Mediator, as man" (*ST* III, q. 26, a. 2). Again: "Although it belongs to Christ as God to take

It is this threefold effect of his priestly sacrificial act as man that Christ, as the risen, empowered Head of the Church, will make present, in various ways, within the sacramental acts, the forgiveness of sin, the grace of salvation, and the perfecting of glory.

Grace was in Christ not merely as in an individual, but also as in the Head of the whole Church, to whom all are united, as members of the head, who constitute one mystical person (*mystice una persona*). And hence it is that Christ's merit extends to others inasmuch as they are his members; even as in a man the action of the head reaches in a manner to all of his members, since it perceives not merely for itself alone, but for all members.[10]

As the Head of the Church, Christ's actions bear upon his Body, the Church, and thus the human actions by which he merited his own glory are the same merit that he now extends to his Body. Aquinas treats this notion more fully when he speaks of the grace of Christ as Head of the Church.

Since the whole Church forms "one mystic body" whose members perform "divers acts," so Christ, as the Head of the Body, performs specific acts that pertain to him as Head. These acts concern "order," "perfection," and "authority." First, as Head of the Church and being nearest to God, his "grace is the highest and first." Second, as Head, Christ "had perfection as regards the fullness of all graces" (this finds its supreme summit in the Beatific Vision).[11] Third, as Head, Christ "has the power of bestowing grace on all the members of the Church."[12] Significantly, there is a progression that leads to Christ's ability to act as Head of the Church. Because he possesses the highest order of grace and the full perfection of grace, he, as Head, has the power and authority to bestow that grace upon the members of the Church. Moreover, because Christ is the Head of the Church, he bestows this grace as man. "To give grace or the Holy Spirit belongs to Christ as he is God, authoritatively; but instrumentally it belongs also to him as man, inasmuch as his manhood is the instrument of his Godhead."[13] Aquinas further

---

away sin authoritatively, yet it belongs to him, as man, to satisfy for the sin of the human race. And in this sense he is called the Mediator of God and man" (*ST* III, q. 26, a. 2, ad 3).

10. *ST* III, q. 19, a. 4.

11. For Aquinas, the highest grace and the most perfect grace in Christ is the beatific vision, which is a necessary result of the incarnational union of the divinity and humanity. See *ST* III, q. 10, a. 4.

12. *ST* III, q. 8, a. 1.   13. Ibid., q. 8, a. 1, ad 1.

accentuates the ability of the Son of God to act as man in the bestowing of grace.

Since everything acts inasmuch as it is a being in act, it must be the same act whereby it is in act and whereby it acts, as it is the same heat whereby fire is hot and whereby it heats … Now … grace was received by the soul of Christ in the highest way; and therefore from this pre-eminence of grace which he received, it is from him that this grace is bestowed on others,—and this belongs to the nature of head. Hence the personal grace, whereby the soul of Christ is justified, is essentially the same as his grace as he is the Head of the Church, and justifies others; but there is a distinction of reason between them.[14]

Because the Son's humanity possesses the fullness of grace, he, as man, is in act such that he is able to bestow grace upon the members of the Church. While Aquinas does clearly teach that, as Head, it is the Son of God as man who bestows grace upon the Church, it is here that I believe he may not appreciate fully the dynamic causal relationship and sequence between Christ's priestly action and his ability to act as Head of the Church.

Although Aquinas does speak of Christ meriting the grace of salvation through his priestly acts, when he actually discusses the headship of Christ, he does so exclusively within the context of the grace that flows into Christ's humanity owing to its singular, intimate union with his divinity. Thus the Son of God bestows grace upon his Church that his humanity first received by the very nature of the incarnational union. As Aquinas later states concerning Christ being Head of the Church, "Now the interior influx of grace is from no one save Christ, whose manhood, through its union with the Godhead, has the power of justifying."[15] Christ's manhood has the power to justify us not simply because of its union with his divinity, but also because of the priestly acts Christ performs as Head of the Church. Aquinas will acknowledge this, but he fails to grasp that this conflicts with his other view, that Christ possesses the fullest and highest grace solely because of the incarnational union of the humanity to the divinity.

14. Ibid., q. 8, a. 5.

15. Ibid., q. 8, a. 6. Aquinas also states that, because Christ's soul possesses the fullness of grace due to the nature of the incarnational union, "it is poured out from it to others" (*ST* III, q. 7, a. 9).

The Priestly Acts of Christ the Head

The reason Aquinas gets himself into this tension is that he insists, as did all the Scholastics, that Christ, from the moment of his conception, when his humanity was united to his divinity, possessed the beatific vision and thus the fullest and highest grace. For Aquinas, Christ always possessed the grace of headship, which he would bestow upon believers. It is this insistence on the beatific vision that is the cause of Aquinas's conflicted positions—between that of Christ possessing the fullness of grace at the moment of his incarnation or also through the merits of passion, death, and resurrection.

I argue that, while Christ possessed the fullness of grace insofar as it pertains to his earthly existence, it was only through the entirety of his life, culminating with his sacrificial death on the Cross, that he merited the glory of his resurrection and thus the complete perfection of his humanity with its perfect heavenly filial vision of his Father.[16] The fullest and highest grace only accrued to Christ's humanity when his humanity was glorified in the Resurrection, and only then did he become the Head of the Church with full power and authority. As the Letter to the Hebrews professes, Christ only became perfect through suffering (2:10, 5:9, 7:28), for it was only through his sacrificial death that he merited for himself and his brethren the glory of the Resurrection. Aquinas rightly contends that a being is able to act only insofar as he is in act, but the Son of God as man is only fully in act as risen, and thus it is only as resurrected, possessing the perfection of grace concomitant with his heavenly life, that he establishes himself fully as Head of the Church and so is empowered to act fully as such, bestowing grace upon it members.

If Christ's grace of headship is founded solely upon the incarnational union, this would undermine the meaning and significance of the sacraments, for the sacraments would then make present merely the grace of the Incarnation. But as Aquinas acknowledges, the sacramental acts do not

16. I have argued that the notion of the Beatific Vision is incompatible with Christ's earthly life and that it is the wrong category to employ with regard to the Son's incarnational state. See my "Jesus' Filial Vision of the Father," *Pro Ecclesia* 13 (2004): 189–201 (chap. 19 in this volume). Thomas Joseph White has argued against my position. See his "The Voluntary Action of the Earthly Christ and the Necessity of the Beatific Vision," *Thomist* 69 (2005): 497–534. I have in turn responded to White: "The Beatific Vision and the Incarnate Son: Furthering the Discussion," *Thomist* 70 (2006): 605–15.

bestow graces that simply flow from the Incarnation; they make present Christ's incarnate priestly graces merited through the Paschal Mysteries—his passion, death, and resurrection. Aquinas founds the instrumental causal efficacy of the sacraments on the "passion of Christ." It is through these Paschal events/acts that Christ obtained for the Church the grace of forgiveness, justification, and the heavenly glory, and it is now the risen Christ, the heavenly High Priest, as Head of the Church, who makes present these saving actions of the sacraments.[17] The Church and sacraments were born not solely of the Incarnation, but from the pierced side of the incarnate crucified High Priest (see Jn. 19:34–5). As Aquinas himself states, "the Church is said to be built up with the sacraments *which flowed from the side of Christ while hanging on the cross*."[18] It is the risen Lamb who was slain who presides over the heavenly liturgy and who makes that heavenly liturgy present and active within the sacraments (Rev. 5:6).

I have labored over these issues because I want to ensure that the proper foundation for the sacraments is securely and correctly laid. In so doing, I have continuously emphasized the dynamic notion of "act." First, the sacraments are primarily acts founded upon the priestly human actions of the Son of God—his passion and death. The glorious and risen High Priest makes present, as Head of his Body, these same saving mysteries through the acts that are the sacraments. We now turn to Aquinas's teaching on how Christ acts, as the Head of the Church, within the sacraments so that these sacramental actions allow believers to be incorporated into the saving mysteries and so obtain their eternal effect.

---

17. Aquinas may be addressing this issue when he makes a distinction between "personal and capital grace" and "the grace of union." "Personal and capital grace are ordained to an act; but the grace of union is not ordained to an act, but to the personal being." For Aquinas, while the grace of union pertains to the fact that the Son of God exists as man, the personal or capital grace pertains to his ability to act as Head of the Church in bestowing grace. But Aquinas proceeds to say that "the grace of union, the capital, and the personal grace are one in essence, though there is a distinction of reason between them" (*ST* III, q. 8, a. 5, ad 3). I believe that there is more than a distinction of reason between them because Christ obtained the capital grace whereby he became the fully empowered Head of the Church only upon his resurrection. Only after, and not prior to, his resurrection did the grace of union and capital grace become one in the person of Christ, for only then was the glorified incarnate Son fully empowered to act as Head in the bestowal of grace. See J.-P. Torrell, "La causalité salvifique de la resurrection du Christ selon saint Thomas," *Revue Thomiste* 96 (1996): 180–208.

18. *ST* III, q. 64, a. 2, ad 3. See also q. 64, a. 3; q. 66, a. 3, ad 3.

Sacraments: Efficacious Signs

Aquinas begins his treatment of sacraments by stating that, having considered "those things that concern the mystery of the Incarnate Word, we must consider the sacraments of the Church which derive their efficacy from the Word incarnate himself."[19] Here Aquinas is clearly acknowledging that the incarnate salvific acts of Christ are the source of the efficacy of the sacramental acts.

As is well documented, Aquinas's understanding of the efficacy of sacramental causality evolved; its most mature expression being found within the *Summa Theologiae*.[20] For Aquinas, a sacrament is not merely "a kind of sign," but a specific kind of sign in that it is a "sign of a holy thing insofar as it makes men holy."[21] While a sacrament is a sign, it is not an inactive sign, but an active sign for the enacting of the sign is in itself what makes men holy. Thus sacramental actions contain within themselves sanctifying causality that effect holiness. As Aquinas states, "Since a sacrament signifies that which sanctifies, it must needs signify the effect, which is implied in the sanctifying cause as such."[22] For Aquinas, the efficacious causality of a sacrament is founded on "Christ's passion." This causality is the source of present "grace and the virtues," and ultimately fosters the goal of "eternal life." "Consequently a sacrament is a sign that is both a reminder of the past, that is, the passion of Christ; and an indication of that which is effected in us by Christ's passion, that is, grace; and a prognostic, that is, a foretelling of future glory."[23]

Aquinas proceeds not only to define the nature of a sacrament, but also to put into place the nature of its causal activity. First, a sacrament by its very nature must be a sensible sign otherwise it would not be intelligible. "Now it is part of man's nature to acquire knowledge of the intelligible

19. Ibid., q. 60, prae.

20. For an excellent study on this development, see B. Blankenhorn, "The Instrumental Causality of the Sacraments: Thomas Aquinas and Louis-Marie Chauvet," *Nova et Vetera* 4 (2006): 255–93. See also J. F. Gallagher, *Significando Causant: A Study of Sacramental Causality* (Fribourg: Fribourg University, 1965); N. Lefler, "Sign, Cause, and Person in St. Thomas's Sacramental Theology: Further Considerations," *Nova et Vetera* 4 (2006): 381–404; P. McShane, "On the Causality of the Sacraments," *Theological Studies* 24 (1963): 423–36.

21. *ST* III, q. 60, a. 1, 2.   22. Ibid., q. 60, a. 3, ad 2.

23. Ibid., q. 60, a. 3.

from the sensible … it follows that the sacramental signs consist of sensible things." Second, the significance (literally what is signified) of these sensible signs can only be grasped by the appropriate sacramental words that make evident the inherent meaning of the sign. "Therefore in order to insure the perfection of sacramental signification it was necessary to determine the signification of the sensible things by means of certain words … When we say: I baptize you, it is clear that we use water in baptism in order to signify a spiritual cleansing."[24]

Third, and of the utmost importance, the sensible sacramental sign and the sacramental words only achieve their effect when they together become the one act that is the sacrament. A sacrament is not merely the union of a sign and words, but the performing of the action that the sign and the words signify and embody.

Aquinas notes that some have thought (e.g., Hugh of St. Victor) with regard to baptism "that water itself is the sacrament."

But this is not true. For since the sacraments of the New Law effect certain sanctification, there the sacrament is completed where the sanctification is completed. Now, the sanctification is not completed in water; but a certain sanctifying instrumental virtue, not permanent but transient, passes from the water, in which it is, into man who is the subject of true sanctification. Consequently the sacrament is not completed in the very water, but in applying the water to man, that is, in the washing.[25]

For Aquinas, sacraments are efficacious acts that are enacted by sensible signs and words. In baptism it is the combined action of pouring the water and the pronouncing of the words that effects what this one action symbolizes and speaks—the cleansing of sin and being incorporated into the life of the Trinity.[26] But we have yet to speak of the nature of this sacramental causal action that affects what it symbolizes and symbolizes what it affects. Aquinas addresses this issue when he treats of the instrumental causality of the sacraments.

24. Ibid., q. 60, a. 6.
25. Ibid., q. 66, a. 1.
26. Walsh rightly states: "The words 'inform' by saying what the action means, rather than simply what the water means. And since both words and actions require a person to make them happen, matter and form can never mean impersonal objects waiting around for someone to pick them up. There is matter and form, and therefore a sacrament, only when persons are doing and saying something significant." "The Divine and the Human," 340.

The Sacraments as Instrumental Efficient Causes

Are the sacramental acts inherently instrumental efficient causes of grace? Aquinas answers this question by noting again that some "say that they [sacraments] are the cause of grace not by their own operation, but insofar as God causes grace in the soul when the sacraments are employed." Aquinas gives as an example a man who presents a leaden coin and, on the king's command, receives a hundred pounds. The leaden coin itself did not influence the giving of the hundred pounds, but the "mere will of the king ... For the leaden coin is nothing but a sign of the king's command that this man should receive the money."

In contrast, for Aquinas, an efficient cause can be twofold: principal and instrumental. "The principal cause works by the power of its form, to which the effect is likened ... In this way none but God can cause grace: since grace in nothing else than a participated likeness of the Divine Nature." The sacraments are instrumental efficient causes "for they are instituted by God to be employed for the purpose of conferring grace."[27] The sensible sacramental action is thus the cause of the interior effect of grace. "For example, the water of baptism, in respect to its proper power, cleanses the body, and thereby, inasmuch as it is the instrument of the Divine power, cleanses the soul: since from soul and body one thing is made."[28]

For Aquinas, the sacraments contain within themselves the power to cause grace. Again, "those who hold that the sacraments do not cause grace save by a certain coincidence deny the sacraments any power that is itself productive of the sacramental effect." However, "if we hold that a sacrament is an instrumental cause of grace, we must allow that there is in the sacraments a certain instrumental power of bringing about the sacramental effects."[29] For Aquinas, the power residing within a sacrament as instrumental cause comes from being moved "by the principal agent." Thus "a sacrament receives spiritual power from Christ's blessing and from the action

27. From *ST* III, q. 62, a. 1. See also ad 1.

28. Ibid., q. 62, a. 1, ad 2. See also q. 62, a. 3. While Aquinas does not state this, instrumental sacramental efficient causality is similar to the theandric actions of the incarnate Son. The Son of God performs a miracle by his divine power, but he does so by the instrumentality of his humanity. So, too, the sacramental acts effect interior grace, but they do so through the sensible outward signs.

29. *ST* III, q. 62, a. 4.

of the minister in applying the sacramental use."[30] We are now at the heart of Aquinas's understanding of the efficient instrumental causality of the sacramental action.

Aquinas brings all the above to bear upon the question of "Whether the Sacraments of the New Law Derive Their Power from Christ's Passion?" He states, as said above, that "a sacrament in causing grace works after the manner of an instrument."

Now an instrument is twofold; the one separate, as a stick, for instance; the other, united, as a hand. Moreover, the separate instrument is moved by means of the united instrument, as a stick by the hand. Now the principal efficient cause of grace is God himself, in comparison with whom Christ's humanity is as a united instrument, whereas the sacrament is a separate instrument. Consequently, the saving power needs to be derived by the sacraments from Christ's Godhead through his humanity.[31]

For Aquinas, since Christ freed us from sin through his passion and since it is through his passion that he perfected the soul "in things pertaining to Divine Worship in regard to the Christian Religion," "the sacraments of the Church derive their power specifically from Christ's Passion."[32] Here we perceive all of the logical, causal connections that bear upon Aquinas's understanding of the causality of the sacramental acts. By the united instrumentality of his humanity, the Son, through his passion, obtains the forgiveness of sins whereby we are reconciled to God and thus also obtains for us the grace whereby we are enabled to worship God properly within the sacraments. The sacraments, through their separated instrumental causality,

---

30. Ibid., q. 62, a. 4, ad 3.

31. Ibid., q. 62, a. 5. Because Blankenhorn is insightful on this issue, I quote him at some length. "It is through the instrumentality of the sacraments that I attain a real participation in the efficacy of past historical events, a spiritual contact with the power of Christ's saving actions. Through the sacraments, I enter into communion with the Christ of history two thousand years ago. I am not simply connected to the power of his hypostatic union, but rather to the power emanating from his humanity, to the 'instrumental flux' that was active in the particular operations of the Jesus of history." "The Instrumental Causality of the Sacraments," 288–89. Yocum states that "the sacraments and the humanity of Christ are connected in the line of instrumental causality." "Sacraments in Aquinas," 170. See also Walsh, "The Divine and the Human," 347.

32. ST III, q. 62, a. 5. See also q. 64, a. 3, 7. Blankenhorn states that "the sacraments effect a real ontological connection with Christ's saving activity. In other words, they cause grace." "The Instrumental Causality of the Sacraments," 287.

make present the meritorious effects of Christ's passion and so Christians are able to worship God in righteousness and holiness.

In the above, Aquinas, it appears to me, rightly founds the sacramental actions, not simply on the grace bestowed upon Christ's humanity owing to its incarnational union with his divinity, but also upon the human salvific actions of the Son of God. The human acts that make up the entire Paschal Mystery are the human instrumental causes whereby the Son obtains our salvation and whereby, I have argued, he merited the perfection of his own glory and ours as Head of the Body, the Church. What I find unsatisfactory, and it pertains to my previous criticisms, is Aquinas's lack of a theological development concerning Christ's action within the sacraments as the risen priestly Head of his Body and, owing to this lack, a somewhat misconceived understanding of the instrumental nature of sacramental causality.

While the incarnate salvific acts of the Son of God as High Priest do bring about humankind's salvation, and so become the source of the sacramental acts, it is as the glorified risen High Priest that he makes these earthly efficacious acts present within the sacraments. It is as the risen Lord, whose blood ever intercedes on our behalf (Heb. 12:24), that he is Head of the Body and as Head acts so as to sanctify his Body through the sacraments. What Aquinas does not appreciate fully is that this action of Christ the Head within his Body demands a new conception and articulation of instrumental causality that is in keeping with this new reality.

As stated above, there are, for Aquinas, two types of instrumental efficient causality. The first is that the principal agent employs what is constitutive of who he is to bring about an effect, as a man employs his body to bring about an effect, or the Son of God acts as man through the instrumentality of his humanity. Aquinas refers to this as a "united instrument." The second type of instrumental efficient causality is that whereby one uses something other than oneself to bring about an effect, such as a man using a pen to write. Aquinas refers to this as a "separate instrument," and he sees the sacraments as possessing this type of instrumental efficient causality. Christ employs the sacraments as separate from himself to bring about an efficacious salvific effect. From within the unity of Christ, the Head, with his Body, however, I argue that there is a third type of instrumental efficient causality unique to the sacraments that allows Christ to act in the sacraments in a much more personally direct and immediate manner.

The Sacraments: Mystical Instrumental Efficient Causes

The Mystical Body, through the shared life of the Holy Spirit, is one living reality. It is composed of the risen Christ as its Head and the members of his Body, the Church. Within this one Mystical Body there is what I call a mystical instrumental causality, by which Christ as Head acts so as to sanctify his Body. This mystical instrumental causality finds its fullest expression within the sacraments (the Eucharist being its definitive expression), for they are his own personal instrumental efficient causes in which he himself acts as Head so as to sanctify his Body. The sacraments are constitutive of the living and life-giving reality of the Mystical Body, for they are the mystical instrumental actions of Christ within his Body, and as such they are personal instrumental causal acts of Christ himself.

Within his incarnate state the Son of God acted as man because that was the manner in which he existed. Within his resurrected state, the Son of God now acts as a glorious man, and as such does so as the Head of his Body. While the sacraments do not accrue to the Son of God's glorious humanity in a manner in which he now exists as a glorious man, because they are distinct from him and in this sense are "separate" from him, they nonetheless accrue to him as to the manner in which he now acts within his Body as its risen human Head. The sacraments are then efficacious instrumental causes because through them Christ himself is personally acting as Head within his Body.

Since Christ and his Church form one the one Mystical Body, Christ's sacramental actions as Head are of a singular causal nature. What makes them unique is that they are "mystical" in that they take place within the one reality that is Christ and his Church, and they are "personal" in that they are the personal actions of Christ as Head by which he sanctifies the members of his own Body.

The Sacramental Character and the Sacramental Act

My argument concerning the unique instrumentality of the sacraments within the Mystical Body of Christ can be clarified and strengthened by examining the nature of the sacramental character. For Aquinas, the sacramental character is a "seal" by which God "imprints his character on us."[33] This seal deputes Christians "to spiritual service pertaining to the worship of God."[34] Significantly, this character or seal empowers the Christian to act in a twofold manner.

Now the worship of God consists either in receiving Divine gifts, or in bestowing them on others. And for both these purposes some power is needed; for to bestow something on others, active power is necessary; and in order to receive, we need a passive power. Consequently, a character signifies a certain spiritual power ordained unto things pertaining to Divine worship.[35]

For Aquinas, the sacramental character empowers a Christian to act either insofar as he is an active minister in the bestowing divine gifts, such as the priest who baptizes or presides over the Eucharist, or insofar as he is an active recipient of the divine gifts, such as the baptized Christian who participates in the Eucharist.[36] Pertaining to the power of the active minister, because this power is sacramental in nature, it is, for Aquinas, instrumental. "But it must be observed that this spiritual power is instrumental ... of the virtue which is in the sacraments. For to have a sacramental character belongs to God's ministers: and a minister is a kind of instrument."[37]

The minister, through his sacramental character, is empowered to be an instrument through which the sacraments are enacted. From where does this sacramental character derive its instrumental power, and in what manner does it exercise such power? For Aquinas, because this sacramental character pertains to divine worship either in the power of bestowing or in the power of receiving divine gifts, "the whole rite of the Christian religion is derived from Christ's priesthood."

Consequently, it is clear that the sacramental character is especially the character of Christ, to whose character the faithful are likened by reason of the sacramental characters, which are nothing else than certain participations of Christ's priesthood, flowing from Christ himself.[38]

---

33. *ST* III, q. 63, a. 1, s.c.   34. Ibid., q. 63, a. 1.

35. Ibid., q. 63, a. 2.

36. With regard to this active and passive power, Aquinas states, "It is the sacrament of Orders that pertains to the sacramental agents: for it is by this sacrament that men are deputed to confer sacraments on others: while the sacrament of Baptism pertains to the recipients, since it confers on man the power to receive the other sacraments of the Church." *ST* III, q. 63, a. 6.

37. *ST* III, q. 63, a. 2. See also q. 64, a. 5.   38. Ibid., q. 63, a. 3.

Through the sacramental characters, Christians are conformed into the likeness of Christ and so come to share in his priesthood.[39] Through the sacramental characters, they are empowered to act in a priestly fashion, either in bestowing or receiving divine gifts within Christian worship. Aquinas further specifies that the sacramental characters are ordained to priestly action.

Since the sacramental characters pertain to the bestowing or receiving divine gifts within Christian worship, they consist "in certain actions: and the powers of the soul are properly ordained to actions, just as the essence is ordained to existence. Therefore a character is subjected not in the essence of the soul, but in its power."[40] For Aquinas, the act of existence empowers the essence to perform acts in keeping with that essence. Similarly, the sacramental character empowers the soul of the Christian to perform actions in a manner in keeping with its Christian nature; that is, to perform actions in conformity with Christ the priest.

In a sacramental character Christ's faithful have a share in his priesthood; in the sense that as Christ has the full power of a spiritual priesthood, so his faithful are likened to him by sharing a certain spiritual power with regard to the sacraments and to things pertaining to the divine worship.[41]

Again, for Aquinas, this spiritual power pertaining to the sacrament character, by sharing in Christ's priesthood, is "an instrumental power."[42]

I argued previously that the risen Christ personally exercised his priestly ministry within his Body, of which he is the Head, through the instrumental causality of the sacraments. Because the sacramental action resides within the one living reality of the Mystical Body, the sacramental actions are not instrumental actions separate from Christ, as a man employs a pen to write, as Aquinas contends, but his own personal and immediate actions within his Mystical Body. In the light of the nature of the sacramental character, we can see more clearly why this is the case. The sacramental character conforms the minister into the likeness of Christ the priest, and so the minister, insofar as he is instrumental in bestowing grace, is empowered

---

39. This further supports my argument that the grace whereby Christ, as Head, sanctifies his Body is derived not merely from the incarnational union of his divinity and humanity, but primarily from his priestly acts.

40. *ST* III, q. 63, a. 4.   41. Ibid., q. 63, a. 5.

42. Ibid., q. 63, a. 5, ad 1.

to act in union with Christ, *in persona Christi*.[43] The sacraments are instrumental causes of grace, not as impersonal causes separate from Christ, but as personal instruments of Christ because they are personally enacted by the minister. By being a member of Christ's Body and through sharing in Christ's very own priesthood, by the power of the sacramental character, the ordained minister acts in the very person of Christ. The acts that are the sacraments are the personal acts of Christ, performed as Head of his Body, because they are enacted by the minister who personally makes present, as a living member of Christ's one Body and through sharing in Christ's one priestly power and activity, Christ's redemptive priestly acts.[44] Aquinas states in relationship to the Eucharist:

such is the dignity of this sacrament that it is performed only as in the person of Christ. Now whoever performs any act in another's stead must do so by the power bestowed by such a one. But as the power of receiving this sacrament is conceded by Christ to the baptized person, so likewise the power of consecrating this sacrament on Christ's behalf is bestowed upon the priest at his ordination.[45]

I have argued that the instrumental causality enacted within the sacraments is unique because it is personally enacted by Christ as the priestly head of his one living Body. The manner in which Christ exercises this sacramental instrumental causality is through the ordained minister, who, by sharing in Christ's priestly power, actually acts *in persona Christi*, and so the priestly sacramental actions that he enacts are the priestly sacramental actions that Christ himself enacts as Head of his Body.[46] In this understanding of the sacramental action, everyone is in act—Christ and the priest—and thus the sacramental actions make efficacious the mysteries that they symbolize.

43. For a study of Aquinas's understanding of the minister acting *in persona Christi*, see B. D. Marliangéas, *Clés pour une Théologie du Ministère: In Persona Christi, in Persona Ecclesiae* (Paris: Éditions Beauchesne, 1978). I am indebted to Germain Grisez for providing me with this reference.

44. Aquinas states: "For, clearly, Christ himself perfects all of the sacraments of the Church: it is he who baptizes; it is he who forgives sins; it is he, the true priest, who offered himself on the altar of the cross, and by whose power his body is daily consecrated on the altar—nevertheless, because he was not going to be with all of the faithful in bodily presence, he chose ministers to dispense the things just mentioned to the faithful" (*ScG* IV, ch. 76, 7).

45. *ST* III, q. 82, a. 1. See also q. 78, a. 1, 4.

46. While the ordained minister acts *in persona Christi*, it is not as if he is absorbed into

Sacramental Acts: The Acts of the Participant

Before concluding, I examine briefly the nature of the acts by which the participants within the sacraments lay hold of their salvific effects. Within the discussion of the nature of the sacramental character, we saw that Aquinas holds that Divine worship consists of either bestowing or receiving divine gifts. For both, a specific power is required. "To bestow something on others, active power is necessary; and in order to receive, we need a passive power." It is through Baptism that Christians are empowered, through the sacramental character, to participate in and so receive the benefits of the other sacraments. While it is a "passive power" in that it is a power to receive, the ability to participate and so receive the benefits of the sacraments is an activity, an act of participation and reception. There is not only a sacramental dynamism in the bestowal of God's gifts; there is also an equal sacramental dynamism in the reception of God's gifts.[47] In terms of this essay, this notion is of the utmost importance, for it is inherent within a proper understanding of the sacraments as acts. They are both acts of bestowal and acts reception.

While Aquinas emphasizes within his treatment of the sacraments the sacramental action of bestowal, he is not ignorant of the sacramental action of participation and reception. He notes, for example, that the priest within the Eucharistic liturgy not only speaks on behalf of Christ but also on behalf of the Church.[48] It is through speaking on behalf of the Church

the hypostatic union. This is probably one of the reasons that Aquinas speaks of the sacraments being "separate" instrumental causes. Christ and the ordained minister are two distinct individuals. It should also be noted as well that, while the minister acts *in persona Christi* as an instrumental cause in what is necessary to enact the sacrament, to do so he must possess the proper intention precisely because he is a rational agent acting in union with Christ. Moreover, the preaching of the ordained minister and the manner in which he presides over the liturgy can be means of grace, but this very much depends upon the holiness, learning, and gifts of the minister and his cooperation with the grace of Christ. I am grateful to John Yocum for pointing out to me these various important nuances.

47. Walsh puts this nicely: "In Christian worship receiving is every bit as active as giving, because it is the taking hold of grace. It is, indeed, the action that lasts forever." "The Divine and the Human," 353.

48. See *ST* III, q. 82, a. 7, ad 3. Aquinas stresses the active nature of the participation and reception when he speaks of the "virtue of religion." Religion, as do all virtues, pertains to acts, which are "proper and immediate acts, which it elicits, and by which man is directed to God alone, for instance, sacrifice, adoration and the like" (*ST* II-II, q. 81, a. 1, ad 1). For the active

that the priest, together with all those participating, offers prayers to the Father in union with Christ through the power of the Holy Spirit. It is through this act of liturgical prayer that the priest and people participate in the sacramental action and so reap its sacramental effect. Within the Eucharist, they find its culmination in the active receiving of Holy Communion, where one receives the body and blood, soul and divinity of Christ, and so are united to him and to the body of believers. Such an active participation and reception is also seen within the sacrament of Penance, where sinners not only actively confess their sins in repentance but also actively receive sacramental absolution through their response of "Amen" and the performing of the act of penance.

What we find, then, in the acts that are the sacraments is the meeting of a twofold act within each of the sacraments. The first is the action of the risen Christ made present through the sacramental action of the minister. The second is the sacramental act of the participant who grasps, in faith and worship, Christ's action. It is the meeting of these acts, the sacramental act of Christ and the sacramental act of the participant, that comprises the completion and efficacy of all sacramental acts. Moreover, it is this sacramental union of act to act that anticipates the fullness of act in heaven. There, in an immediate and nonsacramental manner, the Son of God as man will act so as to bestow the fullness of his risen glory and life and the saints will act so to lay hold of these in the fullness of love and worship. It is the everlasting union of these heavenly human acts between Christ and the members of his Body that will effect full participation within the life of the Trinity and so the fullness of the divine vision and life. Until that glorious consummation, we must satisfy our longing by participating in Christ's priestly acts that are the sacraments.

---

nature of the "virtue of religion" as well as the active nature of "devotion," see *ST* II-II, q. 81, a. 2–7; q. 82, a. 1–3.

As Walsh states, "He [Aquinas] has been criticized for placing an excessive emphasis on the sanctifying movement of sacraments, as God giving grace to humans, and not enough emphasis on their cultic movement, as worship given by humans to God. However, one must remember that the cult movement of all human action, its *ordo ad Deum*, has been established in his theology of religion, and sacraments have been expressly identified as acts of religion." "The Divine and the Human," 332.

PART III

CHRISTOLOGY AND CONTEMPORARY ISSUES

CHAPTER 13

The Case for
Spirit Christology
Some Reflections

In the June 1992 issue of *Theological Studies*, Roger Haight, S.J., of the Weston School of Theology authored an essay titled "The Case for Spirit Christology."[1] In the December 1992 issue of the same journal, John Wright, S.J, of the Jesuit School of Theology at Berkeley wrote a critical response titled "Roger Haight's Spirit Christology."[2] While I fully endorse Wright's reservations, here I wish to offer some of my own criticisms as well as expand upon some of his.[3]

In order for a Spirit Christology to be viable, Haight believes that it must fulfill six criteria: (1) It must adequately explain why Christians be-

Originally published as "The Case For Spirit Christology: Some Reflections," *Thomist* 59 (1995): 173–88. Reprinted by permission.

1. Roger Haight, S.J., "The Case for Spirit Christology," *Theological Studies* 53 (1992): 257–87. All subsequent page numbers given in the text refer to this article.

2. John Wright, S.J., "Roger Haight's Spirit Christology," *Theological Studies* 53 (1992): 729–35.

3. While this essay focuses exclusively on Haight's Spirit Christology, much of what is said here, by way of criticism, can be applied equally to other expressions of Spirit Christology because the various forms are quite similar. Haight relies heavily upon and substantially agrees with G. W. H. Lampe, "The Holy Spirit and the Person of Christ," in *Christ, Faith and History*, ed. S. W. Sykes and J. P. Clayton (Cambridge: Cambridge University Press, 1972), 111–30; *God as Spirit* (Oxford: Clarendon Press, 1977). For other recent examples of Spirit Christology, see Haight, 257n1.

lieve that their salvation is found in Jesus. (2) It must be faithful to the Bible. (3) It must uphold the teaching of the Councils, especially Nicea and Chalcedon. (4) It must be intelligible and coherent. (5) It must respond to contemporary concerns, specifically the relationship of Jesus to the founders of other religions. (6) It must be able to stimulate and empower Christian life (260–62). As in Wright's response, I examine Haight's Spirit Christology in light of these criteria.

I begin with an extensive examination of Haight's second criterion—faithfulness to Scripture—for it is most central to his whole enterprise. Then, more succinctly, I address his other criteria.

Biblical Revelation and Religious Language

The central, and therefore fatal, flaw within Haight's Spirit Christology is that his understanding of "God as Spirit," upon which the whole of his Christology is founded, is itself nonbiblical. To discern Haight's understanding of "God as Spirit," we must first examine his notion of religious language and the philosophy sustaining it.

For Haight, "The medium through which religious experience takes place may be called a symbol, making all religious knowledge symbolic knowledge. A symbol is that through which something else is made present and known; a symbol mediates a perception and knowledge of something other" (263). While the symbol makes the presence of God known, because it is a symbol, God is beyond or transcends what is symbolized. The symbol "both makes God present and points away from itself to a God who is other than itself" (263). The symbolized "is" and "is not" the symbol (263).

Haight argues that the biblical symbol, "the Spirit of God," refers to God and is "materially and numerically identical with God. God as Spirit is God" (266). But God as Spirit "indicates God at work, as active, and as power, energy, or force that accomplishes something" (266–67). God as Spirit refers not to God as he is immanent in himself, but to God as he is "outside of himself" within the order of time and history. Haight recognizes that the Old Testament also uses "Word" and "Wisdom" as symbols along with "Spirit," but "all of these symbols are basically the same insofar as they point to the same generalized experience of God outside of God's self and immanent in the world in presence and active power" (267). While

Haight acknowledges that these symbolic expressions were, at times, personalized in the Old Testament, it would be wrong to hypostatize them; that is, to conceive them as objective and individual. To do so detracts, Haight believes, from the fact that they are symbols of God himself and do not designate some intermediary between the world and God. Thus "In order to preserve this primal quality of the biblical symbol Spirit, against the tendency of objectifying a personification ... [Haight uses] the phrase God as Spirit" (268).[4]

Haight is correct that all religious language is in some sense symbolic. His understanding of symbolic language is not without ambiguity and error, however, which leads him to misrepresent biblical language and thus biblical revelation itself.

First, he speaks at times of religious symbolic language as being metaphorical. For example, Jesus as Savior is a "metaphor of understanding" (264). "God as Spirit" is a "metaphorical symbol" (267). The Old Testament terms "Word" and "Wisdom" are "metaphors [that] contain imaginative virtualities that reveal aspects of God" (267). He refers to the "metaphorical and symbolic character of this term Spirit" (267).

Now a metaphor is a word, phrase, action, or the like that is not literally applicable, such as "raining cats and dogs" or "a glaring error." The Bible uses metaphor—God is said to be a rock or, anthropomorphically, to possess eyes and ears. The statements themselves are not literally true, though they do express something that is true about God—that he is steadfast and faithful or that he perceives human thought and action. But while terms such as "the Spirit of God," "Wisdom," and "Word" are symbolic, they are not metaphors, for they are stating something that, in some sense, is literally true— God acts in time and history by his Word, Wisdom, and Spirit analogous to the way human beings speak and act. There is something literally true about what is expressed, even if what is said is not the whole truth. Missing here in Haight's understanding of symbolic language is the traditional notion of the analogical use of religious language where what is said about God is not just a metaphor, but rather what is said actually lays hold of and literally corresponds to something true about God in himself and his activity. This ambiguous understanding of symbolic language, however, allows Haight to

---

4. Haight is closely following Lampe here and refers to his *God as Spirit*, 37, 115–16, 179.

regard symbolic religious language as merely metaphorical when he wishes to deny something within the Bible that contradicts his notion of "God as Spirit," such as the personification of "Spirit," "Word," or "Wisdom."

Second, this contradiction leads to a more serious problem. Haight wishes to maintain, as the above exposition of his thought confirms, that his notion of "God as Spirit" actually symbolizes, and thus truly expresses, the reality of God and his activity in the world and within history. But for Haight, the symbol itself "mediates" or "makes present and known" God. While Haight then professes that "God as Spirit points to God as active" (268), underlying his understanding of the symbolic nature of religious language is a philosophy that does not see God as actually acting in distinct and different kinds of ways in the world or within history. (This becomes most evident when Haight compares Jesus with the founders of other religions. All religions embody "God as Spirit"; that is, God's universal and generic activity. There may be a difference of degree but not of kind.) Rather, the symbolic language itself mediates God's presence and merely articulates and expresses the continuous, generic manner in which God is always "present" and "active." "The metaphorical symbol of God as Spirit expresses the experience of God's power and energy in creation; this power is seen in its effects. The verbal or conceptual symbol points to the way God is present in the world" (269). The symbolic, for Haight, expresses not a new and specific action of God as such, but rather human insight into the transcendent nature of finite reality. The symbolic gives utterance not to a new action of God, but to a new insight of man. Because God's generic presence is perceived in a new way, God is said, symbolically or metaphorically, "to act."

The philosophy behind Haight's understanding of religious language is hardly biblical. The Old Testament, when it speaks of God ratifying a covenant with the Israelites, or inspiring the prophets, or forgiving sins, or answering the prayers of the poor, is symbolically expressing not just some human insight (although human beings did have to grasp what was happening) but is signifying God's distinctive activity within history and in the lives of individuals. The Israelites came to new knowledge because God acted in a new way. Equally, the primary presupposition of the New Testament is that God acted in a distinctive and new kind of way in and through Jesus.

In summary, for Haight, human insight, expressed symbolically, is the immediate justification of revelation, and thus man is the primary source of its meaning. Within the Bible, God's specific and distinct action is itself revelatory and therefore the source of its meaning, which is experienced and then expressed in a symbolic manner. For the Bible, God (by his revelatory action in word and deed) defines, specifies, and interprets the symbol. For Haight, the symbol (of human origin) defines, specifies, and interprets God.

The Spirit of God versus God as Spirit

What has been said so far now converges upon Haight's use of the term "God as Spirit." Despite Haight's continual appeal to the necessity of a biblical perspective, the phrase "God as Spirit" never once appears in the Bible. The Bible does speak of "the Spirit of God" and Jesus tells us that "God is Spirit" (Jn. 4:24), but Scripture never employs the idiom "God as Spirit." This biblical absence does not necessarily discredit the expression, for the Church uses nonbiblical words and concepts to declare what it believes to be biblical revelation, such as Nicea's homoousios and Trent's "transubstantiation." In this situation, however, its absence is significant.

The Old Testament's perception of the "Spirit of God" differs in three ways from Haight's understanding of "God as Spirit." First, "Spirit of God" refers to God's distinctive activity in history and not just to human insight into God's generic presence in history "as Spirit." Second, while "Spirit of God" in the Old Testament is used to protect God's transcendence, it is used to affirm that the wholly other, *as the wholly other* (without losing his wholly otherness), is in our midst and acting, and not the wholly other manifesting himself in some lesser degree or form "as Spirit." "God as Spirit" makes a nonbiblical separation between the wholly transcendent God and his lesser manifestations in history "as Spirit"—as force, energy, power. Third, "Spirit of God" specifies the personal nature of the God who acts in history. God personally acts in the Spirit and not impersonally "as Spirit." "God as Spirit" subtly but effectively depersonalizes God. "God as Spirit" is no longer an acting subject. Rather, "God as Spirit" becomes the symbolic expression of a philosophical principle—there is something transcendent or beyond (not necessarily a personal God) within the realm of the historically finite that human beings can personal embody, symbolically express, and so come to know. Haight's understanding of "God as Spirit" is closer to the metaphysics of Hegel and to the religious philosophy of Schleiermacher than to the revelation of the Bible.[5]

Jesus and God as Spirit

Because Haight's basic concept of "God as Spirit" is nonbiblical, his Spirit Christology is not founded upon the New Testament proclamation. Haight states that by Spirit Christology he means one "that 'explains' how God is present and active in Jesus, and thus Jesus' divinity, by using the biblical symbol of God as Spirit, and not the symbol Logos" (257). Jesus, then, is not the eternal Son of God who came to exist as a man; rather, he is a man who incarnates in a preeminent manner "God as Spirit."[6] Haight believes that this is more in keeping with the Synoptic portrayal of Jesus as speaking and acting by the power of the Spirit. Also, "God as Spirit" gives rise to his filial consciousness and sense of mission (269). The apparent equating of the Spirit and the risen Christ within the early Church tends to confirm this understanding (270–71).[7]

The symbol of the Spirit more forthrightly makes the claim that God, God's very self, acted in and through this Jesus. This stands in contrast to the symbols of God's Word and Wisdom which, insofar as they became personified and then hypostatized, tend to connote someone or something distinct from and less than God that was incarnate in Jesus even though it is called divine or of God. By contrast the symbol of God as Spirit is not a personification of God but refers directly to God, so that it is clear from the beginning that nothing less than God was at work in Jesus. (272)

---

5. While Haight continually appeals to the importance of historical revelation and our contemporary historical consciousness in order to advocate his notion of "God as Spirit" and his Christology, his theology levels history. History is only the backdrop for man to discern God's generic presence, rather than the divine drama in which God acts in new and distinctive kinds of ways. History no longer bears a divine expectancy.

6. Lampe states: "In this continuous incarnation of God as Spirit in the spirits of men the Jesus presented to us by the Gospels holds his unique place ... In Jesus the incarnate presence of God evoked a full and constant response of the human spirit. This was not a different divine presence, but the same God the Spirit who moved and inspired other men, such as the prophets." *God as Spirit*, 23–24.

7. Again, Haight is much indebted to Lampe's exegesis; cf. *God as Spirit*, 62–94.

Haight argues in the above quote that "God, God's very self, acted in and through this Jesus." He believes that this adequately accounts for Jesus's divinity. But this understanding is scripturally deficient in three ways. First, this "self" is not God, as he exists in himself wholly as God but in the lesser expression of himself "as Spirit." Although Haight claims that it is "nothing less than God at work in Jesus," it is not the "whole fullness of deity" that dwells in him bodily (Col. 2:9). Second, as Wright in his response emphasizes, Haight neglects significant portions of the New Testament, specifically the heart of the New Testament proclamation that Jesus is the unique Son.

That Jesus is Son of God is declared or implied throughout the New Testament. Jesus is not just a son of God like every other believer, but God's "beloved Son" (Mt. 3:17), "his own Son" (Rom. 8:3), to whose image we are predestined to be conformed (Rom. 8:29), "his only begotten Son" (Jn. 1:14, 3:16). Paul's preaching of the Gospel "concerns his Son" (Rom. 1:3). This Son is involved in the creation of the world (e.g., 1 Cor. 8:6; Col. 1:15–17; Heb. 1:2; Jn. 1:3).[8]

Even within the Synoptics, Jesus's divinity is implied and revealed in such passages as the Infancy Narratives and in his unique authority as Son to forgive sins and to augment God's commandments (Lk. 1:32–35; Mt. 1:23, 5:21–48; Mk. 2:1–12). Furthermore, and most obviously, as Wright also notes, "Haight does not take serious account of the Christology of John."[9] Third, while Haight speaks of Jesus's filial consciousness and that "God as Spirit in his life" is the "ground of Jesus' sonship" (269), the concept "God as Spirit" necessarily brings to Haight's Christology an impersonalism that is totally absent in the New Testament. Jesus is not the eternal Son who now as man relates to the Father in love and obedience, but becomes "son" by incarnating "God as Spirit"; that is, the force, energy, and power of God. Despite Haight's disclaimer, this is Adoptionism, or rather "symbolic adoptionism."[10] What Jesus is actually doing is embodying the philosophical

8. Wright, "Roger Haight's Spirit Christology," 730–31.

9. Ibid., 731: "It is not only that he [Haight] neglects John's teaching on the Logos with God in creation (John 1:1–3) and the affirmation of the incarnation of the Logos (John 1:14), but he also takes no account of the 'I am' assertions of the Johannine Jesus."

10. Both Haight and Lampe believe that by saying Jesus embodied "God as Spirit" from the first moment of his existence they have freed themselves from Adoptionism. Haight, 277; Lampe, "The Holy Spirit and the Person of Christ," 125–26. But the issue of Adoptionism is not a question of timing, but a question of *who* Jesus is. Is the historical Jesus the eternal Son of God existing

principle that there is something transcendent within the finite, which is symbolically called "God as Spirit."

Because of the impersonal nature of Haight's Christology, it is not surprising that he never once refers to the Father. Significantly, too, the emerging and even developed personal subjectivity of the Holy Spirit within the New Testament is completely lost within Haight's Christology. The Holy Spirit is not a divine subject who anoints Jesus and sanctifies his followers, but the impersonal force or energy of the transcendent God that Jesus and others embody and so "personalize" in themselves.

Jesus and Salvation

Given Haight's Christology, it is easy to discern his soteriology. Jesus brings salvation in that through embodying "God as Spirit" he discloses, in a preeminent manner and so becomes the paradigm for, how God has always acted and is present. This revelation in turn empowers his disciples to follow his example. It is a "revelational and exemplary theory of salvation" (278). "Jesus saves by being the revealer of God and God's salvation which God as Spirit has effected from the beginning, the revelation of what human life should be, and the empowering example of life for disciples" (278). Haight again professes that this soteriology is biblical in nature. While containing biblical elements, it is far from the whole truth, and what it lacks completely distorts New Testament soteriology.

Haight does not address the biblical notion of sin and its radical effect upon our relationship with God and with others. Nor does he envision the devastating effect that sin has upon us as human beings. For this reason, his notion of salvation is Pelagian and Gnostic. Jesus is the Gnostic redeemer who reveals to us and is the paradigm for how we are to relate to God and so become human. Once we have learned the lesson, we can do it on our own. Haight equally reduces the Gospel to pure moralism, for we are justified and saved not through faith, but by merely imitating Christ through our ethically good actions (278).

---

as a man? Or is he a man who is in some manner united to God and so constituted his son? If the latter is the case, the time or manner does not ultimately matter. It is still Adoptionistic. If the Son is not God, then the sonship is always one of adoption. Only if Jesus is the eternal Son of God, and therefore needs no adoption, since he is Son by nature, can Adoptionism be overcome.

Moreover, once Jesus has revealed to us how we are to live and so furnished the ultimate salvific clue of the universe, his importance ceases. The historical Jesus in himself is not the Savior. He is purely a Gnostic functionary who performed his task of putting us in the know. Gone is the biblical, historical Jesus who took the sins of all upon himself and died, and now, as the risen Lord, pours our his Spirit, intercedes for us in heaven, personally acts within the Church and sacraments, and will come again in glory.

In contrast, the New Testament professes that through Jesus's historical death and resurrection our relationships with God and with one another change not in degree (from good to better) but in kind (from bad to good). Jesus did not supremely reveal an already founded relationship with God, thus enabling those who follow to utilize better the preestablished salvific program; rather, through his death and resurrection, he changed in kind our relationship with God. A whole new salvific order is initiated. We go from being enemies of God to being children of the Father. Moreover, those who now live in Christ possess a relationship with one another that differs in kind from their relationships with those who do not believe. Furthermore, because of and simultaneous to our new relationship to God, those who believe are changed not in degree but in kind. We become a new creation in Christ, for the Holy Spirit now dwells in us in a new kind of way.[11]

The lack of Jesus's contemporary importance can also be seen in Haight's view of Christian prayer. Because Jesus is a human being who incarnates "God as Spirit," one does not really worship Jesus but worships God through Jesus (283–84). Haight admits that there are a few instances of prayer to Jesus in the New Testament. But here again he misrepresents the Scriptures. The recognition of Jesus as Lord and our relationship to him as Lord is one of worship (Jn. 20:28; Phil. 2:10–11). Moreover, the whole of the Book of Revelation is a portrayal of heavenly worship of the Father and the Son. Not to worship Jesus, besides being contrary to the whole Christian tradition, radically transforms the nature of Christianity. Christians by definition worship, adore, and glorify Jesus as their Lord and God.[12]

---

11. For a fuller expression of how salvation "differs in kind," see T. G. Weinandy, *In the Likeness of Sinful Flesh: An Essay on the Humanity of Christ* (Edinburgh: T&T Clark, 1993), 85–88.

12. Wright comments that the "Christian experience of Jesus is expressed in doxologies given to him in the New Testament (e.g. Heb. 13:21; 2 Pet. 3:18; Rev. 5:13) and found in Christian

In light of these criticisms, we are compelled to conclude that Haight's Spirit Christology does not fulfill his second criterion—that of being faithful to the Scriptures.

Spirit Christology and the Councils

Haight believes that his Spirit Christology is fully in keeping with the doctrines enunciated at the Councils of Nicea and Chalcedon—namely that Jesus is truly God and truly man. In claiming that by hypostatizing the Logos one runs the risk of imposing a lesser intermediary between God and man, and by emphasizing instead that in Jesus "not less than God was present to and operative in," Haight actually circumvents the heart of Nicea's teaching.

Nicea proclaimed (against Arius) that the Son was not some semidivine intermediary, but that he was fully divine, *homoousios* with the Father. While Haight consistently quotes Chalcedon's statement that Jesus is *homoousios* with man, he never quotes Nicea's that the Son is *homoousios* with the Father. The reason for this is simply discerned. *Homoousios* bears upon one's ontological status. Haight wants to say that Jesus *is* man, but he does not want to say that Jesus actually *is* God. Yet this is expressly what Nicea wishes to ensure. The historical Jesus, as the Son, is not only "not less than God"—he also ontologically is God. All that the Father is, the Son is. The Son is not just "adverbially" God, as Haight maintains (287).[13] He (verbally) *is* God. This Haight's Spirit's Christology will not allow. Jesus may incarnate "God as Spirit" to the highest degree possible, but God himself, in the whole of his reality as God, is not man.

On the question of preexistence, Haight argues that in order to assure that Jesus is thoroughly like us, one cannot "really think of a preexistence of Jesus" because that would demand that he be substantially different from us. As preexistent he would be a different kind of man (276).[14] This herring

---

worship ever since. An experience of Jesus is expressed in Thomas's profession of faith, repeated by countless believers after him: 'My Lord! and my God!' (John 20:28). These expressions are not directed simply to God as Spirit dwelling in him, but to Jesus himself. Haight's Spirit Christology does not justify this aspect of Christian experience." "Roger Haight's Spirit Christology," 730.

13. As Haight notes, he obtains this notion of Jesus being "adverbially" divine from Lampe, "The Holy Spirit and the Person of Christ," 124.

14. Lampe argues in a similar vein. *God as Spirit*, 120–44.

is so red that even the father of deception must blush in embarrassment. The eternal Son, as God, preexists; not Jesus as man. As Wright remarks, "No one ever understood preexistence in this way, so why trouble to refute it?"[15] We must remember, however, that for Haight, if Jesus did preexist, he would necessarily preexist as a man, since within his Christology there is no preexistent divine Son. Nonetheless, Haight refutes this bogus heresy precisely because, by sleight of hand (or thought), it helps to undermine the preexistence of the Son as God and provides a platform for insisting that Jesus incarnates "God as Spirit," which then guarantees that Jesus is not only fully man but also only a man.

This same contrived confusion is evident in the question of whether Jesus differs from us in kind or in degree. For Haight, to say that Jesus is qualitatively different from us would be "directly contradictory to the doctrine of the consubstantiality of Jesus with other human beings" (279).[16] Again, no orthodox theologian or Council ever held that Jesus's humanity was different in kind from ours. What the Christian tradition has always insisted upon, and what Haight denies, is that Jesus's sonship differs from us in kind because he is the eternal Son, and therefore that God is present in Jesus in a different kind of way: as incarnate. Haight's philosophy will allow only one kind of relationship with God—that is, the embodying of "God as Spirit"—and therefore, by necessity, Jesus can only differ from us by degree in that he incarnates "God as Spirit" more than we do.[17]

Haight obviously wishes to ensure the full humanity of Jesus and believes that the traditional understanding of the Incarnation jeopardizes this humanity because the personhood of Jesus is the eternal Son. While such a discussion cannot be fully undertaken here, it must be said that to specify the divine subjectivity of Jesus in no way implies that he is less than human. He possesses all that pertains to being human, including a human self-conscious "I." What the Councils and the tradition wished to ensure was

15. Wright, "Roger Haight's Spirit Christology," 731.

16. It is interesting that those segments of the tradition with which Haight agrees with are called "doctrines," such as Jesus being *homoousios* with us, but not those with which he disagrees, such as Jesus being *homoousios* with God.

17. While Haight states that he does not believe that the traditional Logos Christology is wrong, but rather wishes "to characterize a Christology that is more adequate to our situation" (259), the traditional Logos Christology is actually the only Christology that is ruled out of court.

that the subjective identity of that human "I" was the eternal Son of God. Not to acknowledge that Jesus is truly the Son of God thoroughly abandons the significance of the full humanity, and thus of the Incarnation itself.[18]

With regard to the Trinity, Haight admits that the traditional language about three persons in one God "is not directly reflected in Spirit Christology" and that "more speculation will be needed" (285–86). He denies that there is any intrinsic or necessary relationship between the developed Trinitarian doctrine and the New Testament (285). "The economic Trinity is distinct from the doctrine of the immanent Trinity ... and the former does not necessarily entail the latter" (285).

In speaking about the Trinity, Haight exposes how truly nonbiblical is his Spirit Christology. The personalism and the communion of life between persons, which is so prevalent in the Bible, is absent. Not only is the being of God no longer a communion of life and love between the Father, Son, and Holy Spirit, but also God no longer shares this communion of life with us. "Father," "Son/Word," and "Spirit" only function as symbols or metaphors of our human perception of a solitary "transcendent being." He is not a God who acts, and is much less a trinity of persons who desire to form a common life with us. Haight is less than an Old Testament monotheist. He is simply, at best, a Unitarian.[19]

Thus Haight does not meet his third criterion of being faithful to the tradition and to the Councils. Nor is his fourth criterion feasible for the viability of his Spirit Christology—intelligibility and coherence. Wright is correct when he writes, "It seems to me that Haight's position is coherent within itself, but not with the experience of most Christians, with the teaching of the New Testament, nor with the Councils of the Church and the Great Tradition generally."[20]

18. For a fuller discussion of how the eternal Son can become man without diminishing his humanity, see T. G. Weinandy, *Does God Change? The Word's Becoming in the Incarnation* (Petersham, MA: St. Bede's Press, 1985), 96–100, 184–86; *In the Likeness of Sinful Flesh*, 11–13. See also Jean Galot, *The Person of Christ* (Chicago: Franciscan Herald Press, 1983); *Who Is Christ?* (Chicago: Franciscan Herald Press, 1981), 279–311.

19. In response to Lampe's *God as Spirit*, E. L. Mascall wrote the essay "Quicunque Vult ...? Anglican Unitarians," in *Whatever Happened to the Human Mind?* (London: SPCK, 1980), 97–127.

20. Wright, "Roger Haight's Spirit Christology," 733.

Jesus and Other Salvation Bringers

Haight's fifth criterion, that Christianity must take into account other religions and their founders, can now be examined briefly. Haight writes: "In an historicist framework and on the basis of a Spirit Christology one also confesses that Jesus is an ontological mediation of God that is decisive, definitive, final, and even absolute, provided that these determinations are not construed exclusively, as negating the possibility that God as Spirit is at work in other religions" (282). Jesus may be decisive and absolute for Christians, but this decisiveness and absoluteness is relative because God is working in the same kind of way in other religions—as Spirit.

This relativity is contrary to the New Testament and to the Christian tradition, however. Granted that God can and does work in other religions, Christians believe that Jesus, as the Son of God incarnate, differs from other founders of religion not only in degree (as Haight maintains) but also in kind. Moreover, unlike the founders of other religions, who in themselves are unimportant but function as couriers of an important religious message that is not about themselves, Jesus is fundamentally significant and not just a proclamation about something apart from himself. Jesus is himself the message. He is the way, the truth, and the life (Jn. 14:6). He is the Resurrection and the life (Jn. 11:25). The Church preaches Jesus Christ and him crucified (1 Cor. 1:23). Before him every knee is to bend and every voice proclaim that he is Lord (Phil. 1:10–11). Jesus was important within his earthly life because only in his death and resurrection is sin and death vanquished so that now *in him*, as the risen Lord, we have a new kind of life with Father, the fullness of the Holy Spirit, and the promise of eternal life. Many people from other religions may get to heaven, but they will do so because in Jesus's name alone do we have salvation (Acts 4:12).[21]

Reason and Inspiration

In light of all that has been said, Haight's position does not uphold his first and sixth criteria—that Christology justify our faith in Jesus and inspire

---

21. Ibid., 734. Wright believes that Haight's Spirit Christology "seems to undercut radically the mission of the Church" to preach the Gospel to all nations.

Christian life. Within Haight's Spirit Christology there is little reason to believe in Jesus. Actually, as noted earlier, the biblical concept of faith has been abandoned. Faith is not an intellectual acceptance of nor a personal commitment to Jesus as Lord and Savior by which we are justified and made holy, but rather it is reduced merely to imitation. What we truly require is the means to discern how to live a "good life" and then live it. A noble philosopher could do equally as well as Jesus, although he would inevitably not practice what he preached. Jesus's perfect example may inspire us, but he is not the eternal Son of God who has actually experienced our human plight, nor is he our Savior who has radically changed our desperate condition.[22] In a world racked with so much injustice and war and in the pain of sin and death that inflicts our personal lives, we need a God who does more than provide us moral encouragement.

This essay could be construed as being merely negative.[23] My goal, however, has not been just to demonstrate the inadequacy of Haight's Spirit Christology, but also to defend the Gospel as it has been passed down to us through the Church. The only message that gives life is this Gospel, revealed and protected by the Spirit of truth and lived out by the saints of all ages.

22. Ibid. Wright states: "At least for myself, as I contemplate a purely human Jesus, though one in whom the Spirit is fully operative, I experience an immense sadness and sense of loss: for this would mean that God after all did not love us enough to become one of us and die for us. But Haight thinks that such a Jesus is one we can follow more readily."

23. This essay should not be interpreted as saying that I see no role for the Holy Spirit in the life of Jesus. Actually, I believe traditional Christology and soteriology have been quite deficient in their understanding of the position of the Holy Spirit. See T. G. Weinandy, *In the Likeness of Sinful Flesh*, 59–60, 97, 102, 150–51.

CHAPTER 14

The Symbolic Theology
of Roger Haight

Roger Haight, S.J., of the Weston Jesuit School of Theology, in his book *Jesus Symbol of God*,[1] has not substantially advanced his arguments nor has he fundamentally altered his conclusions from those first offered in his article "The Case for Spirit Christology."[2] Nonetheless, he has obviously expanded his arguments and so has attempted to substantiate further his theological and Christological position, and for this reason his book deserves careful reading and judicious assessment.[3]

Originally published as "The Symbolic Theology of Roger Haight," *Thomist* 65, no. 1 (2001): 121–36. Reprinted by permission.

1. Roger Haight, *Jesus Symbol of God* (New York: Orbis Books, 1999). All subsequent page numbers given in the text refer to this article.

2. Roger Haight, "The Case for Spirit Christology," *Theological Studies* 53 (1992): 257–87.

3. I responded to Haight's article in "The Case for Spirit Christology: Some Reflections," *Thomist* 59, no. 2 (1995): 173–88 (chap. 13 in this volume), where I critically addressed Haight's historical and systematic arguments and doctrinal conclusions. Because Haight has not substantially changed his thinking, for the most part I do not address these same issues here. Haight has not attended to or even acknowledged my criticisms, and therefore I believe my earlier critique still stands. This essay should be read in conjunction with my previous essay (see chap. 13 in this volume). Here I focus my analysis on Haight's understanding of symbolic religious knowledge and language and its ramifications, as these form the basis of his theological and Christological stance. It should also be noted that Haight has not addressed or even noted in his book J. Wright's critical but insightful article, "Roger Haight's Spirit Christology," *Theological Studies* 53 (1992): 729–35.

In Search of a Hermeneutic

Within each chapter of his book Haight cyclically advances a hermeneutic that allows him to reject what he wants to reject and simultaneously allow him to affirm what he wants to affirm. (This reviewer is convinced that, for Haight, the former is often more important than the latter, in that his rejections are more clearly expressed and more decisively uttered than his affirmations. His book is foremost a book of denial.) He locates such a hermeneutical principle in his understanding of the symbolic nature of religious knowledge and language, which he not only argues is in accord with postmodernity with its rightful emphasis on historical consciousness, but also then the only means for making Christianity credible today.[4]

For Haight, God's transcendence necessitates that theological language be symbolic. As transcendent, God is beyond the confines of this world and its history, and therefore he cannot be an object that is directly experienced and known. Human beings can only directly experience, know, and express as objectively factual that which exists within the this-worldly historical order. But symbols and symbolic language provide an opening, Haight maintains, to the transcendent God, for "a symbol mediates awareness of something else" (8). More specifically, "religious symbols ... point to and mediate transcendent realities in response to religious questioning." For Haight, the knowledge that is obtained through religious symbols "is not an attenuated form of cognition, but an extension of the range of human awareness"; that is, it is not a different way of knowing from that of normal human knowing, but rather "symbols may be called engaged participatory knowledge. This

---

4. For Haight's understanding of postmodernity, see 24–26, 330–34. Historical consciousness, for Haight, is that contemporary intellectual mind-set that founds scholarly assessment solely upon historical and factual data, and thus he places all Christology under the normative eye and the final arbitration of contemporary "Jesus research" (30–40). It also represents the prevailing intellectual posture that all scholarly analysis of past beliefs must be measured from within their relative historical and cultural settings and judged in light of their current existing intellectual, educated, historical, and cultural surroundings. Moreover, all new theological proposals must harmonize with these same criteria. This accounts for Haight's incessant and uncritical partiality to what postmodernity, with its historical consciousness, will or will not tolerate and permit concerning Christian doctrine and religious belief (see 21, 26, 39, 48–51, 120, 126, 217, 221–22, 237, 242, 249, 273–74, 278, 280–81, 290–97, 319, 331–35, 339, 342–45, 348–52, 364, 369, 384, 396, 404–5, 422, 431, 433–35, 439, 445, 447, 458, 461, 465–66, 468, 470, 474, 477–78, 490.

means that it is the product of becoming conscious existentially and experientially of that which is mediated by the symbol." Haight draws two critical "axioms" from this understanding of religious symbols, "which interact dialectically." The first is negative: "because theology is symbolic, its assertions are not direct statements of information about God. Information here connotes a kind of objectified datum that is asserted about God the way information about other things of this world are known." This is in accordance with the transcendent nature of faith and revelation, and thus "theology communicates no immediate information about God." The second axiom is positive: "the symbolic assertions of theology communicate through the engaged participatory experience which they invite and actively engender. The symbolic assertions of theology draw one into the mystery of the transcendent" (9). Haight holds that even though symbolic statements do not give us factual and objective knowledge of God, this "does not lessen their epistemological value," for they (and this is the dialectic) draw one into "a participatory encounter with its object ... the meaning and truth" of which "have to be found in the present-day experience of the community" (9–10). Haight summarizes his position as follows.

The idea of a symbol is essentially tensive, dynamic, and dialectical; a symbol mediates something other than itself by drawing or leading beyond itself to a deeper or higher truth. By conceiving theology as a symbolic discipline and by consistently using the language of symbol, one is able to ensure respect for its elementary character. Symbols do not provide objective information about God; symbols draw human consciousness and life into a deeper world of encounter with transcendent reality. This represents epistemologically a symbolic realism (11, 12).[5]

We find in the above, especially as expressed in the two axioms, the basis upon which Haight is able to deny what he wants to deny and to affirm what he wants to affirm.

---

5. Haight distinguishes "concrete symbols" such as Jesus, who in his person and life "concretely" symbolizes God, and "conceptual symbols" such as Scripture, which are the words or concepts that symbolically mediate a transcendent reality (13–14). Haight sometimes speaks of symbols as metaphorical, which he sees as a conceptual symbol. While Haight holds that "symbolic predication preserves the realism of the analogy of being," it only does so in the sense that the symbolic predication mediates the transcendent reality symbolized and not that one actually possesses objective and factual knowledge of the transcendent reality itself (11–13).

A Clear Hermeneutic of Denial

The negative axiom concerning religious symbolic language allows Haight not only to deny the validity and truth of the central doctrines of Christianity as they have been defined and traditionally understood, but it also permits him to eradicate the premise upon which they were founded. To reduce religious knowledge to symbols that are generated from within the this-worldly order prohibits what has now come to be termed as an "interventionist" view of God acting; that is, God acting in time and history in a manner that is peculiar and singular to himself. As such, these divine actions cannot be accounted for solely by the laws of nature nor merely from within the created order. Traditionally such acts were designated as "supernatural."[6]

By employing this negative axiom, Haight is able to deny that Scripture (and the New Testament particularly) provides any specific objective knowledge about the nature of God and of his actions. Scripture must not be read simply from within its original meaning, but from within the confines of postmodernity, where the prevailing hermeneutic is that of "symbol" (7).

From a doctrinal perspective, Scripture is essentially a book of religious symbols, and thus the mere citation of Scripture, as testimony to past belief, by itself bears little weight for belief today; the dynamic process by which scriptural testimony can win authority is one of disclosure and elaboration; that is, symbolic mediation and argument (12).[7]

Haight can deny the traditional interpretation of the New Testament that gave rise to the defined doctrine of the Incarnation and so deny the doctrine itself. He can now do so because it is precisely here where the Fa-

---

6. Haight explicitly disallows a "supernatural" or "interventionist" view of God acting (66, 434).

7. Scripture undoubtedly employs symbolic language. It speaks symbolically, for example, of God's "Word" or "Wisdom," or "Spirit." Such language is not to be taken literally as if God had a mouth, or that he possesses wisdom in the same manner as humans, or that God acts like the wind. Nonetheless, these scriptural metaphors were understood to articulate something that is objective and factual (and in this sense literal) about God. This Haight's understanding of religious symbolic language will not allow, for it is devoid of the authentic, traditional understanding of the analogy of being, whereby what is predicated of God actually corresponds, in an analogous manner, to something that is objectively true about God and his actions.

thers went wrong. The Fathers and even the early Councils "used scripture in a way that implied that it communicated what amounted to representative knowledge about transcendent reality" (279; see also 247, 261, 270). They did not apprehend the symbolic nature of scriptural affirmations and so objectified the knowledge of God, which led them, falsely, to hypostasize "the Son/Word" as a distinct "being" (Haight's word), rather than recognizing that such terms were symbolic personifications. More specifically, Haight can deny that the Son of God is an eternal divine subject, equal to and one in being with the Father, who came to exist as a man. By not taking into account the symbolic nature of God's presence in Jesus, such a Christology "from above" is viewed today as "fantastic" and "anthropomorphic," for it "depicts a mythological fable" (273; see also 177).[8]

Haight can equally deny the bodily resurrection of Jesus as it has been traditionally understood within the New Testament and articulated within classic theology. Neither the empty tomb, nor the bodily appearances, nor even the Resurrection itself should be taken as historical objective fact, as has been done in the past, but must now be interpreted as symbols of Christ's new life within "the sphere of God" (119–51).[9]

8. Haight interprets all interventionist views of God acting in a supernatural manner as mythological (see 177, 240, 352). The reason is that, in accordance with his notion of religious symbolic knowledge, all theological knowing is initiated from within and confined to this world. Haight also insists that historical consciousness, as found within contemporary "Jesus research," demands that all Christology be "from below" (29–30), which requires for Haight that the historical Jesus not be a divine person but solely a human person (288–97). In his discussion of Christology "from above" and "from below," Haight makes a fundamental error. All Christology, even traditional Christology, begins epistemologically "from below." There is nowhere else to begin than from coming to know the historical human Jesus. Haight draws the false conclusion (though within his symbolic system it is the only conclusion he can draw) that this epistemology "from below" demands an ontology "from below"; that is, that coming to know Jesus though his humanity demands that he ontologically only be a man. The New Testament and the Christological tradition that it spawned, however, concluded that who this man Jesus was was none other than the eternal Son of God, and thus that this Son of God became man ("from above"). Epistemologically, Christology is always "from below." Ontologically, Christology is always "from above."

9. Because the symbol of the Resurrection pertains to God's unknowable transcendent reality, Haight insists that the Resurrection "is not an historical fact" (124). Haight is correct in that the Resurrection was not brought about historically through human or natural causality. But Haight is conflating divine causality with historical effects. Jesus's resurrection is a historical fact if one holds, which Haight does not, that God acted in such a manner that on a given day within history, a man, who actually died, was glorious raised from the dead, and one of the

Similarly, Haight can deny a great portion of traditional soteriology, particularly those aspects where Jesus's death on the Cross is interpreted as sacrificial and atoning or reparational, substitutionary, and reconciling. Because Jesus's redemptive work on the Cross was not in the past interpreted symbolically but understood literally, traditional soteriology became "bizarre, extravagant, and at times grotesque" (237). The language of "Jesus suffering for us, of being a sacrifice to God, of absorbing punishment for sin in our place, of being required to die to render satisfaction to God, hardly communicates meaningfully in our age" (241). Such a literalist and nonsymbolic use of language is offensive and even repulsive to "postmodern sensibility" (241).[10]

Haight's negative axiom also authorizes him to deny that Jesus is the sole definitive revelation of God and the sole indispensable means of humankind's salvation, and so unique among the founders of religions. The early Church and its subsequent tradition read the New Testament in a "literalist manner," which constituted a "lapse into a propositional view of revelation and fundamentalism" when asserting the uniqueness of Jesus and his work of salvation (404). Instead of rightfully conceding that Jesus is a symbol of what God has always been doing and continues to do throughout the whole of history and within all religions, the Christian tradition has falsely, and often arrogantly, insisted that Jesus be the unique definitive revelation of God and the sole and singular cause of humankind's salvation (395–423).[11]

---

bits of evidence is that on a given day his tomb was found empty. The cause of the Resurrection may require an act of God, who exists apart from time and history, but the effect of such an act took place within time and history, and in this sense it is an historical fact.

10. No theologian who argues that Jesus's death on the Cross was sacrificial, atoning, or satisfactory would endorse Haight's crude, stereotypical portrayals of these traditional soteriological themes. For a critique of Haight's own "revelational" and "exemplarist" view of salvation, see Weinandy, "The Case for Spirit Christology" (chap. 13 in this volume).

11. Haight argues that while Jesus is normative for Christianity, God can also be normatively revealing himself in other religions. Jesus is not the universal cause of salvation, but merely reveals and exemplifies, within a Christian symbolic context, what God is doing always and everywhere, and thus within other religions as well (350, 422). As to the different religious symbolic expressions "of ultimate reality, these are always generated historically through particular, individual, specific historical media. The attachment of all-knowing to the sensible historical world accounts for the pluralism of religious experiences" (401, 402). While Haight affirms a plurality of religions and the need to respect such plurality, what he has actually done, in confining "all religious knowing to the sensible historical world," is relegate all religions to differing symbolic expressions of some one deeper and all encompassing philosophical truth. Thus all

Haight can similarly deny that the Holy Spirit is a distinct subject within the Trinity. As with the Son, the early Church and the subsequent Christian tradition hypostasized the New Testament understanding of Spirit as if one now possessed an objective knowledge of God's inner being. Rather, "the metaphorical symbol of God as Spirit expresses the experience of God's power and energy in creation … God's Spirit is not so much a distinct agent of creation but the creative power itself of God" (448).

Lastly, Haight can deny the entire doctrine of the Trinity as defined by the early Councils and developed and taught within the Christian tradition. They did so because they were not sensitive to the symbolic nature of religious language. Again, they falsely believed that they were actually speaking about how God truly exists, and were unaware that, because of God's transcendence, "such language, therefore, is not objectively representational, or immediately referential, or propositionally descriptive, or ostensive in its reference" (471). The one God is not the ontological communion of three distinct subjects, the Father, the Son and the Holy Spirit, but rather "Father/Mother," "Son/Word," and "Spirit" are symbols of God's immanence within the world (467–91).[12]

I have delineated in some detail his denials, for if Haight's use of his negative hermeneutical axiom concerning the symbolic nature of religious language is correct, it strikes a death blow to Christianity as it has been proclaimed, understood, professed, and lived since its conception. So thorough is Haight's denial of traditional Christian doctrine that, whatever he may

---

religions lose their integrity, for now no deference is given to their own unique religious character and theological distinctiveness.

12. Haight argues that his understanding of the Trinity is a form of modalism, though now properly and legitimately set within a symbolic context. This means that "God as Word" and "God as Spirit" are symbolic expressions of the manner in which God is experienced within the world (476–79, 488). Haight is correct that his conception of the Trinity does possess a modalistic flavor, but having placed it within a symbolic framework, it is not modalistic at all. Traditional modalism had the one God actually acting in time and history under various modes. But Haight's God does not act in time and history under various modes. The "modes" are merely our symbolic expressions of how we perceive God's presence and not how God is acting. Moreover, for Haight, because religious symbolic language does not convey objective knowledge of God, "there is no logical connection that demands a correlation of an internal differentiation within God and God's actual self-communication to human existence" (488). The immanent expression of God, as humanly conceived symbolically, bears no correspondence to his transcendent reality. This would appear to be a major quandary within Haight's whole theological enterprise, and it is examined below.

propose as its alternative replacement, it will not be the fine-tuning or development of doctrine but the mutation into an entirely new and different religion. Aside from some recognizable similarities in vocabulary, Christianity will be an entirely different entity, for the meaning of the "Christian" words will now assume an utterly disparate definition. For Haight, such a mutation is not impossible or even undesirable. Since the very nature of religious symbolic language does not lock one into objective or factual truth about God, it not only sanctions one to reinterpret religious symbols but also actively encourages one to create new symbols in a manner that best accords with the prevailing intellectual and cultural milieu.

At this point I want to make a more specific and substantive criticism. Haight believes that in insisting that one cannot possess objective and factual knowledge of God, he is but protecting the very mystery of God's transcendence. He is merely preserving the venerable tradition concerning the apophatic character of theology, whereby God can never be fully comprehended. As seen above, those who formulated the classic doctrines of the Christian faith labored under the misconception that one could obtain factual and objective knowledge of God, but in so doing they shattered the very mystery of God. "God is a mystery, doctrines are not" (480).

God is indeed a mystery and all that pertains to him shares in that mystery, but the doctrines of the Christian faith, though considered to be true, were never thought to be comprehensive statements about God and his actions. The doctrines were definitions of what the mystery of God is and what he has done, and they were historically formulated to protect the mystery of God from those who would make God and his revelation comprehensible. The conciliar doctrines concerning the persons of the Trinity state what the mystery of the Trinity is and are not statements intended to make the Trinity comprehensible. The Chalcedonian definition that Jesus is the eternal Son of God existing as an authentic man is a statement that articulates the very mystery of the Incarnation. What it definitely does not do is make the mystery of the Incarnation comprehensible. In fact, it is because the traditional doctrines do define and so protect the mysteries of the Christian faith that Haight wants to jettison them, for it is specifically these mysteries that he and those who fall under his umbrella of postmodernity find no longer credible. Ironically, but true to his principles, while Haight remains throughout his book scrupulously agnostic about the "mystery" of who God is, his symbolic understanding of "Christianity" becomes comprehensible, for no longer do disconcerting and embarrassing mysteries loiter within his symbolic understanding of Jesus and the Gospel.

An Ambiguous Hermeneutic of Affirmation

In tandem with his denials, Haight also presents his symbolic affirmation of the Christian Gospel. He argues that his reconstruction is in conformity with Scripture and even with the Christian tradition if understood as to their proper intent and authentic purpose—that is, symbolically—though his symbolic interpretation may not concur with their actual former reading or belief. But it is here that his thesis that all religious knowledge and language are symbolic plunges him headlong into theological ambiguity and into a philosophical quandary.

What is ultimately decisive in assessing Haight's book is not merely a critique of the specifics of what Haight wants to affirm about God, Jesus, salvation, and Christianity's relationship with other religions, and the like, but an evaluation of the premises upon which he wants to affirm such assertions. If the premises are flawed, then the affirmations become utterly problematic.

Again, Haight is correct when he states that, since God is wholly transcendent and thus not a member of this-worldly order, we cannot have any direct experience and knowledge of him. For this reason, as is evident from above, he reduces all theological language to the symbolic. How does this symbolic language arise? Haight insists that it does not arise from a manner of knowing that differs in kind from all other human knowing. It arises out of "religious questioning"; that is, from such human experiences as the presence of evil and death and the desire for happiness and well-being (192–93, 254–55). But from where do the answers to such questions come? At this point one encounters much ambiguity and even a dilemma within Haight's presentation.

He consistently states, as seen above, that "religious symbols ... point to and mediate transcendent realities." We become "existentially and experientially" conscious "of that which is mediated by the symbol." Symbols "draw" and "lead" us to "deeper and higher truth." Religious symbols "draw human consciousness and life into a deeper world of encounter with transcendent reality" and so symbols allow us to be "engaged in participatory knowledge" with the transcendent object. As Haight states in his second positive axiom, "The symbolic assertions of theology communicate through the engaged participatory experience which they invite and actively engender."

Notice that, for Haight, it is not some religious experience of a transcendent reality that gives rise to its being expressed in a symbolic manner. Rather, it is the religious symbol itself, such as Jesus, or the symbolic expression itself, such as Scripture, that "draws," "engenders," "leads," or "invites," one into a symbolic experience of the transcendent reality. As Haight states, "The world of religious symbolism, the world of language about God, is not one of facts and digital information; it is a world of religious experience; it is based on a narrative of a symbolic encounter with God in history" (472).[13] For Haight, what is important is not that a religious experience be expressed symbolically, but that "the religious experience" itself, the encounter with God, be symbolic, for it is "based on a narrative of a symbolic encounter with God in history."

A question and problem now arise: If the religious symbolic language, which solely and completely emerges from within historical and cultural experiences of the this-worldly order, what founds the truth and validity of the symbol and its symbolic expression? Religious experience does not found the truth of the symbol because it is the symbol itself or its symbolic expression that gives rise to the symbolic experience. Even if one did allow an experience of something that transcended worldly historical reality, it would mean that one's experience and knowledge exceeded the normal manner of human knowing. In addition, one would then possess, in some sense, a factual or objective knowledge of the transcendent reality, both of which Haight intentionally and repeatedly rejects. Moreover, the symbol and its symbolic expression obviously cannot be due to a specific "interventionist" action on the part of God within history and the world by which he reveals something about himself and so is responsible for its meaning. Haight's negative hermeneutic concerning symbolic knowledge is purposely designed to eliminate such a view.

13. What it means to possess "digital information" about God is a question better left unasked, though it might refer to the Trinity being digitally three in one or that Christ is digitally two in one. In the end, I guess, it does not really matter what "digital information" about God means since it is impossible to have it anyway.

Within Haight's account there appears to be no epistemological connection between the symbol or the symbolic language and the transcendent reality that is meant to be experienced symbolically. For Haight, the symbol arises exclusively from within the culture in which it was formed, or from within "the present-day experience of the community." In so arising it thus fosters a symbolic experience of "the transcendent" in keeping with that culture or community, but this merely informs one as to how a particular culture or community conceives and symbolically experiences the transcendent reality (God). It does not validate as true that cultural or communal religious symbol or symbolic experience. The symbol is purely the seemingly arbitrary conception of a particular culture or community within its historical setting—what it holds to be of transcendent value. Within a Christian culture, God may be symbolized as personal and loving. Within another religious culture, God may be symbolized in a pantheistic manner. But within Haight's theory there is no way for religious symbols and their symbolic expression to leap beyond their historical and cultural bounds from which they were engendered and so make contact with a transcendent reality that exceeds these bounds. Thus, while Haight wishes to hold a "symbolic realism," there is actually no realism to the symbol, for there is no authentic epistemological basis upon which this realism is founded. Its referent is not actually the "real" God, but only the real historical culture or community from which it arises. While Haight continually argues that religious symbolic knowledge puts one in contract with the transcendent reality, there is no basis for such a claim because one's symbolic religious knowledge arises out of and is completely confined within the this-worldly order.[14] The truth of this objection is seen in Haight's own insistence that religious symbolic knowledge, by its very symbolic nature, is not an objective or factual knowledge of the transcendent reality. The reason being, again, that symbolic religious knowledge refers not to the transcendent reality as such but to the

---

14. In defense of his "symbolic realism," Haight argues that it would be erroneous to relegate his understanding of symbol to that of being "merely a symbol," "for a symbol as it is understood here truly reveals and makes present what it symbolizes" (197). Even if this were true, it would still mean that what is revealed and made present is only present in a symbolic manner, and not present as it actually is, and thus its presence would still be merely symbolic. Within the traditional understanding of grace, for example, the Holy Spirit is not present within a person symbolically, in that a symbol mediates the Spirit's "real" presence, but the Holy Spirit is present within the person as the Holy Spirit actually exists.

historical and cultural milieu from which it arises and gives voice. There is no way of knowing whether one's symbolic religious knowledge has any epistemological correspondence to the transcendent reality.

Haight's book is fraught with ambiguity. On one level, Haight makes numerous affirmations founded upon his understanding of symbol and symbolic language, giving the impression that one is actually saying something that is meaningful, objective, factual, and true about God. For example, Haight constantly states that Christian religious symbolism "reveals," especially through Jesus, and so allows one to encounter a personal God who is loving, kind, compassionate, just, and forgiving (113–18).[15] Or, most importantly, Haight argues that Jesus is the Christian symbol of God; that is, in his concrete historical human personhood, he was "the parable of God" (112–22).[16] He not only symbolized what God is like, but through his words and actions also manifested symbolically what God has always been doing and continues to do throughout the world to ensure humankind's salvation. This includes what God is salvifically doing within other religions, though such religions may symbolize God's salvific action in a manner that is in conformity with its own historical and cultural milieu. He tirelessly argues that the religious symbol of "God as Spirit" is the symbolic expression of God's "work, as activity, and as power, energy or force that accomplishes something" (447).[17] "God as Spirit," for Haight, is the symbol of God's con-

15. The term "revelation," for Haight, does not refer to some specific action of God but arises out of a human engagement with the world and is "a form of human experience," whereby "God works within human subjects in a way that corresponds to the structure of human experience itself" (194). But the way "God works," which "corresponds to the structure of human experience," is not actually a work of God at all, but rather revelation simply "occurs in human experience through symbolic mediation" (198–99). It is through humanly manufactured symbols and symbolic language that are symbolically termed "revelation" and "the works of God."

16. Haight is selective in his use of the New Testament. He limits his Christology almost entirely to the Synoptic Gospels, for the obvious reason that they seem to uphold unmistakably Jesus's humanity with little or no reference to his possible divine status. Haight omits almost the whole of the Johannine literature (all references are by way of critique) and the Pauline corpus. There is no mention of any of the other New Testament documents. Although Haight emphasizes the plurality of New Testament Christologies (425–31), the irony is that once these Christologies are filtered through his symbolic prism they lose their uniquely vibrant Christological hue and are homogenized into the same dull and pallorous meaning.

17. To speak of "God as Spirit" as "indicating God's work, as activity, and as power, energy or force that accomplishes something" is to mislead the reader at best, for such terms do not refer to the way God actually is and acts. Again, they are merely symbolic expressions arising out

tinual activity and power within the world since creation and is manifested in Jesus in a supreme manner.

The symbol of the Spirit more forthrightly makes the claim that God, God's very self, acted in and through Jesus ... the symbol of God as Spirit is not a personification of God, but refers more directly to God so that it is clear from the beginning that nothing less than God was at work in Jesus ... This should also be construed as more than a thin functional or "adverbial" presence of God to Jesus, and truly an ontological presence, because where God acts, God is. In this empowerment christology Jesus is the reality of God.[18] (451, 455)

Now, at another level, one must always bear in mind that such and similar affirmations, despite the impression they may initially give, are not making objective or factual statements about the true nature of God and his manner of acting. This Haight will ultimately not tolerate. These are but symbolic statements drawing one into symbolic experiences founded upon one's historical, religious, and cultural milieu, and they have no objective reference to God and his actions at all. They are entirely culturally, historically, and religiously relative.

In the end, as Haight would ultimately agree, despite all of his affirmations, we do not actually know God and thus we do not know whether God is actually "loving, kind, compassionate and forgiving," for such words do not convey any objective or factual knowledge of God.[19] While Haight

---

of a particular historical, religious culture that symbolically designate the symbolic presence of the transcendent. Their frame of reference is contained solely within the historical worldly order.

18. Haight, in his "The Case for Spirit Christology," speaks of God being "adverbially" present within Jesus. Within his book he strengthens his claim by saying that God is "ontologically" present in Jesus. While Haight may claim that God is ontologically present in Jesus, how we would know this, given that we are laboring within the constraints of symbolic knowledge, remains ambiguous at best. Nonetheless, this ontology of "presence" is far removed from saying, as Nicea and Chalcedon do, that, objectively and factually, Jesus is ontologically the eternal Son of God, one in being with the Father. For a full critique of Haight's interpretation of the Councils and the validity of his "Spirit Christology," see Weinandy, "The Case for Spirit Christology" (chap. 13 in this volume).

19. Here we see the full extent to which Haight's book is foremost a book of denial. He not only denies the traditional Christian doctrines, but he also, even within his affirmations, ultimately denies that one can have any objective or factual knowledge of God. What Haight has in effect attempted to do in his symbolic reinterpretation of the Gospel is to affirm those bits and pieces of the Gospel that he finds acceptable, such as God being personal, loving, and kind. He would have no basis for affirming these, however, as the Scriptures make unmistakably evi-

wants us, through religious symbols and their linguistic expression, to be in touch with the incomprehensible transcendent reality of God, neither the symbols nor their expression allow us anything more than for us to be in touch with the mystery and transcendent reality that reside solely and exclusively within this cosmic order.

In fairness, Haight does argue, almost as a subplot when the need arises, that the epistemological connection is founded upon the Creator/creature relationship. "Among other things, the doctrine of creation out of nothing means that God is immediately present to all finite reality and thus to human beings" (392n52). Actually, this Creator/creature relationship is the exclusive relationship upon which Haight founds his symbolic knowledge and language. All religious symbols, including Jesus and salvation, are but the various and diverse symbols through which the religious implications of this Creator/creature relationship are manifested.[20] This ontological Creator/creature relationship provides the epistemological window through which religious symbols, such as Jesus, and religious symbolic language, such as Scripture, acquire their meaning and validity. For Haight, however, while this relationship allows one to be led and drawn into the incomprehensible mystery of transcendent reality through these valid symbols and meaningful symbolic language, one never actually knows, through these valid symbols and meaningful symbolic language, objectively and factually the transcendent reality itself. For Haight the transcendent mystery still remains unknowable. To this reviewer it all seems utterly ambiguous and confusing if not contradictory. How is it possible for symbols to be valid and for symbolic language to be meaningful if the symbols do not convey valid truth and the symbolic language articulate meaningful knowledge?

Haight's argument is nonetheless extremely fascinating. He is adamant that all religious knowledge and language is symbolic, but we profess that God—the wholly mysterious, incomprehensible, and transcendent God— is indeed factually and objectively (digitally, if you like) the Creator. The term "Creator" is not symbolic, though on one occasion Haight does speak of "the symbol of creation," but that hardly accords with his notion of "cre-

---

dent, if God had not actually intervened in the world, historically revealing that he is indeed a personal God who is kind and loving.

20. For the relationship between creation and salvation, see 350–54; between creation and Christology and eschatology, see 392n52; and between creation and revelation and grace, see 453.

ation out of nothing" (453). Moreover, having ruled out of court an "interventionist" view of God acting within history and the world, we have here the literally primordial intervention. If there ever was a "supernatural" act—one that only God can perform and to which neither history, nor culture, nor this world's causality can give account, because they do not exist—it is the act of *creatio ex nihilo*!

Here we see clearly the ambiguity and the dilemma within Haight's position. Religious symbols and their symbolic expression are entirely embedded within this world of history and culture, but he wants them nonetheless to have some ontological and so epistemological connection with transcendent reality, though not an epistemologically objective and factual connection. He calls into play the notion that God is Creator in order to establish such an ontological and so epistemological connection. If the term "Creator" becomes a symbol and if "creation out of nothing" becomes symbolic, however, which they rightly should be so as to conform to Haight's own premises, then the whole religious symbolic system becomes ensnared within this historical, cultural world order. Religious symbols, such as Jesus, and their symbolic expression, such as the sacred texts of all religions, merely provide symbolic knowledge of a transcendence that refers not to a wholly transcendent other called God, but only to the "mystery" that lies completely within the cosmic order. The term "God," for Haight, must now be construed symbolically, as well, for it does not refer to an existing being distinct from the historical, cosmic order but is merely the symbolic expression of the "mystery" that lies within the historical, cosmic order. One wonders whether Haight is not unaware of this contradiction. When speaking more philosophically rather than theologically, he often seems to prefer the phrase "transcendent reality" over the term "God," for the term "God" implies a being distinct from the historical cosmic order, whereas the phrase "transcendent reality" necessarily does not. The reality that is transcendent could very well be within the historic cosmic order. If such be the case, then one would have, in Haight's account, a form of atheism that is merely couched in religious symbolism.

Conclusion

I have not assessed in this essay the specifics of Haight's theological program, having done so in my previous essay. What I have done here is ad-

dress what I consider to be the important issues and critical ramifications
that ensue from Haight's philosophical and theological premises—his understanding of religious symbols, religious symbolic knowledge with its religious symbolic language, and the religious symbolic experiences to which
they give rise. I have been extremely critical of Haight's whole enterprise,
to say the least, but then I believe a great deal is at stake—the heart of the
Gospel and the whole Christian doctrinal tradition. Haight argues that a
radical redefinition of Christianity is necessary in order to make it credible to the contemporary educated person of postmodernity, and he has offered his version of what that redefinition should be.[21] Nonetheless, it must
be forthrightly acknowledged that Haight's reinterpretative enterprise does
not arise from within the Gospel itself but is the importation of a foreign
hermeneutic that has ruthlessly been imposed upon it. If history is a good
teacher, the Christian faithful—not merely of the present but also of the
past—will not tolerate such philosophical and theological colonialism, for
they will demand and seize the Gospel's rightful freedom and integrity.

21. While some have hailed Haight's book as theologically "innovative" and "pioneering,"
it is but one more example of a theological genre that goes back at least to the Enlightenment.
Haight himself affiliates his Christological enterprise with that of Schleiermacher's (304–9,
445–46). Anyone who has kept abreast with contemporary Christology will recognize that
Haight's book bears a striking resemblance to such books as John Hick, ed., *The Myth of God
Incarnate*; John Hick, *The Metaphor of God Incarnate*; John Knox, *The Humanity and Divin-
ity of Jesus*; John Macquarrie, *Jesus Christ in Modern Christian Thought*; *Christology Revisited*;
J. A. T. Robinson, *The Human Face of God*; and many more contemporary selections.

CHAPTER 15

Terrence Tilley's Christological Impasses

The Demise of the Doctrine of the Incarnation

In June 2009 the Catholic Theological Society of America (CTSA) met in Halifax for its annual convention. The theme of its gathering was "Impasse ... and Beyond." At the conclusion of the convention, Terrence W. Tilley, chairman of the Department of Theology at Fordham University, presented his presidential address, titled "Three Impasses in Christology." I was present for this address and found it troublesome on a couple of levels. First, while one would expect a presidential address to a scholarly society to be a work of substantial scholarship, this was not the case. Much of its theological argumentation was superficial and fallacious. Second, although an address by the president of a theological society that calls itself Catholic, much of the address's Christological content and many of its suggested proposals contained doctrinal ambiguities and even errors.

Rhetorically, Tilley's address was a *tour de force*, moving the hearts and minds of many, if not most, of his CTSA listeners, which was not hard to do given the content of the talk and the theological and ecclesial sympathies of many in the audience. Undoubtedly, many who now read the published version will likewise be enthused by its stump rhetoric and pulpit-rousing

Originally published as "Terrence Tilley's Christological Impasses: The Demise of the Doctrine of the Incarnation," *Fellowship of Catholic Scholars Quarterly* 32, no. 3 (2009): 4–10. Reprinted by permission.

style.[1] But it is the rhetoric that hides Tilley's superficial scholarship and thereby camouflages the address's theological ambiguities and doctrinal errors. In this essay I examine Tilley's address in order to demonstrate the validity of my above observations, allowing Tilley to speak for himself, so as to ensure that the reader will hear him and not my summary.

Tilley states at the onset of his address that "impasses are serious." If impasses of consequence, including ecclesial and theological impasses, are not adequately resolved, they become stalemates. "A stalemate is the result of playing a game to the point that neither side can win." Within the academy, stalemates "are resolved more by attrition than intellection, theories go out of style." According to Tilley, what resolves various conflicting claims, the stalemate, is not in determining their respective truth or falsity, but rather, depending on the intellectual temper of the time, one or both "go out of style." It is this "what is in style" or "what is out of style" historical relativism that underlies many of Tilley's negative critiques of the Church's doctrinal Christological tradition—it has gone "out of style." And it is Tilley's historical relativism that allows him to advance his own positive Christological proposals—his "in style" solutions that will go "beyond" the Christological impasses.

Tilley's three Christological impasses concern (1) method, (2) salvation, and (3) the person of Christ. Methodology "has to do with the starting point of Christology." "Does one begin with Scripture and tradition or does one begin with the current situation?" While Tilley admits that such a dichotomy may be questionable, he believes it useful because the Congregation for the Doctrine of the Faith (CDF) has criticized Roger Haight, S.J., and Joseph Sobrino, S.J., for not adhering adequately to Scripture and to the Christological tradition. Instead, they have methodologically founded their respective Christologies on the contemporary situation, what Tilley terms "presentism." Haight founds his Christology within a postmodern culture and Sobrino within the context of the church of the poor.

Tilley criticizes the CDF and defends Haight and Sobrino. First, Tilley points out that the New Testament professes a variety of Christologies. John 1 speaks of "God becoming man," which the CDF endorses. "However, [in criticizing Haight] the Congregation for the Doctrine of the Faith

---

1. Terrence W. Tilley, "Three Impasses in Christology," *Origins* 39, no. 7 (2009): 98–105.

seems to neglect another pattern, that 'God made a human God's Son,' as in Romans 1:4, Acts 2:22–24, 36, and even John 20:31, among other places. Both patterns are clearly discernable in the New Testament but not in the classic dogmas nor in the congregation's notification." Second, Tilley notes that the CDF believes that Sobrino has undermined the classic Christological tradition by holding that the classic doctrines capitulated to the culture of the time. In response, the CDF argues that patristic Christology and the early Councils transformed Greek words and concepts so as to articulate the truth of the Gospel in their day. In light of CDF's critique of Haight and Sobrino, Tilley, in keeping with John Paul II's insistence that the faith must be inculturated, asks rhetorically: "Isn't that what Sobrino and others are trying to do today? If it was the right approach to inculturate the Gospel message in the fourth and fifth century, why not in the twentieth and twenty-first?"

For Tilley, this represents a methodological impasse. "To express the faith in the present we must use terms appropriate to the present while the Congregation for the Doctrine of the Faith demands in effect Christology must be represented in the terms used to inculturate the faith in cultures that exist no longer, terms like *hypostasis, physis, prosopon, persona, substantia*, or modern transliterations. Adhering to the Greek and Latin terms of late antiquity runs the real risk of distorting the meaning of the faith for people today, yet they are alleged to be the right terms to use. Impasse!"

I will take up later the issue of whether patristic concepts and terminology could actually "distort the meaning of the faith for people today." First, while many scholars of Scripture emphasize the varieties of Christology contained within the New Testament, these variations, despite what some Scripture scholars maintain, do not contradict one another. It is not as if the Prologue of John's espousal of an incarnational Christology from above contradicts the professions by Paul and Acts of an Adoptionist Christology from below. The whole of the New Testament professes that Jesus is the eternal Son of God incarnate and that he lived an authentic human life of humble obedience, even to death on the Cross. For this reason, the Father raised him up bodily in glory and in so doing manifested that Jesus is truly the divine Son of God now reigning as man as the risen Lord and Christ. The Resurrection of Jesus is not, as Tilley would have it, God making a human his divine Son, but rather the confirming demonstration that

Jesus is the eternal divine Son of the Father. Such an interpretation of the various texts was common within the patristic Church and has continued through the centuries to the present day. In attempting to revive and authorize a form of Adoptionism (which the Church condemned as heretical early on), Tilley has merely raised the red herring that the New Testament offers a variety of competing and even conflicting Christologies from which to choose. In so doing, he has nonetheless laid the groundwork for conclusions that he wishes to draw as his address progresses.

Second, in keeping with a variety of competing New Testament Christologies, the specter of relativism has again raised its head. Having endorsed the methodology of the Fathers—that is, that they faithfully expressed the Gospel within a Greek and Latin culture—Tilley simply and uncritically presumes that this is what Haight and Sobrino have done or are attempting to do. They may have rejected as "out of style" the incarnational model contained within the New Testament and endorsed by the early Church, but their respective Christologies equally illustrate the New Testament principle that multiple Christological interpretations are available, and these interpretations, such as their own, may now be "in style." Absent within Tilley's proposal is any Christological norm, other than the relative cultural and historical *zeitgeist*, by which one is able to evaluate objectively their Christologies or anyone else's. As we will see, this is a consistent problem throughout Tilley's address.

Third, to inculturate the Gospel is the necessary Spirit-filled task of the Church in every age and within every culture. But there is a difference between inculturating the Gospel so as to allow it to be heard and accepted and in so doing Christianizing the culture, and culturally de-Christianizing the Gospel whereby the culture transforms the Gospel into something other than what it authentically is. Tilley does not address this serious and delicate issue. Because he does not hold for any doctrinal norm that transcends history and culture, Tilley implicitly contends that the present culture always trumps the content and so controls the expression of the Gospel as in the cases of Haight and Sobrino. While Tilley lauds the Fathers for inculturating the Gospel in their day, and insists that Haight and Sobrino are heroically doing the same today, what the latter are actually attempting to do is exactly the opposite of what the former did.

"The second Christological impasse is how to account for God's salvific will being effective beyond the community of the baptized." Tilley rightly perceives that this impasse is particularly acute with regard to the Jews and the enduring nature of their covenants. In the course of his presentation, however, Tilley does not offer any new or creative insights on how to move beyond these interreligious impasses other than the need for continual dialogue. Because there is nothing substantially new here, I will not discuss this second Christological impasse.

The third Christological impasse is "an ancient one: How could Jesus Christ be both divine and human?" Tilley argues that today theologians regard the Creed of the Council of Chalcedon (451 AD) "as a timely resolution of the historic Christological impasse, but no longer take it as a timeless archetype to which all theology must conform." Actually, Tilley believes that "Chalcedon's 'solution' was hardly a solution." Here we find an error and an irony—ones that, as we will see, resurface throughout his talk. The error consists in viewing the doctrinal teaching of the Council of Chalcedon as merely a "timely resolution" to an historic issue that has long since passed and so no longer "a timeless archetype." Rather, the Council of Chalcedon defined the ontological nature of the incarnational mystery, that the eternal Son of God exists as man, and as such Christians of every age are bound to assent to the doctrinal content of that definition. The irony is that, on the one hand, Tilley argued earlier that the Fathers and Councils provided an adequate expression of the Gospel within a Greek and Latin culture and insisted that Haight and Sobrino are admirably attempting to do the same today, yet on the other hand, he now argues that the Fathers and Councils were a complete failure. For Tilley, it is not consistency of argumentation that is important but rhetorical sound bites. This is further exemplified in what immediately follows.

One of the reasons, according to Tilley, for Chalcedon's failure is in the unethical and unscrupulous ecclesial politics of the time, including, quoting G. Hall, the "rigged councils, banished bishops, imprisonments, ecclesiastical witch hunts and even physical fights." The aftermath of the Council of Chalcedon was no better. In the midst of political force and imposition, the Church became splintered into warring theological factions. The "political response to the impasse was to resort to force or divorce—the impasse became a stalemate."

What is the purpose of the above highly rhetorical historical narrative?

It would appear that by detailing all of the political and ecclesial shenanigans, some of which (but not all) are no doubt true, one is able to contaminate the doctrinal content of the Councils (Nicea, 325 AD; Constantinople, 381 AD; Ephesus, 431 AD; and Chalcedon, 451 AD), all of which took place within such a political corrupt and ecclesial power-hungry environment. For Tilley, it is simply guilt by association. Good doctrine cannot possibly associate with such reprehensible company, and because, historically, it did have such nefarious friends, it cannot possibly be good, either. What Tilley does not address is the most important issue of all: Was what the Councils taught in accordance with revelation and so true? In the end, Tilley's historical narrative is merely a rhetorical ploy used to subvert and relativize the teaching of the Councils.

More substantially, Tilley states that the Council of Chalcedon simply restated the Christological problem without offering a satisfactory solution as to how one person could be both God and man. This is exemplified particularly in attempting to predicate divine and human attributes to Jesus. "The problem of how a *person* could have both divine and human *properties* was not resolved." For Tilley, Chalcedon actually exacerbated the problem. "The theological effect of the Chalcedonian strategy of attributing properties to the two natures rather than to the person of Christ basically left the impasse intact."

Two comments are in order here. The first is that Tilley reveals in the above that he is not adequately acquainted with the Creed of the Council of Chalcedon. Chalcedon did not endorse the notion that the divine attributes are to be predicated of the *human nature* and that the human attributes are to be predicated of the *divine nature*. Chalcedon did endorse the Alexandrian Christological tradition of Athanasius and Cyril, both of whom stressed that the divine and human attributes be predicated on *one and the same person* of the Son. Because Chalcedon declared that one and the same Son existed "in two natures"—that is, as God and as man—it is one and the same person of the Son who did not suffer as God, and it is one and the same person of the Son who did suffer as man. The Second and Third Councils of Constantinople (553 and 680–81 AD) were held not to reinterpret or even to clarify the teaching of the Council of Chalcedon, but to ensure that it be understood precisely in this manner, for this was the original mind of Chalcedon itself.

Second, in criticizing Chalcedon for merely restating the impasse of how Jesus can be both God and man rather than finding a satisfactory resolution to the issues, Tilley manifests that he does not understand the true nature of the theological enterprise. The task of theology and the defining of doctrine is not to solve theological problems but to clarify exactly what the mysteries of the faith are. Heresy always solves what is considered to be a theological problem and in so doing renders the mystery of faith completely comprehensible and so depriving it of its very mystery. Arius, a priest from Alexandria, for example, concluded in 318 AD that there is no possible way for both God to be one and for the Son to be God. This, for him, was a theological—an impasse. He resolved the impasse by denying that the Son was truly God. Granted, this resolution may be easier to comprehend, but it also destroyed the Christian mystery that God is one and that the Father, the Son, and the Holy Spirit are that one God. The Council of Nicea, which responded to Arius's heretical position, did not attempt, as he did, to solve a theological problem. Rather, the Council clarified the exact nature of the Christian mystery. The one God is not simply the Father, as Arius maintained; rather, the one God is the Father begetting the Son and thus the Son possesses the same divine nature as the Father. The begetting of the Son by the Father is proper to the very nature of the one God. Granted that the Council of Nicea did not make the mystery of the Trinity comprehensible, but it did clarify what exactly the mystery is. The Council of Chalcedon did the same with regard to the Incarnation. It stated clearly that Jesus is one and the same person of the Son of God who exists in two natures, both as God and as man, and thus the attributes of each manner of existence can rightly be predicated of that same Son. Tilley, it would appear, is into solving theological problems as a way of overcoming theological impasses, rather than clarifying the exact nature of the Christian mysteries, and in so doing allowing these mysteries to shine with even greater splendor.

Tilley once more faults the CDF for demanding that theologians employ Chalcedonian concepts and language rather than use contemporary concepts—"just what the fathers did." He sees in such insistence "another instance of a political imposition." For Tilley, the key failed tactic in attempting to overcome impasses "is stopping the dialogue, often done by silencing theologians." While "notifications and instructions of the Congregation of the Doctrine of the Faith can be and are often helpful theologically and pedagogically," "when the congregation resorts to star-chamber tactics and political sanctions—some direct, some indirect—the Congregation of the Faith may recapitulate the vicious politics of the early Church." Such unseemly tactics only leads to stalemate. The way through an impasse (and so to avoid a stalemate) is "to stay at the table no matter what until we can find a way together around the impasse." Again, for Tilley, "Stopping the dialogue by silencing theologians does not resolve the impasse. You can kill theologians, but you cannot silence them—short of gagging their mouths and tying their hands behind them. The *habitus* of their vocation is too strong to be stopped by human authorities. As I said yesterday, you can't shut us up." Tilley argues that "good theological ideas live despite official authoritarian repression because these ideas capture the old creeds in the new world, using a new idiom for giving voice to new ways in which the old faith can live on in a new context." While theologians who "stubbornly maintain their positions" and are not willing to rethink them—"not necessarily to change them"—do not help in advancing the process, "the guardians of orthodoxy who mobilize the legionaries of repression do little to resolve theological impasses." Once more, Tilley insists that "we must stay at the table of dialogue until we can hear the Spirit, who gets us through the impasse as the impasse moves through and in us. Patience with each other is key."

A few comments are again in order. First, as he has done previously, Tilley pleads that the CDF simply permit theologians today to do what the Fathers did in the past, even though he finds that what they did utterly inadequate, for they created and sanctioned a Christological impasse, and their political and ecclesial behavior was utterly reprehensible.

Second, what Tilley says about the CDF is completely inappropriate, especially within what is expected to be a scholarly and objective context. Such language hardly exemplifies respectful table manners, nor is it conducive to honest and forthright dialogue, the very thing Tilley insists is the proper way to overcome impasses. While the CDF does criticize and condemn particular theological opinions, it always does so in a scholarly, respectful, and professional manner.

Third, though Tilley rightly speaks of good theological ideas living on and thus speaking the old creed to a new world, he does not offer any criteria by which to judge whether a theological idea is good and so captures the old creed for a new world. He is incapable of offering any theological or doctrinal criteria, for, in criticizing the workings of the CDF, Tilley clearly reveals yet again that he espouses a theological relativism—that there is no objective standard of orthodoxy, no authentic rule of faith, by which theological opinion can be judged to be true or false, clear or ambiguous. The CDF, then, possesses no doctrinal base for discerning the adequacy of theological opinion other than "star-chamber tactics." Nor does it posses any rightful divine magisterial authority to make doctrinal judgments. It simply possesses "human authority" that it autocratically exercises with an authoritarian and repressive will. This theological relativism becomes eminently clear as Tilley moves to the conclusion of his address.

Fourth, Tilley gives the impression that the theological academy and the Church's magisterium are equal partners around the table of dialogue. This is obviously not the case, but if one holds that the Church no longer possesses divine authority to defend and proclaim the truth of revelation, one is then able, as Tilley does, to pretend that some dialogical compromise is the only proper way forward within a theological environment that professes that all truth is culturally relative. Moreover, Tilley gives the impression that the entire Catholic theological academy is at an impasse with an intransigent and repressive magisterium. He fails to recognize that not all Catholic theologians agree with his or with the CTSA's theological and ecclesial agenda, and thus he fails to acknowledge that he does not speak on their behalf. Many, if not most, of the creative and scholarly Catholic theologians today are fully in accord with the Church's doctrinal Christological tradition and so would find Tilley's own positions less than adequate.

Nonetheless, how does one progress beyond the present Christological impasses? For Tilley, not only is dialogue essential—the staying at the table—but important also is shared ascetic practices, especially "shared prayer." Thus "Demanding theological conformity in a time of impasse is a divisive practice." It must be remembered that "practice, not theory, is the heart of Christian life together; to insist on ideological identity—one way, one model, one language, especially in a time of impasse—is destructive and, as I said yesterday, idolatrous."

Tilley is correct that shared prayer is important. But the depth of shared prayer depends on the unity of faith that both parties share. A group of Catholics who share the same authentic faith of the Church are able to participate in a depth of shared prayer, such as the Eucharist, that a mixed group of Catholics and Protestants could not possibly achieve. This has further consequences that bear upon Tilley's argument.

Tilley is correct that to demand "theological conformity" is a "divisive practice." For the CDF to demand, for example, that every theologian conform to the theology of Hans Urs von Balthasar would be divisive. But to demand doctrinal orthodoxy—what has been revealed in Scripture and authentically taught within the Church's magisterial tradition through the centuries—is to promote, protect, and defend the very mysteries of the Catholic faith upon which the unity of the Church, as the body of Christ, is founded. Neither the Church nor the CDF in particular is demanding an "ideological identity" or championing a "theory," for the Gospel is neither an ideology nor a theory. What the Church is demanding and what the CDF is furthering and guarding is that the complete faith of the Church is to be believed, professed, and lived, for it is this faith, in its entirety, that is fully salvific. This doctrinal unity is the life-giving source of the Church's corporate prayer and common life. To endorse and promote erroneous conceptions and faulty expressions of this faith—these actions are the "destructive" ideologies and "idolatrous" theories that divisively undermine "shared prayer."

In resolving the impasse over Christological method, Tilley insists that we must "begin where we are." We are not above "in heaven" nor are we in the past or the future. Yet Tilley admits that "many of us cannot but tell a story that begins in heaven: God made the Word flesh." Nonetheless, "for many of us, we cannot but tell a story that begins on earth: God made a human, Mary's child, God's Son." Both, according to Tilley, are found in the New Testament. Tilley proceeds to argue as he has done so often in his presentation. While Nicea's *homoousios*—that the Son is consubstantial with the Father—may have worked in the fourth century, it will not work in the present. "The world has changed, and those ancient words and concepts can no longer express the same meaning as they once did. We need to experiment with multiple models and concepts and may wind up with a host of models for communicating the mystery."

So the methodological impasse is resolved in that some are permitted to tell the old incarnational story, even though these people are not above "in heaven," where one would seem to need to be, according to Tilley, in order for such a story to make sense. Moreover, this model employs words that are ancient and no longer express what they once did. These people presently think that they believe what the Fathers taught and the Councils declared, but in fact they do not because the words that they are employing to express their faith no longer bear the same meanings as when the Fathers and Councils first used them. Yet it must be asked: If the meaning of the ancient words no longer bear their original meanings, how would we know this, given that the only meaning we now know is their contemporary meaning? Tilley appears to be in a singular enlightened position in that he must know what these ancient words originally meant in the past, if he is now able to discern that they no longer bear their original meanings in the present and so to employ them now would be to misrepresent the faith. The point of my critique is simply to manifest the incongruity of the entire argument. Tilley never provides a reason as to why these ancient concepts and words have altered their meaning and so are made ineffectual in communicating the faith today, aside from the fact that they originated in a culture other than our own. But different historical cultures are not self-contained units; rather, they form the continuum of history. Cultures may vary over the course of history, but they bring with them into the present the truths (and falsities) they contain—this is what the growth in knowledge is all about. If Tilley were correct, there would be no point is studying Aristotle, Plato, Dante, or Shakespeare, all of whom lived in cultures other than our own. But any intelligent person can learn to read the Fathers with understanding and can grasp the doctrines proclaimed in the ancient creeds—this is the point of catechesis. Because he ultimately believes that the doctrine of the Incarnation, as defined by the ancient Councils, is no longer believable, Tilley rhetorically attempts simply again to destabilize its credibility.

Allowing for a "host of models" is the way for Tilley to resolve the impasse concerning the relationship between the divinity and humanity in Christ. For Tilley, the success of these models "begins by realizing that *success in accuracy of representation is dependent on success in the practice of communication*, not vice versa." One begins, it would appear according to Tilley, not with accuracy in conceiving and expressing the mystery of the Incarnation with the presumption that such accuracy will allow one to communicate clearly and unambiguously the faith. Rather, one attempts to communicate the faith and, if it is achieved, then one knows that one has expressed it accurately. This is almost a parody of modern subjectivism. How can one attempt to communicate something if one is not reasonably confident that one is communicating it accurately? Moreover, how can a person who has little or no understanding of the mystery of the Incarnation be the judge of whether the person who is attempting to communicate such knowledge has done so accurately? In this situation the hearer makes a subjective judgment, founded upon no objective criteria, on what he or she would like to believe and in so doing validates it.

For Tilley, the heart of the problem is that Christological models, including the ancient "incarnational model," do not conceive and express the ontological or metaphysical reality of the mystery of the Incarnation. Models are simply phenomenological approximate expressions of the mystery, but since we do not know the metaphysical reality of the mystery, we are unable to judge which models are closer approximate expressions and which are not. The acceptance or nonacceptance of a model depends on the subjective judgment of the person—"what speaks to me" or what is "in style." Tilley, I feel confident, would find no problem with this limitation, as it is what he has been arguing for throughout his presentation in his critique of the traditional expression of the Incarnation and in his proposal for the need for "a host" of other "models." This "host" is necessary in order to accommodate everyone's personal preference. Of course, there is no longer any objective revelational content to be known and believed, nor is there any unity and communion of faith. The Church, as the one body of Christ, becomes so fragmented that it ceases to serve any divine purpose.

Tilley fails to recognize and acknowledge that the Trinitarian and Christological doctrines of the early Councils and creeds, as well as the authoritative doctrinal teaching of the Church today, are not models in the sense of approximate expressions of the mysteries. While these doctrines do not make the mysteries entirely comprehensible or offer a complete description of the mysteries, they do provide a true ontological account of the mystery, one that can be known and believed. To say that Jesus *is* the divine Son of the Father existing as man, for example, is to define the ontological nature of the mystery of the Incarnation. This is not one model among many other possible models. All else that is or could be said concerning Jesus must conform to the metaphysical truth of this doctrinally defined incarnational mystery. It is the ontological nature of the mysteries of faith and their ability to known and articulated, and so be doctrinally defined, that Tilley ultimately denies.

To be fair, Tilley does offer a test. The test cannot be whether a specific model conforms to the ancient creeds. "Rather, we shall know relatively adequate models by their practical fruits." These fruits are working "for justice within the church and society," seeking "reconciliation in a world desperate for healing," and keeping "at the table of dialogue so as to keep impasse from degenerating into a deadly stalemate." The fruit of an adequate model is in feeding the hungry, clothing the poor, scattering the proud, and so on. All of these fruits were already present when the old "incarnational model" was revered, venerated, and believed. Nonetheless, Tilley has a point: good doctrine does bear the fruit of a good moral life. Tilley's own criteria undercut his whole theological proposal, however. Those who argue in a manner similar to Tilley with regard to what is to be the content of faith also often espouse contraception, abortion, fornication, adultery, divorce and remarriage, masturbation, homosexual activity, same-sex marriage, euthanasia, embryonic stem cell research, and the like. Tilley states in a footnote: "Laity seem to have been disaffected by the bishops' preaching about sexual morality that is increasingly incredible." While Tilley is not specific, one can presume that he would include at least some of the above list. But the above enumeration is hardly the fruits of a holy life founded upon the truth of the Gospel of Jesus Christ.

While my response to Professor Tilley may be perceived as extraordinarily negative, and for me it was not fun to write, I hope that I have demonstrated the truth of my original concerns: Tilley's lack of scholarship, doctrinal ambiguity and error, and misuse of rhetoric. It is of the utmost importance that we know who Jesus is—that we know metaphysically the mystery of the Incarnation. Jesus *is* the eternal Son of the Father existing as a man, once in humility and now as the glorious Lord and risen Christ.

CHAPTER 16

Gnosticism and Contemporary Soteriology

The abundant variations of Gnosticism in the second and third centuries testify both to its popularity and to the threat it posed to the early Church. This threat is all the more evident in that some forms of Gnosticism were espoused by men; for example, Valentinus and Basilides, who considered themselves faithful Christians. Yet, as is well known, Irenaeus, Hippolytus, Tertullian, and other Church Fathers believed that Gnosticism was radically inimical to the authentic Christian Gospel as professed by "the Great Church." Many contemporary theologians, who equally profess to be Christians, have proposed soteriological theories that are at their heart Gnostic and constitute an equally grave threat to the integrity of the Gospel today.

Before examining instances of what I consider contemporary variants of Gnostic soteriology, I state briefly what I believe to be at the heart of the ancient Gnostic systems. I am not so much interested in the particular details of the various Gnostic schools, but rather I want to highlight what exactly that *gnosis* consisted of for the Gnostics. What did the *Pneumatikoi* know that brought them salvation?[1]

Originally published as "Gnosticism and Contemporary Soteriology: Some Reflections," *New Blackfriars* 76 (1995): 546–54. Reprinted by permission.

1. For recent studies of Gnosticism, see S. Pétrement, *A Separate God: The Origins and Teachings of Gnosticism* (San Francisco: Harper, 1990); K. Rudolph, *Gnosis: The Nature and History of Gnosticism* (Edinburgh: T&T Clark, 1984). For brief accounts of Gnosticism, see "Gnosticism," in *Encyclopedia of Early Christianity*, ed. E. Ferguson (London: Garland, 1990),

The various Gnostic schools taught elaborate cosmological systems or schemes, which were normally composed of the utterly transcendent and often unknowable good God followed by the assorted lesser aeons of spirits (e.g., Sige, Ennoia, Nous, Logos, Zoe, Pneuma, Sophia, angels, etc., depending on the Gnostic school). These made up the pleroma and filled the infinite void between the transcendent God and the world of matter. The evil demiurge, often seen as the God of the Old Testament, was responsible for the creation of the material world and thus for the evil within it. Through a mixture of mythology and philosophy, Gnosticism offered a total cosmological view of reality and what reality was all about. The intention of all this was to properly locate human beings within this total cosmological order and to offer, at least to the elect, a way out of the evil world of matter so as to obtain knowledge of God and thus salvation. Within this cosmological scheme is found the relevance of "the Gnostic Redeemer." This redeemer, however he was portrayed, revealed saving knowledge/*gnosis*. Within Christian Gnosticism, Jesus, "inhabited" by Christ, fulfilled this task.

Now the central question for this study: What does the Gnostic Redeemer/Jesus reveal? What is the saving *gnosis* that is imparted? What does the Pneumatic come to know? The Gnostic Redeemer reveals how the cosmological system works. The Gnostic Redeemer does not change the cosmic blueprint; rather, he makes known what has always been the case. The Pneumatic, in receiving this *gnosis*, is enlightened and thus empowered by this esoteric knowledge to attain union with God and the divine *pleroma*. Through Gnostic mythology and philosophy, the enlightened, being "in the know," can confidently participate in the cosmological enterprise.

In light of this brief description of classic Gnostic thought, I examine some contemporary soteriological theories so as to illustrate their Gnostic tendencies. The theologians discussed below are a representative sampling of what, I believe, is common among many other contemporary theologians and their soteriological theories.

John Macquarrie in his book *Jesus Christ in Modern Thought*[2] contends that, since the Enlightenment, the traditional Christian view of God super-

---

371–76; "Gnosis," in *Encyclopedia of the Early Church*, ed. A. Di Berardino (Cambridge: James Clarke, 1992), 1:352–54.

2. John Macquarrie, *Jesus Christ in Modern Thought* (London: SCM, 1990).

naturally acting within the world is no longer theologically or philosophically defensible. Thus Jesus cannot be seen as the eternal preexistent divine person of the Son now existing as man, but rather "to call him the God-man … is to claim that in him human transcendence has reached that point at which the human life has become so closely united with the divine life that, in the traditional language, it has been 'deified'" (370). Unlike the rest of humankind, Jesus is the human being in whom the divine image is not defaced but manifested in its fullness, and thus he is "God's existence" insofar as "the divine can become manifest on the finite level" (371; see also 372–73). For Macquarrie, Jesus differs from us only in degree and not in kind in that he manifests to a greater degree than we the ever-present God in our midst (346, 358, 361, 377, 392, 415).

How, then, does Jesus save us? "Jesus is the representative human being" (373). For Macquarrie there is an archetype, an ideal, or a lure that draws us to God which "we see fulfilled in a signal way in Jesus Christ … We recognize him as the representative human being, the Word made flesh." Jesus enfleshed the love of God and so a "new humanity was formed" (374). Jesus represents, makes known, and reveals the decisive clue to what God has always been up to in the world (379). Jesus "sums up and makes clear a presence [of God] that is obscurely communicated throughout the cosmos" (381). For Macquarrie, salvation consists in the coming to know what has always been the case: God is ever present in the world, and we, like Jesus, are called to respond and incarnate this self-sacrificing love as he did.

Jesus is not for Macquarrie unique among the founders of world religions. Like Jesus, all "saviour figures were mediators of grace. We have seen what this means in the case of Jesus Christ, yet these others too were emissaries of holy Being. They too had given themselves up to the service of a divine reality, who might work in them and through them for the lifting up of all creatures upon earth" (420). The founders of all religions are all saviors because like Jesus they manifest or reveal, in their various and distinctive ways, the one truth of what God is doing generically and constantly in the world and so what our response should be.[3]

John Hick, though in much more sweeping and conspicuous manner,

---

3. For a critique of Macquarrie, see Charles C. Hefling Jr., "Reviving Adamic Adoptionism: The Example of John Macquarrie," *Theological Studies* 52 (1991): 476–94.

offers a similar view of salvation to that of Macquarrie. In *The Metaphor of God Incarnate*,[4] Hick places Jesus squarely within the context of world religions and contends that Christianity offers the exact same sort of salvation as any other world religion.

Like Macquarrie, Hick finds the traditional view of the Incarnation completely unacceptable to our scientific and enlightened age and so views Jesus as possessing an "immensely powerful God-consciousness." He is "so transparently open to the divine presence that his life and teaching have a universal significance which can still help to guide our lives today" (26).[5] For this reason, Jesus manifests what God is always up to in the world. The idea of the Incarnation is "a metaphorical statement of the significance of a life through which God was acting on earth" (106).

For Hick, other religious traditions have similar metaphorical formulae and thus they are ultimately expressing the same view of salvation as that of Christianity. "I suggest that these different conceptions of salvation are specifications of what, in a generic formula, is the transformation of human existence from self-centeredness to a new orientation centered on the divine Reality" (135). Put more philosophically, Hick states that "our human religious experience, variously shaped as it is by our sets of religious concepts and practices, is a cognitive response to the universal presence of the ultimate divine reality that, in itself, exceeds human conceptuality" (146). The ultimate referent of all religious mythology is "the Transcendent, the eternally Real, experienced in different ways within the different religious traditions" (161).

In Hick we see, more clearly than in Macquarrie, that religious my-

---

4. John Hick, *The Metaphor of God Incarnate* (London: SCM, 1993). Hick also proposes similar arguments in his other works. See *God and the Universe of Faiths* (London: Macmillan, 1973); *An Interpretation of Religion* (London: Macmillan, 1989); "The Non-Absoluteness of Christianity" and "The Logic of God Incarnate" in *Disputed Questions in Theology and Philosophy of Religion* (London: Macmillan, 1993).

Hick notes that his book finds its historical impetus and forebear in the publication of *The Myth of God Incarnate* (London: SCM, 1977), of which he was the editor. He believes many younger theologians today hold similar views to his own. He includes such people as A. Race, P. W. Newman, J. Bowden, P. Fredricksen, K. Ward, and L. Houlden (3). Other recent writers representing this tendency include: D. Cupitt, G. Kaufman, J. Knox, H. Küng, C. M. LaCugna, J. A. T. Robinson, and M. Wiles.

5. Hick acknowledges that his proposal falls within the liberal tradition of F. Schleiermacher (18).

thology, whether Christian, Jewish, or Hindu, is but a metaphorical way of expressing a deeper, "hidden," philosophical truth. Salvation consists in perceiving and living the philosophical truth hidden within the religious metaphor and myth. For Hick, this truth is that divine Reality or the Transcendent is always acting toward us in love and that we manifest this generic and continual presence in our own selfless love. The role of Jesus, Moses, Mohammed, or Buddha is all of one piece. Through their teaching they reveal and in their lives they manifest, at least metaphorically, this common *gnosis* of what the Transcendent and the world are all about.

This same kind of soteriology is found in some expressions of "Spirit Christology." One of its most recent exponents, following G. W. H. Lampe, is Roger Haight. In an article "The Case for Spirit Christology," Haight proposes that the best way of conceiving of God and his work in the world is through the metaphor "God as Spirit."[6] "God as Spirit is God present and at work outside of God's self" (267). Thus Jesus is an "embodiment of God as Spirit" to an exceptional degree (276). "The symbol of the Spirit more forthrightly makes the claim that God, God's very self, acted in and through this Jesus" (272). Haight proposes "a revelational and exemplary theory of salvation" in that Jesus is "the revealer of God and God's salvation which God as Spirit has effected from the beginning, the revelation of what human life should be, and the empowering example of life for disciples" (278). Jesus is "a normative manifestation of what God is like and the pattern of what human existence should be" (278–79). Jesus brings us salvation by being a metaphor of God's generic action in the world, and by coming to know this action we are able to respond to it more easily and readily. Because for Haight, as for Macquarrie and Hick, Jesus only differs in degree from us and not in kind; we, too, possess God as Spirit and so can live as he has manifested to us. Moreover, just as God as Spirit acted in Jesus, so, too, has he acted in other "salvation bringers" (280–82).[7]

---

6. Roger Haight, "The Case for Spirit Christology," *Theological Studies*, 53 (1992): 257–86. For similar examples of this type of Spirit Christology, see G. W. H. Lampe, *God as Spirit* (Oxford: Clarendon Press, 1997); P. W. Newman, *A Spirit Christology* (New York: University Press of America, 1987).

7. For a critique of Haight's Spirit Christology, see John Wright, S.J., "Roger Haight's Spirit Christology," *Theological Studies* 53 (1992): 729–35; T. G. Weinandy, "The Case For Spirit Christology: Some Reflections," *Thomist* 59 (1995): 173–88 (chap. 13 in this volume).

This same pattern can be found, in a more metaphysical manner, within Process Christology. For Process theologians, God is part of the total and unbroken cosmic process where he provides from within his primordial or abstract pole the goods and values that are to be actualized (prehended) within the world, especially by human beings, and so assumed (prehended) into God's concrete pole—that is, God as he actually is. Placing their Christology and soteriology within the general framework of Process Theology, Process theologians see Jesus as incarnating (prehending) God's lure or potential to the highest degree and so concretizing it and making it real. God does not act in a different kind of way in Jesus, but rather in Jesus we find manifested the way God is always acting. For Norman Pittenger, Jesus "is the classic instance of the Divine Activity in manhood."[8] The Incarnation is not an intrusion of God by some supernatural act, but "Jesus Christ is seen as the focal self-expression of God the Word in human terms." In the man Jesus, "the Word who is present and active in the lives of men in their historical situation, is actualized or 'en-manned' in such a decisive and distinctive fashion that we are enabled to say *here*, as nowhere else, we are in the presence of the Word 'made flesh.'"[9]

For Process theologians, Jesus does not establish an entirely new relationship between God and man but makes it possible for the God/man relation, which always was to become more fully actualized. It becomes more fully actualized because Jesus, at least symbolically through his life and teaching, makes it known. David Griffin writes: "The only change in the God-man relation is man's attitude. Through revelation he comes to know things about God that were already true, and this knowledge affects the subjective form of his experience."[10] Jesus saves us by being the mythical or metaphorical expression of what Process theologians *know* to be literally the case through Process Philosophy.[11]

8. Norman Pittenger, *God in Process* (London: SCM, 1967), 29. Other significant works by Pittenger are: *The Word Incarnate* (London: James Nisbet, 1959); *Christology Reconsidered* (London: SCM, 1970). For other examples of process Christology and soteriology, see David Griffin, *A Process Christology* (Philadelphia: Westminster Press, 1973); Schubert M. Ogden, *The Reality of God* (London: SCM, 1967); The Point of Christology (London: SCM, 1982).

9. Pittenger, *Word Incarnate*, 180.

10. Griffin, *Process Christology*, 236.

11. For a critique of the whole of *Process Christology*, see T. G. Weinandy, *Does God Change? The Word's Becoming in the Incarnation* (Petersham, MA: St. Bede's Press, 1985), 124–53.

With a representative sampling of contemporary theories of salvation, we turn now to demonstrating how they are essentially Gnostic in character, something that may already be evident. While the above cases are not exact replicas of classic Gnosticism (e.g., they do not see matter as evil), salvation within these soteriologies similarly consists in coming to know the "eternally" established and unchanging (and unchangeable) cosmological order. Soteriology is reduced to and identified with cosmology.

Because this cosmological order is total, self-contained, and closed, Jesus changes the God/man relation not by establishing an entirely new and different kind of relation, but by making the "old" relation (the only one there is) more workable. Reality (the complete cosmic order) is not ontologically changed or made different by the salvation Jesus brings, but it is changed only gnoseologically. One is not saved by faith but by knowledge that is esoteric and philosophical in nature. As in classic Gnosticism, Jesus is a mythical or metaphorical Gnostic redeemer and Christianity is Gnosticism—the coming to know the cosmological system.

Jesus as a person therefore loses much of his existential and contemporary importance. Having fulfilled his task of imparting the "secret" or "clue" of reality in a metaphorical or mythical manner, he is relegated to being the mere historical revelatory exemplar of a philosophical/religious sect. Like Mohammed, Buddha, or any good moral philosopher or holy person, Jesus's sole task is to put humankind "in the know" so that it might obtain salvation through this knowledge. Having done this, his contemporary relevance vanishes. What is important is purely the *gnosis*.

Moreover, what is ultimately critical within all of these various expressions of contemporary soteriology is not Jesus or for that matter Buddha, Mohammed, or Moses, for they all trade in myth and metaphor, but rather the philosophy contained in and behind their mythical and metaphorical "revelation." Actually, one could live a "saved" life without belonging to any religion, and one might actually be better off for having abandoned the myth and metaphor contained within them, as long as one knows philosophically the cosmological system and lives in accordance with it. Within these contemporary soteriologies it is the traditional believers (whether they be Jews, Christians, or Hindus) who are now—at best—the *Psuchikoi*, and the people who actually *know* the true philosophical cosmology are the new *Pneumatikoi*.[12]

12. It is interesting to note how often Hick, in his *Metaphor of God Incarnate*, contrasts the "unlearned circles" (28), those "unacquainted with the modern study of the Bible" (29), and

Regardless of how one judges the truth and validity of these contemporary forms of Christian Gnosticism, one thing is certain: they are not authentic expressions of the traditional Christian Gospel and the faith of "the Great Church." The Christian Gospel and tradition asserts that the person of Jesus himself is central to salvation and not a message (*gnosis*) apart from him. He himself is the message. To *know* Jesus through faith is to find salvation. Unlike Buddha, for example, who imparts a salvific message (what one must do) that is distinct from himself, Jesus himself is the Gospel of salvation.

The reason for the centrality of Jesus is that God, through him, has radically changed and altered in kind and not in degree man's relationship to himself, and this new kind of relationship is secured not through some *gnosis* that he imparts, but by being united to his very person in faith through the Holy Spirit. Jesus, as the eternal Son of God existing in time and history as man, has through his death and resurrection put in place a whole new salvific order or program that differs in kind from what existed hitherto. Through *faith* in him as the living risen Lord, one receives the Holy Spirit, and through this reception one's relationship with God changes in kind and not in degree. In Christ, through the Holy Spirit, one is transformed from being a sinner and an enemy of God into being a righteous son or daughter now able to call God "Father." Moreover, as implied above, the believer is changed not in degree but in kind. The believer is a radically new creation in Christ. Equally, believers possess a relationship with other believers, as members of the Body of Christ, that differs in kind from the type of relation they have with those outside of Christ.[13]

By reducing the Christian Gospel to the mythical or metaphorical expression of an unalterable philosophical cosmology, contemporary soteriology has deprived and robbed the Christian Gospel of its fundamental integrity and distinctive character. The reason, and this is the heart of the

---

most of all "the fundamentalists" (87, 115, 121, 126, 147, 154, 160) with "educated Westerners" (8), "highly regarded Christian theologians" (11), "the scholarly community" (33), "the New Testament scholar" (34, 42), the "majority of contemporary theologians" (34), "modern New Testament scholarship" (91), "thoughtful Christians" (113, 159), "educated Christians" (116), and "responsible scholarship" (151). The unlearned includes not only those who believe God literally created the world in seven days, but also those who believe in anything "supernatural." The educated are the new elite, the *Pneumatikoi*.

13. For a fuller account of the biblical notion that Jesus brings about changes in kind rather than in degree, see T. G. Weinandy, *In the Likeness of Sinful Flesh: An Essay on the Humanity of Christ* (Edinburgh: T&T Clark, 1993).

problem, is that God, within these contemporary soteriological views, does not exist ontologically distinct from all else—that is, in such a way as to be free to interact with all else that is in ways he freely chooses—but rather he himself is a prisoner to a cosmological order that is self-contained and closed. Because it is impossible for God to interact with humankind in different kinds of ways (traditionally called "supernatural"), contemporary soteriology is forced, by philosophical necessity, to view salvation in a merely Gnostic manner—only as the coming to know of what has always been.

It is regarding this point that the Bible protests loudly. It demands to be taken on its own terms and not reinterpreted within a philosophical hermeneutic that is foreign to it—a philosophy that, if true, would require the biblical proclamation to be false. The Bible refuses to be merely or solely mythical and metaphorical. The heart of biblical revelation, with its own inherent philosophical principles, is that God ontologically does differ in kind from all else that is; that he has nonetheless acted in time and history in distinctive and various ways; and ultimately and lastly that he has acted through his Son. These actions were intended to form relations with humankind that differ not in degree but in kind.

In conclusion I want to comment on the interreligious concerns of the above theologians. All of them propose that, by making Christianity comparable to other religions, specifically by making Jesus just one among many "salvation bringers," they have rightfully denied Christianity its mistaken "elitism," and in so doing they offer an equitable solution as to the inherent unity of all religions. Ecumenically this appears appealing. But by denying Christianity its specific integrity, these theologians have equally denied the specific integrity of all other religions. Now all religions have become mere mythical and metaphorical expressions of a philosophical "truth" that those "in the know" truly discern. The ardent and committed Jew, Muslim, Hindu, and Buddhist are all equally deluded. They do not *know* that they all *really* profess one and the same "faith."

This concept is especially important with regard to the relationship of Christians to the Jews. Hick, for example, virulently castigates Christians for their anti-Semitism and finds its origin in the elitist claim that Jesus is God incarnate.[14] Christians believe that Jesus brought the fullness of salva-

---

14. See Hick, *Metaphor of God Incarnate*, 80–83.

tion. But Hick (as all the above theologians), by making Judaism just another mythical and metaphorical expression of a religious philosophy, has
denied Jews their chosen status. If Hick is correct, all the Jews who died
for their faith died in vain. They did not *know* that Christianity, or for that
matter Hinduism, is really the same as their own faith. If they had only
known, they need not have died.

Christians throughout history have persecuted the Jews. But today most
Christian theologians and Church leaders recognize, unlike many in the past
who held that they ceased to be God's chosen people following their denial
of Christ, that the Jews still remain God's chosen people, and they are so because he established a relationship with them that differed in kind from his
relationship with all other peoples. Hick, Haight, Lampe, and Macquarrie,
by proposing that the Jews are no different from anyone else, are in the end
unwittingly espousing a position that is inherently more anti-Semitic than
anything held in the past. By reducing Judaism to just another mythical and
metaphorical expression of a generic philosophical *gnosis*, they may have performed "the most unkindest cut of all."

CHAPTER 17

The Human "I" of Jesus

On a number of occasions I have proposed that Jesus possesses a human "I."[1] As incarnate, the person of the eternal Son lived, thought, was self-conscious, and spoke within the confines a human "I." Or, conversely, it is a human "I" that gives expression to the divine person of the Son.

Because of the controversial nature of my thesis, I offer here a fuller and more systematic account of it. The original stimulus for this thesis grew out of a desire to defend, against contemporary charges of Docetism and Monophysitism, the traditional view of the Incarnation; namely, that Jesus is the one divine person of the Son existing as man. Many Christologists have recently denied that Jesus is a divine person because they believe that such a claim jeopardizes his full humanity.[2] But what began as an apology on behalf of the traditional view may have become an expression of a deeper insight into the mystery of the Incarnation.

The proposal that Jesus does possess a human "I" must be founded upon and flow from a proper understanding of the Incarnation. Indeed, the Incar-

Originally published as "The Human 'I' of Jesus," *Irish Theological Quarterly* 62, no. 4 (1996/97): 259–68. Reprinted by permission.

1. For example, see T. G. Weinandy, *In the Likeness of Sinful Flesh: An Essay on the Humanity of Christ* (Edinburgh: T&T Clark, 1993), 12–13; *Father's Spirit of Sonship: Reconceiving the Trinity* (Edinburgh: T&T Clark, 1995), 120–22.

2. See, for example, J. Hick, ed., *The Myth of God Incarnate* (London: SCM, 1977); *The Metaphor of God Incarnate* (London: SCM, 1993); J. Knox, *The Humanity and Divinity of Christ* (Cambridge: Cambridge University Press, 1967); J. Macquarrie, *Jesus Christ in Modern Thought* (London: SCM, 1990); J. A. T. Robinson, *The Human Face of God* (London: SCM, 1973); W. Thompson, *The Jesus Debate: A Survey and Synthesis* (New York: Paulist Press, 1985).

nation itself must be the hermeneutical principle for determining whether or not Jesus possesses a human "I." Moreover, such a proposal must be in harmony with the New Testament, especially with the portrayal of Jesus in the Gospels. The argument of this essay comprises three parts. The first investigates the conceptions of the Incarnation found in Nestorius, Cyril of Alexandria, and the Council of Chalcedon so as to assess whether any of these provide the incarnational foundation for the claim that Jesus possesses a human "I." The second argues that a true understanding of the Incarnation allows for, and even demands, a human "I." It also describes the character of this human "I." And the third confirms this claim by examining a brief representative sampling of Gospel passages.

The Starting Point: Nestorius?

Since the thesis that Jesus possesses a human "I" has a distinctly Nestorian ring, one might suspect that Nestorius could provide its incarnational grounding. Nestorius's Christology has recently undergone a marked rehabilitation precisely because he so uncompromisingly defended the complete and full humanity of Jesus. In defending the full and complete humanity and divinity of Jesus, Nestorius argued that Christ must possess two οὐσια (natures), each possessing its own πρόσωπον (the distinctive qualities and attributes of each nature). From this Nestorian perspective, it would appear that one could straightforwardly and simply argue that Christ possessed both a divine and a human "I."

The difficulty is that, having conceived the two natures of Christ not only as distinct but also as separate prior to their union, Nestorius was unable to show how they could be ontologically one without jeopardizing the integrity of each. He rightly saw that any compositional union of the natures would demand that the humanity and divinity be united so as to form a *tertium quid* whose nature would be neither truly divine nor truly human. In order to avoid a compositional union, Nestorius proposed a "prosopic union." In such a union the natures are so closely aligned that the attributes or qualities of each πρόσωπον give off or display one common appearance— the common πρόσωπον of union. (A contemporary analogy might be that of two closely aligned stars that give off one common appearance to the un-aided human eye.) But this prosopic union is the mere phenomenal interplay and mingling of the attributes of the two separate πρόσωπαα of the natures. Like the two stars closely aligned, the humanity and divinity remain ontologically two separate realities. The name "Christ," the πρόσωπον of union, possesses no ontological depth. There is actually no ontological subject, and therefore no authentic "I."[3]

While Nestorius can account for both a divine and a human "I" corresponding to the distinct natures, each "I" retains its own separate ontological identity. Ultimately the divine "I" and the human "I" are two different subjects, two different "who's"—the Son of God and the man Jesus.[4]

While Nestorius's concern for the full and complete humanity must not be lost, a proper understanding of the Incarnation demands that the ontological hypostasis or subject (the "who") of both the humanity and the divinity be one and the same. If Jesus possesses a human "I," that "I" must conform or correspond to (and concur or coinhere with) the divine subject. It must be the divine subject who would possess a human "I," and the human "I" in turn would have to manifest the divine subjective identity. For this reason, Cyril's Christology, somewhat surprisingly, may be a more secure and fruitful starting point.

3. For a fuller presentation and critique of Nestorius's Christology, see A. Grillmeier, *Christ in Christian Tradition*, rev. ed. (London: Mowbrays, 1975), 1:450–63, 1:501–19; T. G. Weinandy, *Does God Change? The Word's Becoming in the Incarnation* (Petersham, MA: St. Bede's Press, 1985), 34–46.

4. In this century a number of theologians, from a "Nestorian" perspective, have proposed that Jesus possessed a human "I." See, for example, Déodat de Basly, *En Christiade Française* (Paris: 1929); "Le Moi de Jésus-Christ, Le déplacement des autonomies," *France Franciscaine* 12 (1929): 125–60, 325–52; P. Galtier, *L'Unité du Christ, Être ... Personne ... Conscience* (Paris: Beauchesne, 1939). Pius XII, in his encyclical *Sempiternus Rex* (AAS 43 [1951] 638) condemned the extreme view of de Basly but left open Galtier's view that Jesus possessed a human psychological "I."

K. Rahner's position on the self-consciousness of Christ also possesses a Nestorian flavor. He sees the man Jesus becoming aware of *his* divinity, through the *visio immediata*, as an *object* to be known, rather than the eternal Son becoming *subjectively* conscious of himself as the Son of God in a human manner. Conceiving the divinity as an object to be known implies an "I" (a knower) that is ontologically separate from the known (the divinity). "Current Problems in Christology," *Theological Investigations I* (Baltimore: Helicon, 1961), 149–200; "Dogmatic Reflections on the Knowledge and Self-Consciousness of Christ," in *Theological Investigations 5* (Baltimore: Helicon, 1966), 193–215. For a contemporary critique of the above authors, see J. Galot, *La Conscience de Jésus* (Paris: Duculot-Lethielleux, 1971), 97–131, 169–72; *Who Is Christ? A Theology of Incarnation* (Chicago: Franciscan Herald Press, 1981), 323–28.

The Starting Point: Cyril?

Cyril, unlike Nestorius, firmly upheld the ontological unity between the humanity and the divinity in Jesus. The question is, did he do so, as Nestorius claimed, by jeopardizing their integrity? While some of Cyril's formulations are ambiguous, such as his μία φύσις formula, and thus easily misinterpreted, I think he did not. Nonetheless, in order to understand Cyril's Christology, and then to found a conception of the human "I" of Jesus upon it, it is necessary to grasp his notion of the incarnational "becoming." What does it mean to say that the Son of God *became* man?

In his Christology, Cyril wanted to uphold three interrelated truths. First, it is *one and the same Son/Logos* who exists as God and man. Second, it is *truly as man*, as incarnate, that the eternal Son now exists. Third, as incarnate, the Son is *ontologically one* with his humanity—that is, the Son truly *is* man. All three points can be expressed by saying that, for Cyril, the one ontological reality of Jesus is the one person of the Son existing as man, as incarnate. A few examples from Cyril's writings illustrate and clarify these three points.

First, "the same even before the Incarnation was Son of God and Word of the Father, and after, he has become man like us and been made flesh."[5] It is one and the same Logos "who is ὁμοούσιον with us in that he has been made man ... and yet he is also ὁμοούσιον with the Father himself, in that he remained God even in human nature."[6] For Cyril, the Incarnation does not bring into existence a new person or hypostasis. Rather, in the Incarnation it is the same person existing in a new manner.

Second, the Incarnation does not mean "that the nature of the Word was changed and made flesh or, on the other hand, that he was transformed into a complete man ... but instead we affirm this: that the Word, having personally (καθ ᾿ ὑπόστατιν) united to himself flesh endowed with life and reason, in a manner mysterious and inconceivable, became man."[7] His celebrated (or notorious) formula—μία φύσις τοῦ θεοῦ λόγου σεσαρκωμένη "the one incarnate nature/person of the Word of God"—also emphasizes that it is the one person of the Word who now actually exists as incarnate.

---

5. *C. Nest.* 2:10.   6. *C. Nest.* 3:3.
7. *Ep. ad Nest.* 2:3, 2:4, 2:7.

It is therefore idle for them (the Antiochenes) to claim that if there is one nature of the Word incarnate (σεσαρκωμένη) it follows there must have been a mingling and merger, with the human nature being diminished by its removal … for to state that he is incarnate gives completely adequate expression to the fact that he has become man.[8]

The σεσαρκομένε specifies the mode or manner of the Logos's existence, and thus all is predicated of him as the one incarnate subject. "Accordingly all the sayings contained in the Gospels must be referred to a single person (ἐνι προσώσοπω), to the one incarnate subject of the Word (ὑποστάσει μῖα τῇ τοῦ λόγου σεσαρκωμενη)."[9]

Third, in a variation of the formula μία φύσις τοῦ λόγου σεσαραρκωμένου, where σεσαρκωμένου modifies τοῦ λόγου, the assertion is not that the humanity and divinity form one third quidity, but that the Logos as incarnate is one ontological reality. "The nature of the Incarnate (σεσαρκωμένου) Word himself is after the union now conceived as one (μία), just as will reasonably be conceived in regard to ourselves, too, for man is one, compounded of unlike things, soul I mean and body."[10]

In this brief sampling of quotations, we find Cyril attempting to define what it means for the Son to become man. While Jesus is one ontological reality, "become" does not mean that the Son changes into man. The "becoming" is not the compositional union of natures forming some third nature. What "become" means for Cyril is that the Son takes on a new mode of existence. "To become man" means "to come to be man," and thus to exist as incarnate. This notion of the incarnational "becoming" is what I have come to call a "personal/existential" becoming; that is, it is one and the same person who comes to be, comes to exist, in a new manner or mode— as man. In the Incarnation the Father, in one and the same act, brings into being (by the power of the Holy Spirit and with the consent of Mary) a humanity and ontologically or substantially unites it to the person of the Son so that the person of the Son now actually exists as a man.

8. *Ep. ad Succensum* 2:3.

9. *Ep. ad Nest.* 3:8.

10. *C. Nest.* 2: proema. Cyril consistently uses the body/soul analogy to demonstrate not that the divinity and humanity in Christ form a common *tertium quid*, but to illustrate that they form one ontological being or reality. See *Ep. ad Nest.* 3:4, 3:8; *Ep. ad Eulogium*; *Ep. ad Succensum* 1:7, 2:3, 2:5. Also see T. G. Weinandy, "The Soul/Body Analogy and Incarnation in Cyril of Alexandria," *Coptic Church Review* 17, no. 3 (1996): 59–66 (chap. 6 in this volume).

By conceiving the Incarnation in a personal/existential manner, Cyril is able to maintain that it is one and the same Son who now exists both as God and man. He has distinguished and established the "who" and the manner of the "who's" existence. The identity of this man Jesus, who this man is, is the eternal Son of God. The manner in which the Son possesses this identity is as man.

Before I elucidate the importance of Cyril's Christology for the present thesis that Jesus possesses a human "I," it would be helpful first to examine briefly the Council of Chalcedon to determine whether it sanctions Cyril's Christological insights.

The Council of Chalcedon

Chalcedon, with almost repetitious monotony, professes that "one and the same" is "perfect in Godhead and the same perfect in manhood ... ὁμοούσιον with the Father in Godhead, and the same ὁμοούσιον with us in manhood." The key to understanding this profession is, as with Cyril, to discern *who* this "one and the same" is. What is his identity? For Chalcedon, to speak of one πρόσωπον and one ὑπόστασις is to designate one and the same "who"—that is, one and the same subject or hypostasis. The one "who," the one person, is identified as the Son of God.

For Chalcedon, the Son exists in two natures: as God and as man. The Son's two modes of existence are "without confusion, without change, without division, without separation." The reason the natures are not confused or changed lies in the fact that the incarnational act, "the becoming," is not the compositional union of natures, forming some *tertium quid* that is neither fully God nor fully man. (This is how Eutyches conceived the Incarnation and what the Antiochenes accused Cyril of doing.[11]) Rather, Chalcedon has grasped Cyril's insight that the incarnational act is that act by which the one person of the Son takes on or assumes a new mode of ex-

11. Both classical and contemporary expressions of Kenotic Christology continue to view the Incarnation as the compositional union of natures. This is why, unlike the Monophysites, who jeopardize the humanity, they insist on "gearing down" the divinity of the Son so as to make it compatible ("user-friendly") with his humanity. They wish to deprive the Son's divine nature of those attributes that would be incompatible, and so "interfere" with, Jesus's human mind, will, and self-consciousness. For a further critique of Kenotic Christology, see Weinandy, *Does God Change?*, 101–23; *In the Likeness of Sinful Flesh*, 8–13.

istence; that is, coming to exist as man. The two natures concur in the one person of the Son, and therefore the two natures are equally without division and without separation. Like Cyril, Chalcedon has sanctioned a "personal/existential" understanding of the Incarnation. Jesus is the person of the Son existing as man, and what has changed is not the natures, but rather the mode of the Son's personal existence. Understanding the incarnational act in a personal/existential manner ensures both that it is one and the same person/subject (the Son) existing as God and man, and the full integrity of what the one person is—God and man.[12]

The Human "I" of the Son

From the above examination of the Incarnation I argue for two conclusions that flow from the "personal/existential" understanding of the Incarnation of Cyril and Chalcedon.

The first conclusion proceeds from the "personal" side of the incarnational equation. Because Chalcedon, following Cyril, professed one and the same person of Son to be both God and man, traditional Christology has rightly concluded that there is only one person or subject in Christ. Thus there is only one "I" corresponding to the one ontological person or subject. The identity of that "I," of that "who," is the person of the Logos or Son. If the "I" is not identified as God the Son, then the true Incarnation has not taken place. If the subject (the who) of that "I" is not the divine Son, then Jesus would differ from us in his relationship to God only in degree and not in kind. (He obviously does not differ from us in his humanity, which is ομοουσιον with our own.)

It might appear that I have undermined the point I set out to prove. If the one ontological person or subject is the eternal Son, if the identity of Jesus is the Logos, if the one "I" is the "I" of a divine subject, then it would seem impossible to contend that Jesus possessed a human "I." But it is precisely at this point that the human "I" can be established.

The second conclusion proceeds from the "existential" side of the incarnational equation. When Cyril argued and the Council of Chalcedon demanded that the identity of Jesus, the "who" or "I," be that of the divine Son

12. For a fuller account of Cyril and Chalcedon's "personal/existential" notion of the incarnational becoming, see Weinandy, *Does God Change?*, 46–66.

or Logos, the whole point was to guarantee that this one person or subject now actually *existed* as man. While the identity—the subject or "who"—of Jesus is the Son/Logos, that identity is now seen as incarnate, as man. The Logos has assumed a human identity and, I propose, lives and reveals himself within the parameters or under the expression of a human "I," for it is truly as man that the Logos now exists. The one "I" of Jesus is the human "I" of the one divine subject.

To profess that the Son of God, the one person, exists as man, confirms that the Son now lives and functions under the conditions of a human being, as a man. Thus the divine Son, as incarnate, not only lives and acts within the confines of a human will and human intellect, but he also is conscious and knows himself within the confines of a human self-consciousness. The Son, as man, wills truly and solely in a human manner. As man, he thinks truly and solely in a human manner. Likewise, as man, he is conscious of himself and expresses himself truly and solely in a human manner. The human "I" of Jesus actualizes and expresses the human psychological self-conscious awareness of the Son in all that he humanly wills, knows, and does. The human "I" is the human psychological center of the one ontological person or subject of the divine Son.

While it is the divine Son, through the Incarnation, who enters time and history and establishes relations with other human beings, he does so at the level of other human beings who also exist in time and within history. The Son of God does not relate to and interact with humankind under the conditions of a divine "I," which would demand that he still relates to and interacts with us in his divine transcendence, but rather he relates to and interacts with us as we ourselves are, under the condition of a human "I." Between the incarnate Son of God and other human beings, there is an encounter of equal "I's."[13]

---

13. Galot is close to the above when he writes, "In becoming man, the relational being of the Son inaugurated horizontal relationships with men. His contacts were no longer directed solely downward from above. They were henceforth to be made on a level of equality with human nature. Through this human nature, a divine relational being entered into human interpersonal relations." *Who Is Christ?*, 306–7. Where Galot would propose that a divine "I" now interacts with human beings on a human level, I would want to go further and say it is a divine person who relates to humankind under the conditions of a human "I" for only then is the Son not relating to us in a "downward fashion," but in a truly "horizontal" manner as equals. See also Weinandy, *Does God Change?*, 174–86.

There are similarities and differences between the "I" of Jesus and the "I" of other human beings. When I say "I am Tom Weinandy," I am stating my unique personal identity. I am saying that the personal subjective identity (the who) of this particular man who is speaking is Tom Weinandy. The "I" of Jesus is also the human "I" of a man, but what makes him qualitatively unique, because of the Incarnation, is precisely that the human "I" does not manifest or reveal a merely human person or subject (a human "who"), but rather manifests and reveals his personal subjective identity as the eternal Son of God.[14]

Succinctly put: Who lives as man? The Son. What is the manner in which he lives? As man. Thus the "I" of God the Son is a human "I," and it must be a human "I" because that is the manner in which the Son now exists. Yes, there is only one "I" and it is ontologically one with the divine person of the Son, but that one "I" is expressed in a thoroughly human manner. It *is* the human "I" of a divine "who," of a divine subject or person. The identity of the Son and of the human "I" are one and the same.[15]

14. The identity between the divine subject and the human "I" has Trinitarian implications. The Son, by identifying himself with a human "I," reveals that, as God, he is himself a person or subject. The Son, as a divine subject, may be more than we are as persons, but he is not less than we are as persons, and we know this because the Son, in the Incarnation, has now identified himself with a human "I." The human "I" of Jesus reveals the personhood or subjectivity of the eternal Son, for the Son's identity is one with that "I." Thus human personhood is the prerequisite for a fully adequate revelation of the very nature of God as a trinity of divine persons or subjects in that one of the persons (the Son) has now identified himself with a human "I." See W. Kasper, *The God of Jesus Christ* (New York: Crossroad, 1984), 155–56; Weinandy, *Father's Spirit of Sonship*, 123.

15. Traditionally, those theologians who have followed the lead of Cyril and Chalcedon from a Thomistic perspective have insisted, in contrast to P. Galtier, that there is one "I" in Christ and that that "I" is the divine "I" of the Son. See, for example, B. Lonergan, *De Constitutione Christi: Ontologica et Psychologica*, 3rd ed. (Romae: Gregoriana, 1961); P. Parente, *L'Io di Christo* (Brescia: Morcelliana, 1951, 1955); A. Perego, "Il 'lumen gloriae' e l'unità psicologia di Cristo," *Divus Thomas* 58 (1955): 99–110, 296–301; M. B. Xiberta, *El Yo de Jesus Christo* (Barcelona: 1954).

This insistence upon one divine "I" lies in the desire to maintain the one person or subject in Christ—that of the Son. While Lonergan, for example, contends that the Son of God, within the Incarnation, is conscious of himself in a human manner, it is still the divine "I" who is humanly self-conscious. While Aquinas rightly upholds that the one person in Christ is the Son, however, he equally insists that the Son actually *subsists* as man. See *ST* III, q. 2, a. 6; III, q. 10; III, q. 17, a. 2; *De Unione Verbi Incarnati* 1.

Even though Aquinas never treats Jesus's human self-consciousness in the modern sense,

I argue that his Christology, as does Cyril's and Chalcedon's, allows for, and even demands, a human "I" because he stresses that it is truly as man that the Son subsists. It would seem to follow, therefore, that the Son subsists under conditions of a human "I." The subject is the Logos, which Aquinas and all his defenders rightly wish to uphold, but what the traditional Thomists have failed to recognize is the manner in which the Son subsists—that is, as a full and complete man. W. Kasper seems to agree with this interpretation of Aquinas, and his position is also quite close to the present proposal. *Jesus the Christ* (London: Burns and Oates, 1976), 248. Similarly, see G. O'Collins, *Interpreting Jesus* (London: Geoffrey Chapman, 1983), 182–90.

More recently, J. Galot proposed a position that is similar to the present thesis, but he, too, would deny that Jesus possesses a human "I." He writes in *Who Is Christ?*:

> Does Jesus possess a human "I"? There can be no doubt that Jesus possesses an "I" perceived in a human way by his human consciousness. But must this "I" necessarily be a human "I"? Are we obliged to admit that there are two "I's" in Christ, one divine and the other human, or must we say, on the contrary, that there is in him only the one identical "I" of the Son of God? (320)

From his examination of Scripture, he concludes:

> Obviously, we are not speaking of a divine "I" that manifests itself as such in its pure state, but of a divine "I" in a human context, of an "I" that asserts itself within a human consciousness and in human language. It is the divine "I" of a man who is living a genuinely human life. (321–22)

Or again:

> The autonomy of Jesus' human psychology likewise accounts for the fact that his divine "I" manifests itself only in an integrally human consciousness. We have already noted that this "I" did not reveal itself in its pure state. It always appeared within a human consciousness, and its expression was entirely human. The reason certain scholars have tended to speak of a human "I" in Christ may stem from their desire to emphasise this fact. However, while the "I" of Christ asserted itself with a profoundly human psychology, it remained the divine "I" of the Son. (334)

The obvious reason Galot wishes to maintain that the "I" of Jesus is divine is to guarantee the same identity of the "I" and of the person of the Son. Jesus cannot possess two "I's." This identity I, too, wish to maintain. I agree that Jesus cannot possess two "I's." It is because it is the divine "I" not in its "pure state" but under "human conditions" that I argue it is more correct to state that it is the human "I" of a divine person, of the Son. I wish to make a distinction between the subject (the who) of the "I" and the manner of the "I's" (the who's) expression. The identity of the "I" (the who) is the same, that of the Son, but the manner of the subject's identity is as man, and therefore the "I" is the human "I" of a divine subject or person. See also Galot, *La Conscience de Jésus*.

For an almost complete bibliography on the question of Christ's human consciousness in this century, up to the time of the writing of his own article, see K. Rahner, "Dogmatic Reflections on the Knowledge and Self-Consciousness of Christ," in *Theological Investigations 5*, 196–98. For other contemporary studies, see Kasper, *Jesus the Christ*, 243–48; B. McDermott, *Word Become Flesh: Dimensions of Christology* (Collegeville: Liturgical Press, 1993), 268–81; R. Sturch, *The Word and the Christ: An Essay in Analytic Christology* (Oxford: Clarendon Press, 1991), 121–41.

The Human "I" of Jesus: Gospel Confirmation

A brief sampling of Gospel texts illustrates and confirms that Jesus has a human "I." I focus on a few texts where Jesus speaks in the first person.

Jesus asked his apostles, "Who do you say that I am?" (Mk. 8:29). Jesus is asking, "Who am I?" and "What is my identity?" The answer is that he is "the Christ." But although he is asking a question that ultimately concerns his divine identity, an identity that he himself became conscious of and knew, the "I" of the person asking the question is a human "I," for Jesus is asking the question as a man. It was a man who stood before the apostles and asked the question using human concepts and words that were formulated by a human mind and self-consciousness. What we find in this question is a divine person asking about his divine identity under the conditions of a human "I." It is the divine identity of that human "I" that is being sought.

Similarly, when Jesus says, "I have come not to abolish the Law and the prophets, but to fulfill them" (Mt. 5:17), he is saying, "I, who have come from the Father and have become man [and thus I who am the Son], I have come to fulfill the Law and the prophets." The one speaking is the divine Son, but he is saying "I" as a man. If the Son were saying "I" in a divine manner (*qua* God), then it would be the Son, as God, speaking *in* a man, like a man inhabiting a space suit. Then he would be saying: "I, as God, have come to fulfill the Law and the prophets." But if the Son is saying "I" in a human manner (*qua* man), which a true understanding of the Incarnation demands because that is the manner in which the Son now exists, then that "I" must be the human expression of a divine person/subject. Jesus is then saying: "I [the Son], as man, have come to fulfill the Law and the prophets."

Jesus frequently expressed ignorance or asked questions. These passages have traditionally posed problems in light of his divinity. How could the Son of God not know something? Why would he need to ask questions? For example, "But of that day or that hour no one knows, not even the angels in heaven, nor the Son, but only the Father" (Mk. 13:32). This passage is significant, for here Jesus uses the term "Son" in an absolute sense. He is "*the* Son," and therefore his unique divine relationship to the Father is alluded to. Yet it is this Son who is saying, "I do not know when the end of the world will come." If the Son as God (under the conditions of a divine "I") is saying he does not know when the last hour will be, he would be a liar because, as God the Son, he must know what God the Father knows. What is important here, however, is that it is actually the divine Son saying that he does not know when the end will come, and he is speaking the truth precisely because the divine Son, as man, knows, speaks, and acts only within the parameters of his human "I." The Son can truly say: "*I, who am the Son, do not know*" only because that "I" is human and not divine.[16]

The Gospel of John would seem to pose the greatest difficulties for the present thesis, for it is there that the divine identity of Jesus is so radically apparent. Jesus says, for example, "Truly, truly, I say to you, before Abraham was, I am" (Jn. 8:58; cf. 8:24). Or, "The Father and I are one" (Jn. 10:30; cf. 17:21); "The Father is in me and I am in the Father" (Jn. 10:38; cf. 14:9–10).

Jesus is revealing his eternal divine identity, that he is God as the Father is God. But it is as man (σάρξ) that the Son is revealing that he is truly God. In these passages Jesus is using human words forged from human concepts and conceived by a human mind. He is revealing what he is humanly conscious of and knows concerning his own self-identity. He is revealing his divine identity in a human manner—he possesses no other way of doing so. Therefore the "I" in these and similar texts is a human "I" of a divine subject. The Son of God is revealing his divine identity, as the Son, under the mode and expression or within conditions of a human "I," for it is under the form of this human "I" that he knows himself to be the eternal Son of the Father.[17]

16. For a recent discussion of the problem of divine and human knowledge in Christ, see T. W. Bartel, "Why the Philosophical Problems of Chalcedonian Christology Have Not Gone Away," *Heythrop Journal* 36 (1995): 153–72. Bartel's discussion is flawed because he sees the Incarnation as the compositional union of natures and thus the compositional union of divine and human knowledge. The problem arises of how Jesus, within one and the same mind, can be both omniscient and ignorant. But the Incarnation does not result in the one and the same mind trying to hold within it omniscience and ignorance. Within a personal/existential understanding of the Incarnation, the Son comes to exist as man, and thus as man is ignorant. The divine omniscience does not and cannot enter into his human existence and thus into his human mind.

17. I believe that Galot and I would similarly interpret the "I" sayings of Jesus. The significant fundamental difference would be that, where he would assert a divine "I" expressed as man, I would affirm a human "I" of a divine subject. See Galot, *La Conscience de Jésus*, 55–91; *Who Is Christ?*, 320–23.

Conclusion

In the Incarnation the Son of God has taken on a human identity, and thus the "I" of Jesus expresses the human identity of the Son. What the Incarnation entails, and the tradition and Councils confirm, is that he who embraced a human "I"—and so willed, thought, spoke, and was self-conscious within the confines of that human "I"—was the eternal Son. The identity of Jesus is the Son, but the manner or mode of that identity is as man. On this understanding, Jesus lacks nothing that pertains to us as human beings. What is unparalleled (and this is the marvelous mystery of the Incarnation) is that it is the divine Son (the subject/person) who, as incarnate, lives, experiences himself, and expresses himself in a totally human manner—with a human self-identity under the conditions of a human "I."

One final personal note: In thinking about and in writing this essay, I often felt as the early Fathers must have felt—I "knew" what I wanted to say, but I was often not sure I was conceiving and articulating my thoughts properly. I hope that others may conceive and say it better than I.

CHAPTER 18

Jesus's Filial Vision
of the Father

The Christian theological tradition teaches that Jesus possessed the beatific vision from the moment of his conception.[1] I am not comfortable with this traditional teaching. Such a claim appears to me to be contrary to Jesus's

Originally published as "Jesus' Filial Vision of the Father," *Pro Ecclesia* 13, no. 2 (2004): 189–201. Reprinted by permission.

1. The first known author to state explicitly that Jesus possessed the beatific vision was Candide in the ninth century. Peter Lombard raises the question in his *Sentences* III, 14, 2–4. Thomas Aquinas taught that Christ possessed the beatific vision. See *ST* III, q. 9, a. 2.

For recent defenses and clarifications of the position of Aquinas and the tradition, see: R. Cessario, "Incarnate Wisdom and the Immediacy of Christ's Salvific Knowledge," in *Problemi teologici alla luce dell'Aquinate*, Studi Tomistici 44:5 (Vatican City: Libreria Editrice Vaticana, 1991), 334–40; F. Crowe, "The Mind of Jesus," *Communio* 1 (1974): 365–84; "Eschaton and Worldly Mission in the Mind and Heart of Jesus," in *Appropriating the Lonergan Idea*, ed. M. Vertin (Washington, DC: Catholic University of America Press, 1989), 193–234; M. Levering, *Christ's Fulfillment of Torah and Temple: Salvation According to Thomas Aquinas* (Notre Dame, IN: University of Notre Dame Press, 2002), 32–33, 38–39, 59–63, 73–75; B. Lonergan, *De Verbo Incarnato* (Rome: Gregorian University Press, 1964); *De Constitutione Christi Ontologica et Psychologica* (Rome: Gregorian University, 1964); *The Ontological and Psychological Constitution of Christ*, trans. M. Shields (Toronto: University of Toronto Press, 2002); G. Mansini, "Understanding St. Thomas on Christ's Immediate Knowledge of God," *Thomist* 59 (1995): 91–124; R. Moloney, "The Mind of Christ in Transcendental Theology: Rahner, Lonergan, and Crowe," *Heythrop Journal* 25 (1984): 288–300; A. Patfoort, "Vision béatifique et théologie de l'âme du Christ: À propos d'un ouvrage recent," *Revue Thomiste* 93 (1993): 635–39; C. Sarrasin, *Plein de grace et de vérité: Théologie de l'âme du Christ selon Thomas d'Aquin* (Vénasque: Éditions de Carmel, 1992); T. J. Tekippe, "Towards Systematic Understanding of the Vision in Christ," *Method* 11 (1993): 77–101.

human life as *viator*. The very nature of the beatific vision, to my mind, is a postresurrectional reality, and thus one that would be incompatible with a preresurrectional life. How could Jesus have lived an authentic human life that is like ours in every way—sin excepted—when he, even during his life on earth, already possessed what we will possess only in heaven? While I have recently become more sympathetic to some of the issues surrounding the need to affirm that Christ possessed the beatific vision, which I will address in the course of this essay, I am nonetheless still convinced that the question of whether the earthly Jesus possessed the beatific vision as traditionally asked and understood is largely misconceived, and therefore that the traditional answer, that he possessed the beatific vision, is radically defective and so misleading for properly discerning the authentic implications of the Incarnation. In this essay I critique the traditional understanding of Jesus's possession of the beatific vision and, more importantly, propose what I believe to be a position that is more in accord with a true understanding of the Incarnation. I conclude by examining some of the implications for Christian believers.

A Nestorian Question and a Nestorian Answer

Besides my preliminary concern that the beatific vision is inappropriate for one living a genuine earthly life, I am convinced that the very question, as traditionally asked and understood, of whether Jesus, during his earthly life, possessed the beatific vision, is a "Nestorian" question, one that, I am equally convinced, Cyril of Alexandria would never have contemplated, at least not in its present form. What makes it a Nestorian question is that the beatific vision is defined as the immediate vision of God by someone who is not God. It is an objective vision, a "seeing" or "contemplating," of the divine essence that not only stands ontologically distinct from, but also then over against, the one "seeing" or "contemplating." Within a Nestorian Christology, where the Son of God and the man Jesus are not ontologically united within "the Incarnation," and so stand over against one another, the question of whether Jesus the man possessed the beatific vision would make sense, and Nestorius would in all probability have answered "yes" to such a question. Such a vision would have sanctioned the special union he saw between the Son of God and the man Jesus.

However, I believe that Cyril would have recognized immediately that this question is not properly framed, and thus it is a flawed question. The proper question is not whether the earthly Jesus possessed the beatific vision. Rather, the proper question is: Did the Son of God as man, within his human consciousness and intellect, possess a vision of the Father such that he (the divine Son) was humanly aware of himself as Son and so knew himself to be the Son, consequently perceiving all that the Father willed for him during his earthly life?[2] This is a more nuanced question to say the least, but it is one that is in keeping with the proper conception and understanding of the Incarnation—one that is in conformity with Cyril's Christology and thus in agreement with the Creed of the Council of Chalcedon.[3] To this

2. Although Aquinas addressed the question of Christ's beatific vision in the manner of his day, he asked the relevant questions in relation not merely to the divine essence but also to the Word: "Whether the Son of God knew all things in the Word?" (ST III, q. 10, a. 2); "Whether the soul of Christ can know the infinite in the Word?" (ST III, q. 10, a. 3); "Whether the soul of Christ sees the Word or the divine essence more clearly than does any other creature?" (ST III, q. 10, a. 4). It would seem that Aquinas realized instinctively that because the Son of God existed as man, what he knew as man was intimately related to the Word and not merely a human knowledge apart from the Word. But Aquinas still answered these questions in a Nestorian manner; that is, as if the man (soul of) Jesus was a distinct subject who possessed objective knowledge apart from the Son. As I argue, it is the Son who possesses the vision, and he possesses it in a human manner—that is, by means of his human "soul" (consciousness and intellect).

3. I have argued elsewhere that the only proper reading of the Creed of the Council of Chalcedon is through the eyes of Cyril. See T. G. Weinandy, Does God Suffer? (Edinburgh: T&T Clark, 2000), 197–98. J. Galot is excellent in framing the proper questions concerning Christ's self-consciousness and knowledge. La Conscience de Jésus (Gembloux: Ducolot-lethielleux, 1971); Who Is Christ? A Theology of the Incarnation (Chicago: Franciscan Herald Press, 1981), 319–43.

Lonergan was also very much aware of this present concern. The main thesis of The Ontological and Psychological Constitution of Christ is that consciousness must be defined as a subjective experience rather than as a perceptive experience or knowledge of an object. He writes:

let us recall that consciousness is not on the side of the object but on the side of the subject, not on the side of the perceived but on the side of the perceiver. Hence it follows that the Son of God or the person of the Word is conscious of himself through human consciousness not because the Son of God is perceived but because the Son of God perceives, nor because the Son of God perceives himself as an object but because the Son of God either senses or understands or chooses or attends to any object whatsoever. (267)

Lonergan similarly states that "the psychological question is not how a human consciousness has a divine subject but how a divine subject experiences through a human consciousness" (285). See also Ontological and Psychological Constitution of Christ, part 2, 175, 287–89; De Verbo Incarnato, thesis 10, 267–310.

question I want to answer "yes." To grasp fully the significance and implications of this newly and now properly formed question, however, and so to articulate a proper answer to it, the various facets of this question must be both clearly distinguished and related.

The Communication of Idioms:
Three Incarnational Truths

Before examining the various aspects of this issue and providing my tentative answer, I want first to articulate three truths that are essential for properly conceiving the exact nature of the Incarnation, and so properly grasping the question at hand. (1) It is truly *the Son of God* who is man. Here emphasis is placed upon the divine nature of the Son, that he who is incarnate is truly the eternal divine Son of God. (2) It is truly *man* that the Son of God is. Here the fullness and authenticity of the Son's humanity is affirmed. All that pertains to the Son within his incarnate state is predicated of him in a genuine human manner. (3) The Son of God truly *is* man. Here the ontological nature of the incarnational "becoming" is affirmed in that it results in the fact that the Son of God actually *exists* as man. There is, then, an "is" that is unique to the Incarnation: the Son of God, who is God, now also simply *is* man.[4]

Significantly, for our purposes here, these three truths find their foremost sanction and exemplification in the Communication of Idioms, for it contains and even accentuates the truth that because the Son actually exists as man, he is the sole subject of all that pertains to his human existence, and, equally, all that pertains to the Son within his incarnate state must be authentically human.[5] Keeping in mind these incarnational truths as displayed within the Communication of Idioms, we now turn to the question of the incarnational characteristics of the Son's vision of the Father.

---

4. See Aquinas, *ST* III, q. 16, a. 1. See also T. G. Weinandy, "Aquinas: God *IS* Man: The Marvel of the Incarnation," in *Aquinas and Christian Doctrine: A Critical Introduction* (London: T&T Clark/Continuum, 2004). (Chap. 8 in this volume.)

5. The Communication of Idioms was actually the catalyst for coming to a proper understanding of the Incarnation and thus for the articulation of these three incarnational truths. See Weinandy, *Does God Suffer?*, 173–77.

The Son's Incarnate Vision of the Father

First, in keeping with the first and third incarnational truths as found within the Communication of Idioms, the subject (the "who") of any vision of the Father is not a subject (a "who") different from that of the divine Son, but *the divine Son himself*, since it is actually the Son who *is* man. Because it is the Son who must be the subject of any such vision of the Father, his vision of the Father cannot be a vision of the divine essence as an object ontologically distinct from and over against himself. As traditionally asked and answered, the question concerning Jesus's beatific vision, by the very nature of the question, always and necessarily posited another subject (another "who") distinct from that of the Son, who possessed an objective vision of God who was other than "himself," and it is this positing of another subject (or "who") that accounts for why this question of Jesus's beatific vision was necessarily asked and answered in a Nestorian manner.[6] While the Son's vision of the Father necessarily distinguishes the Father and Son as distinct subjects ("who's"), the Son's vision is not a vision of a reality objectively and ontologically different from who he himself is. Rather, the nature of the Son's vision must be a subjective vision; that is, a personal vision of the Father whereby the Son comes to know the Father as Son and in so doing becomes conscious of who he is as Son and so comes to know himself to be the Son. Through this vision of the Father, the Son does not obtain an objective knowledge of the divine essence as something ontologically apart from himself, but rather this subjective vision of the Father reveals and so confirms that he, too, as Son, is indeed God.

Second, in keeping with our second and third incarnational truths as expressed within the Communication of Idioms, while the subject of any such vision of the Father must be the Son and not another "who" apart from the Son, it is *as man*, since this is the manner of the Son's *incarnate existence* that the Son possesses such a vision, for it is as man that the Son becomes humanly self-conscious as Son through his human vision of the Father. As the Son eter-

6. While Lonergan does not set this issue within a Nestorian context, his whole emphasis on consciousness as a subjective experience rather than the perception of an object allows him rightly to criticize those who posit the beatific vision as an objective vision whereby Christ came to know that he was the divine Son. This is especially the case regarding P. Galtier. *Ontological and Psychological Constitution of Christ*, esp. 272–77, 277–85.

nally knows the Father as Father and so is eternally personally self-conscious as being the divine Son of the Father, so, as man, the same Son possesses a human cognitive vision of the Father, which would manifest, in a human manner, that his identity, who he is, is that of being the divine Son of the Father.

While Jesus is traditionally said to have possessed the beatific vision, I argue, in keeping with the above, that it is more properly correct, in accordance with the hypostatic union, to speak of a human "hypostatic vision"; that is, the person (*hypostasis*) of the Son possessed, as man, a personal human vision of the Father by which he came to know the Father as the Father truly exists. Moreover, in coming to know the Father as truly Father, the Son equally became humanly self-conscious as Son and so humanly came to know that he is, like the Father, God.[7] To emphasize and so to further clarify this point, the Son, through his human hypostatic vision, in coming to know the Father as the Father truly is, comes to know that he is the divine Son because in humanly perceiving the Father as truly his Father he per-

7. The tradition, through the beatific vision, wanted to assure that Jesus knew God in the fullness of his divine reality, but it did so in a misconceived manner. My understanding assures that the Son possessed, in a human manner, the immediate vision of the Father, which to my mind is more in keeping with the true nature of the Incarnation.

It is here that Lonergan and I both agree and disagree. In *The Ontological and Psychological Constitution of Christ*, Lonergan affirms that it is the Son of God who is the sole conscious subject and he equally adamantly insists that he must be conscious as man. "Therefore, through a consciousness that is truly and properly human, a divine person is conscious of a divine person" (211; see also 209, 213, 269). With this I agree. But Lonergan also insists that Christ must possess beatific knowledge in order for him to have a full and objective knowledge that exceeds that of subjective conscious experience. Through his human consciousness, the Son of God became humanly consciously of *who he is*, but it was only through the beatific vision that he became fully knowledgeable as to *what he is*—God. "For to understand the quiddity of something is to know that thing in its essence; and no created intellect can know God in his essence save through the beatific vision" (217; see also 207, 209, 219, 265). See also Lonergan, *De Verbo Incarnato*, thesis 12, 332–41. In thesis 12, Lonergan includes patristic texts that illustrate the development of the tradition.

Lonergan never sets the Son's human consciousness of himself as Son within the context of his cognitive vision of the Father. While I, in agreement with Lonergan, have argued that the Son's human conscious experience is the subjective experience of the Son and not the perceptive experience of an object apart from himself, I have also argued that he obtained his human conscious awareness of who is as the Son in relation to his human objective vision of the Father. It was in becoming humanly aware of the Father as Father that he became self-consciously aware that he was truly the Son of the Father. While the Son may not have possessed a full knowledge of the divine essence during his earthly life, as Lonergan insists, he did possess a knowledge of the Father and so of himself as the Father's divine Son that was in keeping with his earthly incarnate state.

ceives himself as truly the Father's Son. This is not only more fully in accordance with the Gospels themselves, both the Synoptics and John, but it also actually arises out of the biblical data itself. Within the Gospels one of the foundational ways the full divinity of the Son is revealed and manifested is through Jesus's conscious awareness of being the unique Son of the Father (e.g., Mt. 11: 27, 16:17; Lk. 10:22; Mk. 12:6, 13:32; Jn. 3:16–18, 5:19–26, 6:40, 11:4, 11:27, 17:1). The whole of John's Gospel was written to elicit faith in Jesus as the true and authentic Son of the Father (Jn. 1:18, 1:49, 20:31). Scholars have long argued that Jesus's use of "Abba" is central for perceiving his unique inner consciousness as the divine Son (Mk. 14:36).[8]

The Human "I" of the Incarnate Son

I have argued elsewhere that within his incarnate state the Son possesses a human "I."[9] While the one subject/person, the one "who," is that of the Son, within his incarnate state that one subject/person/who exists within the parameters of a human "I." When the earthly Jesus was conscious of himself as an "I" and expressed himself as "I," that "I" was a human "I" in that it was conceived and expressed in an entirely human manner. Who was conscious of himself and expressed himself within the confines of a human "I" was the Son of God. Within the Incarnation, there is a human "I" of a divine "who." The identity of that human "I" is that of the divine Son, but that divine identity is only consciously conceived and articulated from within the parameters of that human "I." When Jesus said "I," it was the Son of God saying "I," but he was saying "I" in a human manner, for it was as man that he was consciously speaking as an "I," as a subject, as a "who."

8. The International Theological Commission in its excellent 1985 document "The Consciousness of Christ Concerning Himself and His Mission" strongly argues, from the New Testament evidence, that the Son's filial self-consciousness and knowledge was founded upon his consciousness and knowledge of the Father (see First Proposition and 1.1–1.3). This document is published in M. Sharkey, ed., *International Theological Commission: Texts and Documents 1969–1985* (San Francisco: Ignatius Press, 1989). It is fascinating and significant that the commission, while insisting on the Son's human consciousness and knowledge of himself in relationship to his Father, never raises the issue of Christ's beatific vision. See also Galot, *La Conscience de Jésus*, 76–91; *Who Is Christ?*, 113–18.

9. See T. G. Weinandy, *In the Likeness of Sinful Flesh: An Essay on the Humanity of Christ* (Edinburgh: T&T Clark, 1993), 12–13; "The Human 'I' of Jesus," *Irish Theological Quarterly* 64 (1996/97): 259–68 (chap. 17 in this volume); *Does God Suffer?*, 209–11.

In turning to the nature of the Son's human hypostatic vision of the Father, it is through this human "I" that the Son of God as man became humanly self-conscious as the true divine Son. The Son, through his human hypostatic vision of the Father, consciously became aware, in a human manner, that his identity as man, the identity of his human "I," was that of being the divine Son. Again, in coming to know the Father as *his* Father, the Son became humanly self-conscious that he was the Son. In keeping with the truth of the Incarnation, the human "I" of Jesus thus does not possess a human identity, a human "who," but rather a divine identity, that of the Son.

The above intensifies the reality of the three incarnational truths as found within the Communication of Idioms. Because the Son actually *existed* as man, it is actually the *Son* who became aware, through his human hypostatic vision of the Father, *as man*, from within the parameters of his own human "I," that he was indeed the divine Son of the Father. With a human "I" the Son could conceive and articulate the truth: "I am the divine Son of God." The "I" is a human "I," but the identity of that human "I" is the divine Son, and it is precisely the Son's human hypostatic vision of the Father that establishes and authorizes such a self-perception and statement.[10]

The Manner of the Son's Incarnate Vision

How did this subjective cognitive vision of the Father come about within the Son's incarnate state? Within the context of Jesus's beatific vision, the

10. While I have previously articulated the similarities and differences between my understanding of Jesus's human "I" and that of J. Galot in "The Human 'I' of Jesus," 267–68n15, here I note the similarities and differences in relation to Lonergan's position. In *The Ontological and Psychological Constitution of Christ*, Lonergan holds that "inasmuch as the same subject is aware of himself through both the divine consciousness and the human consciousness, there is, absolutely speaking, only one 'I' in Christ just as there is only one person." Because the Son exists as God and exists as man, however, there are equally two "I's" in Christ, that is, "the 'I as divine,' which is aware of itself in its infinite perfection, and the 'I as human,' which experiences itself with the limitations of the assumed nature" (225). On one level I agree with the main thrust of Lonergan's account, that there is only one person/subject (one "who") in Christ. Moreover, the Son as divine is conscious of himself as God within his divine "I." But within his incarnate state I would not want to posit two "I's"—one divine and one human—for within his incarnate state the one divine Son is only conscious of himself as man, within a human manner (as man he cannot be conscious of himself in a divine manner), and thus there is, as man, only one "I" and that human. I believe it better, for clarity's sake, to speak of a human "I" of a divine person or subject (a divine "who"), rather than confuse the issue by positing a second "I" that is divine.

traditional answer is that, because the Son is hypostatically united to his humanity, his humanity by necessity experiences the beatific vision. The beatific vision necessarily flows from the Son to the humanity that is personally united to him.[11] To conceive the vision in this manner gives the impression that the divinity of the Son washes into the humanity or that the humanity runs off "the steam" of the divinity. Such an understanding borders on a Docetic or a Monophysite understanding of the Incarnation. While the Son is the subject or person, the "who," within the Incarnation, I prefer to nuance the manner in which the Son became humanly self-conscious as Son through his human hypostatic vision of the Father.

I have argued elsewhere that the Father lovingly begets the Son in the Holy Spirit and that the Spirit thus conforms the Son to be the loving Son of the Father. The Holy Spirit equally conforms the Father to be the loving Father of the Son.[12] In light of these theological presuppositions, I argue that it is through the Holy Spirit, the Spirit of sonship, that the Son of God as man experienced his human hypostatic vision of the Father and so became humanly aware that he was truly the divine Son of God. As the Son of God became incarnate by the power of the Holy Spirit—and only the Holy Spirit could accomplish such an action—so the Son's human hypostatic vision of his heavenly Father is achieved only through the divine illumination of the Spirit. It is the Holy Spirit who reveals the true nature of the Father to the Son incarnate, and in so doing it is the Holy Spirit who brings to human self-consciousness the Son's self-identity as Son. Although the Son is the subject, the "who," of such a vision, it was by the power and light of the Spirit of sonship dwelling within his humanity that the Son became aware of his filial identity. This now places Jesus's human hypostatic vision within a Trinitarian context. Unlike the traditional teaching whereby Jesus possessed the beatific vision as an objective knowledge of God's essence, the

---

11. G. Mansini rightly argues that for Aquinas Jesus did not possess the beatific vision by metaphysical necessity of the Incarnation, but because of "conveniens"; that is, because it was most fitting for Jesus to possess it since he is the cause of our beatitude "Understanding St. Thomas on Christ's Immediate Knowledge of God," *Thomist* 59 (1995): 93–96. Nonetheless, as Mansini himself quotes, Aquinas believed that because "the soul of Christ is united to the Word in a singular way, it has a singular and more excellent knowledge of God, beyond that of the other creatures" (100). *Super Evangelium Johannis* 8:3n1065; see also *ST* III, q. 10, a. 4.

12. See T. G. Weinandy, *The Father's Spirit of Sonship: Reconceiving the Trinity* (Edinburgh: T&T Clark, 1995), 53–85; *Does God Suffer?*, 114–19.

present conception is more properly focused on the Son's human hypostatic vision of the Father through the illumination of the Holy Spirit, whereby he comes to know the Father truly as Father and so becomes subjectively humanly self-conscious as the divine Son.[13]

The above is also in keeping with the experience of the believer. The love of the Father is poured into the heart of the believer through the Holy Spirit, and so the Holy Spirit reveals to the believer a knowledge of the Father. This knowledge simultaneously allows the believer, empowered by the same Spirit, to cry out "Abba, Father." The Spirit's revelation of the Father is the cause of the believer's recognition that, in the Spirit, he or she is indeed a child of the Father. My understanding of Jesus's experience of his filial sonship now becomes the actual paradigm of that of the believer.

Viator and *Comprehensor*

This conception of Jesus's human hypostatic vision of the Father is more compatible with his incarnate state as *viator*. The Son of God as man did not possess such a vision from the moment of his conception nor at his birth. Rather, the Son advanced in such a human hypostatic vision as he humanly grew in wisdom, age, and grace (Lk. 2:52). As young Jesus studied the Scriptures and as he prayed, the Spirit illuminated his human consciousness and intellect with the vision of the Father such that he became hypostatically aware of Father's glory and love, and within such an awareness he became conscious of his divine identity and so came to know that he was the Father's eternal and only begotten Son. In keeping with ordinary human psychology, the Son became humanly conscious of who he was at the appropriate age, and this is witnessed in his being aware that he must be about his Father's business at the age of twelve (Lk. 2:49).[14]

In keeping with the principle that Jesus's human hypostatic vision of the

13. The International Theological Commission is of the same mind. "This relationship of the incarnate Son with the Father presumes in the first place the mediation of the Holy Spirit, who must therefore be always included in the consciousness of Jesus as Son." "Consciousness of Christ," 2.4. In having a filial vision of the Father, the Son as incarnate is obviously aware of the whole Trinity, for to know the Father necessarily entails knowing the Son and Spirit. But the Son's incarnate knowledge of the Trinity was not an objective knowledge—that is, a knowledge of a being ontologically distinct from himself—but rather a subjective knowledge—that is, a knowledge of who himself is—himself being a person of the Trinity.

Father is in accordance with his earthly state as *viator*, I argue also that the fullness of this vision did not reach its comprehensive and complete maturity until his resurrection. It is there that the Father raises him from the dead by the power of the Holy Spirit and makes him Son of God in power (Rom. 1:4). Only within his glorified and risen state does the Son of God obtain, through the full light of the Holy Spirit, the full human hypostatic vision of his Father and so the full human vision of who he is as the divine Son. This seems to be in accord with the Letter to the Hebrews' claim that he was "made perfect" through his death and resurrection (Heb. 2:10, 5:9, 7:28, 10:14). Only in the Resurrection does Jesus become truly the *comprehensor*. As we will only become fully aware of who we really are in heaven, so does the incarnate Son of God become fully aware of who he really is in heaven.[15]

My understanding of Jesus's human hypostatic vision of the Father raises an important question. Within his *viator* state, and specifically when on the Cross, was the Son of God humanly conscious of those for whom he was dying? Traditionally, this was answered affirmatively on the basis of Jesus's beatific vision. Because Jesus possessed a comprehensive vision of the divine essence, he equally possessed, within that vision, a knowledge of all those for whom he was dying.[16] While I am not happy with the notion of the beatific vision, this concern forced me to reconsider my initial position of simply denying that Jesus possessed the beatific vision. The argument that Jesus must know for whom he is dying does strike me as valid.[17]

14. This does not imply that Jesus only became aware of his divine identity at the age of twelve. Such an awareness would have come much earlier, when individuals typically becomes aware of who they are. The difference is that a human person becomes aware of his or her human identity and the Son incarnate becomes humanly aware of his divine identity as Son. See F. Crowe, "The Mind of Jesus," *Communio* 1 (1974): 368.

15. The Son of God as man did not know that he was the Son of God. Rather, the Son did not fully grasp, as man, the awesome glory and incomprehensible splendor of who he was until he was raised gloriously from the dead.

16. M. Levering rightly, it seems to me, makes much of this point in his defense of Christ's beatific vision. *Christ's Fulfillment of Torah and Temple*, 32–33, 38–39, 59–63, 72–75. Levering also notes other authors who argue in this fashion.

17. The International Theological Commission seems to insist on this as well. Its Fourth Proposition reads:

> The consciousness that Christ had of being the Father's emissary to save the world and to bring all mankind together in God's people involves, in a mysterious way, a love for all mankind so much so that we may all say: "the Son of God loved me and gave himself up for me" (Galatians 2:20).

I now place this question within my own incarnational framework. Within the Son's human hypostatic vision of the Father, he was humanly aware of his Father's will for him, which ultimately found its expression in his death on the Cross. Now, did the Son as man, in knowing the Father's will, humanly know the identities of those men and women for whom he was dying, or did he merely know that he was dying, in some generic sense, for humankind? The Father, within his divine knowledge, obviously knew the identities of all those men and women for whom his Son was dying. I would argue in turn that the Son possessed a human vision in accordance with his vision of the Father of all those men and women for whom he was dying. Here, though, as is the case with the position that Jesus knew for whom he was dying from within the beatific vision, a mystery arises as to the exact manner of that knowing. In a manner in keeping with his human hypostatic vision of the Father, and thus in accordance with his human awareness of the Father's divine knowledge, the Son, as man, knew for whom he was dying. The exact nature and specificity of this human awareness and knowing seem to be part of the mystery of the Incarnation, which in itself can never be fully comprehended.[18]

The Vision of the Blessed in Heaven

The above understanding of Jesus's filial vision of the Father has significant repercussions as to the manner of the vision of the blessed in heaven. Tradition holds that the saints in heaven possess the beatific vision, an immediate vision of God as God exists in himself. The knowledge contained within the beatific vision is an objective knowledge in that the person possessing such a vision is ontologically distinct from God. While, within the beatific vision, God and the saints obtain the fullness of union, God stands over against the saints as an object to be known and loved. It seems to me that it is this notion of the beatific vision that ultimately controlled and governed

18. Some theologians who uphold the beatific vision argue that such a vision is ineffable and so nonconceptual. I agree that Jesus's filial vision of the Father and the knowledge that he obtains from such a vision cannot be fully articulated, and knowing all those for whom he is dying may be a case in point. See, for example, Lonergan, *De Verbo Incarnato*, thesis 12; Crowe, "The Mind of Jesus," 365–84; Tekippe, "Towards a Systematic Understanding of the Vision of Christ," 77–101.

the question and answer as to whether the earthly Jesus possessed the beatific vision. If we allow Jesus's human hypostatic vision of the Father to control and govern the nature of the saints' vision in heaven, however, then a
radical shift in the nature of that vision occurs.

Through faith and baptism a person's relationship with the Trinity fundamentally changes. By the power of the Holy Spirit one is conformed into
the likeness of the incarnate glorious Son and so becomes an adopted son
or daughter of the Father. Thus one shares, as an adopted son or daughter,
in the very Trinitarian relationships as pertains to that of the Son. Through
the Holy Spirit, the Father loves his adopted sons and daughters with the
same love with which he loves the Son, and by that same Spirit his sons and
daughters, after the manner of the Son, cry out "Abba, Father" (Jn. 17:20–
23; Rom. 8:7; Gal. 4:6).

Within this Trinitarian context the beatific vision is no longer simply
the objective vision of God as a being over against the blessed. While God
remains ontologically distinct from the blessed, because the blessed are now
adopted children of the Father, they share in the glorious Son incarnates'
hypostatic vision of the Father, and so it, too, in an adopted manner, is a
subjective personal vision of the Father. Through their heavenly vision of
the Father, in union with the risen Son by the light of the Holy Spirit, the
saints experience God not as a being over against themselves, but as a Trinity of persons in whose life they now subjectively share. This, it seems to
me, is the true meaning of the ancient notion of deification. The saints are
deified because, in being fully conformed into the likeness of the risen Son
though the power of the Holy Spirit, they share in the incarnate Son's glorious filial heavenly vision of the Father and so come to know who they truly
are—sons and daughters of the Father.

This understanding of the "beatific vision" is much more in keeping
with the Trinitarian nature of God, for this vision is predicated upon the
blessed actually being taken into the Trinitarian life. It is in conformity with
the incarnate Son's own human vision, both within his earthly life and his
risen glorious life. His vision is the source and paradigm for the saints' vision.[19] Furthermore, it is in keeping with an authentic understanding of

19. As stated above, Aquinas's primary argument for affirming Christ's beatific vision is
that since all "men are brought to this end of beatitude by the humanity of Christ ... it was necessary that the beatific knowledge, which consists in the vision of God, would belong to Christ

grace. Grace is the work of the Holy Spirit, conforming Christians into the likeness of the incarnate Son and so coming to share in the love of the Father. In heaven this comes to its final completion, whereby the saints are fully conformed, in the Spirit, to the likeness of the risen incarnate Son and so share fully in the Father's love.[20] Lastly and importantly, the humanity of the Son plays a significant role within this heavenly vision. As the Spirit unites the believers to Christ on earth and so through that union they become children of the Father, so in heaven the saints, through the Spirit, come to share fully in the glorious Son's human hypostatic vision of the Father. The saints do not possess a heavenly vision apart from the incarnate Son or an objective vision of God as a being over against themselves; rather, they participate in and so share the same vision of the risen incarnate Son and so possess a subjective vision (adopted human hypostatic vision) of the Father, a vision in which they recognize fully that the life of the Trinity is *their own life* as authentic sons and daughters of the Father.[21]

---

pre-eminently, since the cause ought always to be more efficacious than the effect" (*ST* III, q. 9, a. 2). I argue that Christ not only brings us to the heavenly vision though his human salvific acts, but also that it is by sharing in his risen humanity that we come to share in his heavenly vision of the Father. This notion arises out the Pauline understanding of the Body of Christ in which all believes find their maturity, perfection, and fulfillment in the *one* new Man, Jesus Christ (Eph. 2:16, 4:13–16).

20. Aquinas states, "By natural likeness, because a son is naturally like his father. Wherefore it also follows that one is called a son of God insofar as he shares in the likeness of his natural Son; and one knows him insofar as he has a likeness to him, since knowledge is attained through assimilation [or 'likeness to']." See *Super Evangelium Johannis* 1:18n216 in J. Weisheipl and F. Larcher, trans., *Commentary on the Gospel of John* (Albany: Magi Books, 1980).

21. The risen humanity of Christ traditionally plays no role within the blessed life of the saints. Because the blessed are fully united to Jesus and so are fully transformed into his risen likeness through the Holy Spirit, however, they experience, as Jesus humanly experiences, the beatific vision. Jesus is always the mediator, even in heaven, between the Father and human beings, and while they immediately experience the beatific vision of the Trinity as the Trinity actually is, they do so only through being united, in an unmediated manner, to the risen humanity of the Son.

CHAPTER 19

Thomas Joseph White's Beatific Vision of the Incarnate Son
A Response

There is nothing more stimulating than to ponder the mysteries of the Catholic faith in an attempt to conceive them more clearly and to articulate them more precisely. No mystery is more challenging than the mystery of the Incarnation—even more so, to my mind, than the Trinity itself. My good and longtime Dominican friend Thomas Joseph White has taken up this exhilarating challenge in a thoughtful article on the Incarnation and the necessity of the earthly Jesus possessing the beatific vision.[1] I and Jean Galot were the primary catalysts for this work, for we have argued that a proper understanding of the Incarnation does not warrant the earthly incarnate Son of God possessing the beatific vision, despite the venerable, and to some extent magisterial, tradition to the contrary. I am grateful to *The Thomist* for allowing me to respond to White's article, for while he has marshaled a formidable array of scholarly arguments in support of his position, I believe that his arguments actually undermine what he ardently wants to achieve—to uphold and articulate an authentic understanding of the Incarnation. While White argues that his position is in keeping with the Angelic

Originally published as "The Beatific Vision and the Incarnate Son: Furthering the Discussion," *Thomist* 70 (2006): 605–15. Reprinted by permission.

1. "The Voluntary Action of the Earthly Christ and the Necessity of the Beatific Vision," *Thomist* 69 (2005): 497–534.

Doctor, and it may be, the angels know, as did Aquinas himself, that their doctor is not the arbiter of truth. Thomist though I am, I will not address the validity of Aquinas's arguments or White's interpretation of them. Instead, my response is threefold. First, I briefly summarize White's position. I then offer an assortment of critiques of his position. Finally, I attempt to sort out the whole issue by articulating briefly how I believe it must be addressed.

White: The Incarnation and the Beatific Vision

The answer to the question of whether the earthly Jesus possessed the beatific vision must be found in discerning the incarnational principles or rules that govern the earthly, human life of the Son of God. Given that within the Incarnation it is the Son of God who exists as man, what necessarily follows as to the manner or type of human life that the Son of God lived? White and I disagree on the answer to this question; that is, what does or does not necessarily ensue from the Incarnation as to the human life of the Son of God.

White argues that the nature of the Incarnation demands that the Son of God as man must possess the beatific vision if he is to properly live out his human life. For White, the beatific vision not only ensures that the human intellect is cognizant of "his" divine filial identity, but also that the human intellect knows and the human will acts in complete conformity with the divine intellect and will of the Son. (I have written the above sentence in conformity to White's manner of speaking. I would not articulate the issue in such a manner, as will be seen below.) As White states at the onset:

this unity of personal action in Jesus requires a perfect cooperation between the human will of Christ and his divine will. In effect, Christ's will and consciousness must act as the instruments of his divine subject, being directly specified at each instant by his divine will. For this, knowledge of his own filial nature and will is necessary. The virtue of faith, or a uniquely prophetic knowledge (by infused species), is not sufficient. The unity of activity of the Incarnate Word requires, therefore, the beatific vision in the intellect of Christ, so that his human will and his divine will may cooperate within one subject. (507)

White argues that without the beatific vision the human intellect and will of Christ would exercise an autonomy that would undermine the unity of subject; that is, that the Son acts through the instrumentality of his humanity. The Son can act through the instrumentality of his humanity only if his human intellect and especially his human will are in complete accord with his divine intellect and will, and this assurance is only obtained if the human intellect of Christ possesses the beatific vision. As White again states,

If Jesus is truly the Son of God, and therefore a divine person, then his divine will is present in his person as the primary agent of his personal choices. This means that, necessarily, his human will must be continually subordinate to, informed by, and indefectibly expressive of his personal divine will in its human, rational deliberation and choice making … it is only if Christ's human intellect is continuously and immediately aware of his own divine will (by the beatific vision, and not merely by infused knowledge and by faith), that his human will can act in immediate subordination to his divine will as the "assumed instrument" of his divine subject. (516)

White illustrates the incarnational need for the beatific vision by way of the examples of Christ's obedience and prayer. As seen above, only the beatific vision guarantees that the human will of Christ is conformed to his divine will, for only through the beatific vision is his human intellect conformed to his divine intellect. The beatific vision likewise empowers Christ to pray to the Father, fully aware that he is the divine Son (523–33). For White, this is only possible "due to the correspondence between the human and divine wills of Christ within his *unified* personal action, effectuated by means of the beatific vision" (522).

From the above, I think it is obvious how White conceives the incarnational principles or rules that necessarily govern how the Son orders and regulates his earthly life. Simply put, the Son of God comes to exist as man and in so doing now possesses a divine and human intellect and a divine and human will. These two distinct intellects and wills interact practically within Jesus's everyday earthly life through the beatific vision in that the human intellect possesses the knowledge of the divine intellect and thus the human will is able to be conformed to the divine will by means of the divine knowledge now resident within the human intellect.

This mutual conforming of intellects and wills also ensures that the Son is the sole acting subject. Through the beatific vision, everything the Son does humanly is performed in accordance with his divine knowledge and will. The beatific vision thus mediates between the Son existing as God and *divinity & humanity?*

yes (the Son existing as man so as to ensure that the Son as God and the Son as
man *are both* "on the same page." Without the beatific vision, for White,
the Son of God as man would not (with certainty, but only by faith or prophetic infused knowledge) be able to be "on the same page" as the Son of
God as God because the Son as man would not know with certainty what
the Son as God knows and so would not be certain as to what the Son as
God wills.

*For White
the
Person
that
see
essence
is
divinity +
humanity
conform
to
it.*

A Slight Whiff of Nestorianism

Eyebrows may have been raised at the above words "are both," and rightly they should have been. Despite the fact that White wants to guarantee,
through the beatific vision, a unity of subject and a unity of action between
the divine and human natures, and so avoid Nestorianism, his conception
of the "mechanics" of the Son's incarnational life bears the odor of Nestorianism, even if it be ever so slight. We need to examine more closely his argument.

White rightly wants to hold, and often states, that in the Incarnation
the Son of God came to exist as man, and therefore he is the one acting subject within his human life as man. Yet when it comes to conceiving and articulating the inner dynamics of the Son's incarnational life as man, White's
articulation becomes somewhat imprecise.

For White, within the Incarnation, the manner in which divine knowledge, and with it the divine will, comes to the human Jesus is through the
beatific vision. The beatific vision mediates between the human intellect
and will of the Son and the divine intellect and will of the Son, thus allowing the human intellect to know and the human will to will in unison with
the divine Son. In conceiving the inner workings of the earthly life of the
Son incarnate in this manner, however, White gives the impression that the
human intellect had a mind of its own and that the human will had a will
of its own apart the Son, and that it is only if the human intellect and the
human will are tamed by the beatific vision that we (or, for that matter, the
Son of God) are assured that they will not run autonomously wild on their
own. White's understanding of the Incarnation is here faulty.

Because the Son is the sole person or subject within the Incarnation,
what he knows and wills as man is done by him and so, from the very on-

tology of Incarnation, the human intellect and will are never autonomous "things" in need of being "brought into line," whether by the beatific vision or by any other means. It is the Son of God who exists as man and, like every human being, personally acts through his human intellect and his human will, for they are personally his own. They are ontologically constitutive of who the Son of God is as man and thus are incapable of having a "self" life of their own.

Without realizing it, in his attempt to find a necessary reason for why Christ must possess the beatific vision, White first had to rend asunder the human intellect and will from the divine Son with his divine intellect and will, and then he had to impose, which he so wanted to do, the beatific vision as the necessary means for uniting the human intellect and will with the divine intellect and will within the one Son of God. White does not want to disconnect the human intellect and will from the divine Son, as he himself argues profusely in his article, but his arguments on behalf of the beatific vision of Christ have forced him to do so. This is why the articulation of his position always bears the slight whiff of Nestorianism, and why he is also forced at times to articulate his position in am imprecise manner.

The Ambiguous Use of "His"

White's whiff of Nestorianism can be seen in the fascinating, but highly ambiguous, way that he often employs the term "his" in relation to "the man," "the human intellect," and "the human will." White states that through the beatific vision "the man Jesus knows immediately that he receives his divine will from the Father, and his human acts of obedience bear the imprint of this unique filial certitude" (526). Within the Incarnation, there is no "man" Jesus apart from the Son who "knows," there is no human "he" who receives, and there is no human "who" who possesses the certitude of "his" filial human acts. Within the Incarnation there is only the Son of God existing as man, and thus there is only one "he" and one "his"—the divine Son. Again, as quoted above, "Christ's will and consciousness must act as the instruments of his divine subject, being directly specified at each instant by his divine will. For this, knowledge of his own filial nature and will is necessary" (507).

Who is the subject/person (the "who") of all of these various uses of the term "his"? The first "his" refers to Christ, but this gives the impression that Christ is a different human subject from the latter designated "divine subject." But how can there be a "his" that differs from the divine subject to which the "his" refers? The second "his" appears to shift from referring the human subject of "Christ" to, presumably, referring to the Son of God as God, since it speaks of "his divine will." This may be an attempt at employing the Communication of Idioms, but it fails because, within the Communication of Idioms, divine and human attributes are predicated of one and the same subject and that of the divine Son.

Here the first "his" refers to a human subject other than the Son as God, and the second "his" refers to the Son as God. The third use of the term "his" does not appear to have any incarnational logic whatsoever—"knowledge of his own filial nature." This "his" implies a human "who" that comes to know that "who" he really is is the Son of God, but within the Incarnation one does not have *a man* who comes to know that he is God; rather, within the Incarnation, the Son of God *humanly* comes to know or *humanly* becomes conscious, within his human intellect and human consciousness, that he is the Son of God. Again, the reason White is forced to employ such strained terminology and to state his position in such a tangled fashion is because, in a Nestorian manner, he has separated the human intellect and will from the Son of God with the intention of gluing them back together by means of the beatific vision.

Giving "Subjectivity" to the Human Intellect and Will

The way in which White speaks of the divine and human wills as if they could act apart from the person of the Son, implying that they possess their own distinct subjectivities, also reflects a Nestorian bent. In a passage quoted above, White speaks of "Christ's human intellect" being "immediately aware of his divine will," and it is the beatific vision that ensures that "his human will can act in immediate subordination to his divine will" (516). But an "intellect" is not aware, nor does a "will" act; only a person knows and only a person acts, and he does so through his will. Later White speaks of the "divine will" moving the "human will" (519) as if these were wills of different subjects. It is the Son of God who wills either with his divine will or with his human will, but the wills themselves do not interact apart from the one who is willing, the divine Son.

Within the same passage, White states that "the human will of Christ acts 'instrumentally,' that is to say, through an immediate subordination to his divine will" (519). As man, the Son's humanity is the personal instrument through which he acts in a similar way as I personally act through the use of my hand. But my hand does not act "instrumentally," and neither does Christ's "human will." Moreover, a "will" does not act apart from the one whose will it is, nor does a "will," as if it were an acting subject, subordinate itself to another will. Only persons subordinate their will to another person. To say that one will subordinates itself to another will implies two persons.

One also finds peculiar statements such as, "His human will cooperates indefectibly with his divine will in the unity of one personal subject" (520). "Wills" do not "cooperate"; persons cooperate through a mutual agreement of their wills. To say that the divine and human wills cooperate "in the unity of the personal subject" implies two willing subjects being united to a third. What White wants to say is that, when the Son of God wills and acts as man, his human will and action are always in conformity with his divine will because there is only one willing and acting subject, the Son of God. The reason he cannot simply say so is because, again, within his conception of the Incarnation the human intellect and will would be in competition with the divine intellect and will unless the beatific vision is imposed so as ensure their unity. For White, it is not the *hypostatic* union, the ontological union whereby the Son of God exists as man, that guarantees the unity, and so conformity, of the human intellect and will with the divine intellect and will, but the beatific vision.[2]

Sorting Out the Incarnational Confusion

The reason White has gotten himself in this incarnational tangle is that he has misconceived the incarnational principles that must be operative within the incarnate Son. For White, the manner in which the Son of God as man

2. Part of the problem may reside in White's ambiguous us of the term "Christ." One is not sure at times whether such a designation refers to the Son of God incarnate or to the man Jesus who is distinct from the Son of God. For example, White can state that without the beatific vision the "the human mind of Christ would no longer be moved by the will of the divine person" (320). This implies that "Christ" is a human subject possessing a human mind who is different from the "divine person" who possesses a divine will.

becomes conscious of who he is as God and the manner in which he comes to know the divine will and so act in accordance with it is through the beatific vision. For White, this all takes place within what might be called an inner dialogue between the divinity of the Son and the humanity of the Son, for through the beatific vision the human intellect and will are "hot wired" to the divine intellect and will. The incarnate Son comes to know who he is and he comes to know what to will and to do in relationship to his own divinity mediated through the beatific vision. This, to my mind, is contrary to the very nature of the Incarnation and to the human life that the Son of God lived.

How, then, does the Son of God as man come to know who he is within his incarnate state?[3] He does so through his incarnate relationship to his Father, and he comes to know what to will and to do through his incarnate relationship to the Father. The Son incarnate becomes conscious of who he is and so knows who he is not in relationship to his own divinity mediated through the beatific vision, as White would argue, but through what I have termed his human "hypostatic vision" of the Father. Through his human prayer, in conjunction with his pondering the Scriptures, the person of the Son as man has a vision, though not beatific, of the Father, and in so coming to know his Father he comes to know, he becomes self-conscious, that he is indeed the only begotten Son.[4] White contends that if the Son of God does not possess as man the beatific vision, his divine identity and knowl-

3. Here I am not afforded the space to give a complete account of my argument. I refer readers to my "Jesus' Filial Vision of the Father," *Pro Ecclesia* 13, no. 2 (2004): 189–201 (chap. 18 in this volume).

4. In "Jesus' Filial Vision of the Father" (chap. 18 in this volume), I give two reasons why I believe Jesus did not possess the beatific vision. The first is that the beatific vision is traditionally understood as a heavenly vision and thus a vision that is resurrectional in nature. Such a vision would then be contrary to Jesus's being able to live an authentic earthly life. Moreover, because the beatific vision has traditionally been understood as an objective vision of God obtained by some one who is other than God, to say that Jesus possessed the beatific vision implies Nestorianism, as if the man Jesus, who possessed the beatific vision, were a different subject/being from that of the Son. It is the Son of God as man who has a personal/hypostatic vision of the Father, and within that vision he not only humanly comes to know the Father as his Father, but he also simultaneously becomes humanly conscious of his divine sonship in relation to his Father. White also gives the impression that I agree with Galot that the beatific vision gives a Monophysite skew to the Incarnation. I do not think that such would necessarily be the case. I hold that the traditional understanding of beatific vision is simply contrary to the very nature of the Incarnation and the incarnational principles that are literally embodied within it.

edge of what he should will and do would be reduced to an act of faith or be reduced to prophetic infused knowledge. This is not true. The Son of God, in coming to know who he is in a human manner through his human hypostatic vision of his Father, humanly comes to know the will of the Father and so humanly acts in accordance with it. This, I believe, is in keeping with the Incarnation and the incarnational principles that govern it. Everything concerning the Son of God within his human state as man must be conceived and articulated within that incarnate state—not in relationship to his own divine nature but in his human relationship to his Father and to the earthly human life that he authentically lives. My understanding of the incarnational principles that govern the earthly life of the incarnate Son differs radically from White's.

Let me conclude by adding a new argument, one that may help clarify the issue. Within the life of the Trinity, the Son of God did not come to know who he is as the Son of God, *homoousios* with his Father, within his own self-contained knowledge of himself, similar to the way White wants the Son of God as man to know who he is in relationship to his own divinity through the beatific vision. Rather, the Son of God is eternally self-conscious, and so knows who he is, as Son only in relationship with his Father and so eternally conforms, as Son, his will to the Father's will. Similarly, the eternal Son of God, though his human hypostatic vision of the Father, is humanly conscious of and so knows who he is as the Son, *homoousios* with the Father, in relationship to his Father, and in humanly knowing who he is as Son in relationship to his Father, he humanly wills and does what the Father wills and does (Jn. 5:17–20). The principles that govern the Son's incarnational life are the same principles as those governing his divine life.

I ardently hope that my critique of White has been fair and to the point. White is too good a theologian to dismiss lightly. Nonetheless, I hope that the clarifications I have attempted to offer will further the debate, as there is no greater joy than to contemplate, in unison with the angels and their doctor, the divine mysteries. To ponder, and to debate, the mystery of the Incarnation with my Dominican brother Thomas Joseph will, I am confident, bear much intellectual fruit, and hopefully abundant grace, for both of us.

CHAPTER 20

The Council of Chalcedon
Some Contemporary
Christological Issues

The Council of Chalcedon: Three Christological Truths

I have been asked to address some contemporary Christological issues in light of the Council of Chalcedon. In many ways, the Council of Chalcedon was the culmination of a 451-year-long Christological journey within the early Church. It stated positively what the Church believed with regard to the divinity and humanity of Christ and simultaneously refuted various errors. Before examining some of the contemporary issues that arise from Chalcedon, it would be best to examine first what Chalcedon actually stated so that we have a clear and concise understanding of its teaching.

In agreement, therefore, with the holy fathers, we all unanimously teach that we should confess that our Lord Jesus Christ is one and the same (*hena kai ton auton*) Son, the same (*ton auton*) perfect in Godhead and the same (*ton auton*) perfect in manhood, truly God and truly man, the same (*ton auton*) of a rational soul and body, consubstantial (*homoousion*) with the Father in Godhead, and the same (*ton auton*) consubstantial (*homoousion*) with us in manhood, like us in all things except sin; begotten from the Father before the ages as regards his Godhead, and in the last days, the same (*ton auton*) because of us and because of our salvation begotten from the Virgin Mary, the *Theotokos*, as regards his manhood; one and the same (*hena kai ton auton*) Christ, Son, Lord, only-begotten, made known in two natures

Originally published as "The Council of Chalcedon: Some Contemporary Christological Issues," *Theology Digest* 53, no. 4 (2006): 345–56.

(*en duo phusesin*) without confusion, without change, without division, without separation, the difference of the natures being by no means removed because of the union, but the property of each nature being preserved in and in harmony with one *prosopon* and one *hypostasis*—not parted or divided into two *prosopa*, but one and the same (*hena kai ton auton*) Son, only-begotten, divine Word, the Lord Jesus Christ, as the prophets of old and Jesus Christ himself have taught us about him and the creed of our fathers has handed down.

We must first note that the Council three times employed the phrase "one and the same" and five times used the phrase "the same." Here the Council is emphatically confirming the apostolic tradition highlighted by two outstanding Alexandrian theologians, St. Athanasius and St. Cyril.[1] "The one and the same" and "the same" is none other than the one eternal, only-begotten Son or Word. There are not two "sons" as Nestorius's Christology seemed to imply. There is only one subject or person; there is only one "who," and that one "who" is the one Son or Word of God.

The second aspect Chalcedon repeatedly professed is that this one and the same Son is perfect in Godhead and perfect in manhood. The same is consubstantial with the Father (contrary to the teaching of Arius, who denied the full and eternal divinity of the Son), and the same is consubstantial with us and so possessing a genuine human body and authentic human soul (contrary to all those who deny the full humanity of Christ—the Docetists, who denied the material body, and Apollinarius, who denied a human soul). Because the Son of God actually became man within the womb of Mary, she can rightly be called "*Theotokos*—Mother of God," for the incarnate Son of God was actually born of her (contrary to Nestorius's denial). Moreover, the Council highlights the fact that the Son of God is "made known in two natures" and not composed "out of" two natures and in so doing refuted Eutyches's Monophysitism whereby the divine and human natures were united so as to form one new composite nature, thus jeopardizing the full integrity of the divinity and of the humanity.

Third, what the Council has accomplished in making these distinctions is to establish the hypostatic or, what I have come to call, personal/

1. See T. G. Weinandy, "Cyril and the Mystery of the Incarnation," in *The Theology of Cyril of Alexandria: A Critical Appreciation*, ed. T. G. Weinandy and D. Keating (Edinburgh: T&T/Continuum, 2003), 23–54 (chap. 7 in this volume); *Athanasius: A Theological Introduction* (London: Ashgate, 2007), 81–101.

existential understanding of the Incarnation. It distinguishes the person or subject—the who—and the manner of the person's or subject's—the who's—existing. It is one and the same "who"—the one and the same Son or Word—who exists ontologically both as God and as man.

In clarifying the nature of the incarnational union, the Council has also clarified the nature of the incarnational "becoming." Because the "becoming" unites the humanity to the person of the Son, the divine and human natures are not confused or changed, nor are they divided or separated. Why? The reason the natures are not confused or changed is that the incarnational union—the "becoming"—is not the compositional or organic union of natures, which would give rise to a third kind of being, a hybrid, which would then be neither truly God nor truly man. Because the incarnational union is not a compositional union of natures, Chalcedon can say that "the difference of the natures is not removed because of the union." Yet Chalcedon can also insist that the natures are not separated or divided because they find their unity in the one person of the Son or Word. "The property of each nature being preserved in and in harmony with one *prosopon* and one *hypostasis*." The incarnational act, the incarnational "becoming," is the ontological uniting of the humanity to the person of the Son of God so that the Son comes to exist personally as man. This is a singular and unique understanding of the term "become," establishing a singular and unique ontological union for the Incarnation as a singular and unique event giving rise to a singular and unique being—Jesus—the Son of God incarnate.

Lastly, because the Council conceived and articulated a proper understanding of the Incarnation, it properly clarified and so sanctioned the use of the Communication of Idioms. Because the same Son of God actually exists as God and as man, both divine and human attributes can be predicated of this same Son. The divine Son of God can rightly be said to thirst, hunger, suffer, die, and rise, for the Son actually lived a genuine human life as man.

In light of the Council of Chalcedon, all subsequent Christological questions, issues, and developments must protect and promote the following three incarnational truths, as will become evident below when we discuss the contemporary issues.

First, it is truly *the Son of God* who is man. This truth emphasizes that

Jesus must be truly the divine Son of God. Second, it is truly *man* that the Son of God is. From an incarnational perspective, it is of no value to uphold the full divinity of the Son if that Son is not truly and fully human. Third, the Son of God truly *is* man. This truth accentuates the fact that the incarnational "becoming" must terminate in an incarnational "is." The divine Son and the man Jesus cannot be separate beings. The Son of God actually came *to be* man and so actually *exists* as man. Moreover, the Communication of Idioms embodies and highlights all three of these incarnational truths. To say that "God suffers and dies," for example, demands that the Son be truly *God*, for if he were not truly God, it would not be God who suffers; the Son must be truly *man*, for if he were not truly man, he would not be able to suffer and die humanly; and the Son must truly *be* man, for only if Son truly is man can he truly suffer and die as man.[2]

Having examined the decree of the Council of Chalcedon and delineated the three incarnational truths that flow from it, we now turn to some contemporary Christological issues, issues that the Fathers of Chalcedon probably would never have imagined but would find extremely fascinating and important if they lived today. All of these issues and the questions they raise, as the Fathers of Chalcedon would insist, must be discussed and answered within the context of Chalcedon. Karl Rahner stated correctly, "we have not only the right but the duty to look to it [the Chalcedonian formula] as end *and* as beginning."[3] All discussions and arguments surrounding new Christological issues and questions must begin with Chalcedon, and when they reach the truth of their conclusions, they will have helped deepen, intensify, and expand Chalcedon by humbly being in accord with it.

Christology from Above and Below

Contemporary authors frequently discuss what is perceived as two approaches to Christology.[4] One is referred to as Christology "from above,"

2. For a more complete discussion of the Council of Chalcedon, see T. G. Weinandy, *Does God Change? The Word's Becoming in the Incarnation* (Petersham, MA: St. Bede's Press, 1985), 63–66.

3. K. Rahner, "Current Problems in Christology," in *Theological Investigation* (Baltimore: Helicon Press, 1961), 1:150.

4. See, for example, K. Rahner, "Two Basic Types of Christology," *Theological Investiga-*

which emphasizes that the transcendent divine Son of God came down from heaven and became man. While this approach to the Incarnation ensures the full divinity of Jesus, it is sometimes criticized, usually without warrant, for undervaluing the humanity of Jesus and so his historical life and Jewish cultural milieu. The other Christological approach is named Christology "from below," which emphasizes the humanity of Jesus and so his historical life and cultural conditioning. But some authors confuse two points when discussing this Christological approach "from below"—one of which is true, and so is in conformity with the Council of Chalcedon, and the other is false, and so is not in conformity.

It is true that the only way we can come to know who Jesus is as the divine Son of God and also the significance of what he humanly achieved is through his humanity, through what he historical said and did as a man. Epistemologically, Christology must always, by necessity, be "from below"; that is, we can only come to know who Jesus is by listening to his human words and observing his historical actions. As the apostles themselves experienced, his humanity is the necessary sacramental reality or means through which the deeper truth that Jesus is the Son of God is revealed.

Yet some contemporary theologians confuse our way of coming to know that Jesus is the Son of God with the way Jesus himself actually did become the Son of God. We come to know that Jesus is divine "from below," from and through his humanity, but Jesus himself did not become divine "from below." It is not through some form of human openness to the transcendent that the man Jesus—through his prayer, love, faithfulness, and obedience—was taken up into the divine and so became "God." Such a Christology would merely be a form of Adoptionism and not the Son of God actually coming to exist as man.

The Council of Chalcedon, and the apostolic tradition it embodies, demands that Christology must always be ontologically "from above"; that is, that the Incarnation is always the Son of God ontologically assuming a human nature and so coming to exist as man. Since the Council professes that it is truly man that the Son of God is, epistemologically Christology must always be "from below"; that is, we can only come to know Jesus to be the

tions 13 (New York: Seabury Press, 1979), 213–23; W. Thompson, The Jesus Debate (New York: Paulist Press, 1985), 45–78.

eternal Son of God incarnate through his historical and earthly humanity. By correctly recognizing the ontological nature of the Incarnation on the one level and the epistemological nature of our coming to know Jesus as the Son of God incarnate on the other, the full significance of Jesus's divinity and humanity is properly balanced in accordance with the Council of Chalcedon.

The Miracles of Jesus

You might be surprised that I have chosen the miracles of Jesus as our second example of a contemporary Christological issue. I chose it not because some theologians deny that Jesus actually worked miracles, though some do, but because the manner in which Jesus actually worked his miracles is often misconceived, even by faithful Christians. This misunderstanding stems from a deficient grasp of Chalcedonian Christology. Allow me to give my rendition of a familiar Gospel story with added bits and pieces.

Jesus went to the home of Mary, Martha, and Lazarus for dinner. Martha served as a starter (the English term) raw carrots and garlic dip (a yet-to-be discovered American fare), which Jesus ate. Who was it who ate the carrots? It was the Son of God who ate the carrots. Did he eat the carrots as God or as man? He ate the carrots as man. God as God cannot eat carrots for obvious reasons. But because the Son of God now actually existed as man, he could eat carrots just like every other human being. Moreover, he was pleased that he had created them as God since they were quite delicious to eat as man. Lazarus also ate the carrots, but unfortunately he got a rotten one and died of food poisoning. Four days later, Jesus returned and raised Lazarus from the dead. Who was it who raised Lazarus from the dead? It was the Son of God who raised Lazarus from the dead. Did he raise Lazarus from the dead as God or as man? Here is where a proper understanding of the Council of Chalcedon and of the Communication of Idioms comes into play.

The Son of God ate the carrots as man because the Son of God truly existed as man. Some readers, like many of my past students, might want to say that the Son of God raised Lazarus from the dead *as God*. But to say so is to forget our three incarnational truths. It is true that who performed the miracle was the Son of God. But it was performed by the Son of God existing as man, and so it was *as man* that the Son of God performed the miracle. It was the Son of God as man who wept at the death of Lazarus, and it was the Son of God as man who cried out with a human voice: "Lazarus come forth!" In raising Lazarus from the dead, the Son of God performed a divine action (or, even better, an action empowered by the Holy Spirit), but he did it in a human manner—he did it as a man. Miracles are traditionally termed "theandric" actions, or divine deeds done humanly. Everything that the Son of God did within his incarnate state was done as a man, whether it was eating carrots or raising someone from the dead. If we do not uphold this, we would have the Son of God doing some actions *as a man*, such as eating carrots, and some actions as God *in a man*, such as working miracles. This an authentic understanding of the Incarnation will not allow. All earthly actions (and postresurrectional heavenly actions) performed by the Son of God must be done in a human manner, for that is the manner in which the Son now exists—as man.[5]

Let us now turn to the contemporary issue of Christ's suffering. Did he suffer as God or as man or as both?

The Suffering of the Incarnate Son

The vast majority of contemporary Christian theologians contend that God as God suffers in solidarity with our suffering. God, perhaps echoing the noble words of President Bill Clinton, would say, "I feel your pain." How can God be loving, they ask, if he does not suffer in union with the innocent and down trodden? The paradigm for such suffering, they claim, is Jesus himself. While the Christian tradition has consistently held that the Son of God suffered as man, he did not suffer as God, for God as God cannot suffer. Nevertheless, the present wisdom holds that it is because the Son of God became man that he suffers not merely as man, but equally as God. In so doing, he illustrates that God, in his very divine nature, always lovingly suffers in solidarity with those who suffer.

I cannot possibly address here all of the complex issues and erroneous presuppositions and conclusions that are involved in this seemly simple

---

5. For a fuller discussion of this issue, see T. G. Weinandy, *Does God Suffer?* (Notre Dame, IN: University of Notre Dame Press, 2000), 199–206.

and, to many, all too obvious conclusion that God suffers.[6] Nonetheless, we must first remember that God is not a member of this created order, and thus he is not a being who undergoes, as do human beings, a multiplicity of emotional changes depending upon the present state of affairs. The evil that occurs within the created order, which causes us to suffer, cannot reverberate back into the uncreated divine order, and so God does not suffer in any literal sense. Nonetheless, God is perfectly and unchangeably loving—he is love perfectly in act—and so he embodies perfectly and unchangeably all facets of love: kindness, compassion, justice, mercy, correction, forgiveness, and so on. His perfect and unchanging love responds to all situations appropriately, and we experience these various facets of God's perfect and unchanging love differently depending on our present state of affairs. If we have sinned, we experience God's perfect, unchanging love as a call to repentance. If we repent, we experience God's perfect, unchanging love as mercy and forgiveness. Thus God is not aloof and indifferent. To those who innocently suffer for the sake of justice, his love is experienced as compassion and the fostering of courage. With this in mind, we must now return to Jesus and our three incarnational truths confirmed by the Council of Chalcedon.

Those who champion a suffering God want Jesus to suffer not only as man but also as God. Only if he suffers as God, they claim, does God really experience and so know our human suffering. The Father of love sent his Son into the world to suffer and die so that we might be saved. But what is redemptive is not that the Son of God suffered as God, but that he truly suffered as man—in a manner exactly as our own. If the Son of God suffered as God, it would mean, contrary to the Council of Chalcedon, that there was a confusion and mixing and so a changing of natures. If the Son of God suffered as God, he would not have experienced human suffering in an authentic human fashion, but he would have experienced human suffering in a divine fashion, which would not be the authentic experience of human suffering. Chalcedon demands that it truly be the person of the divine Son of God who suffered, and equally that he personally suffered as man, for it is the human suffering of the Son of God that is redemptive. What is redemp-

6. For a thorough study of divine impassibility and all of the issues related to it, see Weinandy, *Does God Suffer?*. For a shorter summary of my arguments, see "Does God Suffer?," *First Things* 117 (November 2001): 35–41.

tive is that the Son of God as man took upon himself our sin and death, and in so doing he, equally as man, lovingly offered his holy and innocent human life (not his divine life) to the Father as a sacrifice for our sin. Again, in keeping with our three incarnational truths, it is not what the Son of God experienced or did as God that is redemptive, but rather it is what the Son of God experienced and did as man that is redemptive. Those who advocate a suffering God completely miss the point of the Incarnation and so completely undermine its redemptive significance.[7]

Did Jesus Know He Was God?

The early Church confirmed, in keeping with the truth that he is genuinely human, that Jesus possessed a human will and intellect (Second and Third Councils of Constantinople; 553 and 680–81 AD). In the nineteenth and twentieth centuries, however, with the rise of historical consciousness and psychology, a new question arose: Was Jesus conscious, and so knowing that he was God?

The first thing we need to do is properly frame the question. The question is not "Did Jesus know he was God?," as if Jesus the man was a different person or subject (a different "who") from the Son. The proper question is, "Was the Son of God conscious of himself and so know that he was God *in a human manner*, through his human consciousness and mind?" Again, in keeping with our three incarnational truths affirmed by the Council of Chalcedon, who was humanly self-conscious was the Son of God and the manner in which he was self-conscious was as man. The answer to our question must now be "yes." If the Son of God incarnate was not humanly conscious and so did not humanly know that he was the Son of God, he could not have revealed to us that he was the Son of God, for he would have been ignorant of his own identity. For Jesus to be ignorant of his own identity would be absurd. There is something psychologically amiss when a person does not know who he or she is.

How did the Son of God become humanly conscious and so humanly come to know that he was indeed God's Son? Traditionally, many theologians, including the great Scholastics St. Thomas Aquinas and St. Bonaven-

---

7. This is more fully treated in Weinandy, *Does God Suffer?*, 172–213.

ture, taught that Jesus from his conception possessed the beatific vision and so from his conception knew he was the Son of God. But I do not find this lesson in keeping with the Son of God living an authentic human life, one like our own. Moreover, the beatific vision is traditionally understood to be the immediate vision of God possessed by the blessed in heaven—precisely by those who are not God. Jesus is God, however, and so whatever "vision" he might have possessed, it could not be a "vision of God" whereby he viewed God as a being over against and other than himself.

I argue that the Son of God became humanly conscious of who he is and so knows that he is the Son of God in a manner that is in keeping with normal human beings. I have been told that children normally come to perceive themselves as distinct persons around the age of four, when they begin to use the word "I" in a meaningful manner. It would be around this age, in conjunction with Mary and Joseph teaching him to pray, that Jesus began to perceive in a human manner, through the Holy Spirit dwelling within him, his divine sonship. Later, as he prayed the Psalms and read and studied the Scriptures—as he grew in wisdom, age, and grace—his self-understanding as the Son of God would have become more clearly perceived and defined, so that by the age of twelve he would have clearly known as man that he, as the Son, must be about his Father's business. This self-understanding may best be illustrated by a statue I once saw in France.

In an ancient monastery that now belongs to a charismatic community, I saw a statue, carved from a huge old tree trunk, of Joseph sitting with the child Jesus (about seven or eight years old) on his lap. Joseph, with his expansive, muscular arms around Jesus, held open before them a scroll of the Psalms. Joseph and Jesus, with mouths wide open, were together singing the Psalms. It is in this kind of setting, praying with his earthly father, that the Son of God became humanly conscious of his heavenly Father and so became conscious himself that he was the Father's Son. It was in coming to know the Father, through the light of the Holy Spirit dwelling within him, that the Son of God became humanly conscious and so humanly came to know himself to be the divine Son of the Father.

I have argued elsewhere that the earthly Jesus, as the incarnate Son of God, possessed, through the Holy Spirit, a human filial vision of the Father—a vision of the Father such that he became conscious of his own divine sonship and so came to know his own self-identity as the Father's eternal Son. I believe that this vision is in accord with the Council of Chalcedon. The one who is self-conscious and so knows himself as the divine Son, and the manner in which he is self-conscious and so knows himself to be the divine Son is as man.

It seems to me that this is also in keeping with our own Christian experience. By the power of the Holy Spirit we are united to Jesus, the Son, and so are transformed into his divine likeness; in union with Jesus through the Spirit, we come to experience the paternal love of the Father and so come to know that we are his adopted children in Christ his Son. We perceive our true identities, who we really are as sons and daughters only as we come to experience and know, like Jesus, in union with him, our heavenly Father. The love of the Father is poured into our hearts and minds through the Holy Spirit, and so with Jesus the Son, we, too, can cry out, in the same love of the Holy Spirit, "Abba, Father!"[8]

Is Jesus a Human Person?

In light of the Council of Chalcedon, we can now progress to the next question, of whether Jesus is a human person. In keeping with our three incarnational truths, the one person of the divine Son is traditionally said to exist as man. This is the meaning of the term "hypostatic union": the human nature is united to the person/hypostasis of the Son so that the person of the Son actually exists as man. But some contemporary theologians argue that if Jesus is a divine person and not a human person, then he is missing something essential to being authentically human, meaning therefore that he is not fully human. They argue that Jesus must be a human person, but in so doing they unavoidably deny that Jesus is the divine Son of God.[9] This whole issue is entirely misconceived.

First, while it is absolutely crucial that Jesus's full and authentic human-

---

8. For a more detailed treatment of my position and the debate surrounding it, see "Jesus' Filial Vision of the Father," *Pro Ecclesia* 13, no. 2 (2004): 189–201 (chap. 18 in this volume); "The Beatific Vision and the Incarnate Son: Furthering the Discussion," *Thomist* 70, no. 4 (2006): 605–15. Also, see T. J. White, "The Voluntary Action of the Earthly Christ and the Necessity of the Beatific Vision," *Thomist* 69, no. 4 (2005): 497–534; "Dyotheletism and the Instrumental Human Consciousness of Jesus," *Pro Ecclesia* 17, no. 4 (2008): 396–422.

9. For example, see J. Macquarrie, *Christology Revisited* (London: SCM, 1998), 43–60.

ity be maintained, it must be done to ensure what the Son of God is—an authentic man. To uphold the full humanity at the expense of the divinity is to jettison the most important reason for upholding his humanity; that is, to ensure that the Son of God actually is a man.

Second, the term "person" is not some sort of "thing" that must be added to a human being in order for that being to be complete. The term "person" denotes that a particular being is a "who" rather than a "what" and possesses a singular identity. In all cases but one, human beings possess a specific human identity, a specific human "who." When asked "Who are you?," we answer by giving our name, which identifies us as a particular and unique human being. The difference between Jesus and us is that, while he possesses everything that pertains to being authentically human—a body, intellect, will, self-consciousness, and the like—he does not possess a *human* identity but rather a *divine* identity as the Son of God. The identity of this particular and unique human being, Jesus, is that of the Son of God. To say that Jesus is a divine person or subject (a divine "who") and not a human being or subject (a human "who") is not to deprive him of a full humanity but rather articulates the very mystery of the Incarnation—that the person of the Son of God has come to exist as man, and therefore the identity of this man (who he is) is the Son of God. It appears to me this is what Jesus was getting at when he asked his apostles, "Who do you say that I am?" He wanted them to acknowledge his divine identity, his divine personhood, who he really is. Peter got it right when he answered, "You are the Christ; the Son of the living God."

The Human "I" of Jesus

Theologians who have followed the Doctrine of Chalcedon have argued that there is only one "I" in Christ—the divine "I" of the Son of God. The obvious reason is to confirm, in accordance with Chalcedon, the singular divine identity or personhood of Jesus as the Son of the Father. Bernard Lonergan, S.J., holds that, inasmuch as the same subject is aware of himself through both the divine consciousness and the human consciousness, "there is, absolutely speaking, only one 'I' in Christ just as there is only one person." In a qualified manner, however, Lonergan argues that one can also speak of a human "I." Since Christ possesses two natures and so two consciousnesses, divine and human, he possesses, as a human psychological subject, an "I" as human, "which experiences itself with the limitations of the assumed nature."[10] More recently, Jean Galot, S.J., has emphasized that while there is one divine "I" of the Son, that divine "I" is manifested to others in a human, self-conscious manner. When Jesus said "I," that was a divine "I" speaking and acting in a human manner.[11] While I, too, in keeping with the Council of Chalcedon, profess and maintain the divine identity of Jesus as the Son of God, I also argue, in keeping with Chalcedon, that it is nonetheless more correct, within his incarnate state, to speak simply of the human "I" of the divine Son.[12]

Within the Incarnation, the person/subject—the "who"—is the Son of God. Nonetheless, the Son of God humanly experiences and humanly acts within the parameters of a human self-conscious "I." There is a human "I" of a divine person/subject—a divine "who"—the Son of God. Let us again examine Jesus's question: "Who do you say that I am?" Jesus is asking his apostles to identify "who" he is. The answer to this question, as Peter stated, is that Jesus is the Christ, the Son of the living God. Jesus's divine identity was here confirmed. But while Jesus was eliciting from his apostles the affirmation of his divine identity as the Son of God, his divine "who," the manner in which he asked the question was as a man, and so within the parameters of his own human self-consciousness. Thus the "I" in "Who do you say that I am?" is a human "I." The Son of God as man, within the confines of a human "I," is requesting that the divine identity of his human "I" be affirmed—that the one who is humanly saying "I" be identified as the Son of God.

I believe this understanding of the Incarnation—that the divine Son of God possesses a human "I"—upholds and even intensifies Chalcedonian

10. B. Lonergan, *The Collected Words of Bernard Lonergan: The Ontological and Psychological Constitution of Christ* (Toronto: Lonergan Research Institute, 2001), 225.

11. See J. Galot, *Le Conscience de Jésus* (Paris: Duculot-Lethielleux, 1971); *Who Is Christ?* (Chicago: Franciscan Herald Press, 1981), 319–43.

12. I have addressed this issue on a number of occasions: *In the Likeness of Sinful Flesh: An Essay on the Humanity of Christ* (Edinburgh: T&T Clark, 1993), 12–13; *The Father's Spirit of Sonship: Reconceiving the Trinity* (Edinburgh: T&T Clark, 1995), 120–22; "The Human 'I' of Jesus," *Irish Theological Quarterly* 62, no. 4 (1996/97): 259–68 (chap. 17 in this volume); *Does God Suffer?*, 209–11. In the latter two citations I discuss the differences between my position and Galot's.

Christology. It accentuates that who is man, the person or subject, is none other than the divine Son of God, and it simultaneously heightens the fact that he actually became fully human even to the extent of speaking and acting within the parameters of a human self-conscious "I."

The Council of Chalcedon and Religious Pluralism

Recently there has been a great deal of theological discussion concerning global religious pluralism, specifically Christianity's claim that Jesus is the singular and universal savior. Some theologians, often with great ambiguity, argue that Jesus is merely one of any number of religious founders and that these other religions are of "salvific" value in their own right. Such a position is contrary both to the proclamation of the New Testament and to the Christological tradition as canonized by the Council of Chalcedon.[13]

No other founder of a religion—for example, Buddha or Mohammed—claimed to be God, and their adherents do not make such claims of them. But Christianity believes that Jesus revealed that he was the eternal Son of God and the conciliar tradition, especially at the Councils of Nicea, Ephesus, and Chalcedon, solemnly defined that Jesus was the Son of God, one in being (*homoousion*) with the Father. It is the fact that Jesus is not simply a prophet or a holy man but the Son of God incarnate that gives him a status that is singular in nature from all other founders of a world religion. Jesus is not simply "better" than the other founders of religions by way of degree, revealing more truth or living a holier life, but rather he differs in kind from other founders of religion for he is the definitive, unique instance of the Son of God existing as man.

13. See, for example, J. Dupuis, *Toward a Christian Theology of Religious Pluralism* (Maryknoll: Orbis Books, 1997); R. Haight, *Jesus: Symbol of God* (Maryknoll: Orbis Books, 1999); P. C. Phan, *Being Religious Interreligiously: Asian Perspectives on Dialogue* (Maryknoll: Orbis Books, 2004).

The Congregation for the Doctrine of the Faith has responded to the writings of Dupuis and Haight. See , Notification on the Book *Toward a Christian Theology of Religious Pluralism* by Father Jacque Dupuis, S.J. (24 January 2001) and Notification on the Book *Jesus Symbol of God* by Father Roger Haight, S.J. (13 December 2004). The United States Conference of Catholic Bishops Committee on Doctrine has responded to Phan. See Clarifications Required by the Book *Being Religious Interreligiously: Asian Perspectives on Interfaith Dialogue* by Reverend Peter C. Phan (10 December 2007).

As the Son of God incarnate, Jesus accomplished what no other founder of a religion is able to do. First, he is able, as the Word of the Father, to reveal the fullness of divine truth. Second, through his sacrificial death Jesus reconciled us to the Father, and through his resurrection he conquered death and obtained for us eternal life. Third, as the glorious Lord and Savior, Jesus poured out the Holy Spirit upon the Church at Pentecost. Fourth, only by being united to his risen humanity through the indwelling of the Holy Spirit are we transformed into the children of the Father and so come to share in the very divine life of the Trinity. Jesus is therefore the universal and definitive savior of the whole of humankind, and his salvific work is predicated upon the Chalcedonian faith that he is uniquely the Son of God incarnate.

Conclusion

Contemporary Christology is alive with many issues and questions.[14] This should not be surprising since it is the Holy Spirit, the Spirit of truth, who constantly leads Christians of every age to a deeper knowledge and love of Jesus—who he is and what he has done for us. Because the Council of Chalcedon is the ever-new beginning of Christology, the truth it proclaimed will never be changed. Nonetheless, its truth will be ever deepened and clarified. I hope that this discussion has offered some clarity, though there may be many questions left unanswered. Theology is about the clarification of divine mysteries, the discerning of what the mysteries are. It is not about making the divine mysteries comprehensible and so thoroughly known.[15] This is impossible, and those who attempt to do so become heretical. Again, my only hope is that the mystery of the Incarnation has now become a little clearer in light of contemporary concerns, renewing and fostering a greater understanding and love of Jesus.

14. Many, but not all, of the topics treated here have also been discussed in T. G. Weinandy, *Jesus the Christ* (Huntington, IN: Our Sunday Visitor Press, 2003).
15. For a fuller discussion of this point, see T. G. Weinandy, "Doing Christian Systematic Theology: Faith, Problems, and Mysteries," *Logos: A Journal of Catholic Thought and Culture* 5, no. 1 (2002): 120–38; *Does God Suffer?*, 27–39.

CHAPTER 21

Dei Verbum
The Centrality of Jesus and Islam

I am pleased and honored to be a participant in this interreligious dialogue. While I have participated in many ecumenical events involving various Christian denominations, I have never had the opportunity to gather with members of another religion to discuss common religious concerns and theological issues. In a way I am following in the footsteps of the founder of my religious order, St. Francis of Assisi, who during the Fifth Crusade came to Egypt and in early September 1219 met with the Sultan Malik al-Kamil, though I doubt if either of them considered their gathering "a dialogue." So I come filled with anticipation at what I will learn today and at the positive outcome of this dialogue.

I have been asked to address the issue of Catholicism and the necessity of revelation, especially as it has been articulated in the Second Vatican Council's Dogmatic Constitution on Divine Revelation, *Dei Verbum*. I do this within the context of examining the opening verses from St. Paul's Letter to the Ephesians. Ephesians 1:3–14 is the *locus classicus* for expressing succinctly and clearly the Christian understanding of God's eternal plan for human beings and the manner in which he brought that plan to fulfillment.

St. Paul exhorts the Ephesian Church to bless "the God and Father of our Lord Jesus Christ" (Eph. 1:3). The reason for such an exhortation is that the

Originally published as "Dei Verbum: The Centrality of Jesus and the Necessity of Revelation," *Chicago Studies* 48, no. 2 (2009): 207–13. Reprinted by permission.

Father has "blessed us in Christ with every spiritual blessing in the heavenly places" (Eph. 1:3). St. Paul next explicates exactly what these blessings are, and it is here that we enter into the necessity of revelation. St. Paul proclaims that the Father chose us in Christ "before the foundation of the world" and that he did so that we might be "holy and blameless before him" (Eph. 1:4). Moreover, St. Paul states that the Father "destined us in love to be his sons through Jesus Christ, according to the purpose of his will" (Eph. 1:5).

Inherent in what St. Paul proclaims are a two interrelated points that are essential for discerning the Christian understanding for the necessity of revelation. First, we learn what our loving Father desires for us. The Father's eternal desire is that we be as holy as he is holy, and therefore blameless of all sin, for sin is absolutely contrary to his holiness. Moreover, in being holy and blameless the Father wants us to be his sons. Our destiny is to possess an intimate and familial relationship with the Father and so share in his own divine life. Second, we learn that the Father's predestined will for humankind is only accomplished in and through his eternal Son who became man, Jesus Christ. By our own efforts we are not capable of making ourselves holy, nor can we transform ourselves into sons of the Father and so share in his divine life. Only Jesus Christ, the *holy* Son of the Father, can make us holy, and only Jesus Christ, the *proper* Son the Father, can fashion us into adopted sons of the Father. This is why St. Paul stresses that it is "in" Jesus Christ that we were eternally chosen by the Father, and it is "through" Jesus Christ that we become adopted sons of the Father. What is fascinating is that St. Paul professes that Jesus Christ, as the Father's incarnate Son, was not simply a necessary response to human sin and so a divine afterthought, but was from the onset the preordained means for accomplishing the Father's eternal plan of making humankind holy and blameless and thus his sons.

Our next point is equally important. Revelation and its necessity for St. Paul are not simply or solely to impart knowledge of God that would otherwise be unknown or to enlighten human beings as to how they are to live in relationship with God and with one another, such as through obeying his divine commands. Rather, revelation is essentially those acts of the Father, carried out through his incarnate Son, Jesus Christ, by which he accomplishes his eternal plan for humankind. *Dei Verbum* espouses and confirms this notion of revelation: "This economy of Revelation is realized by deeds and words, which are intrinsically bound up with each other. As a result, the works performed by God in the history of salvation show forth and bear out the doctrines and realities signified by the words; the words, for their part, proclaim the works, and bring to light the mystery they contain" (2). Words articulate the divine content of revelation, but what these words articulate is primarily the divine revelatory deeds and actions of God of himself, what *Dei Verbum* calls "the divinely revealed realities" (11). This is clearly exemplified in what St. Paul next proclaims.

He states that even in the midst of sin the Father was not deterred. So lavish is the Father's grace that we have redemption through Jesus's blood, "the forgiveness of our sins" (Eph. 1:7). Again, we perceive the necessity of revelation not simply as the communicating of the unknown, but as the redemptive actions of the Father's incarnate Son; life, death, and Resurrection. The inspired words of the apostles and of the New Testament articulate the significance of who Jesus is and the salvific meaning of his actions—that he is the eternal Son of the Father who became man and as man died on the Cross and rose gloriously for our salvation. Through Jesus's loving sacrificial death on the Cross, sin, which separated us from the love of the Father, is expiated and so we are reconciled to the Father. In Jesus's glorious resurrection, human death is vanquished and we are now capable of sharing in his risen and glorious life through the outpouring the Holy Spirit. St. Paul further states that through faith we "were sealed with the promised Holy Spirit, who is the guarantee of our inheritance until we acquire possession of it" (Eph. 1:13–14). Through the indwelling of the Holy Spirit we are united to the risen Lord Jesus and so share in his holiness being transformed into his own divine filial likeness. In union with Jesus, through the indwelling of the Holy Spirit, we come into communion with our heavenly Father as his adopted children sharing in his own divine life of love and goodness.

For St. Paul, the mystery hidden from the foundation of the world has now been revealed. "For he [the Father] has made known to us in all wisdom and insight the mystery of his will, according to his purpose which he set forth in Christ as a plan for the fullness of time, to unite all things in him, things in heaven and things on earth" (Eph. 1:9–10). The Father's eternal plan for humankind finds its fulfillment only when human beings are united to Jesus Christ through the indwelling of the Holy Spirit, for only in union with Jesus Christ do we become holy and blameless, and only in union with him do we become sons in communion with our Father. *Dei Verbum* echoes the words of St. Paul: "It pleased God, in his goodness and wisdom, to reveal himself and to make known the mystery of his will. His will was that men should have access to the Father, through Christ, the Word made flesh, in the Holy Spirit, and thus become sharers in the divine nature" (cf. Eph. 1:9, 2:18; 2 Pet. 1:4).[1]

We find in St. Paul's proclamation that through the person and work of Jesus Christ a whole new salvific order has been set in place; that is, what was not possible prior to Jesus salvific work is now possible. Prior to Jesus's death on the Cross the scourge of sin and quilt had not been adequately dealt with, but now we have obtained forgiveness and reconciliation with the Father. Prior to Jesus death reigned, but now we can share in his risen life and so the guarantee of our own resurrection. Prior to Jesus we could not have full communion with the Father, but now, through the indwelling Spirit, we are united to the risen Jesus and so are transformed into the Father's sons and daughters. The revelation of Jesus Christ is not the message of a prophet who simply speaks on God's behalf. Rather, Jesus himself is the message, for in his own person and acts the fullness of revelation, the fullness of the Father's preordained plan, finds its fulfillment. This is why *Dei Verbum* states that "the most intimate truth which this revelation gives us about God and the salvation of man shines in Christ, who is himself both the mediator and the sum total of Revelation" (2). Again: "Therefore, Christ the Lord, [is the one] in whom the entire Revelation of the most high God is summed up (7; cf. 2 Cor. 1:20, 3:16–4:6)."

It is probably already clear, but because I want to emphasize the centrality and necessity of Jesus within Christian revelation, I belabor the point once more. What uniquely distinguishes Jesus and sets him apart from all other prophets or holy men is not only that he establishes the divine economy of salvation through Incarnation, passion, death, and Resurrection with the subsequent sending forth of the Holy Spirit upon those who believe, but also that one can only enter into or have access to this new salvific order by being united to the person of risen Jesus Christ. Only by being united to Jesus, through faith and the Holy Spirit, is one able to reap the benefits

---

1. See also *Lumen Gentium* 2–4, the Second Vatican Council's Dogmatic Constitution on the Church.

of all that Jesus accomplished in becoming man, dying, and rising. As *Dei Verbum* states, "Christ established on earth the kingdom of God, revealed his Father and himself by deeds and word; and by his death, resurrection and glorious ascension, as well as by sending the Holy Spirit, completed his work. Lifted up from the earth he draws all men to himself (cf. Jn. 10:31 Gk. Text)" (17). Only as one is drawn to and is ultimately united with Jesus Christ does one have access the Father in the Holy Spirit.

Let me close these comments on Christian revelation by stating that this is why for Christians Jesus's name is above every other name, and why he is supreme above all, Lord of lords and King of kings, for only through him and in union with him is the Father's predestined eternal plan fulfilled. Only in Christ Jesus do we become holy and blameless in the Father's sight and so become his sons and daughters sharing in his eternal life and perfect love, and so inconceivable joy, forever and ever.

Having articulated, hopefully clearly and accurately, the Catholic understanding of revelation and its necessity, by way of conclusion I consider briefly the ways this understanding of revelation may find some communality with other religions. *Dei Verbum* does affirm in conformity with St. Paul (cf. Rom. 1:20) and the First Vatican Council that all human beings can come to a true, though limited, knowledge of God by perceiving his presence in the works of his creation (cf. 6). But can there be a deeper communality that exceeds this natural knowledge of God?

As you may know, some of the early Christian Fathers, Justin Martyr for example, speak of "seeds of the Word" (*Logos Spermatikos*) being spread and planted throughout the whole of human history. They held that since the eternal Word of God embodied the fullness of divine truth and since all human beings were created in his image as rational and intelligent, whatever religious truth human beings obtained throughout all of history, in whatever culture, must find its source in that one eternal Word.

Nostre Aetate confirms this notion when it says that "throughout history even to the present, there is found among different peoples a certain awareness of a hidden power, which lies behind the course of nature and the events of human life. At times there is present even a recognition of a supreme being, or still more a Father" (2). For Catholics the Word of truth, while lacking in fullness, is not absent from our brothers and sisters of other faiths, for what ever is true must first reside within God himself. Thus *Nos-*

tre Aetate states that "the Catholic Church, rejects nothing of what is true and holy in these religions. She has a high regard for the manner of life and conduct, the precepts and doctrine which, although differing in many ways from her teaching, nevertheless often reflect a ray of that truth which enlightens all men" (2).[2]

The source of our communality could possibly reside within some common understandings of the Word of God. For Christians, the Word of God as the eternal Son of the Father is a distinct person/subject (a distinct "who") within the one nature of God, yet all might be willing to acknowledge that God's revelation and communication with all peoples and religions is through his Word, with its goal to enlighten the hearts and minds of all humankind. If the human ear is not deaf to God's voice, then it is his Word that we hear when he speaks.

2. See also *Dominus Jesus* 2, issued by Congregation of the Doctrine of the Faith on August 6, 2000.

PART IV

CHRISTOLOGY AND THE CHRISTIAN LIFE

CHAPTER 22

On the Grace of Humility

The University Church of St. Mary
the Virgin, Quinquagesima Sunday,
February 13, 1994

The title of this University Sermon is significant. Observe that I am to speak "On the *Grace* of Humility." Humility is a grace, which suggests two points. First, humility is not a natural human endowment like one's intellectual ability or artistic aptitude. As human beings we do not innately possess humility. It is not a part of our genetic makeup. We are born in a humble state—naked and helpless—but we are not born humble. Second, the title of this sermon intimates that humility, being a grace, is a work of God in each of our lives. He alone bestows humility upon us as a free gift, as a *gratia*, as a grace. Precisely because humility is a grace, it must come from God.

But if humility comes from God as a free gift to us, it must be that God is himself humble. The medieval schoolmen were fond of the maxim *Nemo dat quod non habet* "no one gives what he does not possess." God can give us humility only if humility is his to give.

Normally we do not think of God being humble. As a matter of fact, humility seems incongruous with how we normally conceive him. Within the Jewish/Christian tradition, God is believed to be almighty, all-powerful, all-knowing, and all-perfect. He is the fullness of life and being. He exists in and of himself, and thus he is eternal.

Originally published as "On the Grace of Humility," *Oxford Magazine* 104 (1994): 8–10. Reprinted by permission.

God is the all-powerful Creator who creates, as only he can do, *ex nihilo* "out of nothing." Only by his habitual will does anything continue in existence. Nothing escapes his Lordship. He governs creation with his inscrutable wisdom and guides the course of history with his universal providence. The prophet Isaiah asks, "Who has measured the waters in the hollow of his hand and marked off the heavens with a span, enclosed the dust of the earth in a measure, and weighed the mountains in scales and the hills in a balance?" Isaiah answers that "It is [God] who sits above the circle of the earth and its inhabitants are like grasshoppers; [it is he] who stretches out the heavens like a curtain and spreads them like a tent to live in; [he] brings princes to naught, and makes the rulers of the earth as nothing" (Is. 40:12, 40:23–24).

These divine attributes, qualities, and titles hardly seem to be the endowments out of which humility is fashioned. How can someone of this stature be humble? One might even argue that God may be the only being who could actually be proud without sinning. Could not God, rightly and in truth, be proud of himself? What we discover, however, is that God is not proud. Instead he defines what it means to be humble.

It is in fact, within the very act of creating, an act that only he can perform, that the almighty and all-powerful God first manifested his humility. In the act of creating, God revealed his desire to associate with someone other than himself, someone immensely beneath his own status as God, for anything that is not God is by definition immensely inferior to him. As the above passage from Isaiah implies, the act of God creating us would be similar to our creating grasshoppers, doing so only because we wanted to live in fellowship with grasshoppers. But God did not make us grasshoppers. He created us in his own image and likeness not for his benefit but for ours. Being in the image and likeness of God, we are endowed with intelligence and will. Thus we are empowered to associate with the all-powerful and almighty God in a rational and personal way. We can know God and know that he knows us. We can experience his love and in turn we can love him. In humility, God created us so that as human beings we could participate in his own divine life. So humble is God that he did not hoard his divine prerogatives, but instead desired to share his divine status with us even though we in ourselves are far beneath his divine stature.

In light of creation a rather curious question now appears on the horizon. The question is not whether God is humble enough to be found in our presence. The act of creation itself reveals that he is. The question is: "Are we as human beings humble enough to associate with God?" The absurdity of answering "no" is readily apparent, and yet that is exactly what we as the human race have done. "No" resounds throughout the whole of human history, and its echo today reverberates louder than ever before.

The story of the Fall of Adam and Eve is the story of us all. Adam and Eve were tempted not just to eat some forbidden fruit—the real temptation was the prospect of becoming gods themselves. The serpent assured them that, if they ate from the tree, their eyes would be opened and they would become like God, knowing good and evil (Gen. 3:4–5). We as human beings, in the end, are not humble enough to walk with God. We as mankind separated ourselves from God, and we as individuals continue to do so for the sole end that we ourselves might become gods. Pride—the desire to be God, to determine for ourselves what is right and wrong, to live separate from and independent of God—is the primordial and ever-present sin, rooted in us all.

But notice the type of god we have become. In our rebellion we have not become like the humble God who created us. We have become gods of pride who seek our own power, well-being, and self-indulgence. In our defiant attempt to become like God, we have not become like God at all.

Now it is in this situation that the humility of God is most clearly manifested. So great is God's humble desire to live with us, and so great is his love in wanting us to live with him, that, despite our prideful rebellion, he determined to do everything in his power to win us back to himself. And how was this divine power manifested? It was manifested in supreme humility.

God the Father sent his eternal and beloved Son into the world of creation, into the world infected by sin. The Son of God came to exist as a man. The Creator came to exist as a creature. As Paul states, "For you know the grace of our Lord Jesus Christ, that though he was rich, yet for your sake he became poor, so that by his poverty you might become rich" (2 Cor. 8:9). The grace of our Lord Jesus Christ resided in his humility. Though rich in divinity, he became poor in our humanity that we might become rich in his divinity.

The Son of God did not just assume some generic humanity or a humanity sanitized from evil. He came in the likeness of sinful flesh (Rom. 8:3) and so experienced all the evil effects that our sin has begotten. He was not immune from suffering. He was not immune from death.

The hymn in Paul's Letter to the Philippians is a hymn to the humility of God, an anthem to the humility of Jesus (Phil. 2:6–11). "Though he was in the form of God, he did not count equality with God a thing to be grasped." Jesus did not cry out in divine pride, "I am God! I will not demean my divine status! I will not become a mere man—a grasshopper." Rather, he "emptied himself, taking the form of a servant, being born in the likeness of men." Jesus hid his eternal glory not just by becoming a man, but also by becoming a servant, a slave to us who were sinners. "And being found in human form he humbled himself and became obedient unto death." So humble was Jesus that as an obedient servant he died for us, offering his life for us in love, so that we might be cleansed of sin and reconciled to the Father who created us. But his death was not a death with dignity. So humble was he that he died, "even death on the cross." The Cross is the supreme icon of the humility of God. To gaze upon the Cross and to recognize in faith that it is the eternal Son of God in the flesh who hangs there is to perceive that no one is more humble than God himself. And it is in this supreme act of humility, a humility that first showed itself when he created us, that God destroys our pride and makes possible once more our life with him. As Paul states, "For the foolishness of God is wiser than men, and the weakness of God is stronger than men" (1 Cor. 1:25). Ultimately, the humility of God triumphs over the pride of men.

Jesus's resurrected glory, his supreme Lordship, is founded upon his supreme humility. The Philippian hymn concludes that because of the humility of Jesus, even to death on the Cross, "God has highly exalted him and bestowed on him the name which is above every name, that at the name of Jesus every knee should bow, in heaven and earth and under the earth, and every tongue confess that Jesus Christ is Lord, to the glory of God the Father" (Phil. 2:8–11). There is no one greater than Jesus because there is no one more humble. He is exalted in glory above everyone else because no one has been more lowly. Every knee should bow before him because no one has been more abject. He alone should be proclaimed as supreme Lord of every race and nation and people because no one else is more a servant. Jesus's exaltation by the Father is in direct proportion to his humility.

Nemo dat quod non habet "no one gives what he does not possess." In light of creation and especially in light of the Cross, we recognize that only God can give us the grace of humility. But how do we receive this gift of humility, which will once more transform us from being prideful gods, which is not to be like God at all, into being in the true likeness of God? We receive the grace of humility by associating ourselves with the humble acts of God. As Paul states just prior to beginning the Philippian hymn, "Have this mind among you as was in Christ Jesus" (Phil. 2:5). Our mind should be that of the humble bearing of Jesus.

If God was humble enough to create us so that he could associate with us, his creatures, our first act of humility, the first grace of humility, is for us to acknowledge that we are indeed creatures whom God has created. In humility we acknowledge that God is God the Creator and we are his creatures. The grace of humility demands that we do not attempt to usurp the place of God, to make ourselves into gods. We associate with and relate to God not as his equals, but as the creatures we truly are. It is upon this foundational truth that we establish our life with God.

Ultimately, all that we possess as individual human beings comes from God the Creator. We are not the source of our intelligence, or our freedom, or our human dignity. They were given to us when God created us in his own image. Therefore, as Paul states, "What have you that you did not receive? If then you received it, why do you boast as if it were not a gift?" (1 Cor. 4:7). As human beings we are unique in all of creation, but this boast of ours finds its source in the Creator God, who humbly made us in his own likeness.

If the Son of God was humble enough to become man in the likeness of sinful flesh, then our second act of humility, the second grace of humility, is for us to acknowledge that we are indeed the sinful flesh in whose likeness Jesus came. If Jesus was humble enough to die for our sin, then we, in humility, must acknowledge that it was for our sin, my sin, that he died. If Jesus humbly accepted our condemnation in humility, it is only right that we acknowledge that it was our condemnation, my condemnation, that he assumed. The Cross not only makes visible the humble love of God, it also makes visible the sinful pride of man, and it is in humility that we acknowledge the truth that we are indeed the sinners for whom Jesus humbly accepted the Cross.

Repentance, the acknowledgment of our sin in sorrow and the accepting of forgiveness in Christ, is truly a humble act, but it is an indispensable feature of the grace of humility. Without the humble act of repentance, we are incapable of drawing near to the all-holy God. Yet this humble act of repentance brings with it a boast. Paul could cry out, "Let him who boasts, boast of the Lord" (2 Cor. 10:17). Why could Paul boast in the Lord? He could boast because, in and through repentance, he gloried "in the cross of our Lord Jesus Christ, by which the world has been crucified to me, and I to the world" (Gal. 6:14). Paul knew that, through the Cross, Jesus had freed him from the world of sin. In Christ, Paul was now dead to the world of pride.

He could boast in the Lord also because it was in the risen Lord that he boasted. Jesus is risen, and through faith and baptism Paul not only died to sin, but he had now also risen with Christ. In Christ, Paul had become a new creation. In Christ, Paul was a new man. No longer did Paul need to live in the flesh of sin, for he could now live by the power of the Spirit who dwelt within him. No longer was he an enemy of the Father, but in Christ, through the Spirit, he had been transformed into a son of God. In Christ, Paul's life was now hidden in God. And being a son of the Father, he could look forward to becoming an heir, with Christ, to the same glorious Resurrection. This was Paul's boast—by humbly uniting himself to Jesus, he came to share in the glory of God.

The acknowledgment of our sin in repentance is a humble act. To place our faith in the risen Jesus as our Lord and Saviour is a humble act. As exemplified in the life and words of Paul, however, by humbly associating ourselves with Jesus we come to share in his glory. As it was for Jesus, so it is for us. Our glory, our exaltation by the Father, is in direct proportion to our humility. To assume the likeness of God, to be transformed into the glory of Jesus, is to assume the humility of God, the humility of Jesus. The work of the grace of humility in our lives now becomes the source of our eternal grandeur.

But the original question once more looms upon the horizon, the question that confronted our first parents, Adam and Eve. While God is humble enough to associate with us, are we humble enough to associate with him? Are we humble enough to associate with Jesus—in the folly of the Cross—so as to be transformed into his likeness?

The question today is not just whether you and I are humble enough to believe in God or place our faith in Jesus within the solitude of our own hearts. If left to ourselves, each of us may possess the humility needed to associate with God and Jesus through repentance and in faith. Today it is the public nature of faith that is the greatest test to humility. The question today is whether we possess the humility to associate with God, to have faith in Jesus, within a culture where such belief is often belittled and those who believe are often thought naive. In the past, to believe in God or to be a Christian was what was expected. It required less humility. But today a person not only needs to be humble before God in order to believe, but a person also must be willing to be humble before men, for the believer today faces cultural opposition and even contempt.

The Holy Spirit must double the grace of humility when it comes to us who live and work within today's academic community, for it is within the academy that all the cultural and intellectual opposition to faith converges and is encountered most intensely. Within the academic community today the prospect of believing in God has become an embarrassing proposition. One might say that within the polite society of our technological, scientific, and sophisticated world of academe, it can be rather humbling—"humiliating" might be the better word—to be caught fraternizing with God, unless it be on formal and established occasions such as the present one. Even more, to regard Jesus as any more than a good man is considered fanatical by many. So embarrassing have God and Jesus become that even some of those who say they do believe, even Church members and theologians, can be at times tempted to assure everyone, especially the intellectually sophisticated, that they do not really believe anything that seems incredible to the unbeliever.

The heart of the problem for us academics today, who are faced with questions of faith and humility, is that to believe in God, in all that that entails, could be viewed as jeopardizing our academic credentials. Not only could we be considered devotees of archaic superstitions, but also, even worse, such religious persuasion could be regarded as undermining our objectivity and credibility as scholars and as intellectuals. Faith is perceived to subvert our academic freedom and our intellectual autonomy. Belief in God so prejudices our minds, it is thought, that our whole integrity as serious scholars is called into question. To be a Christian scholar, to take Jesus and his Gospel seriously, to hold in faith the teachings of the Christian Church, and at the same time be an academic looks to some to be a metaphysical impossibility. Such an animal cannot exist.

This may be called the third grace of humility, a grace not absent from the great Christian scholars of Oxford past and present—that of humbly identifying with the visible body of Christ, the Church, and so regarding our lives within the visible Church as our greatest temporal honor. If there is any truth to what I have just said, to be a man or woman of faith within the academic community today, one may need to speak not of the *grace* of humility but of the *miracle* of humility, for only if one is humble will one be willing to profess one's faith in a milieu that is often hardly conducive to or appreciative of it.

I conclude this sermon by asking a few questions of all of us who are giving our lives to the noble adventure of education and to the pursuit of knowledge. Although we may be experts in our own respective disciplines, does not the knowledge of our own ignorance—that which we are striving mightily yet to know—give voice to humility within us, whispering that there must be a God who knows it all because he is ultimately responsible for its creation? Is not he the one whom we ought humbly to reverence in awe? While we may rightly boast of our academic achievements, do we not have to admit that these accomplishments have not stopped us from sinning? We may be professional scholars, but we are also personal sinners whose minds are often ruled not by wisdom but by greed, lust, rivalry, resentment, and the fear and anxiety that spring from pride. Is not the recognition of our own sinfulness the voice of humility whispering that we need the transforming grace of the Holy Spirit? Do not our own lives whisper the humble truth that we need Jesus to save us from ourselves and to provide us, as our Lord, with the wisdom and power that comes from God? Finally, does not the prospect of our own death allow the grace of humility to whisper to our hearts that to know everything without the knowledge of God is to know nothing of lasting value—that to know God, even if we are ignorant of a great deal, is to know everything of eternal worth?

The Letter of James proclaims: "Humble yourselves before the Lord and he will exalt you" (Jas. 4:10). We have seen that the omnipotent and eternal God possesses the grace of humility needed to exalt us. But do we possess the grace of humility needed to allow him to do so?

And now to that same God, Father, Son, and Holy Spirit be ascribed as is most justly due, Majesty, Dominion, and Power henceforth and forever more. Amen.

CHAPTER 23

You Shall Call His
Name Jesus

Names: The Genealogy of Jesus

In the opening chapter of his Gospel, Matthew names forty-six people. The vast majority are the names that make up Jesus's genealogy. They are his ancestors going back to Abraham.

Most of these people are significant in many ways—Abraham was the father of the Jewish nation; the Moabite Ruth was faithful to her Israelite mother-in-law, Naomi; David was the great king who killed Goliath and conquered the Philistines; Solomon, the Wise, built the temple. The primary reason these people are included in this genealogy, and so categorically named, is for the sake of the genealogy itself. What each may have done, good or bad, during the course of their lives finds its ultimate significance in that they begot a son or a son was begotten of them. Abraham may be the exemplar of obedient faith, but his importance lies in the fact that he begot Isaac. If he had not begotten Isaac, his faith would have not been remembered. Ruth may have devotedly followed Naomi, but her virtue would not have been recorded within history if she had not married Boaz and became the mother of Obed. David may have conquered nations and so became Israel's greatest king, but that would be of little import had he not begotten Solomon. Solomon may have been wise and built a magnificent temple to the one true God, but if he had not begotten Rehoboam, his reign would hard-

Originally published as "You Shall Call His Name Jesus," *Voices: Women for Faith and Family* 28, no. 1 (2013): 27–29. Reprinted by permission.

ly merit a footnote in an obscure scholarly journal. What gives all of these named people historical (and theological) significance is that they make up a genealogy, a history of begetting that terminates with a man named Joseph.

After so many hundreds of years, this genealogy comes to an abrupt halt because Joseph did not beget anyone. While all of his named male ancestors merit to be included in this genealogy because they each begot a son, Joseph merits to be included in the genealogy ironically because he did *not* beget a son. Joseph is present in the genealogy because of whom he married, not because of who he begot. He is "the husband of Mary, of whom Jesus was born, who is called Christ" (Mt. 1:16). The history and nature of Jesus's genealogy teach us two divinely revealed truths.

The Name "Jesus": A Divine Father and a Human Mother

The first truth is that, unlike all of his ancestors, Jesus has no human father. Jesus has no earthly, historical, human father because he has a heavenly, eternal, divine Father. Prior to the Incarnation, he possessed no human name, but he did possess a divine name. From all eternity, God the Father begot God the Son. As the Father eternally and simply bears the name "Father," for that is wholly who he is in the begetting of his Son, so the Son eternally and simply bears the name Son, for that is wholly who he is in being begotten of the Father. To name God the Father "Father," and to name God the Son "Son," is to define exactly who they are. God the Father is wholly and completely the Father of the Son, and God the Son is wholly and completely Son of the Father.

The second truth is that, while Jesus has no human father because he is the eternal divine Son of the heavenly Father, he *does* have a human and earthly mother. The eternal Son of the eternal Father became flesh in the womb of Mary through the overshadowing of the Holy Spirit. Having become man, the Son now possesses not only the divine name "Son," but also the human name "Jesus." Having been conceived and born of Mary, this human name of the Son of God incarnate—Jesus—is extremely important.

Although the name "Jesus" is a human and earthly name, the person who bears it does so by divine decree. The infancy narrative in Matthew's Gospel makes this evident. In a dream the angel of the Lord said to Joseph, "Joseph, son of David, do not fear to take Mary your wife, for that which is conceived in her is of the Holy Spirit; she will bear a son and you shall call his name Jesus, for he will save his people from their sins" (Mt. 1:20–21). Mary conceived by the Holy Spirit, and so the Son has not a human father but the divine Father. Nonetheless, who is conceived in her is a human being—a man—and so that man, who is the Son of the Father, is to be called by a human name: Jesus. Joseph did not have relations with his wife prior to the birth of her son, and when this son was born of Mary, Joseph "called his name Jesus" (Mt. 1:25). As God the Father eternally bestowed the divine name "Son" upon his only begotten, so Joseph, the earthly icon of the heavenly Father, bestows, on behalf the heavenly Father, the temporal name "Jesus" upon the incarnate Son of the Father.

At this juncture, it is important to perceive one marvelous divinely revealed truth. Just as the divine name "Son" fully designates that the Son is wholly and entirely simply the Son of the Father, so does the human name "Jesus": "Yahweh-YHWH Saves" fully designates that Jesus is wholly and entirely simply our divine Savior. The Name of God, YHWH, revealed to Moses, is considered unpronounceable. In the Bible the "unpronounceable tetragrammaton" (four letters of YHWH) is traditionally rendered as "LORD" (in Hebrew, *Adonai*; in Greek, *Kyrios*; in Latin, *Dominus*), sometimes as "Jehovah" or "Yahweh."

As the divine name "Son" reveals who the Son personally is in his *divine* totality, so his human name "Jesus" reveals who he personally is in his *incarnate* totality. As the name "Son" defines him as God, so the name "Jesus" defines him as man. "You [Joseph] will call his name Jesus, for he will save his people from their sins" (Mt. 1:22). Human names such as Henry, James, Susan, and Jane do not define the person who bears the name. But the name "Jesus" does define, and so reveal, who he is; the heavenly Son is in our midst as an earthly man, and he is in our midst as "Yahweh-YHWH Saves." When Joseph, in accordance with the will of the Father, named the son of Mary "Jesus," he defined precisely, accurately, and completely the one who bears that name. A few examples illustrate and develop this divine truth.

The Word Became Flesh and the Name of Jesus

When we consider a painting of the Annunciation or peer into the Christmas crib, what do we see? In the Annunciation we find Gabriel appearing to

Mary, informing her that she "will conceive in her womb and bear a son" by the overshadowing of the Holy Spirit and that his name is to be called Jesus (Lk. 1:26–38). In the act of assuming our sinful humanity, the Son of God initiated our salvation, and in so doing Jesus became *Jesus*—the One who would save us from our sins. The incarnational act, the act of being conceived in Mary's womb by the power of the Holy Spirit, is itself a saving act, and so it is the first act by which Jesus does not simply receive his name but actually *acquires* his name by *enacting* his name, for in this act of becoming one with mankind he begins to actualize who he is—Jesus, the One who saves.

Similarly, when we gaze upon the nativity scene, we see a child who just came forth from the womb of his mother Mary. This birth, as with his conception, is a saving act by which the Son of God incarnate is once again becoming who he is. In being born into the world, Jesus more fully enacted his name. Being named "Jesus" defines his act of birth as a saving act, and this saving act of birth more fully conforms Jesus into the very likeness of his name—the God who saves. Joseph can rightly, without any hesitation, name his foster son "Jesus," for through his incarnation and birth he has truly become who he authentically is—Jesus.

The Paschal Mystery and the Name of Jesus

The Paschal Mystery of Jesus's death and resurrection are two of the most notable examples of Jesus fulfilling his name. When we gaze and meditate upon the Cross, we see a crucified man suffering and dying. This man has a name, and his name is Jesus. His name manifests to us that the action that he is performing on the Cross is an act of salvation. Jesus, the Son incarnate, is offering his holy and innocent life to his Father as a pure sacrifice for the salvation of the world. On the Cross, Jesus is fully enacting his name and so totally conforming himself into the very definition of his name—"Yahweh-YHWH Saves." Jesus crucified is the perfect living icon of his name, of who he is.

In raising Jesus gloriously from the tomb, God the Father verifies that his Son's sacrificial death on the Cross saved us from sin and so reconciled us to him. In the Resurrection the Father does not simply confirm that his incarnate Son was not misnamed, but he elevates Jesus to the fullness of being Jesus—the risen glorious Savior and Lord.

On the first Easter evening Jesus appears to his disciples, breathes upon them, and proclaims, "Receive the Holy Spirit" (Jn. 20:22). Jesus is *re-creating* those who believe in him. He is making them a new creation through the indwelling of the Holy Spirit. He is transforming them into children of his Father (Rom. 8:12–17). This Easter breathing-forth of the Holy Spirit, as confirmed at Pentecost, is an *everlasting* breathing-forth. In this endless heavenly outpouring of new life, Jesus, as the risen Lord and Savior, conforms himself into who he is—Jesus, in whom we have the forgiveness of our sins and the eternal life of the Holy Spirit. At the throne of his Father, our crucified and risen Lord will forever bear the humble name Jesus, for he is now and will forever be "Yahweh-YHWH Saves."

The Eucharist and the Name of Jesus

As the risen Lord, Jesus continually makes present in his very person his saving mysteries and so continually enacts his name as Savior. This is especially true within the seven Sacraments. The Eucharist, as the consummate sacrament, illustrates this act.

Within the Eucharistic liturgy, Jesus, in making himself present within time and history, makes his one sacrifice present, the sacrifice by which he reconciled us to the Father. Those who participate in the Eucharistic liturgy unite themselves to this one sacrifice, and so share in and reap the benefits of the act by which Jesus saved us. By sharing in his one sacrifice, we are empowered by his Spirit to receive the risen Jesus—truly and really present in the Eucharist. In the Eucharist, in his sacrifice, and in his risen presence, we are in communion with Jesus *being* Jesus, for here and now he is enacting his saving name on our behalf, the name/person in whom we, through the indwelling Spirit, have access to the Father.

The name "Jesus" does not simply inform us of who he was and what he did in the past, but his person and name possess ever-contemporary consequences. Since Jesus is risen, he continually enacts his name as the one in our midst—as he who saves. For the Eucharist, being is the most eminent manner through which his name continues to embody the *living reality* of who Jesus is.

The Second Coming and the Name of Jesus

All of the above past events, from the conception of Jesus to his resurrection, anticipate the future. This future is clearly perceived in the liturgy of the Eucharist. In the Eucharist the past salvific deeds, the Paschal Mysteries, are made present in order that we might share in them now, and the present partaking of these mysteries is already in itself a participatory foretaste of their fulfillment in the future. The earthly Eucharistic banquet is a living prefiguring of and anticipatory communion in the heavenly banquet.

When he comes again in glory, Jesus will fully become our Savior and thus fully become "Jesus." Coming in glory, Jesus will raise all of the faithful gloriously from the dead so that they might share in the fullness of his glory, and thus obtain everlasting life with the Father in the fellowship of the Holy Spirit. In this final and consummate act of salvation, this concluding act of history, Jesus will fully consummate his name. He will be Jesus *fully in act* because he will be our Savior fully in act. Having fully enacted his name, we, as members of Jesus's Body, will be fully in act, fully who we were eternally meant to be; for now, in full communion with the risen Christ, we will finally be transformed by the Spirit into the perfect likeness of Jesus himself.

In our becoming fully who we are at the end of time, Jesus will give us a new name that, like his own, will precisely define and so reveal completely who we are in our personal identity. Our new name and who we are in our totality will, like Jesus and his name, be one. "To him who conquers ... I will give him a white stone, with a new name written on the stone which no one knows except him who receives it" (Rev. 2:17). (Revelation, chapter 2, tells of Christ addressing the seven churches, admonishing them to be faithful and announcing their reward for conquering sin. Though the churches are addressed singly, the Lord's message can be seen to apply to all members of his Body.) This secret name will become manifest to all of the saints and angels so that the whole of creation will recognize who we truly are and therefore why we, in communion with Jesus our Savior and Lord, have conquered sin and death and merited in him our eternal reward.

In this present sacred interim where we look forward to and grow into the likeness of Jesus, we groan to be set free from sin and death as we await the full revelation of our sonship (Rom. 8:18–25). But our groaning is merely a faint echo of the groaning of Jesus himself. As the head of his Body, the Church, Jesus groans more intensely and deeply than we as he resolutely endeavors and relentlessly labors to perfect this Body. Only when his Body comes to full maturity, and so ceases to groan, will Jesus cease to groan, for only then will he have attained the fullness of his name—Jesus, God who saves.

Jesus: In No Other Name

From the above it is clearly evident why we have salvation in no other name than Jesus (Acts 4:12). Only Jesus rightfully bears the name "Jesus," because only Jesus, through who he is as the incarnate Son and what he has done through his life, death, and resurrection, has become the universal and definitive Savior, and thus the singular and only Lord of heaven and earth. No one else deservedly, rightly, or properly bears the name of Jesus—neither Buddha, nor the Hindu gods and goddesses, nor Mohammed, nor anyone else to come—for they have not enacted nor will any ever enact that name; they have not become nor will any ever become "Yahweh-YHWH Saves." Only Jesus is Jesus.

The hymn in St. Paul's Letter to the Philippians proclaims the truth of Jesus and His name:

Though he was in the form of God, he did not count equality with God a thing to be grasped, but emptied himself, taking the form of a servant, being born in the likeness of men. And being found in human form he humbled himself and became obedient unto death, even death on the cross.

Therefore, God has highly exalted Him and bestowed on Him the name which is above every name, that at the name of JESUS every knee should bow, in heaven and on earth and under the earth, and every tongue confess that Jesus Christ is Lord, to the glory of God the Father. (Phil. 2:6–11)

CHAPTER 24

The Lifting-Up
of Jesus

In the course of Lent, the Paschal Triduum, and the subsequent Easter season of 2010, I pondered the biblical image of the "lifting-up" of Jesus. The Gospel of John, frequently proclaimed in the liturgy during these seasons, provides the biblical basis for this image. The first reference begins with Jesus telling Nicodemus, "No one has ascended into heaven but he who descended from heaven, the Son of Man. And as Moses lifted up the serpent in the wilderness, so must the Son of Man be lifted up, that whoever believes in him may have eternal life" (Jn. 3:13–14). As Moses's lifting-up of the serpent brought healing to the sinful Israelites, so the lifting-up of the Son of Man will bring eternal life to those who believe in him. What are the people to believe? "When you have lifted up the Son of Man, then you will know that I am he" (Jn. 8:28). In the lifting-up of the Son of Man, people will come to recognize and so believe that Jesus is truly God—*ego emi* "I am he." Moreover, it is in this lifting-up that Jesus will draw all men to himself. "'I, when I am lifted up from the earth, will draw all men to myself.' He said this to show by what death he was to die" (Jn. 12:32–33). The Jews protested that Christ is to remain forever and so not die. "How can you say that the Son of Man must be lifted up?" (Jn. 12:34). With these passages in mind, I develop their biblical, liturgical, and theological significance.

Originally published as "The Lifting Up of Jesus," *Adoremus Bulletin* 16, no. 4 (2010): 5, 8. Reprinted by permission.

The Cross

The "lifting-up," in the first instance, refers to the Cross. It is on the Cross that Jesus fulfills and completes the prefigurement of Moses lifting up the serpent. Through Jesus's death on the Cross, humankind is healed of the evil of sin and reconciled to the Father. Although the lifting-up on the Cross was intended to be an instrument of death, in being lifted-up on the Cross, Jesus put death to death. Death died on the Cross because the Cross is the supreme expression of Jesus's love both for the Father and for all of humankind. Love is stronger than death. So much did Jesus love the Father that he was willing, as the obedient Son, to offer in love his life to the Father as an atoning sacrifice for sin. So much did Jesus love humankind that he willingly offered in love his life as an atoning sacrifice on our behalf. It is the twofold offering in love that humanly manifests Jesus's divine love and so reveals, as the centurion recognized, that Jesus truly is the Son of God (Mk. 15:30)—the great "I AM." Through the Cross, Jesus draws humankind to himself, for it is as the crucified Savior that people will come to faith in him as the loving divine Son of the Father and so obtain eternal life. This lifting-up on the Cross is "the hour," for through it the Father reveals his Son's eternal divine glory. He "lifted up his eyes to heaven and said, 'Father, the hour has come; glorify your Son that the Son may glorify you, since you have given him power over all flesh, to give eternal life to all whom you have given him. And this is eternal life, that they know you the only true God, and Jesus Christ whom you have sent'" (Jn. 17:1–3).

This threefold Johannine proclamation of Jesus being lifted up upon the Cross finds its liturgical expression in the Good Friday *Celebration of the Lord's Passion*, where the crucifix is lifted up before the congregation three times and the minister thrice proclaims: "This is the wood of the cross, on which hung the Savior of the world." Through this liturgical action, Jesus draws to himself all who gaze upon the crucifix, calling them to believe that he truly is the divine Son of the Father—"I am he." Although it is the crucified Jesus that is displayed before the congregation, such a lifting-up bears witness to the hour of Jesus's glory as the divine Savior of the world. The faithful are therefore summoned to adore him: "Come, let us worship." The king of the Jews has now also become the Savior of all humankind throughout all ages.

The Resurrection and Ascension

While the "lifting-up" initially refers to the Cross, there is also embedded within that lifting-up the reality of Jesus's resurrection and ascension. Actually, it is because Jesus willingly, in love, allowed himself to be lifted up upon the Cross that the Father lifts him up to the new and glorious life of the Resurrection. "When he had made purification for sins, he sat down at the right hand of the Majesty on high, having become as much superior to angels as the name he has obtained is more excellent than theirs" (Heb. 1:3–4). The lifting-up of the Resurrection bears witness to the salutary effects of Jesus's twofold loving atoning sacrifice. "We see Jesus, who for a little while was made lower than the angels, crowned with glory and honor because of the suffering of death" (Heb. 2:9). So pleased was the Father with Jesus lifting himself up upon the Cross that he would not allow his holy one see corruption, and so the Father lifted Jesus up from the dead so that he might ascend and sit at his right hand in glory (Acts 2:25–33). Even though the Son was divine by nature, he humbled himself by becoming man. Being found in human form, "he humbled himself and became obedient unto death, even death on the cross." It was because of his humble, obedient love that the Father "highly exalted him and bestowed on him the name which is above every name, that at the name of Jesus every knee should bow, in heaven and on earth and under the earth, and every tongue confess that Jesus Christ is Lord, to the glory of God the Father" (Phil. 2:6–11).

Jesus reaps the first fruits of the efficacy of his own sacrificial lifting-up by being the first to be lifted up gloriously from the tomb—sin and death having been vanquished in his very person as the Son of God incarnate. "Although he was a Son, he learned obedience through what he suffered, and being made perfect he became the source of eternal salvation to all who obey him, being designated by God a high priest after the order of Melchizedek" (Heb. 5:9). The Resurrection is the perfection of Jesus's humanity, for through his priestly offering of that humanity on the Cross, he conquered through obedient love, sin, and death and so obtained perfection not only for himself but also for all who believe in him. Jesus, in exaltation, is lifted up as the everlasting glorious High Priest, forever making intercession on behalf of humankind (Heb. 7:25). The Resurrection and ascension is the Father's answer to the question put to Jesus by the Jews: Since the Christ must remain forever, how can the Son of Man be lifted up (Jn. 12:34)? The lifting-up is twofold: the Cross and Resurrection, the first in time and the second forever.

As with the Good Friday celebration, so there is a threefold lifting-up of the risen Jesus at the Easter Vigil under the symbol of the Paschal Candle. With each lifting-up the minister intones, "Christ our light." It is the lifted-up crucified and risen Savior who is now the salvific light in the darkness of the world of sin and death and it is this light—the light of divine truth and the light of divine life—that draws all humankind to Jesus, the lamb once slain who now lives forever (Rev. 5:9–14). The light of the Paschal Candle also bears witness to the triumphant glory of the Cross and so now to Jesus's never-ending resurrected/ascended glorification by the Father in the Holy Spirit. The Paschal Candle is also the light of our hope, for as we die with Jesus in our baptism, sharing his tomb, so are we lifted up with him to newness of life (Rom. 6:3-4). The indwelling of the Holy Spirit is the guarantee, the first down payment, of our own anticipated glorious lifting up at the end of time (2 Cor. 1:22; Eph. 1:13–14).

The Begetting of the Son

Jesus prayed that the Father would give him the glory that he possessed from the beginning. The Father answered that prayer both in the lifting-up on the Cross and in the lifting-up of the Resurrection/ascension. This twofold historical lifting-up provides a revelatory window to what is eternally the case. The Cross and Resurrection may be the earthly referent to the lifting-up, but the primordial referent to this lifting-up is the Father's eternal begetting of his Son. Here is the eternal heavenly foundation for the earthly lifting-up on the Cross in time and the historical lifting-up of Jesus into heaven at his Resurrection. From all eternity, the Father, in begetting his Son in the love of the Holy Spirit, lifted him up in that he shared with him the whole of his deity. In the paternal love of the Spirit, the Father poured out the whole of himself in the begetting of his Son, and in so doing he lifted up his Son so that his Son would be God as he himself is God.

The Son, as the true image and perfect likeness of the Father, gives himself completely to the Father in the filial love of the Spirit. As the Father is defined as Father in the complete giving of himself to the Son in the love of the Spirit, so the Son is defined as Son in the complete giving of himself to the Father in the same love of the Spirit. The Father eternally rejoices in the Son's complete love for him as his Son, and the Son eternally rejoices in the Father's complete love for him as his Father. This mutual love of the Holy Spirit motivates the Father to glorify the Son and motivates the Son to glorify the Father within their eternal Trinitarian life, and it also motivates them to desire to glorify one another before others. Creation, especially the creation of human beings, provides the Father the opportunity to lift up his Son so that all would recognize what he sees from all eternity—the glorious splendor of his all-loving and faithful Son. Creation also provides the opportunity for the Son to lovingly glorify his Father, in the very act of being lifted up, thus manifesting to all of humankind the eternal loving kindness of his Father. The Cross and Resurrection thus become the earthly historical events, events for all to see and hear and even touch, through which the Father lifts up and glorifies the Son in the love of the Spirit, and the Son, in being lifted up in glory, glorifies the Father in the same love of the Spirit. Having witnessed, in the lifting-up upon the Cross and in the Resurrection, the divine splendor of the Son, human beings and all of the creation are drawn to him and in faith proclaim him Lord and Savior to the glory of God the Father (Phil. 2:11).

The Eucharistic Liturgy

The sacrifice of the Mass not only recalls the past historical events of the Cross and Resurrection, but also makes present these mysteries so that the faithful are able to share in their reality and partake of their benefits. In numerous words and actions, Jesus is lifted up within the Eucharistic liturgy. These words and actions are efficacious in that through them the reality of which they symbolize is made present so that the faithful can partake of them.

The Mass is composed of two parts—the liturgy of the Word and the liturgy of the Eucharist. In both parts, Jesus is lifted up in various ways. In the liturgy of the Word, this is primarily enacted in the proclaiming, the lifting up, of the Word, especially in the process of the Book of the Gospel, the solemn incensing of it, and its being lifted up at the end of the proclamation with the intoning "The Gospel of the Lord." The congregation responds, "Praise to you Lord, Jesus Christ." In the proclamation of the Scriptures, particularly the Gospel, with the accompanying actions, Jesus as the eternal Word, the eternal Truth of God, is being lifted up, but not simply as the eternal Word begotten as Son before the ages. It is primarily Jesus, the incarnate Word, who spoke human words and who performed human bodily deeds who is being lifted up. This historical Gospel draws humankind to Jesus, and it is through faith in these revealed mysteries—Jesus and his salvific death and resurrection, proclaimed now in the midst of the faithful—that eternal life is obtained. Jesus is also lifted up in the homily, where the minister expounds the Scriptures so as to enflame the hearts of the faithful with love for Jesus and so profess the creed with the conviction of the Holy Spirit.

There are multiple lifting-ups within the liturgy of the Eucharist. The first is at the Offertory, where the minister offers, lifts up, the bread and wine, expressing the desire of the faithful to offer their lives in union with Christ and confidently acknowledging that the Father will find these gifts acceptable and so transform them into "the bread of life" and "spiritual drink." The second lifting-up is after the consecration of the bread and the wine. The Father having transformed through the power of the Holy Spirit the bread and wine into the risen body and risen blood of Jesus, the minister lifts them up so that the faithful in contemplating the crucified and risen Jesus might be drawn to him as their divine Savior and so obtain eternal life through faith in him. The doxology is the pinnacle of Jesus being lifted up; the rubrics themselves instruct the minister to take "the chalice and the paten with the host and, lifting them up, sings or says." The minister, speaking on behalf of the faithful, offers the risen Lord Jesus in union with his mystical body, the Church, as the one and everlasting atoning sacrifice to the Father. It is this lifting-up of Jesus that gives glory to the Father, for in this lifting-up Jesus gives to the Father the everlasting gift of himself for the salvation of the world. "Through him, with him, in him, in the unity of the Holy Spirit, all glory and honor is yours, almighty Father, forever and ever." This lifting-up is also the supreme liturgical glorification of Jesus, the supreme drawing of all to himself, for the faithful throughout the ages acknowledge through their "great Amen" that Jesus is indeed the one through whom, with whom, and in whom they are reconciled to the Father. Moreover, it is through him, with him, and in him, by the indwelling of the Holy

Spirit, that the faithful obtain eternal life with all of the saints and angels. The sacrifice of the Mass, to which all of the faithful are now united, is also symbolized by the minister slightly lifting up the host and breaking it as the sign of Jesus's broken, crucified body. The minister then places a small piece in the sacred blood, saying, "May this mingling of the body and blood of our Lord Jesus Christ bring eternal life to us who receive it." Having been united to Jesus's one sacrifice and lifted up with him to the Father, the faithful are now prepared to share in this Eucharistic sacrifice by receiving the sacred body and blood of Christ. The minister once more lifts up the host and proclaims that indeed "this is the Lamb of God who takes away the sin of the world. Happy are those who are called to his supper." In this lifting-up, Jesus is once more drawing the faithful to himself so that by receiving him in Holy Communion they might happily share in his heavenly banquet. Before receiving the body and blood of Jesus, the faithful are to make one last expression of their faith in him. As they approach the minister, he lifts up the host and proclaims, "The body of Christ," to which the faithful respond, in faith, "Amen"—so be it. The faithful now fully share in the fruit of Jesus being lifted up—lifted up on the Cross, lifted up in the Resurrection and ascension, lifted up within the Eucharistic liturgy—for they are now in communion with him, partaking in the Spirit of his risen body and blood and so becoming more fully members of his mystical body. They, too, share in his glory and sit with him at the right hand of the Father. In the begetting of his Son, in the love of the Holy Spirit, the Father eternally lifts up his Son. Now, in the same love of the Holy Spirit, the Father lifts up his adopted children by allowing them to share, through his Son's risen humanity, the same intimacy of life and love that exists within the Trinity itself.

The Definitive Lifting-Up

As the Eucharistic liturgy makes present the past lifting-up of Jesus—the Cross and Resurrection—and in so doing allows the faithful to unite themselves to these realities and partake of their benefits, so the Eucharistic liturgy foreshadows and anticipates the final and definitive lifting-up—the Second Coming of Jesus at the end of time. While Jesus will "come down" from heaven, this coming-down is actually the consummate lifting-up. As the Father bestowed all glory on his Son in the eternal begetting, the eternal lifting-up, so he will display and lift up his incarnate Son in all of his risen glory at the end of time. The whole of creation will then jubilantly cry out, "Worthy is the Lamb who was slain, to receive power and wealth and wisdom and might and honor and glory and blessing" (Rev. 5:12). This consummate lifting-up will also be the consummate drawing, for here Jesus will draw to himself all faithful men and women of every age. Here, too, the faithful will acknowledge him, in the Holy Spirit, to be the great "I AM"— the Lord of lords and King of kings. In the new Jerusalem there will be no temple, "for its temple is the Lord God the Almighty and the Lamb. And the city has no need of sun or moon to shine upon it, for the glory of God is its light, and its lamp is the Lamb. By its light shall the nations walk; and the kings of the earth shall bring their glory into it, and its gates shall never be shut by day—and there shall be not night there; they shall bring into it the glory and honor of the nations" (Rev. 21:22–26). In so doing the nations will share in the fullness of Jesus's risen life and so be lifted up with him, body and soul, to the glory of heaven. As one new man in Christ, the Son the faithful, in this consummate and everlasting lifting-up, will experience, as Spirit-filled sons and daughters, the fullness of their own fraternal fellowship and the full love and life of the Father.

CHAPTER 25

Holy Thursday and Good Friday

Jesus's Eucharistic Commentary on the Paschal Mystery

Does Jesus Present a Theology of the Cross in the Synoptic Gospels?

Many years ago, I wondered why Jesus, as portrayed in the Synoptic Gospels, did not present a more detailed understanding of the Cross. He says that he "came not to be served but to serve, and to give his life as a ransom for many (Mk. 10:45). On three occasions, he predicted that he would be handed over, be put to death, and rise on the third day (Mk. 8:31, 9:31, 10:33–34). These prophecies provide merely facts; they do not indicate why this would be the case, what its purpose would be, or what it would accomplish. No wonder the apostles did not understand what it all meant (Mk. 9:32).

St. Paul appears to have a more developed understanding of what Jesus's death on the Cross meant and what it accomplished. He tells us that because of one man's disobedience, sin and death entered the world and that through the obedience of one man many are made righteous and live (Rom. 5:12–21). He also speaks of Jesus's death as being an expiation for sin (Rom. 3:25). He also proclaims that on the Cross Jesus put to death the old sinful nature that he inherited from Adam and rose from the dead with a new and

Originally published as "Jesus' Eucharistic Commentary on the Paschal Mystery," *Adoremus Bulletin* 17, no. 5 (2011): 3–4. Reprinted by permission.

glorious humanity. In so doing he became the new man, the new Adam, the father of a new human race (Rom. 6:1–11; 1 Cor. 15:45). The entire Letter to the Hebrews offers a developed understanding of Jesus's death on the Cross and describes how it led to his glorification and our own entrance into the heavenly sanctuary. Why did Jesus not explain the theology of the Cross in a fuller manner? Humorously I surmised that although Jesus may indeed be the Word of God, he is not a very good theologian.

I pondered this point for a number of years. I knew that Jesus must have a theology of the Cross; it must be somewhere in the Synoptic Gospels, and I just had to find it. It took a while, but it finally dawned on me. Jesus did have a developed understanding, as one might expect, but he revealed it in a manner that one would not expect—at least in a manner that I would not have expected. He did not simply tell us, as did Paul, what the meaning and purpose of the Cross is. He did not say, "I am going to die on the Cross and this is what it means and this is what it will accomplish." He communicated as much in an imaginative and revelatory manner. He acted out the meaning and purpose of the Cross and in a way that we could not only understand, but also in a manner in which we ourselves could participate, and in so doing reap the benefits of his death and resurrection. (I focus primarily on the meaning and purpose of the Cross, but the Resurrection is presumed throughout this essay, and its importance will become evident, especially toward the end.)

We might think that Jesus's crucifixion and death teaches us about the meaning and purpose of the Eucharistic liturgy, and that we understand the Eucharist in the light of the Cross. Only in understanding the Cross do we perceive the reality of the Eucharistic mystery. This is not true! Actually, it is the other way around. What I finally grasped is that we understand the Cross in the light of the Eucharist. The Last Supper and its subsequent liturgical enactment reveal the meaning and purpose of the Cross and, in so doing, how his resurrection is the fruit of the Cross. The Last Supper, the Eucharistic liturgy, is Jesus's theology of the Paschal Mystery—his passion, death, and resurrection. The Eucharist is Jesus's commentary on the Paschal Mystery, a commentary that he acts out and in which he allows his apostles to participate. Jesus's theological commentary is a sacramental commentary—a liturgical commentary composed of words and actions, and into which words and actions Christ unites us to himself and so to the mystery of his saving death and life-giving resurrection. Jesus's liturgical commentary on his death and resurrection is best explained by examining the words of institution as they appear in the Roman Canon, Eucharistic Prayer One.

This Is My Body

The religious setting of the Last Supper is the traditional Jewish Passover, though scholars debate whether the Last Supper took place on the actual evening of the Passover. The Synoptics and John place the Last Supper on different days. Nonetheless, in order to grasp that the Last Supper is Jesus's commentary on his death and resurrection, it is important to place Jesus's meal with his apostles within a Passover context. As the blood of the lamb, placed on the lintels of the Jewish homes, alerted the angel of death to pass over such homes, so Jesus's death on the Cross will be his passing over from death to life. Jesus is the new Passover lamb of sacrifice who will save the people from death and allow them to pass over into life. He is also the priest of the new Passover, for he will offer himself, his own blood, his own life to free humankind from death and so empower them to enter the true Promised Land—the kingdom of God.

With this in mind, the words of institution from the Roman Canon begin: "The day before he suffered, he took bread in his sacred hands." The "day before he suffered" alerts that what Jesus does on Holy Thursday bears upon what he will do on Good Friday. Jesus's hands are sacred because his hands are the human hands of the Son of God. This is an incarnational statement: because the Son of God assumed our humanity, he possesses human hands, and because these human hands are those of the Son of God, they are sacred. These are the same holy hands that healed and blessed. Now Jesus takes bread into these same holy hands; that is, he takes himself into his hands, he takes into his hands his very own life: "and looking up to heaven, to you his almighty Father, he gave you thanks and praise." In looking up to heaven, to his almighty Father, Jesus is offering the bread that will become, momentarily, his very self. In this liturgical gesture and action, we perceive the truth of the Cross. There Jesus will actually take his life in his hands and will offer himself, his life, to his almighty Father, and he will do so with thanks and praise. As the Eucharistic liturgy illustrates, Jesus, on the Cross, looks up to his almighty Father and thanks him for the very act of salvation that he himself is now enacting on behalf of the whole of humankind. He is praising and glorifying his Father, as the author of our salvation, for his goodness and love. Jesus's act of looking up is one of love, adoration, praise, and thanksgiving to his Father. It is also a holy and loving offering of himself to the Father. We see this clearly in the continuation of the liturgical action.

"He broke the bread, gave it to his disciples, and said, 'Take this, all of you, and eat it: this is my body which will be given up for you.'" The breaking of the bread is an action that gives meaning to the Cross. On the Cross, Jesus's body will be broken, or Jesus, as priest, will break his own body in the offering of himself to the Father as a loving sacrifice for the forgiveness of sins. Not only does Jesus, in the breaking of the bread, offer his innocent and holy life to the Father in sacrifice, but he also gives the bread "to his disciples." There is a twofold sense of giving here, each bestowing meaning and understanding upon one another. The breaking of the bread is a liturgical act that finds its reality on the Cross where Jesus offers his life in sacrifice to the Father, and this action on the Cross finds its sacramental reality in Jesus giving the broken bread to his disciples. This liturgical action is a participation in Jesus's sacrifice so as to share in and reap its benefits—the forgiveness of our sins and reconciliation with the Father. The Eucharistic action confers understanding of the action of the Cross—a sacrifice to the Father, and in turn the action of the Cross provides a commentary on the Liturgical action—that those who participate in the liturgical action participate in Jesus's sacrifice of forgiveness and reconciliation.

We explicitly observe this interweaving of the liturgical action and the action of the Cross in the words and actions of institution. "Take this, all of you, and eat it: this is my body which will be given up for you." Jesus hands his disciples the broken bread, the "this" that Jesus is giving to them. What they will actually eat is not broken bread, however, but his body that will be given up for them. The "this" of broken bread is the "this" of Jesus's broken body offered in sacrifice. This liturgical action accompanied by his words is Jesus's clear commentary on the Cross. On the Cross, Jesus will give up his life to the Father for them. In turn, the life that he gave to the Father on their behalf is the same life that is now given to them in the Eucharist, and so they are made one with the one sacrifice of Jesus for the forgiveness of sins. But this is merely the first half of Jesus's Eucharistic commentary on the Paschal Mystery.

This Is My Blood

"When supper was ended, he took the cup. Again he gave you thanks and praise, gave the cup to his disciples, and said, 'Take this, all of you, and drink from it: this is the cup of my blood, the blood of the new and everlasting covenant. It will be shed for you and for all so that sins may be forgiven. Do this in memory of me.'" As Jesus took the bread in his sacred hands, so he takes the cup of wine into his sacred hands; however, now this cup will be the cup of his blood. Once again, Jesus's liturgical actions portray and his words declare that he is taking his lifeblood into his own hands. On the Cross, Jesus will actually take the cup in his own hands and offer his blood to the Father. Jesus, as he did with the bread, also gives thanks and praise to the Father in anticipation of the Cross, for the offering of his blood to his Father will be the supreme act of thanks and praise to him.

The above liturgical words and actions are confirmed in the following words of institution. "Take this, all of you, and drink from it: this is the cup of my blood, the blood of the new and everlasting covenant." The apostles are to take the cup of wine and drink from it, for it is no longer a cup of wine, but the cup of his blood. This cup contains "the blood of the new and everlasting covenant." Again, in these liturgical words and actions Jesus is informing us that on the Cross he will be offering his blood as a new covenant that will last forever. As the old covenant between God and the Israelites was confirmed in blood and so established the living union between them, so now Jesus, as the new High Priest, will offer, in love, his own holy and innocent blood to the Father. Such a sacrifice, unlike the previous sacrifices of old, truly actualizes an unbreakable and everlasting covenant of reconciliation and life between the Father and all of humankind. As Jesus declares, "It will be shed for you and for all so that sins may be forgiven." The cup of Jesus's blood, which the apostles are now to drink, is an anticipatory commentary concerning the shedding of the same blood on the Cross. Jesus's Eucharistic words and actions divinely reveal the truth contained within the Paschal Mystery of his passion, death, and resurrection—he will be shedding his blood for the forgiveness of sin and so establish a new covenant in his blood—an everlasting communion of life with his Father.

As we perceived in the words of institution over the bread, so we now recognize the same truth concerning the words over the cup; that is, while the Eucharistic words and actions manifest what will take place on the Cross, so now, having grasped the truth of the Cross, we recognize what is also actually taking place in the Eucharist. The Eucharist makes present the Paschal Mystery, and so we actually participate in the salvific work of the Cross, in the shedding of Jesus's blood, and thus reap the benefits of the Cross: reconciliation and everlasting life with the Father. Jesus makes this evident in his final sentence: "Do this in memory of me." The "do this" refers to the Last Supper, the Eucharistic liturgy, and in doing "this" we not only recall Jesus's death on the Cross, but we also participate in Jesus's saving activity embracing its effects.

A Complete Sacrifice: The Body and the Blood

Why, at the Last Supper, did Jesus not take the bread and simply say, "This is me"? Why did he not take the cup and simply say, "This is me"? Why did he intentionally insist that the bread is his body and the wine is his blood? The answer lies in the symbols of bread and wine along with the words "This is my body" and "This is my blood," revealing the true and complete nature of Jesus's sacrificial death on the Cross. While the whole of the risen Jesus is present under the appearance of bread and under the appearance of wine, it is the risen Jesus who sacrificed his life on our behalf. The designation that the bread is his body and the wine is his blood assures us that this sacrifice is efficacious and so merits Jesus's resurrection. Moreover, only by designating that the bread is his body and the wine is his blood did Jesus reveal to us that we, within the Eucharistic liturgy, are actually participating in the one and same efficacious sacrifice of the Cross.

The Eucharist Interprets the Paschal Mystery and the Paschal Mystery Makes Efficacious the Eucharist

There is also a relationship between the words of institution over the bread and wine and the Paschal Mystery. I have emphasized that Jesus's Eucharistic words and actions interpret and give meaning to his death on the Cross. Moreover, what he enacted on the Cross makes real the Eucharistic words and actions. For example, when Jesus (and now the priest) at the Last Supper proclaimed, "This is the cup of my blood, the blood of the new and everlasting covenant. It will be shed for you and for all so that sins may be forgiven," he revealed to the apostles the meaning of his crucifixion. Jesus's liturgical words and actions were a prophetic interpretation of what he would accomplish on the Cross. In turn, what took place on the Cross makes the liturgical and sacramental words and actions efficacious. While the Eucharistic words and actions symbolically reveal the meaning of the Cross, Jesus's sacrificial death on the Cross empowers the sacramental actions to effect what they symbolize and to symbolize what they effect. At the Last Supper, Jesus simultaneously revealed through the Eucharist that his death on Cross is efficacious and that the Cross makes efficacious the Eucharist. In the Eucharist, we, in union with Christ, participate in the salvific work of the Cross and so share in its efficacious benefits.

The Resurrection

Just as the Eucharistic liturgy of the Last Supper allows us to interpret the Cross and vice versa, so does the whole of the Paschal Mystery—the passion, death, and resurrection of Jesus. In fact, Jesus's resurrection is what undergirds his liturgical commentary on the Cross. There could not be a sacramental and liturgical commentary on the Cross if Jesus did not rise gloriously from the death because without his resurrection, Jesus's death on the Cross would be meaningless, for there would be no commentary to enact liturgically. Jesus's offering of his body and blood on the Cross is salvific only if the Father raises him gloriously from the dead. Not only does the Resurrection manifest the Father's acceptance of Jesus's sacrificial death, which reveals its efficacy, but it also makes possible our sharing in that efficacy within the Eucharist. Without the Resurrection, the Eucharistic liturgy would be devoid of benefit because the Cross would be inefficacious, bearing no salvific effect. Only because the Father raised Jesus from the dead by the power of the Holy Spirit can the Father, by the same Spirit, make the living and glorious crucified Jesus present within the Eucharist. Only because the risen Jesus is truly present in the Eucharist are we able to unite ourselves to him, and so in the same Spirit obtain the fruit of the Cross—reconciliation and communion of life with the Father through the living Jesus. The Last Supper is not only Jesus's sacramental commentary on the Cross, it also presupposes and anticipates his resurrection. Jesus's resurrection makes his liturgical commentary on the Cross literally come to life, for he himself—the crucified Savior and risen Lord—is present through the sacramental words and in actions.

While the body and blood that we receive in the Eucharist represent the body that was given up for us and the blood that was shed for us, in the Eucharist we receive the risen body and blood of the crucified Jesus. The bread and wine are changed into the risen Jesus, and it is this risen Jesus that we receive. In so doing, we are united to the living Christ who died for our sins and so have, in the Spirit, a living communion with the Father.

Jesus's Commentary on the Commentary

For Holy Thursday, the Church reads a liturgy not one of the institution narratives from the Synoptic Gospels, but the episode from John's Gospel where Jesus washes the feet of his disciples on the night before he was betrayed. Just as Jesus liturgically acted out his commentary on the Cross within the Synoptics, so within the Gospel of John Jesus acted out his commentary on the Eucharistic liturgy. The washing of the disciples' feet is a commentary on a commentary, and the washing of the feet therefore interprets the Eucharistic liturgy that in turn interprets the Cross. Following the reciprocal pattern that we discerned above, the Cross not only gives reality to the liturgical words and actions, but it also provides the proper interpretation of the feet washing.

John begins his narration in this manner: "Jesus, knowing that the Father had give all things into his hands, and that he had come from God and was going to God, rose from supper, laid aside his garments and girded himself with a towel" (Jn. 13:3–4). As the institution narratives within the Synoptics are set within the context of the Passover, so the washing of the feet is set within the same context—"and that he had come from God and was going to God." Jesus then commences with washing the disciples' feet. He is brought up short with Peter's protest. Jesus replies, "What I am doing you do not know now, but afterward you will understand" (Jn. 13:7). Having put his garments back on and assumed his place at table, Jesus interprets his actions for the disciples. "Do you know what I have done to you? You call me Teacher and Lord; and you are right, for so I am. If I then, your Lord and Teacher, have washed your feet, you also ought to wash one another's feet. For I have given you an example, that you also should do as I have done to you. Truly, truly, I say to you, a servant is not greater than his master; nor he who is sent greater than he who sent him. I you know these things, bless are you if you do them" (Jn. 13:14–17). We are to enact the Eucharist in our daily lives by giving our lives for one another—washing one another's feet. Jesus's washing of his disciples' feet is a parable about the Eucharist; as he gives himself to us, so we are to give ourselves to one another. In addition, we find the source of the truth of this parable, as mediated through the liturgical and sacramental words, in the Cross itself. It is on the Cross that Jesus truly washes our feet, for it is there that he gives up his body and sheds his blood for us.

Every time we do what is good, in all of its various forms—acts of charity, kindness, forgiveness, courage, and so on—we are washing one another's feet in imitation of Jesus. In so doing, we are making concrete, in our daily lives, the meaning of the Eucharist that finds its source in the reality of the Cross. Through our acts of sacrificial love, we are saying, "This is my body given up for you." Through our acts of mercy and compassion, we are saying, "This is my blood poured out for you." Here we perceive that Jesus's feet washing is a commentary, a parable, about the meaning of the Eucharist within the lives of Christians, the basis of which is found in the Cross. Likewise, as Jesus through the Cross—the giving of himself, his washing of feet—obtained for him the new life of his resurrection, so, too, does the Cross—the giving of ourselves, the washing of feet—obtain for us the reward of everlasting life.

Conclusion

In the Eucharist, Jesus nourishes us on the living body that he gave up for us, and on the living blood that he poured out for us. This will find its completion in the heavenly banquet, where the life that we live is forever nourished on the risen life of Jesus. As Jesus nourished us on earth, so he will fully nourishes us in heaven. And as we nourish one another here on earth in the giving of our bodies and blood in acts of sacrificial charity, so we will completely nourish one another in heaven, for there, in union with Jesus, we will give ourselves fully and completely to one another.

CHAPTER 26

The "Our Father"
Prayer of the Crucified

What was Jesus's mental disposition during his crucifixion? What was the form and content of his prayer? Despite the unimaginable physical pain and emotional distress, we know that during the course of his crucifixion Jesus's heart and mind were consumed with love—love for his Father and love for every person. We know, too, that Jesus was not undergoing his crucifixion in a passive manner, as if he was merely submissively enduring what was happening to him. Rather, he was using what was being done to him as a divinely ordained event by which he would ardently give his life as an act of sacrificial love to the Father. This Spirit-filled offering of his life to his Father was lovingly done in our stead and on our behalf. Jesus on the Cross must have prayed to his Father out of love for him, and he must have prayed for us out of love for us. We know that, in his cry of abandonment, Jesus prayed the whole of Psalm 22, in which, in the midst of horrendous suffering, the afflicted man trusts in the Lord and is confident that he will be delivered from the present evil only to manifest God's glory among all the nations.

With this in mind, I believe that one of the prayers that Jesus prayed while on the Cross was one he taught his disciples to pray—the Our Father.

Originally published as "The Our Father, Prayer of the Crucified: In Tribute to Ralph Del Colle, Who Prayed the Our Father with Jesus His Savior," in *A Man of the Church: Honoring the Theology, Life and Witness of Ralph Del Colle*, ed. M. R. Barnes (Eugene, OR: Pickwick Publications, 2012), 96–106. Used by permission of Wipf and Stock Publishers. www.wipfandstock.com

This thought first came to me when I was recently celebrating Mass. When it came time for the Our Father, I looked up from the Missal (it was one of the few prayers of the new Roman Missal that I knew by heart) and looked at the crucifix before me. I thought to myself, "Jesus prayed the Our Father when he was on the Cross." Immediately the Our Father, in its totality, took on a fuller and richer meaning. Some may immediately object that there is no biblical evidence that Jesus prayed the Our Father during his crucifixion. That is true. Nowhere do the Gospels state that Jesus did so. But only if Jesus did pray the Our Father while he was nailed to the Cross does it assume its most profound significance and acquire the fullness of its truth. Only because Jesus prayed the Our Father on the Cross was the fullness of its salvific potential and historical consequence actualized. Moreover, everyone else who prays the Our Father does so only in union with and in imitation of the crucified Jesus, and they do so with it having been imbued with the meaning and authority that the Cross has indelibly conferred upon it. Thus I assume, for the sake of this essay, that the crucified Jesus actually did pray the Our Father. Allow me, then, to examine the Our Father in light of Jesus having prayed it while upon the Cross.

Our Father

Most scholars are confident that when Jesus taught his disciples to pray "our Father," the Aramaic word he spoke for "father" was *abba*, so designating their filial, loving intimacy with the Father and the Father's paternal loving intimacy with them. Two interrelated truths can be perceived in the crucified Jesus saying the Our Father. First, Jesus, as man, addressed God as Father because he alone is the eternal Son of the Father, begotten and not made, consubstantial with the Father. Jesus therefore enjoys the privilege and the right to address God as Father, as *Abba*, in a singular and definitive manner.

Second, Jesus did not say "my Father" or simply "Father." He addressed his Father as "our Father." He did so because it is specifically on the Cross that Jesus was obtaining the salvation of all who would become, throughout the whole of human history, members of his body, members of his Church, and so adopted children of the Father. Jesus was praying the Our Father not simply for himself but as the head of his body and thus for all men and women. It is only because Jesus reconciled us to the Father through his sacrificial death that we now obtain, through faith and the indwelling of the Holy Spirit, the privilege and the right to address, in union with Jesus, God as our Father, as *Abba*.

Who Art in Heaven, Hallowed Be Thy Name

With the words "who art in heaven, hallowed be thy name," Jesus confessed who the Father is and thus in what manner he and all of us are to appear before him. First, Jesus confessed that his and our Father is in heaven; that is, he lives and exists in a divine manner that differs in kind and not simply in degree from all else. The acknowledgment that his Father is in heaven, within the context of the Cross, was also an act of faith in that he trusted that his Father, as the heavenly Father, providentially governs all earthly events—even the crucifixion—and so continues to have his loving and protective hand upon him. Jesus, having said "our," included all of humankind under the care of his heavenly Father. When we pray the Our Father, in union with Jesus, we are confessing with him that we also trust, in all circumstances even in the midst of our own suffering and death, that we are in the safety of our heavenly Father's hand.

Second, because the Father is the heavenly Father, his name is to be hallowed; that is, acclaimed to be holy and separated from all that is profane. The Father's name is hallowed by the fact that he is the Father of all, including his Son. Everyone has a sacred duty to hallow the name of the Father, however, to acknowledge and bear witness to the Father holiness. Even the divine Son, from all eternity, hallowed the name of his Father because the divine holiness that was bestowed upon him comes from the Father. What is significant, under the present circumstances of the Cross, is that Jesus, as the incarnate Son, was perfectly hallowing the name of his Father. Jesus's suffering and death on the Cross was in itself the supreme acknowledgment and the ultimate testimony to his Father's holiness, for in this act of laying down his life on the Cross, Jesus is ardently worshipping and fervently glorifying his Father. The offering of his holy and innocent life was the perfect sacrifice of praise. On the Cross Jesus was doing away with all that is not holy—sin and death as well as the devil, the father of all that is sinful and profane. We also hallow our Father's name not only when we pray the Our Father, but also, and especially, when we do so within acts of sacrificial love on behalf of others, for we are imitating the sacrificial love of our crucified savior.

Third, when Jesus prayed that the name of his Father be hallowed, hidden within that proclamation is an entreaty that his own name would be hallowed, as well. In his high priestly prayer, Jesus prays: "Now is the Son of man glorified, and in him God is glorified; if God is glorified in him, God will also glorify him in himself, and glorify him at once" (Jn. 13:31–32). As his perfect Word and eternal Image, the Father forever hallows and glorifies the name of his Son, for the Son expresses his own name in its entirety. The Son eternally hallows and glorifies his Father, from whom he was begotten as the Father's perfect Word and Image. The event of the Cross is the earthly historical act by which and in which the Father and Son mutually hallowed and glorified one another. "Father, the hour has come; glorify your Son that the Son may glorify you … I glorified you on earth, having accomplished the work which you gave me to do; and now, Father, glorify you me in your own presence with the glory which I had with you before the world was made" (Jn. 16:1, 16:4).

Of course, this is true of all of us who are in communion with the Son and like him glorify the Father in our sacrificial acts of love. In these same acts the Father glorifies us, for he allows us to manifest the working of the Spirit in our lives. This mutual glorification finds its supreme expression in the act of martyrdom, where the crucifixion is most fully replicated and so the mutual hallowing and glorifying is most fully witnessed. Through the Cross both Jesus and all of us hallow the name of the Father.

Thy Kingdom Come, Thy Will Be Done, on Earth as It Is in Heaven

The three declarations of "thy kingdom come, thy will be done, on earth as it is in heaven," found their full significance when Jesus prayed them in the midst of his passion. His passion and death were the culminating acts by which Jesus, in his very person, was establishing his Father's kingdom. Through his sacrificial death the reign of sin was destroyed and the power of death was vanquished. Jesus, in conquering this twofold evil on the Cross, opened the gates to God's kingdom—the kingdom of the resurrected life of holiness and immortality. While Jesus, through his resurrection, was the first to experience the fruit of his Cross, his prayer for the coming of his Father's kingdom was prayed on behalf of all. Now all who believe in him can, in union with him, enter the kingdom of God—the kingdom of the Spirit of life and truth.

The coming of God's kingdom is predicated upon the doing of his will. Jesus, unlike Adam and Eve, did the will of his Father, for all eternity in heaven and now here on earth. "I can do nothing on my own authority; as I hear, I judge; and my judgment is just, because I seek not my own will but the will of him who sent me" (Jn. 5:30). This seeking to do his Father's will found its ultimate expression in the Garden of Gethsemane. Echoing the Our Father itself, Jesus prayed, "*Abba*, Father, all things are possible to you; remove this cup from me, yet not what I will, but what you will" (Mk. 14:36). In filial love and obedience, Jesus confidently entrusted himself to his *Abba*, his Father. The Cross was Jesus's supreme act of obedience: "And being found in human form he humbled himself and became obedient unto death, even death on a cross" (Phil. 2:8). This loving obedience was what destroyed the reign of sin and death. The Letter to the Hebrews tells that Jesus received a body so that as man he could willingly offer his life for our sanctification. "By that will we have been sanctified through the offering of the body of Jesus Christ once for all" (Heb. 10:10). Because of this filial and loyal obedience, his Father "highly exalted him and bestowed on him the name which is above every name, that at the name of Jesus every knee should bow, in heaven and on earth and under the earth, and every tongue confess that Jesus Christ is Lord, to the glory of God the Father" (Phil. 2:10–11). This filial submission to the will of the Father also ushered in the new creation. "Then as one man's trespass led to condemnation for all men, so one man's act of righteousness leads to acquittal and life for all men. For as one man's disobedience many were made sinners, so by one man's obedience many will be made righteous" (Rom. 5:18–19). Here we discover the depth and significance of Jesus's praying the Our Father as he suffered on the Cross. Not only did Jesus pray the words of the Our Father on the Cross, but the Cross itself is also the enacting of the Our Father. By faithfully doing the will of his Father on earth, even unto death, the incarnate Son established the kingdom of God on earth, the kingdom for which he prayed. These three declarations are now fulfilled in Jesus and will come to complete fulfillment at the end of time, when all who have done the will of the Father on earth, and so continued to make real the kingdom of God on earth, will forever, in loving joy and gratitude, do the will of the Father in heaven.

As implied above, Jesus made these three avowals not only on his own behalf but also on behalf of his body, the Church. As the head of his body, Jesus declared in the name of the whole Church—"thy kingdom come, thy will be done, on earth as it is in heaven." Whenever we echo the words of Jesus, we do so in union with our heavenly Lord. With one voice, in the one breath of one Spirit, the head and members pledge to further the kingdom of God by doing the Father's will both on here on earth and in heaven. It is in the midst of the suffering body of Christ here on earth, too, that this threefold affirmation finds its most vivid expression. For, as Jesus established the kingdom through his loving obedience to the Father even unto death, by sharing in and completing his suffering, the Church most clearly bears living testimony and contributes to the continuing reality of the Father's kingdom.

Give Us This Day Our Daily Bread

The Last Supper is Jesus's commentary on his imminent passion and death. In the course of the meal he took bread, blessed and broke it, and gave it to his disciples, saying, "Take, eat; this is my body." He then took the cup filled with wine and said, "Drink of it, all of you; for this is my blood of the new covenant, which is poured out for many for the forgiveness of sins" (Mt. 26:26–28). Jesus, through his words and actions, was prophetically revealing that his passion and death on the Cross would be the new Paschal sacrifice that would establish a new and eternal covenant with God, his Father. It would be a covenant of new life. Jesus, in the Last Supper, was dramatically portraying and anticipating his own sacrificial death on the Cross, and already he was allowing his disciples to share in it through the reception of his body and blood under the forms of bread and wine—the bread of life and the cup of salvation.

After Adam sinned, God said to him, "In the sweat of your face you shall eat bread" (Gen. 3:19). As the new Adam, Jesus, through his sweat and blood of the Cross, gained the new bread of eternal life both for himself and his Church. The Cross freed Adam and his descendants (including Jesus himself) from the curse, and so the new Adam would provide the new bread of life that his Father would send down from heaven.

When Jesus prayed on the Cross, "give us this day our daily bread," he had in mind a twofold interrelated meaning. He was petitioning his Father both that he would give him the bread of everlasting risen life, and, as head of the Church that is born from his pierced side, he was also petitioning that the Father would give the bread of new life to the members of his body. In raising him from the dead by the power of the Holy Spirit, the Father answered Jesus's twofold petition. "He who eats my flesh and drinks my blood abides in me, and I in him. As the living Father sent me, and I live because of the Father, so he who eats me will live because of me" (Jn. 6:56–57). There is a threefold communion here. Jesus as God and now as the risen Savior lives because of the Father, and when we partake of Jesus's risen body and blood we abide in him and he in us, and thus we, in union with Jesus, abide with the source of all life—the Father. Because Jesus vanquished sin and death through the sweat of his brow, the Father truly makes him the bread of life. In light of the Cross and the Resurrection, Jesus could truly declare: "I am the living bread which came down from heaven" (Jn. 6:51). Being the living bread, he now provides his body, the Church, with living bread; that is, he nourishes his body on and with his own risen self and in so doing makes us one in him. "Because there is one bread, we who are many become one body, for we all partake of the one bread" (1 Cor. 10:17).

When we, as members of the body of Christ, petition our Father for our daily bread, we do so in union with him. We pray not simply for natural bread, though that be important, but we pray especially that we would receive the living bread that is Jesus's resurrected body. The Father answers this petition by providing for us the Eucharist in which we both share in the one sacrifice of Christ and partake of his risen body and blood: we obtain communion with the risen Christ and so in his Spirit commune with the Father.

By praying the Our Father within the liturgy of the Mass, we are uniting ourselves to that same event in which Jesus himself prayed it most fittingly—within his passion and death. It is thus most apt that we pray the Our Father immediately after the Eucharistic prayer, for we have conjoined ourselves to the one sacrifice of Christ, having placed ourselves on the Cross with and in him. Cleansed of sin, we can most fittingly cry out "*Abba*, Father," the Father who will provide for us, now properly disposed and appropriately prepared, our daily bread—Jesus himself.

This petition also contains an eschatological entreaty. While we wish to share here on earth the living bread that is Christ, we also, along with him, yearn for the day when we will be fully transformed into his likeness by living fully in and with him, who is our eternal and heavenly bread. As the crucified Christ entreated the Father to make him into the living bread through the Resurrection, so we within the sacrifice of the Mass entreat the Father to bring us also to the fullness of life because we already, here on earth, partake of the bread of immortality—the risen Lord Jesus Christ. As we have already participated in the heavenly supper here on earth, so we long to share in its full reality in heaven. We do so in the hope of Jesus's promise: "He who eats my flesh and drinks my blood has eternal life and I will raise him up at the last day" (Jn. 6:54).

And Forgive Us Our Trespasses as We Forgive Those Who Trespass against Us

In the Cross we find the forgiveness of our sins. When Jesus prayed, "forgive us our trespasses," he did so as our Savior, as the head of his body, the Church. Only when Jesus spoke the words on the Cross did they achieve their true end, for on the Cross Jesus is truly offering his holy and innocent life to the Father as a sacrificial petition for the forgiveness of our sins. It is precisely because Jesus prayerfully enacted these words from the Cross that the Father heard and answered his prayer once and for all. The Resurrection confirmed that Jesus's appeal for forgiveness has been realized.

It is only because the Father looked favorably upon his Son's plea from the Cross, specifically because it was from the Cross that it was made, that we are able confidently to say to the Father "forgive us our sins." We say these words in union with our crucified and risen Savior, and this union is the sole assurance that the Father will look kindly upon our entreaty. Without the Cross and Jesus's petition from it, there would be no forgiveness of sins, and thus for us to petition the Father would be pointless and futile.

But the plea for the forgiveness of our trespasses is predicated upon the next phrase: "as we forgive those who trespass against us." As we forgive others, so we are asking the Father to forgive us. Again, Jesus, on the Cross, fulfilled this requirement perfectly. "Father, forgive them; for they know not what they do" (Lk. 23:34). While the primary referents were those who had condemned him and had now crucified him, Jesus was also forgiving all of those who would persecute the members of his body or would harm the just and injure the innocent.

As Jesus prayed, so he has directed all of us to pray. In and with him we, too, ask the Father to forgive us as we forgive others, even in the midst of our suffering for righteousness's sake. "For if you forgive men their trespasses, your heavenly Father also will forgive you; but if you do not forgive men their trespasses, neither will your Father forgive you your trespasses" (Mt. 6:14–15). To forgive reflects the merciful love of the Father. "In this is love, not that we have loved God but that he loved us and sent his Son to be the expiation for our sins" (1 Jn. 4:10). The Father's perfection resides in his mercy (Mt. 5:48; Lk. 6:36). The Father is the source of all mercy and only Jesus is as perfect as the Father, for only he is as merciful as the Father. Nonetheless, in communion with the Father and the Son, sharing in the merciful love of the Holy Spirit, we are also able to forgive.

Lead Us Not into Temptation, but Deliver Us from All Evil

As mentioned above, we know for sure that Jesus prayed at least one prayer, Psalm 22, while on the Cross. The first verse is a cry of dereliction: "My God, my God, why have you forsaken me?" While Jesus had committed himself to drink the cup during his agony in the garden, now on the Cross he suffered the emotional experience of being abandoned by his Father. In trust and faith, Jesus humanly knew that this was not true; nonetheless, the loss of his loving *Abba*, Father, was also his greatest human temptation. "Why are you so far from helping me, from the words of my groaning?" (Ps. 22:2). In praying the Our Father, the crucified Jesus, in the midst of feeling abandoned, also prayed that his Father would "lead him not into temptation," that his Father would free him from the grip of this lying fear and deceitful anguish. He was praying that the Father would send upon him the comforting love and enduring strength of the Spirit.

Jesus was also praying on behalf of his body, and when we pray "lead us not into temptation," we are doing so as members of his body. He was interceding on our behalf that the Father would always send us the wisdom to see the lie within every temptation and to provide us the strength of the Holy Spirit to overcome every temptation. In the midst of the Church's suffering, cares, and concerns, she must likewise pray that the Father will free her from the greatest of all temptations—temptation of being abandoned by God. We, too, at times feel that we no longer reside in the loving presence of the Father, and yet, in union with Jesus, we know, in confident faith and unwavering trust, that this temptation, despite it seeming reality, is simply that—a temptation. If the Father never abandoned his crucified Son, we know he will never abandon the Church or any of us who now live in communion with his risen Son.

The final solution to being led into temptation is to be delivered from evil, the evil from which temptation arises. For this reason, Jesus concluded with the request that the Father "deliver us from evil." The evil that Jesus wished to be delivered from is not simply the evil of being subject to the hands of evil men and so his suffering of the Cross. Rather, Jesus requested that the Father deliver him and all of us from the source all evil—sin—and thus also from the curse of sin—death. Jesus ultimately wanted to be freed from kingdom of Satan, the father of lies from whom all evil comes.

The Cross portrays a marvelous irony. When the crucified Jesus prayed that the Father "deliver us from evil," his prayer was simultaneously being answered. The Cross is the petition, and the Cross is the answer. In his sacrificial passion and death, the definitive petition, Jesus, as one of us, reconciled us to the Father and so obtained the Father's loving forgiveness. On the Cross Jesus put death to death. The Cross was the instrument of Satan's downfall, and thus the Cross is the agency by which Jesus and all of us in him are delivered from evil. The Cross was the Father's answer to Jesus's and our plea for deliverance.

The Resurrection was the Father's complete answer to Jesus's plea for deliverance, for in the Resurrection the Father inaugurated his kingdom—a kingdom free from sin and death, a kingdom of righteousness and immortality. In answer to Jesus's petition for deliverance from evil, the Father made Jesus himself the answer. Jesus crucified prayed to the Father that we be delivered from evil, and the Father's answer to this petition is Jesus risen. The person of Jesus, our crucified Savior and risen Lord, is our deliverance from all evil. Through faith and Baptism we unite ourselves to the risen Jesus as our Savior and Lord, and so share in his victory over evil and obtain the new life of his Holy Spirit.

What we see here is that the first petition of the Our Father, "thy kingdom come," and the last petition, "deliver us from evil," go together. The coming of God's kingdom delivers us from all evil. Moreover, the acts that bring about God's kingdom and deliver us from evil are one and the same—the death and Resurrection of Jesus. In Christ we live within the Father's kingdom and so are delivered from evil.

Although the Resurrection is the assurance that our plea for deliverance from evil has been answered, Jesus, ever before the throne of his Father, continually intercedes for us who are members of his body. When we pray the Our Father, we are joining our voices with Jesus's, confident that the Father is always watching over us and protecting us even within the evil world in which we still reside. The petition "deliver us from evil" is thus inherently eschatological. Only at the coming of Jesus in glory at the end of time will our deliverance from evil be fulfilled and the fullness of the life in Christ be ours. "Therefore are they [the saints] before the throne of God, and serve him day and night within his temple; and he who sits upon the throne will shelter them with his presence. They shall hunger no more, neither thirst anymore; the sun shall not strike them, nor any scorching heat. For the Lamb in the midst of the throne will be their shepherd and he will guide them to springs of living water, and God will wipe away every tear from their eyes" (Rev. 7:15–17).

Conclusion

Even if one is not convinced that Jesus actually prayed the Our Father during his suffering on the Cross, I hope it is evident that, at the very least, he prayed the content of the Our Father. Only if Jesus prayed the Our Father was the content of the Our Father fulfilled. The Cross is the doing of the Our Father. On the Cross, Jesus addresses his heavenly Father in sacrificial love and perfectly hallows his name. Because of this, all petitions of the Our Father are fulfilled. The Cross makes possible the Father's kingdom, because on the Cross Jesus accomplished perfectly on earth the will of his heavenly Father. In raising Jesus from the dead, the Father provides for us the daily bread of eternal life—Jesus himself. In his sacrificial death, Jesus obtained the forgiveness of our sins and reconciled us to the Father. In the Father's forgiveness we are empowered in the Spirit to forgive others. Lastly, the Cross enables us to overcome all temptation and delivers us from all evil, even death itself. The Father testifies that Jesus fulfilled the Our Father by raising him from the dead. In the risen Jesus we find the Father's unqualified answer to all the Our Father's petitions. In perfectly enacting the Our Father on the Cross, Jesus himself becomes the Father's perfect response.

Having been conformed into the likeness of Christ through the indwelling of the Holy Spirit, we can now pray the Our Father in spirit and in truth. As members of Christ's body, we also enact and so make real the Our Father through our deeds of sacrifice. In so doing, we hallow the Father's name by doing his will and thus further his kingdom on earth. We also long for Jesus's coming in glory, when we will worship the Father in the fullness of the Spirit and love one another as perfect sons and daughters of the Father.

CHAPTER 27

Giving the Doubter
His Due

For close to two thousand years, St. Thomas the Apostle has been maligned, known for so long as "Doubting Thomas." Any man who bears the name Thomas and has ever questioned anything, justifiably or not, is regularly accused of being another "Doubting Thomas."

Yes, Thomas doubted that Jesus was raised from the dead. He refused to believe what his fellow apostles told him, "We have seen the Lord" (Jn. 20:25). But in his doubt, Thomas performed an invaluable service for every generation that has come after him, a service unparalleled among those who bear witness to the reality of the Resurrection.

By his doubt, Thomas forced the issue. He pushed the question of Jesus's resurrection to its ultimate point. He wanted proof—concrete, sensible, perceptible proof. "Unless I see in his hands the print of the nails, and place my finger in the mark of the nails, and place my hand in his side, I will not believe" (Jn. 20:25). Thomas would not tolerate some vague, romantic, and ethereal spiritualism. He wanted to see with his own eyes—and even touch with his own hands—Jesus.

The physicality of Thomas's proof is evidently twofold. He physically wanted to see and touch, and what he wanted to see and touch had to be physical. Implied in his demand to see and touch Jesus's wounded body was the guarantee that the one whom he would see and touch would be the

Originally published as "Giving the Doubter His Due," *Canadian Catholic Review* 8, no. 4 (1990): 159–60.

same person who actually died on the Cross and not some new "spiritual" impostor. For Thomas, the Jesus of history must be the Christ of faith. We could not ask for a better proof than Thomas's.

What effect would Thomas's challenge have had upon his contemporaries (and upon future generations) if it were known and not resolved? Not only would it undermine the witness of the other apostles, but also ultimately would have jeopardized Jesus's own testimony concerning his risen glory. Belief in the Resurrection might have actually crumbled. Thomas's challenge rightly struck at the heart of the Resurrection claim and the faith that this claim demanded.

Jesus took up Thomas's challenge. He appeared to Thomas and not only allowed him to see his physical, risen body, but he also permitted him to probe his wounded hands and side (Jn. 20:27). Thomas's doubt—and this is the service he has performed for all future generations—called upon Jesus to manifest his risen glory to such a degree that it left no doubt that he was physically raised to new life, body, and soul. No longer need we wonder or question whether Jesus is risen in the completeness of his humanity. Thomas obtained verification of this truth and continues to witness to it for all generations.

But Thomas's importance does not stop here. Upon seeing Jesus, he fell to his knees and professed, "My Lord and my God" (Jn. 20:28). While Thomas doubted and has suffered the scorn of Christian history ever since, he has given in this gesture and in these words the clearest and most forceful personal profession of faith in the entire New Testament.

First, Thomas's profession was the result of seeing the risen man Jesus. In seeing the glorified Jesus, he declared him to be "Lord" and "God." When the Jews read the Hebrew Scripture in the synagogue, the word Adonai "Lord" was substituted for the divine and all-holy name Yahweh out of deference and respect. In turn, the Septuagint employed the Greek word Kyrios "Lord" to translate Yahweh. By transference of meaning, Kyrios thus became a divine title for God. In professing the crucified and risen Jesus to be Lord (Kyrios), Thomas attributed to him divine and regal status. As a crucified and risen man, the Son of God now reigns as absolute Lord of the universe. Thomas here anticipated Peter's first Pentecost sermon: "God has made him both Lord and Christ, this Jesus whom you crucified" (Acts 2:36). He likewise anticipated Paul, who proclaimed that the Gospel of

God's Son "descended from David according to the flesh and designated Son of God in power according to the Spirit of holiness by his resurrection from the dead, Jesus Christ our Lord" (Rom. 1:3–4).

Second, Thomas professed this risen man to be God. No one else in the New Testament personally addresses the man Jesus, with regard to his divinity, in such an unambiguous manner. While he is primarily remembered for his lack of belief, Thomas's profession of faith is the clearest personal testimony both to the reality of the Incarnation and to the glorious Lordship of the incarnate Son. In word and action, Thomas is the first to embody the exhortation contained in one of the earliest Christian hymns. "At the name of Jesus [the incarnate, crucified and exalted one] every knee should bow, in heaven and on earth and under the earth, and every tongue confess that Jesus Christ is Lord, to the glory of God the Father" (Phil. 2:10–11).

Jesus said to Thomas, "Have you believed because you have seen me? Blessed are those who have not seen and yet believe" (Jn. 20:29). We who believe without seeing are blessed indeed. But our faith comes easier thanks to Thomas. He is our eyes and he is our hands, for he has done for us—we who question and struggle with faith—what we cannot do for ourselves. He is our reliable witness, the one who demanded and received the clearest manifestation of Jesus's glorious humanity.

Ultimately, of course, we must thank Jesus. He is the one who had compassion for Thomas's weakness, and thus for our weakness, too. He did not belittle Thomas's challenge, but recognized its seriousness and importance. St. Paul wrote that we know "that in everything God works for good with those who love him" (Rom. 8:28). In Thomas's case, God even worked great good from his lack of belief. Because of Thomas, many people of every race and nation have in the past, do now in the present, and will in the future boldly profess Jesus, on bended knee, to be "My Lord and my God."

CHAPTER 28

The Cosmic Christ

I first want to thank the Franciscan Association of Great Britain for inviting me to give the first of this Jubilee series of lectures marking the second millennium of Jesus's birth. It is an honor to speak to you about the place that Jesus occupies within our own lives, within the scope of human history, and even within the compass of the whole cosmos. I especially want to thank Sister Mary Readman for her kindness in ordering the various bits and pieces that have helped me give this lecture.

In sponsoring a series of lectures, the Franciscan Association obviously believes that St. Francis and the Franciscan tradition and family have something important to contribute to this Jubilee year marking the two thousandth anniversary of Jesus's birth. Undeniably, St. Francis is one of the best known and best loved of all the saints of the past millennium, if not of the entire history of the Church. Among Christians and non-Christians alike, he is universally admired and acclaimed. Within the Catholic community, his popularity is surpassed only by Mary, the Mother of Jesus, and by two of his followers, St. Anthony of Padua (of Lisbon, if you happen to be Portuguese) and now more recently by my Capuchin confrere Blessed Padre Pio. Catholics instinctively realize, and rightly so, that Christianity is a practical religion—whether it is the defeating of sin and the obtaining of eternal life, or the mere finding of lost objects. So the popularity of St. Anthony and Padre Pio lies chiefly in their uncanny ability to get things done.

Originally published as "The Cosmic Christ," *Cord* 51 (2001): 27–38. Used by permission of Franciscan Institute Publications.

They are, as we say, good value for money, though best value for prayer is probably a better, and less scandalous, manner of putting it. Nonetheless, St. Francis, while not a practical man in many ways, is loved by Catholics and Christians, and even admired by those of other faiths or no religion at all. The reason is that he literally embodied the person and teaching of Jesus. Moreover, he has made Christ present not only in his own person, but also through those thousands of men and women, religious and laity, who over the past eight hundred years have striven to follow his evangelical way of life. They, and presently we, like St. Francis himself, have wanted and continue to want to be "troubadours of the Great King." In being such troubadours, Franciscans have made and continue to make a substantial contribution to Christology—to the significance of who Jesus Christ is and to the place he holds within the whole created order of time and history.

I have been asked to speak on the Cosmic Christ, a Franciscan Christological theme. To speak of the Cosmic Christ is to speak of the primacy of Jesus. Within all of creation, within the whole cosmos, Jesus alone holds primacy of place. His name is above every other name. He alone is supreme. He alone is Lord. Not only was everything created by him, but also, and more so, all was created for him. We Franciscans, in accordance with our Christological tradition, proclaim that the principal reason the Father created the world in all its magnificent variation, crowned as it is by human beings, is to give glory to his incarnate Son, Jesus. The primary task of the Holy Spirit is to gather the whole cosmic order into union with Christ and for all human beings, from Adam and Eve to the last person conceived, to confess that Jesus Christ is Lord. Such a Spirit-filled profession of faith is to the Father's glory, for this is the supreme desire of his paternal heart. As Franciscans we realize that to proclaim that Jesus is indeed Lord, that he alone holds primacy of place, not only rightfully redounds to his glory but also to our own. The glory of every Franciscan, as is the case with every Christian, is to be a troubadour of the Great King. There is no greater calling, no greater honor, no greater vocation.

The Primacy of Christ: The Historical Setting

We are all probably aware that the Franciscan theology of the Cosmic Christ, the primacy of Jesus, was forged within controversy. Since the fourteenth century, two schools of theological thought—the Franciscan and the Dominican—have engaged in a protracted debate over the rationale for the Incarnation. For the great Scholastic Franciscan and Dominican theologians of the Middle Ages, the question revolved around whether the eternal Son of God would have become man if human beings had not sinned.

The Dominicans, following their esteemed brother St. Thomas Aquinas, advocated the theory that the Incarnation was primarily for the salvation of fallen humanity. If humankind had not sinned, the Son of God would not have become man. Aquinas argued that such a view was more in accord with Scripture and tradition. He thought it was impossible to give, with any certainty, an affirmative answer to such a hypothetical question. Nonetheless, in his Commentary on The Sentences of Peter Lombard, he admitted that, because the exaltation of human nature and the consummation of the universe are achieved through the Incarnation, the other opinion could also be seen as probable (cf. *In III Sententiae* d.i,l,3).

The Franciscans, following their esteemed confrere Blessed John Duns Scotus, championed the view that because God the Father created everything for Christ, the Son of God would have become man in order to rightfully claim his kingdom, regardless of humankind's fall. The primacy of Christ could not be founded upon sin because sin, an evil, dictates the necessity for the Incarnation and thus becomes the principal cause of the Incarnation. It is impossible for Jesus's primacy to be predicated upon the mistake of sin, rectified only by the Father inaugurating a secondary and supplementary plan—that of the Incarnation. For Scotus, the Father predestined that his Son incarnate would hold primacy of place within creation, and, while sin became a secondary reason for the Incarnation, the glorification of Jesus must nonetheless be the primary purpose for which all was created.

As a good Franciscan (I hope) and because of my desire to know the truth, I argue for the primacy of Christ, that the Father did indeed intend the Incarnation from all eternity, and that he created all for the glorification of his Son. Jesus is the Cosmic Christ in whom the whole of creation finds its source and end. All was created for his glory, and the supreme glory of each human person is to give glory to Jesus. But I wonder, within the Scholastic and subsequent debates, whether the Franciscan tradition has not lost sight, somewhat, of Francis's charisma to be the troubadour of the Great King. I wonder whether, in attempting to assure that sin did not dictate the

Incarnation and so undermine the primacy of Jesus, the Franciscan Christological tradition has not unwittingly deprived Jesus of his true glory as the Cosmic Christ.

To address this concern, I first sketch briefly and broadly how I believe Francis perceived and grasped the primacy of Jesus. Second, in a more scholarly (but not too scholarly) fashion I examine some New Testament passages that are foundational for an authentic understanding of the primacy of Christ.

St. Francis and the Primacy of Christ

We must first return to St. Francis, for he is the source and inspiration of our Christological tradition on the primacy of Jesus. Francis was not a speculative theologian. He did not dabble, as did later theologians, in hypothetical or theoretical questions. He took reality as it is, and in this sense he was a practical man. To turn to Francis and to the life that he lived in relation to Jesus as his Lord and King places the issue of why the Son of God became man out of the realm of the hypothetical and theoretical, and places it squarely in the realm of factual history. Francis was concerned with who Jesus actually was and what Jesus actually did. So we must examine why Francis is the fount from which the theology of the primacy of Jesus, the Cosmic Christ, flowed and still flourishes. Why did Francis, as the troubadour of the Great King, see his supreme glory in living and singing the praises of Jesus?

For Francis, there never was any separation between the primacy of Christ and the Jesus who died on the Cross for our sin. For Francis, it is precisely the Jesus who actually died for our sin that is now the Lord of glory. In fact, for Francis, Jesus is the Lord of glory, and all primacy belongs to him because he mounted the wood of the Cross. This is where I think the subsequent Franciscan Christological tradition may have gone astray somewhat. It tended to found the primacy of Jesus solely upon the Father's will to create—all was created for Christ. In relating Christ's primacy solely to the order of creation, however, it became separated from the Cross and so undermined the glory of Jesus's primacy, which finds its supreme expression in the Cross. For Francis, there never was any such separation. Yes, all was created for Jesus and the Father willed his primacy before the world began, but the manner in which Jesus's primacy is historically established and manifested is through the Cross, from which his cosmic glory actually flows. Francis perceived that the Cross reveals the supreme glory of Jesus and why everything was created for him.

For Francis, in the Incarnation, the eternal Son of God humbled himself, taking on the poverty of our sinful humanity. This is the lesson of Greccio that Francis so wanted to portray. The poor, innocent, and vulnerable child in Francis's arms on that cold Christmas night was the Lord of glory, and his glory was manifested in his poverty, innocence, and vulnerability. It was in this humble state that Jesus offered his holy and pure life to the Father as a sacrifice for our sin. It was the humble and poor Jesus, the crucified Jesus, whom Francis loved and sought to imitate. It was the crucified Jesus who spoke to him from the Cross, but that same crucified Jesus, as the San Damiano crucifix portrays, is the living Lord of glory. Francis learned to embrace the leper and in so doing learned that Jesus embraced our leprous humanity in the Incarnation. And as Francis was healed of his delicate and refined middle-class values and lifestyle in embracing the leper, so he learned that Jesus had healed all of humankind of sin in embracing our sinful humanity. Francis could be the troubadour of the Great King, he could sing the praises of Jesus, he could proclaim him as supreme within the whole of creation, because he witnessed and knew the source of such glory and supremacy. For Francis, the glory of Jesus, his primacy, why he is the only Lord raised to supreme glory by the Father, is found in his weakness, his poverty, his humility, his lowliness, his gentleness, his mercy, and above all his cross.

I have, in brief and broad strokes, wanted first to reconnect the primacy of Jesus with the Cross because this is what I believe Francis did. Second, to separate the primacy of Jesus from the Cross places his primacy outside of history, outside of who he truly was and what he truly did. Not taking account of sin and death, and the Cross by which both were vanquished, makes the primacy of Jesus as the Cosmic Christ a mere fairytale disconnected from reality. It is not true to life. Third, in placing Jesus's primacy back into history, we learn why Jesus holds primacy of place. Jesus is Lord, the Cosmic Christ, because he defeated sin, Satan, and death—the whole cosmic order of evil—and in so doing established a whole new cosmic order of life and holiness where he and those who believe in him reign in eternal glory. Francis, I maintain, was aware, at least instinctively, of all of these concerns, and his awareness sprang from his knowledge and love of Scripture. Some New Testament passages ground biblically what I believe is the authentic Franciscan understanding of Jesus's primacy as the Cosmic Christ.

The Colossian Hymn (1:15–20): Preeminent in Every Way

The author of the Letter to the Colossians wrote to that Christian community because he feared that its members were flirting with empty philosophies, probably Gnosticism, "the elemental spirits of the universe," and so were not remaining loyal to the Gospel "according to Christ" (Col. 2:8).

Contained within this letter is the early Christological hymn that was Scotus's theological inspiration (Col. 1:15–20; cf. Eph. 1:10, 1:20–23; Heb. 1:1–4). This Christological hymn can be divided into two stanzas (verses 15–17 and 18–20).[1] The first stanza proclaims that the beloved Son is "the image of the invisible God." He is the image of God not only because, as the divine Son, he perfectly images the Father, but also because, as the incarnate Son, he is the perfect visible icon of the invisible Father. He is "firstborn of all creation," again not only because, as the divine Son, he existed externally, and thus prior to all of creation, but also because, as the incarnate Son, he was the first to be conceived within the Father's divine plan for creation. Here we find the primacy of Jesus predicated upon both his divine and human states, for he is within both states the perfect image of the Father, and as such he rightly holds pride of place within the Father's creative plan.

As the divine Son, all was created "in him"—"things visible and invisible, whether thrones or dominions, or principalities or authorities—all were created by and for him (eis auton). He is before all things, and in him all things hold together" (Col. 1:15–17; cf. Heb. 1:3, 1:6; Jn. 1:3, 1:18). Here again we find the primacy of Jesus clearly expressed within the order of creation. The Father creates all in and through his Son, and so everything, even thrones and principalities, is subordinate to him. Everything is dependent

---

1. For a discussion of this and other texts concerning the primacy of Christ from a Scotistic perspective, see J.-F. Bonnefoy, *Christ and the Cosmos* (Paterson, NJ: St. Anthony Guild Press, 1965); M. Meilach, *The Primacy of Christ* (Chicago: Franciscan Herald Press, 1964); J. Carol, *Why Jesus Christ? Thomistic, Scotistic and Conciliatory Perspectives* (Manassas, VA: Trinity Communications, 1986).

upon him for their existence, and thus he is before all things not only in time but also in rank, for in him everything is held together in harmonious existence. But equally, then, everything is created for the Son. The reason everything exists is to give glory to him who is their Creator and, as such, the source of their consequent unity. That everything was created "for Christ" is a clear expression of his cosmic primacy.

The second stanza also declares that Jesus is likewise supreme within the order of redemption. "He is the head of the body, the church; he is the beginning, the firstborn from the dead, that in everything he might be pre-eminent (*en pasin autos proteuon*) [literally, in all things he holds the first place]" (Col. 1:18). Because Jesus is the gloriously risen firstborn from the dead, and thus the beginning of a whole new creation, he is the Lord of a whole new cosmic order. To be a new creation in Christ is to be a member of that new comic order, and that new cosmic order finds expression in his body, the Church, of which he himself is the head.

What has Jesus done that attests to his preeminence both within the order of creation and within the order of redemption? The Colossian hymn answers: "For in him all the fullness of God was pleased to dwell, and through him to reconcile to himself all things, whether on earth or in heaven, making peace by the blood of his cross" (Col. 1:19–20).

Jesus's preeminence resides in his being the eternal Son who shares fully in the Father's divine nature, for the fullness of God dwelt within him (Col. 2:9). The Father gave to his Son a ranking equal to his own. But Jesus's supremacy is not the result of divine nepotism. Rather, as the obedient Son, he reconciled to himself all things, and so is supreme. This reconciliation was accomplished at a great price—as one of us, within our sinful condition. Reconciliation is the fruit of Jesus's sacrificial offering himself on the Cross (the mark of sin and condemnation), and so peace is obtained through the shedding of his holy blood.

The Colossian hymn testifies to the many faceted and intertwined aspects of Jesus's primacy. (1) The primacy of Jesus pertains to his being the eternal Son of God incarnate. (2) As the eternal Son of the Father, he is supreme not only in that all was first created through him and for him, but also in that all was re-created through him and for him. The primacy of Jesus as the Father's Son is founded upon both the act by which he created everything, and so as Creator is the source of all unity, and also on his act of redemption, and so as Redeemer is the new source of a re-created unity. Thus as Creator and Redeemer he is preeminent in every way. (3) The primacy of Christ, as historically revealed, cannot be separated from the condition of sin. Rather, Jesus's primacy in the order of creation is ratified and established within the order of redemption. What the Father established in creating everything for Christ finds its fulfillment in that all is redeemed for Christ. Jesus's primacy is perceived in that all was created through him and all was redeemed through him, and thus all was created for him and all was re-created for him—to give him glory both as Creator and as Redeemer.

The Colossian hymn reminds us that the Christian Church is primarily the gathering of those who have been ransomed from sin, reconciled to the Father, and have now given their lives to Jesus as their Lord. The Church is that Spirit-filled body of people who acknowledge and live under the headship of Jesus, and so find their unity in him. Christians recognize the primacy of Jesus and profess that they have indeed been created and redeemed *for Christ*.

The Letter to the Ephesians (1:3–14): The Father's Grand Plan

A similar argument can be found within the opening chapter of Paul's Letter to the Ephesians. We are to bless "the God and Father of our Lord Jesus Christ" because he has "blessed us in Christ with every spiritual blessing in the heavenly places." Before the foundation of the world, the Father chose us in Christ. The Incarnation is not simply a derivative and so secondary response to the advent of sin, but lies at the heart of the Father's cosmic plan, for we were already chosen in Christ prior to creation. Moreover, through Jesus we were to possess the same attributes that he possessed. We were to be holy and blameless. Ultimately, the Father "destined us in love to be his sons through Jesus Christ." We were to become sons as Jesus is the Son.

While all of this was predestined in and through Christ before the world began, Paul does not hesitate to declare that this was actually accomplished by way of redemption, through the shedding of Jesus's blood by which we have forgiveness of our sins. What was predestined from the beginning and what was actually accomplished in our redemption is ultimately, for Paul,

the revelation of the mystery of the Father's eternal will, which he "has set
forth in Christ ... to unite all things in him, things in heaven and things on
earth." This uniting of all heavenly and earthly things in Christ, reminiscent
of the Colossian hymn, could only be accomplished through his death, and
so manifests his cosmic primacy that was eternally willed by the Father. In
addition, we have been sealed with the Holy Spirit, who is "the guarantee of
our inheritance until we acquire possession of it."

What we find in this Ephesian passage is a clear proclamation of Jesus's
cosmic primacy, a primacy that was willed by the Father before the foundation of the world. Yet Jesus's cosmic primacy, in which we would be blessed
by finding our unity in him, could only be achieved through his death, for
it was only with his vanquishing of the divisions brought about by sin that
such cosmic unity could be established under his Lordship.

Letter to the Philippians (2:5–11):
Above Every Other Name

The Christological hymn in Paul's Letter to the Philippians equally testifies to this same pattern. God has highly exalted Jesus and has "bestowed
on him the name which is above every name." Whenever the name of Jesus is expressed and heard, every knee is to bow whether one is in heaven,
on earth, or even under the earth, and every tongue is to confess that Jesus
Christ is indeed Lord. Such worship and proclamation give glory to God
the Father. But why is Jesus's name supreme? Why has the Father exalted
him above everyone else? Why must everyone, no matter where they may
abide within the cosmos—the angels and blessed in heaven, men and wom-
en on earth, and even Satan and the damned under the earth—bow at the
name of Jesus and proclaim him Lord of all? The answer is founded upon
the humility of the Son.

Though the Son was indeed God, he did not consider his glorious divinity something to which he must egoistically grasp. Rather, he willingly emptied himself of his divine glory and came not simply in the form of
man, but more so as a servant. It was in this humble, subservient state that
he was obedient not only to the Father but also obedient unto death, even
to death on the Cross. The great "therefore" of the Philippians hymn finds
its cause in the humble salvific work of Jesus. It was Jesus's extremely hum-

ble, lowly, and vulnerable actions that compelled the Father to *therefore* exalt him and make his name above every other name. Again, the comic Lordship of Jesus is intimately and causally entwined to the cross.

The Gospel of John: Behold Your King!

The Gospel of John also witnesses the intrinsic relationship between the Cross and Jesus's primacy. Surprisingly, it has been little used throughout history to argue for the primacy of Christ, but it, along with the Book of Revelation, presents the most thorough and sustained argument on behalf of Christ's primacy. I believe that the Gospel of John perceives that what is enacted in time is but the playing-out in history what eternally transpires within the Trinity—the drama of the Father glorifying the Son and the Son in turn glorifying the Father. This mutual glorification is done in and through the reciprocal love of the Holy Spirit.

John proclaims that we have seen the glory of the only begotten Son (cf. Jn. 1:14). The Father sent his Son into the world for our salvation, but inherent in this salvific plan was the Father's desire to reveal the Son's glory (Jn. 3:16). Actually, for John, the salvation of the world is the principal effect of the glorification of the Son. While the glory of Jesus and the salvation of the world are fully achieved and consummated in one and the same act, the exaltation of Jesus is logically prior to and the cause of our redemption. Only in manifesting the preeminent glory of Jesus did the Father bring about the salvation of the world.

Jesus did not seek his own glory, but there is "One who seeks it … It is the Father who glorifies me" (Jn. 8:50, 8:54). It was and is the Father's desire that all may honor his Son as they honor him (cf. Jn. 5:22–23). The Father redeemed us in Jesus not for our own sake but that we might be the Father's acceptable and holy gift to his Son, for the praise of his Son's glory. Jesus prayed that the Father would glorify him so that those who believe might behold the glory the Father had given him before all time (cf. Jn. 17:1, 17:5, 17:22): "Father, I desire that they also, whom you have given me, may be with me where I am, to behold my glory which you have given me in your love for me before the foundation of the world" (Jn. 17:24).

Where did the Father most thoroughly manifest the glory of his faithful and obedient Son, the glory that he possessed from all eternity? Where did the Father declare that his Son deserves all glory, praise, and honor, that all primacy is his? It was on the Cross.

The Cross depicted both Jesus's affinity to our sinful condition and his glory as the only begotten Son. The glory of Jesus resides directly in his willingness to do the Father's will even to dying a sinner's death on the Cross. At the moment when Judas left the upper room, in the utter darkness of the world's and history's sin, Jesus proclaimed, "Now is the Son of man glorified, and in him God is glorified; if God is glorified in him, God will also glorify him in himself, and glorify him at once" (Jn. 13:30–32).

Jesus gave glory to his Father through obediently completing his Father's work, and the Father simultaneously glorified Jesus. The Cross, as the mutual giving and receiving of glory between the Father and the Son, was a historical dramatization of the heavenly relationship between the Father and the Son. In the Cross, both the Father and Jesus revealed why primacy belongs to Jesus alone—the Father, by allowing the world to see under the most severe conditions of sin how obedient and loving his Son is; and the Son, by being obedient and loyal even within a humanity contaminated by sin and burdened by the condemnation he assumed. This is beautifully illustrated in a couple of scenes from the passion narrative.

In the passion narrative, the true nature of Jesus's kingship or primacy is revealed. For John, the trial before Pilate prefigured, anticipated, and thus helped interpret the Cross. During his interrogation of Jesus, Pilate asked him if he were the King of the Jews (cf. Jn. 18:33). Jesus answered that his kingship was not of this world (cf. Jn. 18:36). At Pilate's insistence that he was nonetheless a king, Jesus responded, "You say that I am a king. For this I was born, and for this I have come into the world, to bear witness to the truth. Everyone who is of the truth hears my voice" (Jn. 18:37–38).

The phrase "For this I was born, for this I have come into the world" is purposely equivocal. It indicates that the Son became man in order to be king, and yet, as it is spoken within the context of his trial, it also refers to his imminent passion and death, which is equally the result of his becoming man (*sarx*). This is exactly what John wishes us to grasp, the twofold truth to which Jesus will soon bear witness and those who are open to the truth will accept in faith. The primacy of Jesus the king is to be manifested on the Cross.

An equally revealing scene for John, the central scene of Jesus's trial, takes place at his scourging, for there the soldiers ironically declare the truth of who Jesus is: "And the soldiers plaited a crown of thorns, and put it on his head, and arrayed him in a purple robe; they came up to him, saying 'Hail, King of the Jews!' and struck him with their hands" (Jn. 19:2–3). Without knowing it, these men ironically proclaimed the truth that would resound both in heaven and on earth. Jesus is the king over all. There is no one greater, not because he conquered by arrogant worldly power but because he was meek, humble, and rejected.

John continues with his progressive typology, which uses one scene as a type to prefigure, illuminate, and interpret the next. John skillfully composed as parallels the climactic judgment scene before Pilate and the crucifixion. In so doing, he helps the reader perceive the true significance of both. We can see this more easily when we set these texts side by side:

Gabbatha (Jn. 19:13–15)	Golgotha (Jn. 19:17–22)
Pilate ... brought	Jesus ... went out ... to the
Jesus out and sat [him]	place of a skull, which
down on the judgment seat	is called in Hebrew
at a place called the	Golgotha. There they crucified
Pavement, and in Hebrew,	him ... Pilate wrote
Gabbatha ... He said	a title ... "Jesus of Nazareth
to the Jews, "Behold	the King of the Jews." ... The
your King!" They cried out,	Jews then said to Pilate:
"Away with him, away with	"Do not write."
him, crucify him."	

The poetic resonance between Gabbatha and Golgotha suggests that John saw a correlation between the events of the trial and the crucifixion. Likewise, Jesus's movement helps to establish the parallelism. He moved from inside the Praetorium to the court scene outside; he moved from inside Jerusalem to Calvary outside the city. More importantly, what did John wish us to see through our eyes of faith?

At Gabbatha, Pilate sat Jesus upon the imperial seat of judgment, and in so doing ironically declared that the one who is being judged is the true judge. He likewise prophetically proclaimed Jesus, a man despised and detested, to be king. On the Cross, this prophecy was fulfilled. For John, the Cross was the consummate sign of contradiction. The Cross—loathsome and revolting—was Jesus's throne of glory because in and through his

most abject lowliness and humility—the burden of our sin—he manifested his absolute faithfulness to the Father and his unconditional and all-
consuming love for us. The Cross affirmed the primacy of Christ, the fullness of his glory.

Again ironically, Pilate wrote in three languages for the whole world/
cosmos to read the Father's verdict and nailed it on the Cross: "Jesus of Nazareth, the King of the Jews" (Jn. 19:19). This man Jesus, suspended upon the
Cross, is King and Lord. In him, the fullness of glory dwells and to him belong all praise and honor. When challenged (by the people then and now),
Pilate prophetically echoed the eternal words of the Father: "What I have
written I have written" (Jn. 19:22). The Cross is the Father's final, definitive,
and unalterable decree of Jesus's primacy.

As we noted in the Colossian hymn, so, too, in John's Gospel: the
Church is composed of those who recognize the truth that their king is the
crucified Jesus. Mary and John, standing beneath the Cross and gazing up
in faith, having been washed clean in his blood and reborn in the water of
the Spirit, represent and prefigure the Church of all time (cf. Jn. 19:25–27,
19:31–37). Even Doubting Thomas became the epitome of a man of faith.
By placing his fingers into the nail marks in Jesus's hands and his hand into
his side, he is the first to proclaim publicly that the one who took upon
himself our sin (manifested in the now glorious wounds) is "My Lord and
My God" (Jn. 20:28).

The Book of Revelation: Worthy Is the Lamb Who Was Slain

The Book of Revelation anticipates the heavenly worship where the glory
of Christ's primacy will be revealed in full. Yet even in heaven, the Lord of
lords and the King of kings, the Alpha and the Omega, the First and the
Last still bears the brands of sin now made radiant: "He is clad in a robe
dipped in blood" (Rev. 19:13). For it is the slain Lamb who is honored and
glorified, and he alone is exalted and praised expressly because he bore our
sin and died on our behalf (cf. Rev 5:6):

Worthy are you to take the scroll and to open its seals, for you were slain and by
your blood did ransom men for God from every tribe and tongue and people and
nation, and has made them a kingdom and priests to our God, and they shall reign
on earth. (Rev. 5:9–10)

Worthy is the Lamb who was slain, to receive power, and wealth and wisdom and
might and honor and glory and blessing! ... To him who sits upon the throne and
to the Lamb be blessing and honor and glory and might for ever and ever! (Rev
5:12–13)

Multitudes in white robes washed clean in the blood of the Lamb—
the heavenly church, "the wife of the Lamb"—acclaim their crucified Lord:
"Salvation belongs to our God who sits upon the throne and to the Lamb!"
(Rev. 21:9. 7:10; cf. Rev. 7:14, 12:11, 19:6–9). The glory of the Cross, the
lamp of the Lamb, eternally illumines the whole of heaven (Rev. 21:22–23).

We need to examine one final controverted passage. Revelation 13:8
is variously translated as "And all who dwell on earth will worship it [the
beast], every one whose name has not been written before the foundation
of the world in the book of life of the Lamb that was slain" (cf. *Revised
Standard Version, New Revised Standard Version, New Jerusalem Bible*, and
New American Bible) or as "All the inhabitants of the earth will worship it
[the beast], all whose names have not been written in the book of life of the
Lamb, slain since the foundation of the world" (cf. *Revised English Bible*
and *New International Version* as an alternative translation). What was from
the foundation of the world—the names written in the book of life, or the
Lamb that was slain?

The structure of the Greek text is such that it would seem that "from the
foundation of the world" (*apo kataboles kosmou*) modifies the Lamb who
was slain and not the names written in the book of life. The reason that the
majority of contemporary English versions do not prefer this translation
seems to be twofold. Revelation 17:8 expressly states that the names of those
who will be saved were written in the book of life from the foundation of
the world, so confirming Revelation 13:8. Also, this translation seems to
make more sense because Jesus was slain in time and history and not from
the foundation of the world.

Within the eternal plan of God, however, it is only because the Lamb,
burdened with our sin, was slain that he conquered all his enemies (the
beast), procured his throne, and secured those whose names are written in
his book of life. In other words, the Father, from before the world began,
predicated and preordained the primacy of Christ the Lamb, totally and exclusively, on the Cross. Within the Father's mind, the Cross is not an afterthought to the glorification of his Son, but rather the preeminent demon-

stration and actual attainment of Jesus's primacy. The First Letter to Peter confirms this judgment:

You know that you were ransomed from the futile ways inherited from your fathers, not with perishable things such as silver or gold, but with the precious blood of Christ, like that of a lamb without blemish or spot. He was destined before the foundation of the world but was made manifest at the end of the times for your sake. Through him you have confidence in God, who raised him from the dead and gave him glory, so that your faith and hope are in God. (1 Pt. 1:18–21).

Manifestly, even from our brief study, the salvific reasons for the Incarnation converge with and enhance the truth of Jesus's primacy. Our approach has been wholly biblical and historical, and thus in keeping with Aquinas's concerns, and it yet has upheld Scotus's insight that the supremacy of Jesus was first in the Father's mind. These valid convictions of Aquinas and Scotus form parts of a deeper and more central truth. The primacy of the incarnate Son, as the Cosmic Christ, is achieved and most fully manifested in the Cross. It is there that the cosmic glory of Jesus is beheld in all its luminous splendor and grandeur. It is this truth that I believe Franciscan Christological tradition has failed to fully appreciate, but a truth that Francis himself knew well. He was the troubadour of the crucified King. In his own stigmatized body he proclaimed that the Cross transfixes, in all of its celestial radiance, the whole cosmos and in so doing testifies to the primacy of Jesus as the Cosmic Christ.

Conclusion

How should we, as Franciscans, respond to the truth that the crucified Jesus is the Lord of glory, the Cosmic Christ in whom all primacy belongs? First, during this Jubilee year such truth should be our pride and joy as Franciscans. In the two thousand years since its revelation, we are the ones, more than any others, who have fostered and promoted the primacy of Jesus, and we should continue to do so. I am confident that the Father has been and is well pleased. Second, there ought to be deep sadness in our hearts, a grief that arises from the fact that so few people in our day love Jesus and acknowledge his primacy. This is so not only among those who have not come to faith in Christ, but also even among professed Christians Jesus is often not honored with the respect he deserves as their Lord and Savior.

As Franciscans, troubadours of the Great King, this is a cause or should be a cause of profound distress. Third, this sorrow should move us, as Franciscans, to proclaim fearlessly and wholeheartedly the glory and the splendor of Jesus. As Franciscans, because of our love for Jesus, we are to sing his praises in word and deed. This is our glory—to glorify, to honor, to adore Jesus. Fourth, this desire to magnify the name of Jesus should find its greatest expression in evangelization, especially within Great Britain, where so few of our compatriots know Jesus. We must ardently, and without apology, proclaim the Gospel of Jesus so that all men and women might come to the living and transforming knowledge of Christ, and so, in union with us, acknowledge him, in the Holy Spirit, to be the supreme and only Lord and Savior. Lastly, we should long for the day when Jesus will return in glory, for on that day, finally, what we all desire will come to fulfillment. Then the primacy of Jesus as the Cosmic Christ will be definitively and undeniably manifested. Then, finally, every knee will bow—whether in heaven or on earth or under the earth—at the name of Jesus, and every tongue in every language will proclaim that Jesus is Lord. This is the day we await with anxious and ardent longing. This will be the day of most profound joy for us troubadours of the Great King, for on that day the eternal Jubilee of praise of Jesus will commence in all its cosmic fullness. Come, Lord Jesus!

CHAPTER 29

Eucharistic Adoration
Encountering the Mysteries

Over the last decade or so there has been a renewed and ongoing growth in the practice of Eucharistic adoration, the practice of displaying the reserved sacrament for public worship. This has been especially true within parishes, even to the point of instituting perpetual adoration before the Blessed Sacrament. Eucharistic adoration is also becoming more common within the monasteries and friaries of male religious. Other than the monasteries of cloistered nuns whose vocation entails the adoration of the Eucharist, this trend is less evident within many of the convents of older orders of women religious. This is not the case among the newer and more forward looking orders of women religious. What may have not kept pace with the renewed practice of Eucharistic adoration is a revitalized theology of Eucharistic adoration that would deepen and assist in fostering this authentic renewal. This essay is an attempt to contribute, in a small way, to a renewed theology of Eucharistic adoration.

Encountering the Real Presence of Jesus

Eucharist adoration is doctrinally founded upon the belief that Jesus, the risen Lord and Savior, is truly present in the Eucharist—body, blood, soul, and divinity. Within the Mass, the host, upon which we now gaze in ad-

Originally published as "Eucharistic Adoration: Encountering the Mysteries," *Adoremus Bulletin* 15, no. 7 (October 2009): 3–4. Reprinted by permission.

oration, was transformed into the reality of the risen Jesus. Without this belief in the doctrinal truth of transubstantiation, that the substance of the bread (and wine) has been changed into the substance and reality of the risen Lord Jesus, Eucharistic adoration would be idolatry. Given the truth of the doctrine of transubstantiation, Eucharistic adoration expresses a proper, holy, and loving form of Christian piety, for we give praise, honor, and glory to Jesus here present in our midst.

While we adore Jesus in the Eucharist, however, we may not always fully appreciate the doctrinal and theological implications of our adoration. It is because Jesus is truly present in the Eucharist that all of the mysteries that accrue to him are also equally present. These mysteries, embedded within Eucharistic adoration, provide a spiritual depth and cultivate an even more robust form of Eucharistic worship. When we adore Jesus in the Eucharist, we are encountering not only the mystery of his Eucharistic presence, but also the mysteries of his divinity; his Incarnation; his public life; his death on the Cross; his resurrection and ascension into heaven; his pouring out of the Holy Spirit at Pentecost; his headship over his mystical body, the Church; and finally his Second Coming at the end of time. How is this so? To answer this question, we need to examine these mysteries within the context of Jesus's Eucharistic presence.

Encountering the Son of God

The Jesus we adore in the Eucharist is the eternal Son of God, who is "God from God, Light from Light, True God from True God, begotten and not made, consubstantial [of the same substance or being] with the Father." Our Eucharistic worship is founded upon the truth of Jesus's divinity. It is Jesus's divine presence in the Eucharist that demands and necessitates our worship of him. We adore, praise, and honor him within the Eucharist because we believe that the one before us is truly the eternal Son of the Father. Within our Eucharistic adoration we encounter the divine Son and so are united to him in our adoration of him.

In encountering the Son of God within our Eucharistic adoration, we likewise encounter the Father and the Holy Spirit. Because Jesus, as Son, is consubstantial with the Father, to encounter him is to encounter the Father as well. "He who has seen me has seen the Father ... Believe me that I am in the Father and the Father is in me" (Jn. 14:9, 14:11). "I and the Father are one" (Jn. 10:30). Moreover, to encounter the Father and the Son within the Eucharist is to encounter the Holy Spirit who proceeds from both as their mutual and reciprocal love. Our Eucharistic adoration of Jesus gives us entrance into the mystery of the Trinity, where we experience not only the divine presence of the Son but also the love of the Father and the fellowship of the Holy Spirit (2 Cor. 13:14). We are expressing and experiencing, in our Eucharistic adoration, the reality of our baptism—that we were baptized into and so presently live within the triune life of the Father, the Son, and the Holy Spirit (Mt. 28:19).

Encountering the Incarnation

Within our Eucharistic adoration, however, we are not encountering the Son of God separated from his humanity. It is the incarnate Son of the Father whom we worship and adore. The Son of God became man and dwelt among us (Jn. 1:14). We are able to worship the Son of God within the Eucharist only because he first was present to us as man. His incarnational earthly presence is the prerequisite foundation of his Eucharistic heavenly presence, and so it is the incarnate Jesus we still encounter in our adoration. As the Son of God humbled himself, not grasping after his divinity but assuming the form of a servant and being born in our likeness so as to be present to us, so the Son of God incarnate continually humbly makes himself present to us in the Eucharist (Phil. 2:6–7). St. Francis and St. Clare, like all of the saints, grasped that though he was rich in his divinity, the Son of God became poor in our humanity that we might share in the riches of his divinity (2 Cor. 8:9). In the Eucharist, the Son of God still becomes poor for us, and when we adore him in the Eucharist, we come to share in the riches of his divinity. Men and women professed their faith in Jesus as the Father's only Son while he was on earth—one whom they could see, hear, and touch. Today we follow our faith-filled ancestors, expressing our faith in him who is present to us in the Eucharist—the one whom we can still see, hear, and touch (1 Jn. 1:1–3). With St. Peter we profess that Jesus is "the Christ, the Son of the living God" (Mt. 16:16).

Encountering the Public Life of Jesus

Encountering the incarnate Son of God within our Eucharistic adoration means that we also encounter Jesus in his public life. In his public ministry, Jesus proclaimed the Gospel of salvation. He taught and instructed the people, for example, through his Sermon on the Mount. Through his human words and human deeds he revealed that he was truly the Son of the Father. Through his humanity he manifested his divine love, mercy, and compassion. He was the shepherd who had pity upon his sheep. He healed the sick, raised the dead, cast out demons, forgave sinners, miraculously fed the hungry, and so on. When we adore him in the Eucharist, we are still encountering Jesus in all these facets of his public earthly ministry as he speaks and acts from his glorious heavenly throne.

When we come before Jesus Eucharistically present, we encounter the Jesus who wishes to instruct us in the ways of the Gospel. He continues to reveal himself to us as our Savior and Lord. He continues to teach us how we are to live as priests and religious, as married couples and parents, as children and young adults, as grandparents, as widows and widowers, and as single people serving his kingdom. He hears our petitions and answers our pleas just as he did during his earthly existence. He pours out his compassion and mercy upon us. He continues to heal the sick, to bind up the broken hearted, to forgive sinners, and to nourish those who hunger for him. In our Eucharistic prayers of repentance and acts of faith, Jesus, as he did of old, fosters our virtuous life and nurtures our holiness. In our Eucharist adoration Jesus continues to be our Good Shepherd who has pity on us and leads us, in his Spirit of love, to our heavenly Father. "I am the way, and the truth, and the life; no one comes to the Father, but by me" (Jn. 14:6).

Encountering the Cross

In the Mass we unite ourselves to the one sacrifice of Jesus, the offering of himself to the Father on our behalf. In our Eucharistic adoration we continue to unite ourselves to that saving sacrifice. We acknowledge that Jesus is the Good Shepherd who laid down his life for us (Jn. 10:11). We thank and praise Jesus for dying on our behalf, for us who continue to be sinners and so still need his forgiveness. We express our gratitude for freeing us from our guilt, embarrassment, and shame and so reconciling us to the Father. We revere him as our one Savior and only Redeemer. In his name alone do we obtain salvation (Acts 4:12). We pour out our love for him because he loved us to the end, humbly being obedient to the Father even unto death, death on the Cross (Phil. 2:8). When we come before our crucified Savior in the Eucharist, he continues to pour forth from his pierced heart his cleansing blood, the blood of the New Covenant, and the living water of the Holy Spirit (Jn. 19:34). Through our worship, we place ourselves within the human heart of our crucified Savior so as to experience, in the Holy Spirit, the divine love of the Father. In our Eucharistic adoration we encounter the saving Cross of Jesus, and in so doing our love for him renews, deepens, and grows. In each church that St. Francis entered he would pray, "We adore you, O Christ, and we bless you, here and in every church throughout the world, because by your holy cross you have redeemed the world."

When we encounter our crucified Lord in the Eucharist, we also bring before him our own trials and sufferings, the concerns of our family and friends, the needs of the Church and of the world. We especially place before him our persecuted brothers and sisters throughout the world who are suffering and dying for the sake of the Gospel. In our Eucharistic contemplation we continually unite ourselves to the Cross of Jesus so that, together with him, we offer ourselves to the Father, in the love of the Spirit, for the salvation of all. We complete in our own flesh "what is lacking in Christ's affliction for the sake of his body, that is, the Church" (Col. 1:24). It is in our Eucharistic worship that we conform ourselves, as did all of the saints, to the crucified Jesus, willing to die to sin so as to live sacrificial lives of holiness. Our Eucharistic prayer becomes, then, a sacrifice of praise—an offering of praise to Jesus for all that he has done for us. Such a Eucharistic sacrifice of praise gives rise to heartfelt joy and inner peace, for we have become one with him who has conquered all evil—sin and death itself.

Encountering the Resurrection

While we adore Jesus who died for us, we adore him presently as the risen Lord of glory. We adore him as the one who has ascended into heaven and now reigns at the right hand of his Father as the Lord of lords and the King of kings. On the Cross the Son, as man, died and shed his blood, and it is now the Son of God in his risen humanity—with his risen body and blood—whom we receive in Communion, and it is the Son of God in his risen humanity—with his risen body and blood—whom we adore and worship in the Eucharist. In our Eucharistic worship we encounter and so enter into the risen life of Jesus. We are assured that even though we may suffer many trials, burdens, and even death, we will rise because we have partaken of the risen Lord, whom we now worship in this reserved sacrament. "He who eats my flesh and drinks my blood has eternal life, and I will raise him up at the last day" (Jn. 6:54). Already our life is hidden with Christ in God, and to this heavenly realm, with all of the saints and angels, we raise our hearts and minds when we come before Jesus (Col. 3:304).

In contemplating the risen Lord Jesus, we do so as members of his mystical body, the Church. At Pentecost, Jesus, the Lord of life, sent forth his Spirit of life and so gave birth to the Church, for which he died. Through our faith and baptism we, too, have received this Spirit of life and so become members of that Church. As living stones, with Christ as the cornerstone, we are being built up, through our Eucharistic adoration, into a Spirit-filled temple in which we give praise and honor to the Father (1 Pt. 2:4–5). In the unity of the Spirit with Christ our head, we are entering more deeply into the very mystery of his body, of which we are all living members. This means that to worship and adore Jesus as head of the body of which we are all brothers and sisters, we are also in a real sense giving praise and honor to our brothers and sisters in Christ, those in heaven, those in purgatory, and those on earth—the *totus Christus*. We are rejoicing in him and in one another—who are his brothers and sisters. This is a marvelous mystery, one filled with wonder and awe.

Encountering Jesus's Return in Glory

In contemplating the crucified and risen Jesus in the Eucharist, we are anticipating his coming in glory. His presence in the Eucharist is a foreshadowing of his coming at the end of time. Now we worship he whom we see through the eyes of faith, as in a dark glass, and when he comes again in glory, we will adore him, whom we see face to face. In contemplating in all his brilliance, glory, power, and might the risen Lamb who was slain, we ourselves will be transformed and transfigured completely into his own risen image—a likeness that we progressively assumed through our Eucharistic communion and in our Eucharistic adoration. "Beloved, we are God's children now; it does not yet appear what we shall be, but we know that when he appears we shall be like him, for we shall see him as he is" (1 Jn. 3:2). While our present earthly Eucharistic liturgy is a foreshadowing of the heavenly liturgy, when Jesus comes in glory, the heavenly temple will become a full reality, and we will worship Jesus in the heavenly Jerusalem. Here the body of Christ finds its full maturity in the Spirit and, in that Spirit of love, will experience fully, in Christ, the love of the Father. We will also love and rejoice in one another as Christ has loved us.

Through and in our Eucharistic adoration of Jesus we foster our longing, expectancy, anticipation, and desire for Jesus to return in glory. We await anxiously the day when every tear will be wiped away, when justice and truth shall kiss, when Satan and all of his cohorts will be forever vanquished, and death will eternally lose its sting. In contemplating Jesus we grow in our earnest yearning for our own resurrection so that we can live forever in the heavenly courts of the Lord, the New Jerusalem and celestial household of God, with our royal, holy, and priestly brothers and sisters (1 Pt. 2:4–10). Above all, we look to the day when Jesus will finally receive all of the glory, praise, honor, and adoration that he rightly and properly deserved and never fully received in the long course of the world's history. For at his coming in glory, all men and women of every nation, race, and people, of all cultures and epochs, some in fear and trembling and others with hearts full of the Spirit's love and gratitude, will proclaim in unison on bended knee that Jesus Christ is indeed Lord to the glory of God the Father (Phil. 2:11). On this day our present Eucharistic adoration will find its everlasting realization and jubilant fulfillment.

Conclusion

In this essay I have provided the biblical and doctrinal basis for the various mysteries that form part of our Eucharistic adoration. Each of these mysteries could easily be scripturally expanded and doctrinally developed, but they provide the theological foundation from which this further advance can begin. Although I have presented many of mysteries that accrue to Jesus and so form part of our Eucharistic adoration, there are other mysteries not discussed here, such as Jesus's role in the act of creation and his providential governance of the world. In addition, it is not possible, nor even desirable, to focus on all of the mysteries of Jesus in each individual period of Eucharist adoration. I recommend, in our contemplation of Jesus in the Eucharist, that we concentrate on one or two, and perhaps the same ones, over a period of time. This will allow us to deepen our understanding and love for these mysteries, as well as foster our appreciation of the other mysteries as well. Lastly, our Eucharistic adoration will deepen our love for the Mass and for receiving Jesus in Holy Communion. It will deepen our appreciation of the sacraments we have already received—Baptism, Confirmation, Marriage, and Holy Orders—for we will strive to live out more fully these sacraments in our daily lives. Such Eucharist adoration will also intensify our repentance and so our indebtedness to the sacrament of penance. As we grow in our love for the Eucharist, we are preparing ourselves to receive him when we are seriously ill within the sacrament of the anointing and so readying ourselves for our final reception of Jesus in viaticum—this last reception is but the prelude to our full reception of Jesus when we enter into his heavenly glory.

CHAPTER 30

Athanasius's Letter to Marcellinus

A Soteriological Praying of the Psalms

There is common consensus among scholars that Athanasius is the authentic author of the Letter to Marcellinus and that he wrote it toward the end of his life, probably around 367. Whether Marcellinus was an actual existing person or a literary fiction is more contested. But there is no real evidence that he did not exist, and the fact that Athanasius mentions his unspecified illness or tribulation, during which he has not neglected "the discipline," lends credence to his actuality.[1] Athanasius also notes that, as part of his discipline, he has maintained "a studious attitude toward all of the holy Scripture, but that you read most frequently the Book of the Psalms." What may be less likely is the veracity of Athanasius's statement that he "had a conversation with a learned old man" and that he wished to write about "those things that old master of the Psalter told me about it" (1). While this "old man" could be an elderly monk, it could equally be Athanasius himself.[2]

Originally published as "Athanasius' Letter to Marcellinus: A Soteriological Praying of the Psalms," in *Studia Patristica XLVI*, ed. J. Baun, A. Cameron, M. Edwards, and M. Vinzent (Leuven: Peeters, 2010), 275–79. Reprinted by permission.

1. Translation from R. C. Gregg, trans., *Athanasius: The Life of Antony and the Letter to Marcellinus* (New York: Paulist Press, 1980). Paragraph numbers are cited in the text.

2. On these various issues, see J. D. Ernest, "Athanasius of Alexandria: The Scope of Scripture in Polemical and Pastoral Context," *Vigiliae Christianae* 47 (1993): 341–62; *The Bible in Athanasius of Alexandria* (Leiden: Brill, 2004), 332–33; M. R. Rondeau, "L'Épître à Marcelli-

In his letter Athanasius has tightly woven three interrelated ends. First, that while the individual books of the Old Testament possesses their own genre and purpose—history, prophecy, wisdom, and the like—"the Book of Psalms is like a garden containing things of all these kinds, and it sets them to music, but also exhibits things of its own that it gives in song along with them" (2). Second, the Psalter must be prayed Christologically, for it proclaims in its own unique manner who Christ is as well as his mighty deeds. "When you desire, in private, to extol the events concerning the Savior, you find such things in nearly every psalm" (26). Third, and most importantly for Athanasius, praying or singing the Psalms is in itself a means of appropriating and interiorizing the salvation wrought by Christ. "For just as we discover the ideas of the soul and communicate them through the words we put forth, so also the Lord, wishing the melody of the words to be as a symbol of the spiritual harmony in the soul, has ordered that the odes be chanted tunefully, and the psalms recited with song" (28).[3]

For Athanasius, the Book of the Psalms not only contains, in its own singular way, the whole history of the economy of salvation as found in the Old Testament, but, because that economy finds its source, center, and summit in Jesus Christ and his salvation, it also, when prayed, unites the person to Christ, allowing the person to be fashioned into Christ's likeness. For Athanasius, the singing of the Psalms not only objectively proclaims the mysteries of salvation but also actively places the one praying into the reality of these mysteries.

Athanasius perceives that the Psalms profess the foundational truths of the Christian Gospel. They proclaim the truth that God is the Creator of all and that the whole of creation in turn tells of the glory of God (3).[4] The Psalms narrate the celebrated and mighty triumphs found in Exodus, Numbers, and Deuteronomy as well as Joshua and Judges (3–4).[5] Most impor-

---

nus sur les Psaumes," *Vigiliae Christianae* 22 (1968): 176–97. On the above issues as well as the history of the text, see E. Ferguson, "Athanasius' 'Epistola ad Marcellinum in Interpretationem Psalmorum,'" *Studia Patristica* 16 (1975): 295–96.

3. Ferguson divides Athanasius's concerns into five topics: devotional, liturgical, Christological, doctrinal, and catechetical. See Ferguson, "Athanasius' 'Epistola ad Marcellinum in Interpretationem Psalmorum,'" 298–308.

4. Athanasius quotes Psalms 18 and 23. Athanasius employs the Greek/Latin numbering of the Psalms.

5. Athanasius quotes or refers to Psalms 77, 113, 105, 106, and 19. (Note that here, as well as below, Psalms are given in the order that Athanasius quotes them.)

tantly, "nearly every psalm" echoes and confirms "the pronouncements of the Prophets" (5).[6] The Psalms thus tell of the coming of the Savior as well as of his divine identity. Psalm 106 speaks of the Father sending his Word, and because the Psalter knows that this Word is the Son of God, it chants the voice of the Father in the Psalm 44: "My heart has uttered a good Word." And again in Psalm 109: "I have begotten you from the womb before the morning" (5). The Psalms furthermore tell of the virginal conception and of the Son becoming man (6).[7] "And having declared that he [the Son] would become man, afterwards the Psalter also points to his passibility in the flesh" (7). Not only do the Psalms speak of the incarnate Son's passion and crucifixion, but they equally "[foretell] his bodily ascension into heaven," where, with the Father, he will reign in glory (8).[8] From his throne, the Psalms profess that the risen Jesus is "calling the nations" to himself (8).[9]

According to Athanasius, the Holy Spirit, as the common author, accounts for why the same truths are proclaimed throughout all of the books of Scripture, each in their distinctive manner (9, 10). That Athanasius sees an interrelationship between the various books in the Old Testament is not surprising, for such an understanding was common among the early Fathers, especially within Origen's exegesis. Nor is Athanasius adding any novelty in his Christocentric interpretation of the Psalms and in their Christocentric relationship to similar scriptural passages in their various genres. This, too, had already become commonplace by Athanasius's time. What is new is Athanasius's insightful appreciation that "these things [the truths of revelation] are sung in the Psalms, and they are foretold in each of the other books of Scriptures" (8). With regard to the Psalms, one is not merely reading and so learning what God has revealed, as in the other books of the Bible. Rather, one is actually singing and praying and so *professing* what God has revealed. The singing of the Psalms is a prayerful profession of faith, and so a snatching hold of the truths of faith within one's own heart and mind. Singing the Psalms, then, is a soteriological activity. In prayerfully acclaiming in faith the saving mysteries wrought in Christ, one simultaneously appropriates in faith their saving grace.

---

6. Athanasius quotes Psalms 49 and 117.
7. Athanasius quotes Psalms 86 and 44.
8. Athanasius quotes Psalms 2, 21, 87, 68, and 137.
9. Athanasius quotes Psalm 46 and 71.

For Athanasius, the saving grace that accompanies the chanting of the Psalms is specifically ordered to promote emotional harmony or proper spiritual accord within the person's heart and mind.

For in addition to the other things in which it enjoys an affinity and fellowship with the other books, it possesses, beyond that, this marvel of its own—namely, that it contains even the emotions of each soul, and it has the changes and rectifications of these delineated and regulated to itself. (10)

The Psalms not only teach what virtuous emotions are to be fostered and what evil emotions are to be shunned, but the very praying of the Psalms excites and engenders the virtuous emotions and removes and heals those that are disordered (10–11).[10] The reason is that the person, in praying the Psalms, makes the words and the truth that these words express his or her own (11, 12). The Son of God became man so that as man he might be the perfect exemplar of what it means to be human. While "a more perfect instruction in virtue one could not find than that which the Lord typified in himself," "just as he [Jesus] provided the model of the earthly and heavenly man in his own person, so also from the Psalms he who wants to do so can learn the emotions and dispositions of the soul, finding in them also the therapy and corrections suited for each emotion" (13).

Christ's heart and mind were perfectly conformed to the Psalms. He prayed the Psalms in a perfect manner because his interior heart and mind—the seat of his emotions—corresponded perfectly with what the Psalms professed. For Athanasius, the Christian must acquire the same harmonious conformity. The Christian achieves this harmonious conformity in singing the Psalms. In praying the Psalms, the Christian conforms his or her heart and mind to the truth that is professed and so assumes and expresses an emotional state that is appropriate to the Psalm. The Christian thus gradually and increasingly acquires the heart and mind of Christ himself.

For thus beautifully singing praises, he [the chanter] brings rhythm to his soul and leads it, so to speak, from disproportion to proportion, with the results that, due to its steadfast nature, it is not frightened by something, but rather imagines positive things, even possessing a full desire for future goods. And gaining its composure

10. See P. R. Kolbert, "Athanasius, the Psalms, and the Reformation of the Self," *Harvard Theological Review* 99, no. 1 (2006): 85–101.

by the singing of the phrases, it becomes forgetful of the passions and, while re-joicing, sees in accordance with the mind of Christ, conceiving the most excellent thoughts. (29)[11]

This singing of the Psalms advances, for Athanasius, growth in holiness. It is a sacred soteriological action.

In paragraphs 14–29, Athanasius provides a plethora of illustrations. For example, in praying the Psalms of repentance the person does not simply learn of the evil of sin and the need for repentance. Rather, the praying of the Psalm itself actually convicts the person of his or her own sinfulness and simultaneously provides the words of sincere and heartfelt repentance. This admission of sin with its accompanying repentance forms an enduring humble and contrite heart. The Christian gradually acquires the virtue of repentance. Similarly, the Psalms foster in their singing a love for God as the Creator of all, the mighty works of his hands. They also prompt a love for Jesus as Savior and Lord. In both of these instances they also provide the words of praise, adoration, and thanksgiving by way of response. This response of praise, adoration, and thanksgiving form an attitude of mind and a habit of heart whereby the Christian is continually grateful for what God has done in his mercy. In times of distress or persecution, the singing of the Psalms, for Athanasius, fortifies the emotions of heart and disciplines the thoughts of the mind so as to trust in God. This is achieved in the per-son professing God's steadfast love, his enduring faithfulness, and his ever-present protection. Athanasius summarizes his lengthy discussion on how the Psalms conform the Christian into the likeness of Christ by fostering virtue, healing the emotions, and joyfully professing the goodness of God as follows:

I believe that the whole of human existence, both the dispositions of the soul and the movements of the thoughts, have been measured out and encompassed in those very words of the Psalter. And nothing beyond these is found among men. For whether there are necessity of repentance or confession, or tribulation and trial befell us, or someone was persecuted, or, being plotted against ... or if, moreover, someone has become deeply sorrowful and disturbed and he suffers something of the sort that is described in the things just mentioned, and he either attends to himself as one who is advancing, being set free from his foe, or he wants to sing

11. See also paragraphs 27 and 28.

praises and give thanks to the Lord—for any such eventuality he has instruction in the divine Psalms. Let him therefore select the things said in them about each of these circumstances, and reciting what has been written as concerning him, and being affected by the writings, lift them to the Lord. (30)

In conclusion, what we find in Athanasius's letter to Marcellinus is a soteriological approach to praying the Psalms that is both doctrinal and moral. Chanted with the breath of the Holy Spirit, the Psalms become a profession of faith in Jesus Christ the Savior and Lord. This Spirit-induced chanting of the faith equally engenders in the Spirit a moral and spiritual harmony within the person, conforming the emotions of the heart and the thoughts of the mind to those of Christ. The result is that the chanter, for Athanasius, is ever more empowered to live faithfully the life of Christian virtue and holiness.

CHAPTER 31

Huckleberry Finn and the Adventures of God

I am a Capuchin priest by vocation and a theologian by trade. Every August, which often slips into September, I allow myself to read a few books that I don't normally—works of literature or secular history. Over the past five years I have read, on three occasions, Mark Twain's *The Adventures of Huckleberry Finn*. I have enjoyed it immensely. It is a whopping good tale. I have become convinced that Twain has not only narrated the adventures of Huckleberry Finn and Tom Sawyer, but that he has also woven within them the adventures of God. I believe that Twain presents within *The Adventures of Huckleberry Finn* his understanding of salvation history, or what might be called "Twain's soteriology."

In this essay I present the basis for this thesis. I have not done any academic research on this topic other than studying the text. The only other work of Twain that I have read is his biography of St. Joan of Arc. I have presented my thesis to a number of scholars who are versed in American literature, and they have all said, always with a smile and occasionally with laughter, that they were not acquainted with any books or articles that proposed my thesis. Nonetheless, if there is anyone who has already said what I am about to say, I apologize.

Originally published as "Huckleberry Finn and the Adventures of God," *Logos: A Journal of Catholic Thought and Culture* 6, no. 1 (2003): 41–62. Reprinted by permission.

Giving Notice

It would appear that an interpretation of *The Adventures of Huckleberry Finn* is in itself forbidden. In his opening "NOTICE," Twain vehemently warned—and I believe that he must be taken seriously—that "persons attempting to find a motive in this narrative will be prosecuted; persons attempting to find a moral in it will be banished; persons attempting to find a plot in it will be shot." Twain seems to be cautioning the reader that the tale he is about to tell is just a "good yarn," narrated for the pure entertainment of the telling and the reading. Any intellectual rapscallion who attempts to read some profundity into it should be prosecuted, banished, and shot.

But the first clue to my thesis is in the "NOTICE" itself. In it I am convinced that Twain is forewarning not his readers, but his own characters. He is warning Huck, Jim, Tom, and the Duke and the Dauphin what will happen to them if they attempt to find or place a motive, a moral, or a plot in their adventures. They recklessly but innocently pay no heed to the "NOTICE" and so suffer the consequences. Huck and Jim are banished because they are putting a moral in the story. The Duke and Dauphin are prosecuted because they place a motive in the story. Tom is shot because he, most of all, is desperate to add a plot to the story. The motive, moral, and plot that these characters, each in their own distinctive ways and unbeknownst even to themselves, place within the story relate to my thesis that Twain is presenting his history of salvation—the adventures of God.

Huck represents a reluctant Moses leading the slave Jim, who embodies the whole of sinful humanity, to freedom and the promised land, and in so doing they are banished from their homes. The moral of the story is that truth and goodness succeed despite ourselves, or that God uses those who often appear to be of no account to serve his purposes, even when they are unaware of it.

The Duke and the Dauphin personify all that is false and deceptive (including hypocritical religion) and so are prosecuted, tarred, and feathered, and run out of town on a rail. The motive of the story, a major theme around which the moral unfolds, is to discern truth from falsehood. All of the characters are motivated by either truth or falsity, and Huck and Tom even tell lies in order that truth might succeed. Sometimes Huck even tells lies because he wants the lies to succeed, but the truth nonetheless wins out despite his best efforts. Throughout the book Huck believes that what is false is true and what is wrong is right, but he always does what is true and right despite his convictions to the contrary.

Tom, who is at pains to free Jim in the most noble and proper manner, even when he knows that Jim is already free, acts in a most godly fashion and so is shot for his efforts. In this way Tom represents Jesus. The plot that Tom wittingly gives to the story, a plot that he himself conspires, is that all good deeds must be done in an heroic manner, for doing so makes them good. But as the representation of Jesus, Tom unwittingly reveals that God also acts in a classic heroic manner (death on the Cross) in setting us free, even when he knows that he could have done it more easily. God is the author and, in Jesus, the chief exemplary of heroism. Tom Sawyer would have said "God did it by the book," and he did it by the book because he wrote "the book."

Before fleshing this all out, and to alleviate the unbelieving smiles that are now present on the faces of the readers as such a fandangled interpretation, I must say that Twain does not make all of this abundantly evident. One will not find a great deal of one-on-one correspondence, in either words or action, between Huck and Moses or between Tom and Jesus. Twain is much too good of a writer to make obvious his moral, motive, and plot. I believe that Twain continually plays with the reader. He provides the reader with an abundance of tempting interpretative bait to nibble on, but never enough at any one time to make him bite. Twain in one sense does not want to catch the reader, for if the reader catches on to what Twain is doing, then he himself is caught. This would be the last thing Twain would want. Thus what we will find are allusions by way of scenes, actions, and words that embody or suggest Moses- or Jesus-like actions and words. This is usually accomplished through irony; that is, what is said or done is the antithesis to what is literally being said or done. For example, Huck is literally attempting to tell a lie, but in actual fact he is telling he truth.

Moses and the Bulrushers

The title of the first chapter is the key clue to the present thesis: "Discover Moses and the Bulrushers." Huck begins his narrative by telling how the Widow Douglas, who cared for him, "cried over me, and called me a lost lamb." Then "After supper she got out her book and learned me about Moses and the Bulrushers, and I was in a sweat to find out all about him; but by and by she let it out that Moses had been dead a considerable long time; and so then I didn't care no more about him, because I don't take no stock of dead people." When Huck wanted to smoke his pipe and the Widow refused to allow him, he said, "They got down on a thing when they don't know nothing about it. Here she was a-bothering about Moses, which was no kin to her, and no use to anybody, being gone, you see, yet finding a power of fault with me for doing a thing that had some good in it."

The irony is that although Huck writes off Moses as irrelevant, having lived so long ago and being dead, he himself will live out in his adventures the life of Moses. In addition, Huck will continually be doing things that he believes others will find "a power of fault with" (and often he does too) but that actually have "some good in it," like helping Jim to freedom.

When Huck prayed for fishing line and hooks and only obtained fishing line, the Widow straightened out his theology. She said:

I must help other people, and do everything I could for other people, and look out for them all the time, and never think about myself. This was including Miss Watson, as I took it. I went out in the woods and turned it over in my mind a long time, but I couldn't see no advantage about it—except for the other people; so at last I reckoned I wouldn't worry about it any more, but just let it go.

Again ironically, Huck, as the "lost lamb" of the Old Testament, will risk his own life to help Jim to freedom, and in so doing prefigures Tom, who will become the "lamb of sacrifice" who actually sets Jim free. While Huck does not put "stock in dead people," such as Moses, he does put a great deal of stock in Tom (Jesus), who is alive. Nonetheless, Huck is not always happy with Tom's heroic daydreams and escapades, which will become evident in Tom's elaborate and contrived plot to free Jim, making the escape much more difficult than it ever need be. Even early on, Huck commented that he figured that Tom actually believed in "the A-rabs and the elephants," which were part of their games. "But as for me I think different. It had all the marks of a Sunday-school." This is precisely the point. All that Tom does has the marks of the majestic and noble, yet unbelievable, stories of the Bible, and the irony is that Huck, too, as Moses, will live out these same grand "adventures" without realizing it. His life also has "all the marks of a Sunday-school." In the first chapter we do "Discover Moses," and he is Huck.

I do not think it is a mere coincidence either that, when Huck discusses Tom's gang of robbers, the sign of the gang is a "hacked" cross on their breasts, and only gang members can "use that mark." When it is proposed that the families of any gang member who reveals the gang's secrets must be killed, the boys note that Huck does not have any family and, like Moses, is an orphan. Besides, even though no gang member, including Tom, knows what "ransom" means, this is what must be done with all of the captives. When asked how this can be done when no one knows what it is, Tom retorts, "What, blame it all, we've *got* to do it. Don't I tell you it's in the books? Do you want to go to doing different from what's in the books, and get things all muddled up?" Throughout Tom is insistent that things be done according to "the books," for this is the only proper and noble way. To which books is Tom referring? I suggest Twain has at least these in mind: the books of the Bible. Even though no one knows what "ransom" means, Tom in the end will ransom Jim, the captive, through the shedding of his own blood. The items just mentioned do not prove a great deal, but I believe that they illustrate Twain's playing with the reader. They provide tempting bait for the present thesis.

Assuming the Responsibility of Moses

The bulk of the novel takes place as Huck and Jim float down the Mississippi River on their raft. Jim has run away in the hope of finding freedom in the promised land of the Northern free states. But Huck, again without fully realizing it, is also trying to escape. He, too, is enslaved. He is enslaved by his father who holds him hostage for a time and from whom he escapes, having fabricated his own death in the process. His father refers to him in a drunken stupor as "the Angel of Death." Huck's father might be considered a type of Pharaoh. He is afraid that Huck might "get religion." He represents Huck's (Moses's) past, which still haunts him and will haunt him right to the end. While Huck never considers himself a slave, it is only as he helps Jim obtain freedom that he actually obtains freedom for himself. And as Tom keeps the secret of Jim's freedom, so Jim keeps the secret of Huck's freedom; that is, that his father is dead.

Huck then lives out his life as the reluctant Moses on the Mississippi River. He is reluctant because he believes that in helping Jim escape he is doing something wrong. The closer Huck and Jim come to Cairo, Illinois (a name that may itself be significant for the present—leaving Egypt and entering into the Promised Land), the more excited and bold Jim becomes at his imminent freedom. More, too, does Huck's conscience trouble him.

I begun to get it through my head that he *was* most free—and who was to blame for it? Why, *me*. I couldn't get that out of my conscience, no how nor no way. It got to troubling me so I couldn't rest; I couldn't stay still in one place. It hadn't ever come home to me before, what this thing was that I was doing. But now it did; and it stayed with me, and scorched me more and more. I tried to make out to myself that *I* warn't to blame, because *I* didn't run Jim off from his rightful owner; but it warn't no use, conscience up and says, every time, "But you knowed he was running for his freedom, and you could a paddled ashore and told somebody." That was so—I couldn't get around that no way. That was where it pinched.

Huck also recalls that Miss Watson, who owned Jim, did him no wrong. "Why, she tried to learn you your book, she tried to learn you your manners, she tried to be good to you every way she knowed how. *That's* what she done." Here again we perceive the irony that while Huck's conscience told him he was doing wrong, based upon a false notion of religion ("the book") and social manners, he was actually going to live out the true teaching of "the book"—God desires our freedom, and to do good is to do what will help others be free.

The critical test comes when Huck sets off in his canoe to snitch on Jim and is approached by two men looking for runaway "niggers." Huck "hadn't the spunk of a rabbit" to tell them the truth, so he told them that the other man on his raft was his "pap" and intimated that he was ill, but "it ain't anything much." The men, now suspicious, conclude that his "pap" has smallpox and beat a hasty retreat.

They went off and I got aboard the raft, feeling bad and low, because I knowed very well I had done wrong, and I see it warn't no use for me to try to learn to do right; a body that don't get *started* right when he's little ain't got no show—when the pinch come there ain't nothing to back him up and keep him to his work, and so he gets beat. Then I thought a minute, and says to myself, hold on; s'pose you'd a done right and give Jim up, would you felt better than what you do now. No, says I, I'd feel bad—I'd feel just the same way I do now. Well, then, says I, what's the use you learning to do right when it's troublesome to do right and ain't no trouble to do wrong, and the wages is just the same? I was struck. I couldn't answer that. So I reckoned I wouldn't bother no more about it, but after this always do whichever come handiest at the time.

Huck blames his upbringing, as he does throughout, for doing what he thinks to be wrong. But he actually has "started right," and his "lying" is actually promoting the good in spite of himself. Moreover, while Huck believes that it is "troublesome to do right and ain't no trouble to do wrong," by doing what was seemingly wrong, he has actually assumed much more trouble for himself than if he had done what he thought was right. Now he has to stick with Jim and help him obtain his freedom rather than abandon him and go his merry way.

Without realizing it, Huck has assumed the responsibility of Moses. Like Moses, Huck reluctantly cares for Jim, a "nigger," even though this will cause him pain and hardship. Moses complained to God about the burden of caring for a stiff-necked and no-account people—a people who might have been considered "niggers" in the eyes of the Egyptians and even at times (as with Huck) in the eyes of Moses. Ironically, Moses knew what he was doing; Huck does not.

It is here that the motive and moral of Twain's story begin to come together. Huck is unwittingly motivated by truth and right, within a cultural setting where what was thought to be morally good is evil and vice versa. The moral of the story begins to come into clearer focus: truth and goodness will win out even despite our human frailty, or that God will have his way despite our misplaced attempts to foil it. Huck, in assuming the responsibility of a Moses, is banished, as Twain warned, from the (evil) culture and society that he has now left behind, for his own actions have become the moral of the story.

On and Off the River

The Mississippi River is not only the primary setting of Huck's adventures but also the way to freedom for both himself and Jim. The Mississippi is the American Red Sea, the Jordan River, and the wandering in the desert rolled into one grand symbol. As long as Huck and Jim stay on their raft, and thus stay within the protection of the river (and God), they are safe and free. On more than one occasion Huck makes statements such as, "We [Huck and Jim] said there wasn't no home like a raft, after all. Other places do seem so cramped up and smoothery, but a raft don't. You feel mighty free and easy and comfortable on a raft."

But every time Huck and Jim leave the raft and the river they entangle themselves in trouble. The reason is that they have left the path to the promised land—a land of truth and goodness (a land already anticipated in the river)—and have once more returned, like the Israelites of old, to the old ways of evil and deception, the flesh pots of Egypt.

This is first seen when Huck narrates the feud between the Grangerfords and the Shepherdsons. While these chapters are filled with humor, they are the most violent of the whole book, and the violence is senseless. No one can remember the historical reason for the feud, and yet the merciless killing continues from one generation to the next. All of this hatred and violence is placed within the setting of a God-fearing people who, dressed in their finest, went to church weekly and read their Bible daily. "Col. Grangerford was a gentleman, you see. He was a gentleman all over; and so was his family. He was well born, as the saying is, and that's worth as much in a man as it is in a horse, so the Widow Douglas said."

Among all of this gentility, Huck lived in the finest house he ever did see, and he was almost deceived by it all. Shortly after Huck's arrival, Buck, the youngest Grangerford son, poses a riddle. "He asked me where Moses was when the candle went out. I said I didn't know; I hadn't heard about it before, no way ... 'Why, he was in the *dark*! That's where he was!'" Huck never heard of this before because it wasn't in his "book." Nonetheless, while living with the Grangerfords, Huck (Moses) was in the dark because truth and deception, right and wrong, and true and false religion were all mixed up. It is ultimately these opposing forces, as in the Bible itself, that are at war with one another in Twain's "book."

This is evident in Huck's description of Sunday service, which both sides attended with their guns between their knees.

It was pretty ornery preaching—all about brotherly love, and such-like tiresomeness; but everybody said it was a good sermon, and they all talked it over going home, and had such a powerful lot to say about faith and good works and free grace and preforeordestination, and I don't know what all, that it did seem to me to be one of the roughest Sundays I had run across yet.

The Grangerfords and the Shepherdsons thought they were motivated by truth, good, and Bible Christianity, and yet it was deception, evil, and the false veneer of religion and gentility that made up their lives. This is the ironic motivation of Twain's characters. Those who seem to be motivated by what is good—both individual and the society they represent—are deceived. Those like Huck and Jim—as well as Miss Sophia (Wisdom) Grangerford and Mr. Harney Shepherdson, who ran off and got married (reminiscent of Romeo and Juliet) and who seemingly are motivated by evil—are actually living in the light of truth. The Duke and the Dauphin play this theme of motivation out to the full and, as Twain warned, they are prosecuted for so doing.

The Art of Deception and the Act of Providence

A significant portion of Twain's book consists of Huck's adventures with the Duke and the Dauphin. I believe that these adventures fully portray Twain's theme of lying and deception versus truth and goodness. The characters are motivated more by either deception (the Duke and the Dauphin) or truth (Huck). This theme of deception and truth is intricately woven within the moral of the story: truth will be victorious because it is guided, in the midst of deception, by Providence—God. Also, while Huck gets caught up in all of the Duke and Dauphin's shenanigans, he never loses sight of his primary responsibility of caring for Jim. He never forgets, under Providence's guidance, that he has taken on the responsibility of Moses leading Jim to freedom. Lastly, it is in his attempt to care for Jim, of being the reluctant and unwitting Moses, that his crisis of conscience is ironically resolved.

The Duke and the Dauphin personify deception. They embody all that is false. No truth abides in them. This is so much the case that neither Huck nor Jim, nor anyone else—not even the reader—ever finds out their true identity. They have no true names, and all the names they assume are false. Moreover, they trade in deception. When they inquire of one another what their "line" is, their response is predictable.

Jour printer by trade; do a little in patent medicines; theater-actor—tragedy, you know; take a turn to mesmerism and phrenology when there's a chance; teach singing—geography school for a change; sling a lecture sometimes—oh, I do lots of things—most anything that comes handy, so it ain't work. What's your lay?

I've done considerable in the doctoring way in my time. Layin' on o'hands; and I k'n tell a fortune pretty good when I've got somebody along to find out the facts for me. Preachin's my line, too, and workin' camp-meetin's, and missionaryin' around.

Most of these "lines" concern occupations where truth is of the utmost importance—journalist, doctor, teacher, and preacher—and yet they use these vocations to deceive.

Now Huck, who has been somewhat gullible in the past, sees through them from the start. "It didn't take me long to make up my mind that these liars warn't no kings nor dukes at all, but just low-down humbugs and frauds." Jim is fooled and is surprised at how a duke and a king could carry on such. Huck responds, "Well, it don't, because it's in the breed. I reckon they're all alike." Jim hopes that they don't run into any more dukes and kings for "Dese is all I kin stan." Huck is of like mind. "'Sometimes I wish we could hear of a country that's out of kings.' What was the use to tell Jim these warn't real kings and dukes? It wouldn't a done no good; and, besides, it was just as I said: you couldn't tell them from the real kind." While Twain is here expressing his own disdain for lying politicians, he is also commenting on the society that breeds such charlatans. For Huck, they made "a body ashamed of the human race." The whole of humanity must be freed from deception and led to the truth.

Confronted with all this deception, especially the Duke and Dauphin's attempt to deprive an innocent young lady of her inheritance, Huck decides it is time to tell the truth even though it is contrary to his nature and good sense.

I says to myself, I reckon a body that ups and tells the truth when he is in a tight place is taking considerable many resks, though I ain't had no experience, and can't say for certain; but it looks so to me, anyway; and yet here's a case where I'm blest if it don't look to me like the truth is better and actually *safer* than a lie. I must lay it by in my mind, and think it over some time or other, it's so kind of strange and unregular. I never see nothing like it. Well, I says to myself at last, I'm a-going to chance it; I'll up and tell the truth this time, though it does seem most like setting down on a kag of powder and touching it off just to see where you'll go to.

Ironically, Huck has never taken the "safer" path. His lies were always for the sake of truth, and for this reason he is constantly taking "resks" and "setting down on a kag of powder." He is actually experienced with the consequences of "doing" the truth if not with "telling" the truth. This is why, while he tells Miss Mary about the swindlers, he does not make it common knowledge. "I'd be alright; but there's be another person that you don't know about who'd be in big trouble. Well, we got to save *him*, hain't we? Of course. Well, then, we won't blow on them." Huck's first responsibility is to "save" Jim and assure his escape and freedom.

Although Huck considers himself a darn good liar—for it comes easy with his upbringing—he often gets caught in his own lies. When the doctor and the lawyer interrogate Huck about his relationship with the Duke and the Dauphin, the lawyer says, "Set down, my boy; I wouldn't strain myself if I was you. I reckon you ain't used to lying, it don't seem to come handy; what you want is practise. You do it pretty awkward." Such a comment is contrary to Huck's whole self-understanding. "I didn't care nothing for the compliment, but I was glad to be let off anyway." Huck never grasps that he has been guided by the truth all along and that his lies, paradoxically, actually bear witness to this. In the end, Huck is deceiving no one but himself. He believes himself to be liar when he is not. The Duke and the Dauphin may have mastered the art of deception, but Huck has not. Huck, to the contrary, incarnates Providence.

Huck's self-deception reaches its climax when he finds out that Jim has been captured and is now held by the Phelps family. Huck begins by rationalizing that it is probably better for Jim to be a slave since he could at least be with his family again. He considers writing Tom a letter to give to Miss Watson telling her where Jim is. He gives up on that idea because everyone would give Jim a hard time upon his return.

Everybody naturally despises an ungrateful nigger, and they'd make Jim feel it all the time, and so he'd feel ornery and disgraced. And then think of *me*! It would get all around that Huck Finn helped a nigger to get his freedom; and if I was ever to see anybody from that town again I'd be ready to get down and lick his boots for shame. That's just the way: a person does a low-down thing, and then he don't want to take no consequences of it.

The more Huck thought about his situation, the more his conscience condemned him.

And at last, when it hit me all of a sudden that here was the plain hand of Providence slapping me in the face and letting me know my wickedness was being watched all the time from up there in heaven, whilst I was stealing a poor old woman's nigger that hadn't even done me no harm, and now was showing me there's One that's always on the lookout, and ain't a-going to allow no such miserable doings to go only just so fur and no further, I most dropped in my tracks I was so scared.

Huck again blames his upbringing, and so it was not entirely his fault. But then he thinks that he could have gone to Sunday school, where "they'd a learnt you there that people that acts as I'd been acting about this nigger goes to everlasting fire."

Huck decides that the best he can do is to kneel down and pray that he would be a better boy, but he can't. The words will not come.

Why wouldn't they? It warn't no use to try and hide it from Him. Nor from *me* neither. I knowed very well why they wouldn't come. It was because my heart warn't right; it was because I warn't square; it was because I was playing double. I was letting on to give up sin, but away inside of me I was holding on to the biggest one of all. I was trying to make my mouth *say* I would do the right thing and the clean thing, and go and write to the nigger's owner and tell were he was; but deep down in me I knowed it was a lie, and He knowed it. You can't pray a lie—I found that out.

Huck decides to write the letter and then try to pray. At first he "felt good and all washed clean of sin for the first time I had ever felt so in my life." But the more he thought about Jim and all that they had been through together and all that Jim had done for him, he could do nothing but tear up the letter, saying: "All right, then, I'll go to hell."

It was awful thoughts and awful words, but they was said. And I let them stay said; and never thought no more about reforming. I shoved the whole thing out of my head, and said I would take up wickedness again, which was in my line, being brung up to it, and the other warn't. And for a starter I would go to work and steal Jim out of slavery again; and if I could think up anything worse, I would do that, too; because as long as I was in, and in for good, I might as well go the whole hog.

The amount of irony that Twain has packed into this scene is phenomenal. First, while Huck throughout condemns himself for stealing a "nigger," and so doing wrong he is ultimately not concerned about himself, but his heart is moved by his love, care, and commitment to Jim. Reminiscent of Paul's words concerning his desire for his fellow Jews' salvation, Huck says he is willing to go to hell for Jim's sake. Second, while Huck says he is not willing to face the consequences of his actions, yet again, he has been facing them from the beginning, and that is why he is in a heap of trouble. Third, Huck has learned what is right and just even though he did not go to Sunday school. Actually, if he did learn what he thought he would learn in Sunday school, he would have not learned what was true and just. Fourth,

Huck says he learned that he could not pray a lie. That is the heart of the matter. For Huck to pray the prayer he wanted to pray would have been to pray a lie. The prayer he wanted to pray was not a prayer to reform and do good, as he thought, but a prayer to turn from his godly ways to do evil. Providence would not allow such a prayer. Fifth, Huck concludes that since he was going to do evil and steal Jim back, he might as well be "in for good" and "go the whole hog." Throughout the whole of Huck's adventures, especially in helping Jim, he has been into "evil" "for good." Huck's "evil" is the embodiment of "good." Lastly, Huck believes that Providence has slapped him in the face. There is One who was watching over his orneriness all along and was not going to stand for it any longer. Actually—and again this is the moral of the story—Providence was caring for Huck all along, watching over and guiding him in every "ornery" move he made. Providence assured that Huck's "evil" actually was "good." Huck states later that he must trust in "Providence to put the right words in my mouth when the time comes; for I'd noticed that Providence always did put the right words in my mouth if I left it alone." This is said by Huck "the liar." But Huck is correct. Providence did put all the "lies" in Huck's mouth because all of his "lies" were more true than not.

It is fascinating that Twain has his characters speak at least four times of Providence in the latter part of the book. It is almost as if he sees more clearly that God is guiding his characters as the story progresses, and thus the moral of the story becomes more evident.

Even the Duke and Dauphin in the end say they must trust in Providence. The Dauphin states, "Thish yer comes of trust'n to Providence. It's the best way, in the long run. I've tried 'em all, and ther' ain't no better way." For once the Dauphin is speaking the truth, and Providence has its way with both of them. They are so perverse that they, like the devil, are liars by nature. For this reason, Providence, as Twain warned from the onset, will see to it that they, like the devil, will ultimately be prosecuted, tarred, feathered, and run out of town on a rail.

Shot by a Dream

Huck arrived at the Phelps' family farm where Jim was locked up, and in one of the cleverest turns in all literature, he is mistaken for their nephew,

Tom Sawyer. Amidst the rejoicing of the Phelps, Huck states that "it warn't nothing to what I was; for it was like being born again, I was so glad to find out who I was." Huck, as Moses, prefigured Tom, as Jesus, up to this point. Now he is going to be born into his full likeness by sharing in Tom's great adventure of setting Jim free. There is even an allusion to Huck's "resurrection" as a new man. Since Huck fabricated his own death, when Huck and Tom meet, Tom thinks Huck has come back from the dead to "ha'nt" him. Huck assures Tom: "I hain't come back—I hain't been gone … No, I warn't ever murdered at all—I played it on them. You come in here and feel of me [note Twain's biblical phrase "feel of me"; different from Huck's normal way of speaking] if you don't believe me." The "Doubting Tom" not only came to believe that Huck was alive, but he also "wanted to know all about it right off, because it was a grand adventure, and mysterious, and so it hit him where he lived." Huck's adventures of leading Jim to freedom hit Tom where he lived because they again prefigure the ultimate adventure, contrived by Tom himself, of actually setting Jim free. Huck had been playing Moses to Tom's Jesus, and now they will join together in the last "mystery" of redemption.

Huck is beside himself with scandal that Tom is willing to help him steal Jim. "Well, I let go all holts then, like I was shot. It was the most astonishing speech I ever heard—and I'm bound to say Tom Sawyer fell considerable in my estimation. Only I couldn't believe it. Tom Sawyer a *nigger-stealer*!" It is here that the plot of Twain's book comes into focus. God, like Tom, is a "nigger-stealer" and he sets the whole of "no account" humanity free through Jesus. If Huck was figuratively "shot" upon hearing Tom's affirmative response to his proposal, Tom will literally be shot and so shed his blood on Jim's behalf. He is shot, just as Twain warned, because he has put a plot in the story, a story about the adventures of God.

In his *Summa Theologiae*, Thomas Aquinas frequently notes that God could have done things differently than he did, often in a manner that would appear to be easier and simpler. For example, God could have achieved our salvation by a mere act of his will rather than by sending his Son into the world to die on the Cross. But according to Aquinas, God did what he did because it was the "most fitting" way to do it. If there ever was a person, real or imaginary, who took this principle to heart and applied it with absolute consistency, it is Tom Sawyer.

Tom's response to Huck's plan to set Jim free embodies his whole persona and that of God's as well.

Work? Why, cert'nly it would work, like rats a-fighting. But it's too blame' simple; there ain't nothing to it. What's the good of a plan that ain't no more trouble than that? It's as mild as goosemilk. Why, Huck, it wouldn't make no more talk than breaking into a soap factory.

Tom's plan involved all kinds of trouble. Instead of going through the door to visit Jim, they dug a hole using, at least at first, not shovels and pick-axes but knives. They used a rusty saw to cut through the bed leg to which Jim was chained and ate the sawdust, when all they needed to do was to lift up the bed. They stole a candlestick to make a pen, and made a pie to hide it in. They made a hickory-bark ladder for Jim to use even though none was necessary. They rolled a grindstone into Jim's hut so that he could have something upon which he could write his "mournful inscription." They placed snakes and rats in his shack. They wrote letters to the Phelpses telling of the impending escape, knowing that guards would then be stationed and watching. Why all of this and more?

There is but one refrain throughout the last section of the book, one that has been echoing from the beginning.

Why, drat it, Huck, it's the stupidest arrangement I ever see. You got to invent *all* the difficulties. Well, we can't help it; we got to do the best we can with the materials we've got. Anyhow, here's one thing—there's more honor in getting him out through a lot of difficulties and dangers, where there warn't one of the furnished to you by the people who it was their duty to furnish them, and you had to contrive them all out of your own head.

For Tom, the whole escape must be done properly: according to "the books" and "the regulations." When Huck protests that it may all be a little unnecessary, Tom retorts, "Don't you reckon I know what I'm about? Don't I generly know what I'm about." In one sense, Tom does know what he is about. He knows there is honor and rightness in doing things heroically. All good actions are heroic actions. What Tom, the young lad, does not perceive but to which his words allude is that he is "about his Father's business." God always does his good deeds heroically. Tom's whole contrived plan to set Jim free is but the mimicking of God's whole "contrived" plan to set humankind free. Tom is living out the adventures of God. It is the only proper way to do them—it is part of the regulations. Or, as Aquinas would say, "It is the most fitting way." Besides, if God did not do unnecessary heroic deeds, they would make "no more talk than breaking into a soap factory." The Good News is proclaimed precisely because it tells of God's heroic adventures.

Tom's plan worked, and Jim was set free. Huck tells Jim, "*Now*, old Jim, you're a free man *again*, and I bet you won't ever be a slave no more." Jim adds, "en a mighty good job it wuz too Huck. It 'uz planned beautiful, en it 'uz done beautiful; en dey ain't *nobody* kin git up a plan dat's mo' mixed up en splendid den what dat one wuz." Huck states, "We was all glad as we could be, but Tom was the gladdest of all because he had a bullet in the calf of his leg."

The above is Twain's theory of salvation. Because of Jesus's adventure of becoming man and dying on the Cross, humankind is once more free, and will never be enslaved again, and nobody can find fault with "a plan dat's mo' mixed up en splendid den what dat one wuz." Moreover, Tom is the true hero because, like Jesus, the plan was carried out at the cost of his own blood. Likewise, no one was more pleased with himself than Tom, just as Jesus was. Tom's dream was fulfilled. When the doctor queried Huck about how Tom got shot, he responded: "He had a dream, and it shot him." Tom's dream of doing what was honorable and proper got him shot, making him a true hero.

When it was discovered that Jim had already been set free and that Tom had known about it all along, Aunt Polly asked, "Then what on earth did *you* want to set him free for, seeing he was already free?" Tom found such a question incomprehensible, hardly deserving an answer: "Well, that *is* a question, I must say; and *just* like women! Why, I wanted the *adventure* of it; and I'd a waded neck-deep in blood—goodness alive, AUNT POLLY!"

God's dream of setting humankind free in a proper and fitting manner equally "got him shot." And why? He already in a sense knew we were free. God wanted "the adventure of it!" He, too, would have "waded neck-deep in blood," and did. And when mankind continually asks why, all God can do is echo Tom's frustrated and desperate cry: "Goodness alive, AUNT POLLY!" Huck summarizes Tom's and God's thirst for adventure on behalf of another, saying "Sure enough, Tom Sawyer had gone and took all that trouble and bother to set a free nigger free!" Jesus incarnates the heroic adventures of God—"Goodness alive"—on behalf of all of us "niggers."

It is fascinating that Jim in the end helps both Tom and Huck. Jim helps the doctor operate on Tom's leg, and he is the one who at the very end tells Huck that his "pap" is dead. Not unlike Christians, he freely becomes a slave of freedom to his redeemer.

Who Should Be Shot?

More could be said by way of illustrating my thesis, but I think I have said enough, and maybe too much. In summary, I offer some concluding comments.

In *The Adventures of Huckleberry Finn,* Mark Twain has presented a tale about truth and deception, freedom and slavery, and the heroic deeds by which truth and freedom are victorious. On one level this is a story about Huck and Tom helping to set Jim free by their own heroic deeds, but, as I have argued, they have through these heroic deeds also told the story of God's heroic adventures throughout history to bring truth and freedom to humankind. It is primarily through irony that Twain tells this second tale, his characters being unaware of the deeper significance of what they were doing. Yet his characters did pay the price, as Twain gave "NOTICE" that they would, for adding a motive, moral, and plot to their adventures.

After pondering this book, I do not find it surprising that Twain considered his biography of St. Joan of Arc his most beloved and greatest work. What Huck and Tom were in fiction, Joan was in real life. For Twain, she was the most heroic of all human beings. Her deeds come right out of "the book" and according to "the regulations." God could have conquered the English in an easier fashion, but then it would not have been a heroic adventure. It would not have been fitting. Twain's life of Joan of Arc is the "true" counterpart to his fictitious adventures of Huck and Tom. In both works, it is God who is the actor behind the scene. He is the true hero manifested in the heroic deeds of others. For Twain, God is the ultimate hero who governs and orchestrates by his providence and so ensures that, in the face of evil and deception, the heroic deeds of others succeed, thus bringing salvation.

I also believe that Twain is saying something about children entering the kingdom of God. Only children—Huck, Tom, Jim, St. Joan, and those like them—possess the godly innocence to do the heroic and noble deeds of truth and goodness. They live out the adventures of the kingdom of God. The clever and the crafty never do heroic deeds, for they achieve their devious purpose through deception. Liars, like Satan, are never heroes.

Some may point out that I have forgotten that Twain was an agnostic, and that he had a reputation for being irreligious. This may be true, but I believe that Twain's real enemy was the "tame," and thus hypocritical, religion he perceived within institutional Christianity of his day. For Twain, institutional Christianity had taken out all the adventure and heroism of the Gospel and fashioned it instead into a comfortable endorsement of a decadent culture. Twain knew that if God did exist, he must truly be the adventurous and heroic God of the Bible—the God of Huck and Tom and St. Joan.

My interpretation of Twain may be preposterous. My thesis may illustrate Twain's worst fears. Then again, some young PhD student in American literature may find here a promising topic for a newfangled thesis. I end confident of one thing, something of which Twain himself is also darn well aware. If anyone should be banished, prosecuted, and shot for placing a motive, a moral, and a plot in this book, it is Samuel Langhorne Clemens.

Index

Index of Subjects